W9-AUM-783

Society
and the
Environment

Society
and the
Environment

∙∙∙∙∙∙∙∙∙∙∙∙∙∙∙∙∙∙∙∙∙∙∙∙∙∙∙∙∙∙

*Pragmatic Solutions
to Ecological Issues*

∙∙∙∙∙∙∙∙∙∙∙∙∙∙∙∙∙∙∙∙∙∙∙∙∙∙∙∙∙∙

Michael
Carolan

Colorado State University

**WESTVIEW
PRESS**
A Member of the Perseus Books Group

Westview Press was founded in 1975 in Boulder, Colorado, by notable publisher and intellectual Fred Praeger. Westview Press continues to publish scholarly titles and high-quality undergraduate- and graduate-level textbooks in core social science disciplines. With books developed, written, and edited with the needs of serious nonfiction readers, professors, and students in mind, Westview Press honors its long history of publishing books that matter.

Copyright © 2013 by Westview Press
Published by Westview Press,
A Member of the Perseus Books Group

All rights reserved. Printed in the United States of America. No part of this book may be reproduced in any manner whatsoever without written permission except in the case of brief quotations embodied in critical articles and reviews. For information, address Westview Press, 2465 Central Avenue, Boulder, CO 80301. Find us on the World Wide Web at www.westviewpress.com.

Every effort has been made to secure required permissions for all text, images, maps, and other art reprinted in this volume.

Westview Press books are available at special discounts for bulk purchases in the United States by corporations, institutions, and other organizations. For more information, please contact the Special Markets Department at the Perseus Books Group, 2300 Chestnut Street, Suite 200, Philadelphia, PA 19103, or call (800) 810-4145, ext. 5000, or e-mail special.markets@perseusbooks.com.

All images are by the author unless otherwise specified.

Library of Congress Cataloging-in-Publication Data

Carolan, Michael S.
  Society and the environment : pragmatic solutions to ecological issues / Michael Carolan.
    p. cm.
  Includes bibliographical references and index.
  ISBN 978-0-8133-4594-9 (pbk. : alk. paper) — ISBN 978-0-8133-4595-6 (e-book)
1. Environmental sociology. I. Title.
  GE195.C38 2013
  304.2—dc23
                          2012040677

10 9 8 7 6 5 4 3 2 1

For Nora, Elena, and Joey

Brief Table of Contents

Expanded Table of Contents

Part II: At the Intersection of Ecology and Society

11 Governance: Biases and Blind Spots   211

12 Inequality and Growth: Prosperity for All   228

Preface

Society and the Environment: Pragmatic Solutions to Ecological Issues was born of my personal frustration as an educator. In my department at Colorado State University, we have an undergraduate concentration in environmental sociology; I teach the intro-level course in that concentration, called Global Environmental Issues. Every semester in this class, I engage with roughly 130 students about the environmental state of affairs, while also going to great lengths to explain how sociology can inform our understanding of how we've arrived at this state. It's an incredibly fun class to teach, not only because it deals with subject matter that's close to my heart, but because the students tend to be really interested in the material as well. But over the course of the term, my students' early excitement changed to something cooler. They were becoming, to put it in a word, depressed.

Sociology students talk frequently about their desire to make the world a better place. Yet in our environment classes, day after day, we focused on all that was wrong with the world. I was feeding my students a steady diet of pessimism—about how they can't really make it better—yet still asking them to take individual (and collective) responsibility for our environmental future. No wonder they were getting indigestion.

When I realized this—when the CFL went on over my head—I began to make *solutions* a central component of my class. My students still occasionally feel disheartened or upset, but these days I rarely see a true cloud of depression settle over them.

I talk about solutions in two ways. Think of the first like a steady drumbeat: problem/solutions, problems/solutions. . . . Each chapter, following this arrangement, begins by stating environmental issues and their implications for society. At each chapter's midpoint, the discussion becomes solution oriented, tackling the possible solutions to the problem immediately at hand. Yet in the end, solutions—*real* solutions—to our environmental ills come not from fiddling around at the margins but from deep systemic change; we need to also come up with solutions that take us *in other directions*. The second way I therefore talk about solutions takes the form of an argumentative arch that builds throughout the entire book. Think of it as a complementary drumbeat that slowly crescendos until the cymbals crash in Parts III and IV, where attention centers on collectively reorganizing a sustainable society.

I have found this two-part technique for talking about solutions to be particularly useful in the classroom. Sociologists have long been suspect of bolt-on solutions; after all, we are trained to see the root causes of problems . . . sometimes to a fault. But I would argue that small changes to behavior (such as turning down the temperature on one's hot water heater) and technological fixes (like compact fluorescent bulbs) have their place as long as they are met with an equal zest to create deeper structural change, though I also realize such short-term fixes risk creating short-term apathy, which can derail attempts to solve today's environmental problems at their root. To those reading and assigning this book, I recommend a critical reflection upon the solutions proposed in each of the following chapters. Ask yourself: what do they fix and what do they miss?

Much of the material that populates the book comes from my Global Environmental Issues class, so you could say it has, from a student's perspective, been truly *peer* reviewed. It is loaded with figures, tables, and images as well as a variety of "boxes": the Case Study, to briefly highlight case studies; the Ethical Question, to highlight the value disputes that underlie environmental conflicts; and the ECOnnection, which allows me to interject additional information into a subject. I also include at the end of every chapter, which I again draw right from class material, suggested additional readings, discussion questions, relevant Internet links, and suggested videos. Finally, I take time at the end of every chapter to highlight particularly important concepts. Definitions of these terms are then provided in the Glossary located near the end of the book.

Talking, thinking, and learning about environmental issues in a pragmatic way may also require going beyond the pages of the book in your hands. With that in mind, I have posted a number of "beyond the book" resources online at www.westviewpress.com /carolan. These resources will link you to the social web by way of video clips, podcasts, and interesting, informative blogs and websites. Slides of the figures, tables, and images as well as a variety of slides expanding on issues raised in the "Boxes" are available to help bring the subject matter alive during lectures. Sample quiz questions are available for use as a study guide to give to students, or as a starting-place for crafting your own exams. Additionally, the website provides a selection of exercises, scenarios, and games (such as an adaptation of the "wedges" game developed by the Carbon Mitigation Initiative at Princeton University), all of which are designed specifically to promote active learning in the classroom. If you have suggestions for additional resources, please feel free to share them with me via the website.

Before you dig into the book, I want to say a few words about my very intentional use of the term *pragmatic* in the book's subtitle (indeed, originally the plan was to call this book *Pragmatic Environmentalism*). As with solutions, my understanding of *pragmatic* operates at two levels. At one level, the term is meant to evoke a very common-sense understanding, relating to practical matters of fact where results are of greater importance than philosophical debates. Yet as is also plainly made clear in the chapters that follow, the world is not that black and white. Matters of fact, for example, particularly when dealing with environmental issues, are rarely self-evident. In fact, philosophical and ethical debates are often embedded within debates around what ought to constitute a fact. I would therefore caution anyone from operating solely according to this understanding of the term as they search for answers to the environmental problems that plague us. Yet you could say this book is *pragmatic* insofar as short-term solutions go.

This brings me to the second interpretation of *pragmatic:* as *pragmatism.* For those unfamiliar with this term, it references a distinct philosophical tradition—a tradition whose relevance for environmental sociology I delve into in Chapter 13. At the moment, I will say only that I appreciate the pragmatist approach, for it offers an alternative to overt structuralism, on the one hand, and methodological individualism, on the other. The way it does this, I should also add, makes it inherently *hopeful,* as the changes it seeks are deep and therefore lasting. But you'll have to read the rest of the book to find out how this optimistic story ends.

Acknowledgments

How does one begin to "acknowledge" people when their career is filled with supportive relationships and enlightening encounters? From my graduate student days, when I was lucky enough to have Michael Bell as my PhD adviser, to today, when I have the good fortune of being chair of a Sociology Department full of faculty and students interested in issues related to environment sustainability and justice, scholarship is inherently collective, and this book is a reflection of this fact. So I'll focus on naming those with a presence more directly felt. First, Evan Carver, the original acquisitions editor at Westview Press who talked me into taking this project on. Without you there would be no book. Period. I also owe a debt of gratitude to Brooke Maddaford and Leanne Silverman. More competent, helpful, and responsive development and acquisitions editors, respectively, I could never find.

I also leaned on a number of colleagues for images and articles and in a couple cases used some as sounding boards for ideas and arguments. Those colleagues include Brett Clark, Maurie Cohen, Jennifer Cross, Riley Dunlap, Cornelia Flora, Jan Flora, Lori Hunter, Aaron McCright, Kari Norgaard, Thomas Rudel, and Richard York.

A heartfelt note of thanks must also be extended to these scholars who provided constructive comments and criticisms of the book: Dr. Shaunna L. Scott (University of Kentucky), Dr. Krista E. Paulsen (University of North Florida), Dr. Manuel Vallee (University of Auckland), Dr. Kooros Mohit Mahmoudi (University of Northern Arizona), Dr. Jesse T. Weiss (University of the Ozarks), Dr. Susan G. Clark (Yale University), and Dr. Christopher Oliver (University of Kentucky).

The book proposal and final manuscript were extensively reviewed by a list of scholars known only to me as "Reviewer 1, 2, 3, ..." There were a lot of you who sacrificed a great deal of time to anonymously involve yourselves in this project. Your comments were invaluable. Thank you.

I am also grateful to all those students whom I have had the good fortune of learning from each semester in my Global Environmental Issues class (the "intro" class for our environmental sociology concentration at Colorado State University). This book is the culmination of a lot of trial and error in that class as I sought to make the material interesting, relevant, and, importantly, hopeful in tone.

Finally: to Nora. Thanks to you I am assured that my days will be full of nonmaterial contentment, while in our children (Elena and Joey) I find hope that the future will be in good hands.

Introduction: Individuals, Societies, and Pragmatic Environmentalism

Why must books on the environment be so gloomy? Chapter after chapter detail what's wrong, followed by, if you're lucky, a chapter or two on what could be done to turn things around. No wonder my students express bewilderment and, in a few cases, something akin to borderline clinical depression when, during the first week of my Global Environmental Issues class, I ask about their thoughts on the ecological state of the world. A quick title search of my university library's catalog reveals 311 books with the term *environmental problems* somewhere in the title or subtitle. A search of the term *environmental solutions*, conversely, brought up 2 books, both published in the 1970s. Sex, apparently, isn't the only thing that sells books. We can add apocalyptic ecological predictions to that list.

I understand why, historically, all this attention has been paid to environmental problems. People are not much interested in reading about solutions until they've been convinced that there's a problem in need of solving. It has been fifty years since the publication of Rachel Carson's *Silent Spring* (which was first published in 1962). Since then we have been exposed to a steady diet of problem talk, with measurable effect. An April 2009 Marist poll asked, "Thinking about how you live and the things you buy, overall, do you personally do a great deal, a good amount, a fair amount, a little, or nothing at all to help the environment?" Eighty percent responded by saying "a fair amount" or greater (Cohen, S. 2010). Even friends of mine who would rather lose a limb than be called an "environmentalist" acknowledge the problematic ecological conditions that surround us. (Granted, they might still be in denial about climate change, but not much else.) Who is left to convince? Isn't it time to turn the corner and talk about—and even celebrate—instances of positive socioecological change?

This book is a bit of both: a bit about problems, a little bit more about solutions. By focusing on ecological *solutions*—rather than entirely on *problems*—I am striving to make this book hopeful, recognizing that if we can't at least think and talk about and point to sustainable alternatives, we really are in trouble. But I am a realistic dreamer, as indicated by my evoking the term *pragmatic* in the book's subtitle. Although it never hurts to be imaginative about what could be, we must be realistic about what can be.

Pragmatism decries grand narratives—those totalizing theoretical views of the world that claim to explain human mind, body, and society since the beginning of time. As someone who finds social theory interesting, I admit that it is fun to try to "scoop up" the world in one all-encompassing conceptual framework. Grand narratives are like flying at thirty thousand feet: they are great for discussing the big picture—things like global capitalism and world political and economic systems. When the time comes to roll up one's sleeves and talk about practical policy solutions, however, I find these approaches less helpful, especially when issues revolve around sustainability. (I realize grand narratives have their "solutions" too, but they are often terribly unrealistic and usually rather nebulous and even polemical. In a word, they're not pragmatic.) Theoretical grand narratives aside, the nontheoretical "green" literature is equally rife with overly simplistic, one-size-fits-all solutions. Single-handed praise for such phenomena as eating local (Nabhan 2009), a hydrogen economy (Rifkin 2003), algae-based biofuels (Demirbas and Demirbas 2010), and downshifting (a movement whose tagline is "working less and enjoying life more") (Drake 2000) generates considerable interest in and excitement around a topic. As a professional sociologist, however, I cannot help but cringe when the pilots of these tomes spend the majority of their time at cruising altitude. Fine-grain details matter; often they determine whether a "solution" will work in a particular space. A pragmatic environmentalist enjoys big pictures like anyone else. But he or she also realizes that there is no substitute to having one's feet planted firmly on the ground for establishing what works—and what's sustainable—for any given situation.

Individualism: Too Much and Not Enough

The pragmatic value of many environmental books is further limited still due to what I call the problem of individualism. That is, they place either too much or not enough emphasis on individual action. As for ascribing too much weight to individual action, the standard argument goes something like this: saving the environment starts with each of us "doing our part"—so go plant a tree, buy organic food, ride a bike, install solar panels on your house, recycle, and so on. You don't have to be a sociologist to know that our actions, every one of them, are shaped by a whole host of factors. Evidence of this is all around. Most people, for example, already have a good basic understanding of how they can reduce their ecological footprint—who hasn't heard of the three Rs of reduce/reuse/recycle, for example? Yet people's actions seemingly belie this knowledge. I see this all the time in my students: they recognize the negative ecological impacts of many of their actions yet still do them. (I am certainly just as guilty of this.) While we act in ways that reflect our wants and interests, those very wants and interests are heavily shaped by existing structures—cultural, technological, infrastructural, political, organizational, legal, and so forth. It is not that individual action has no value when it comes to creating meaningful socioecological change. Individual action devoid of collective mobilization, however, will never produce the same level of change as, for example, a well-organized social movement.

Too much focus on the individual can also create dangerous blind spots that risk making circumstances worse for some people. We see this occasionally in the "sacrifice talk" that abounds in the environmental literature—downshift, buy less, give up your car, stop shopping, and so forth. For one thing, I have found this sacrifice talk to be somewhat demoralizing among people genuinely concerned about the environment. Focusing on what one can't do, rather than on what one can, contributes to the malaise described by many of my students. Moreover, not everyone can afford to sacrifice. To give up something requires you to have something to give up. But not everyone wants to sacrifice, or they are willing to sacrifice only so much for the environment. And in some cases, even wanting to sacrifice may still not be enough to elicit a particular behavior—I know someone, for example, who despises driving his car, yet when the temperature drops below freezing, he makes the choice to drive his child to day care to avoid exposure to the elements. This is why environmental education, as a strategy to change behaviors, can take us only so far: because behaviors do not occur in a vacuum. In order for people to make a "greener" choice, they must have viable greener choices to choose from. And to have those choices often requires collective (not just individual) action.

Then there's the other extreme: the world-without-people perspective. I encounter this often in material written by specialists who obviously know a lot more about technoscientific matters than they do about human behavior and social change. These are the books, essays, and research papers that tout impressive technological solutions to a variety of our social and ecological ills, from powering the world with hydrogen (Rifkin 2003) to geoengineering our climate to combat climate change (Crutzen 2006). Don't misunderstand my critique; I enjoy reading these materials. Moreover, they contain just the type of outside-the-box thinking that we need. Nor do I doubt the technological feasibility of many of the solutions proposed; indeed, the authors usually go to great lengths to convince us of their long-term practicality. Yet just because something is technologically *possible* does not automatically mean it is socially, economically, politically, and organizationally *probable*. Too often the two are conflated, leaving the reader guessing as to how to take something that works in a lab or on paper and scale it up to the level of city, state, nation, or entire world.

The Contribution of the Social Sciences

One explanation for why books with an environmental focus tend to concentrate on problems, and superficially on what ought to be done to change things, is the nature of how "expertise" has historically been attached to the subject. They are called *environmental* problems, after all. The discussion is therefore dominated by natural or environmental scientists and engineers. All are very competent to tell us *what* the state of things is (though even so-called objective facts, as is made clear in later chapters, are mediated and conditioned by social variables and are often premised on the making of subtle value judgments). Yet by nature of their training, they lack a strong grasp of *why* we got ourselves into this mess and *how* we might be able to get ourselves out of it. These "why" and "how" questions inevitably require a firm working knowledge of social, political, economic, and cultural variables, which makes these questions better suited for social scientists. Feelings of doom and gloom arise when too much focus is placed on the "what" and not enough on the "why" and "how." To be fair, the social sciences share some blame in this. They spent a good part of the twentieth century turning away from the material world, preferring instead to focus almost exclusively on phenomena such as language, nonmaterial culture, and, later, **social constructivism** (an approach that focuses entirely on the sociologically dependent knowledge of a phenomenon rather than on any inherent qualities that the thing possesses itself) (Catton and Dunlap 1978; Carolan 2005a, 2005b). For much of the last century the "worlds" studied by the social and natural sciences had been distinct—indeed, to some degree, even mutually exclusive.

Of my various professional identities, one is "environmental sociologist." Although I am proud to identify myself with this subfield of sociology, I admit to being tired of answering the question, "What does sociology have to do with the environment?" Much of this, I realize, stems from a general misunderstanding of how the so-called social and natural worlds interact—the very fact that we separate the social from the natural sciences at universities underscores the pervasiveness of this misunderstanding. Yet the longer I study the world, the blurrier this division becomes for me. What does sociology have to do with the environment? More than most realize.

Sociology has a long history of sidestepping environmental variables, phenomena historically understood as under the purview of the natural sciences. It is important to remember that early social thought was developed, at least in part, as a reaction to social Darwinism, which sought to explain much of social life by way of biology. To avoid a repeat of this dark chapter in sociology's history, social thinkers found safer territory studying phenomena they took to be largely decoupled from the natural world. The problem with environmental issues, however, is that they make a terrible mess of this historically rooted division of labor between the "social" and the "natural" sciences. I do not want to say much more about this now, as the remainder of the book details ways that the social sciences can contribute to discussions about today's most pressing environmental issues. I will, however, add this: I cannot think of a single environmental problem today that does not touch, in some way, human society. All environmental controversies are the result of social action, and none can be resolved without social action.

Figure 1.1 gives us a way to visualize this interrelationship while marking the terrain that is comfortably within the realm of what social scientists study. As the figure illustrates, environmental sociologists are *equally* as interested in material (or ecological) and social variables. Although acknowledging the fallibility of all knowledge claims, the "emphasis [among environmental sociologists] tends to be on analyzing linkages between the symbolic, social-structural and material realms" (Dunlap 2010:23).

One could argue that the **sociological imagination**—a way of thinking that involves making connections over time and across scales between the particular and the general—knows no limits, as evidenced by the fact that sociologists have studied such seemingly "natural" phenomena as quarks (Pickering 1999) and genes (Carolan 2010a). I will leave it to someone else to determine exactly where the boundaries of the sociological imagination lie. That said, for students wondering if something falls within what the figure refers to as the "operational space for the social sciences," they need only ask themselves: has human society ever been of consequence to the phenomenon's existence?

Let's take, for example, the sun. Whereas our *understanding* of the sun is an entirely relevant subject for sociological analysis, I would argue that the sun *itself* is not (since the existence of human society has been of no consequence to the sun's life cycle). While we are shaped by the sun daily, there is no evidence that the relationship is symmetrical.

FIGURE 1.1 Operational Space for the Social Sciences

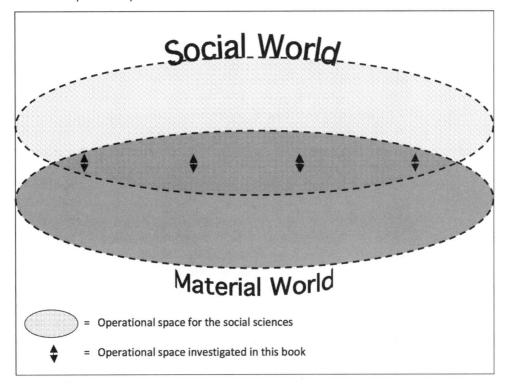

Social World

Material World

⬭ = Operational space for the social sciences

↕ = Operational space investigated in this book

So-called natural ecological processes and phenomena, on the other hand, are very much shaped by our presence and us by them, making them prime candidates for a thorough sociological treatment. Thus, as Richard York (2006) has astutely noted, sociologists who study, for example, environmental controversies or the framing or discursive construction of environmental problems—rather than the interactions between the social and material worlds—might best be described as practicing "sociology of environmental issues."

The double-headed arrows in Figure 1.1 are a key component of the image. Although on paper they may appear insignificant, they represent the figure's conceptual heart. If you want to understand—*really* understand—environmental problems, with the hope of devising practical solutions, then you've got to understand how these two realms interact with each other. And I am not just talking about understanding how society impacts ecological conditions (which implies a unidirectional arrow). We are shaped as much by the material world as the material world is shaped by us. Shying away from this basic fact will only distract us from what's really going on.

Material Things Have Momentum

Environmental controversies are never just about any one thing. The above discussion ought to have made this clear. Context matters.

It is important to remember, however, that this context also changes over time, a point that is particularly salient when discussion turns to behavioral, and ultimately socioecological, change. Structures—social, economic, political, legal, and even technological—can gather what could be thought of as *sociological momentum* over time. I am drawing here upon the term *technological momentum*, which was coined and developed by the famed historian of technology Thomas Hughes (1969).

According to Hughes, society has the greatest control over a technology when it is first introduced. As a technology matures, however, and becomes embedded within society—and society becomes further intertwined with the technology—it becomes increasingly difficult to change paths. Today's gas-powered automobile, for example, would be of considerably less effect were it not for oil, roads, automotive engineers, gas stations, car companies, government fuel taxes, proautomobile cultural imperatives, and the like. The movie *Back to the Future, Part III* (1990) illustrates this perfectly. Marty McFly (played by Michael J. Fox) finds himself in 1885 with a gasoline-powered DeLorean, and his "futuristic" vehicle is worthless: cars are nothing more than processed raw materials when abstracted from the system out of which they emerged. Even understandings of "fuel" are conditioned by these contextual conditions. Nothing is inherently fuel. *Fuel* is simply a term for a carrier of energy. A system must be in place that utilizes a particular carrier of energy if said carrier is to be called fuel. Even oil—before society organized around it, thereby giving it the designation of "fuel"—was once viewed "with indifference or annoyance" (Bolles 1878:772).

When thought of in abstract isolation, technological artifacts—indeed, all "things"—appear innocuous and highly mutable. In reality, however, as contexts change, and as society organizes itself around particular ways of doing things, these artifacts can gather momentum. What I like about the metaphor "momentum" is that it keeps us from reducing discussions of issues to unembedded things.

I frequently come across comparisons between the truly impressive public transportation systems in western Europe and Japan and the truly abysmal system found in the United States. Pointing to the widespread use of mass and individual (e.g., biking) transit in parts of Europe, a number of people have told me, "There's no reason we can't duplicate that system here." True enough; there is no reason we can't duplicate that system in the United States. But there are a lot of reasons we have not.

Before World War II, US cities arguably had the best public transportation systems in the world. Following the war, the nation found itself at a crossroads: should those systems be rebuilt and updated (as was being done throughout Europe), or should another transportation model be adopted, namely, the car? We all know the outcome of that decision. And since then, over the course of more than a half century, the country as a whole has slowly organized itself around the automobile. In doing this, the United States has "sunk" literally trillions of dollars of capital into this transportation model, virtually guaranteeing that the car will remain a central fixture in our lives for decades to come. Here are some examples of how we have stacked the deck in favor of the "choice" to drive a car over other methods of transportation: by building parking lots and by making space for cars to park on taxpayer-funded streets; the government has provided an extensive infrastructure of roads and bridges that in many cases can be used only by automobiles; restaurants like Starbucks and McDonalds have incorporated the automobile into their architectural plans by offering drive-through lanes; and the proliferation of urban sprawl, which simultaneously was made possible because of the car while further making ownership of one a necessity. This level of organization—this *momentum*—makes using the car quite attractive. On the other hand, policy decisions make public transportation, the bike, and walking less convenient and therefore less attractive. This is especially apparent when comparing the United States to other countries, where the decision was made long ago to structurally organize around multiple modes of transportation, which explains why in the Netherlands 27 percent of all trips are by bike versus less than 1 percent in the United States (L. Brown 2009:153).

In short, the automobile, as the dominant mode of transportation in the United States, has a significant amount of momentum behind it. This is not to suggest that our hands are tied, that we cannot move away from the car and replicate a transportation system more like what's found in, say, the Netherlands. Rather, it is an acknowledgment that change of such magnitude comes with significant transaction costs. The question is: are we willing to pay them (and should all in society pay these costs equally)?

The Messy Relationship Between Behaviors and Attitudes

In the small rural Iowa town where I grew up, my parents carefully separate their recyclables from the other rubbish that ends up in the garbage truck. They also have to dutifully study every plastic container and verify its number (only certain numbers, and very few numbers at that, can be recycled). Finally, they have to haul their recycle bins to the nearest pickup site, which, fortunately for them because they live in town, is only about three-quarters of a mile away. It would be so much easier if my parents just threw everything away. But they don't. They put up with the "cost" of recycling. I know many in my hometown, and especially those living in the surrounding countryside, however, who do not. For them, all household waste ends up in either the landfill or the burn pile.

Once, one of my more ecologically passionate friends, after hearing this story, looked at me with disbelief, unable to accept that people choose not to recycle. "Why do they do this? Don't they care about the environment?" I remember one asking me. I think his question missed the mark. These divergent behaviors seem not to reflect vast differences in attitudes. For example, one individual from my hometown who does not recycle, a lifelong friend, has been a card-carrying member of the Sierra Club for as long as I can remember. He has a hard time walking, lives far from town, and prefers not to drive, which makes the practice of recycling very difficult. Similarly, I know some people in the town where I now live, Fort Collins, Colorado, who admit to having very little interest in reducing their impact on the environment but still diligently recycle.

Fort Collins has a mixed-recycling program. In other words, if it is recyclable—and, unlike in my parents' town, every piece of plastic is recyclable—it goes into a massive blue bin that is wheeled out with the trash to be picked up. That's it. Easy. Moreover, unlike my parents, whose garbage fee allows them to set out as many trash bags as they wish, there is an economic incentive in Fort Collins to divert waste into the recycle stream; namely, you pay more for larger trash cans. To put it in cost-and-benefit terms: whereas it costs my parents to recycle—in terms of time, hassle, and braving the elements (Iowa winters can be brutal)—it costs residents of Fort Collins *not* to.

This goes back to a point I made earlier about the need to contextualize social behavior. I recently supervised a visiting student from Russia for six months who wanted to learn more about the field of environmental sociology. One of the things that interested her was how attitudes toward the environment in the United States differed from those in Russia. Coming across a statistic about the amount of solid waste that Colorado State University—my employer—recycles (something like 56 percent), she assumed this behavior was evidence of deep attitudinal affinities toward the environment. After noting how comparatively little her Russian university recycles, she asked, "What do they do here to develop these green attitudes?" Holding up a ubiquitous recycle bin and pointing to the words *mixed recycling*, I proceeded to tell her about how socio-organizational changes now make recycling as easy as throwing things away (if not easier, as rubbish bins are notoriously difficult to find in certain university buildings).

The moral of these two stories: structural changes go a long way toward changing behavior. And many times, these changes go further than attitudinal changes alone. As my nonrecycling but otherwise environmentally minded friend from my hometown reminds us, having the "right" attitudes does not do anyone (or the environment) any good if society fails to provide cost-effective ways to act upon those beliefs.

I realize that the idea of changing behaviors *prior to* attitudes is somewhat counter-intuitive. Yet, for some people at least, perhaps that is what we ought to be shooting for. Just to be clear, I am not talking about making people do something that they don't want to do. In fact, I am saying just the opposite. Recognizing that sacrifice is not for everyone, we should strive to reorganize society in such a way that individuals choose a more sustainable path—like those I know who recoil at the thought of being labeled an "environmentalist" but still diligently recycle. Sacrifice is not only a rather uninspired solution but it's not terribly helpful, either, as my experience has been that the message tends to turn people off (especially among those with exceedingly large ecological footprints). How can we, to evoke the language of economics, incentivize those behaviors that lessen our ecological footprints and disincentivize those that do not?

I lay no claim to having the answers about what ought to be done. That is a question best left for us all, collectively, to decide. But I do know we will never be able to answer it comprehensively until we have a grasp of the level of complexity involved. The road ahead is not going to be easy, but, as the following chapters explain, there are viable ways forward.

The Journey Ahead

Some readers (and colleagues) might wonder why, as a professionally trained environmental sociologist, I did not include the term *environmental sociology* in the book's title. You might say it was a pragmatic move to select a title that does not tie me to any one particular disciplinary narrative. Citing my own earlier plea (see Carolan 2005b) to social scientists to expand their sociological imaginations and see the explanatory power of nontraditional sociological variables, Riley Dunlap calls for the "*pragmatic* employment of environmental indicators in empirical research investigating linkages between social and biophysical phenomena" (2010:23; emphasis added). This book takes this pragmatic call to heart. The conceptual and analytic approaches discussed in the forthcoming chapters come from many disciplines: sociology, to be sure, but also anthropology, geography, political science, science and technology studies, and economics (among others). As I tell my students, there are many ways to make sense of today's ecological state.

Undoubtedly, there will be those who find fault with how I go about discussing a particular environmental issue, thinking I should have used "theory X" or "analytic device Y." I accept such criticism. I make no claims that the analyses that follow are the only ways—or even the "best" ways—to make sense of the environmental issues discussed. Space constraints limit the amount of detail that can be conveyed in any particular issue. But that's okay. The chapters are meant to *start* discussions, not stifle them by claiming to be the last word on any given subject. I urge you to critique, elaborate, and refine what is said in the following chapters.

The following chapters are problem *and* solution focused. In addition to describing what is wrong (and why), they also discuss alternative institutional, cultural, technological, ethical, and political forms that seek to facilitate more sustainable outcomes. Each chapter follows a similar organizational structure: a brief overview on the current state of the issue, an overview of some of the ways social scientists have explored it, followed by a sociological (and thus still critical) discussion of solutions.

Although each chapter is written to stand alone, the full pragmatic force of the text is best felt when it is read cover to cover. The reason for this is simple: the most sustainable solutions (in other words, the *real* solutions) rarely apply to just one problem. In fact, if we dig deep enough, we would discover that many of today's environmental problems share similar roots. Having already admitted to dismissing grand narratives, it should not come as a surprise that I reject the view that environmental problems are the result of any one thing. Yet I do not symmetrically assign fault, either. The problems that we face may not be entirely the product of any one thing, but some things certainly deserve their fair share of the blame. Thus, as the book progresses from "Living in a Material World" (Part I) to "At the Intersection of Ecology and Society" (Part II) to "Organizing a Sustainable Society" (Part III) and, finally, to "Shifting the Focus to Results" (Part IV), critiques sharpen and solutions proposed become more complete, as the discussion moves closer to those notably culpable sociological artifacts, which I zero in on in the latter chapters. You might say that with each section, I attempt to drill further down to uncover the really real social dynamics upon which considerable blame can be laid and which, once changed, point to opportunities for true sustainability.

Thus, if the solutions proposed early in the text seem shallow, they are. This does not lessen their importance, recognizing that when you're sick, you need to treat the symptoms as much as the cause. Yet the pragmatist in me wants more; after all, pragmatic solutions need to not only be realistic but actually resolve that which ails us.

The first part focuses on issues related to certain environmental phenomena. Specifically, time is taken in this part of the book to examine problems and solutions linked to greenhouse gases (Chapter 2), waste (Chapter 3), biodiversity (Chapter 4), and water (Chapter 5). In reference to the aforementioned Figure 1.1, topics discussed in Part I lie "lower" in the figure (while still within what I call "the operational space for the social sciences"). Part II moves slightly "up" the figure with the investigation of issues that weave the "social" and "natural" realms together in complex and fascinating ways. The problems and solutions discussed here revolve around issues relating to population (Chapter 6), transportation (Chapter 7), food (Chapter 8), and energy production (Chapter 9). Part III offers the most pointed response to the question, "What does sociology have to do with today's environmental problems?" To put it plainly: everything. By highlighting the phenomena driving today's environmental problems—which are located "higher" still in Figure 1.1—my wish is to approach the closing chapter on a sincerely hopeful note. Only by naming the root dynamics of today's environmental ills—from the political economy (Chapter 10) to issues of governance (Chapter 11) and inequality and growth (Chapter 12)—can we expect to have a real chance of naming truly sustainable solutions. Part IV concludes our journey. Whereas a considerable amount of attention is given throughout the book to structural phenomena (like the aforementioned sociological momentum), the book concludes by elaborating on how social change ultimately hinges on people behaving and thinking in particular ways (Chapter 13). Change ultimately starts with us. Lest we forget, although social forces act upon us as if independent from us, they are not—they are products of our making. Knowing this is perhaps the most hopeful message of all.

The reader will also find a number of features provided in the forthcoming chapters. In addition to many figures, tables, and images, a variety of "boxes" are interspersed throughout to add either further detail or an illustrative case study to bolster a point, concept, or theme in the main text. These take three forms: the Case Study, which briefly highlights a case study relevant to points made throughout the text; the Ethical Question, to highlight the value judgments that lurk everywhere when talking about environmental phenomena; and the ECOnnection, which I use to interject additional information into the text with minimal disruption to the flow of the main narrative. Finally, suggestions for additional readings are provided at the end of every chapter, as are questions to help spur further thought and discussion on the subject matter. Other features to conclude each chapter include "Important Concepts," "Relevant Internet Links," and "Suggested Videos" (the latter two including short summaries of each).

IMPORTANT CONCEPTS

- ecological complexity
- environmental sociology
- sociological imagination
- sociological momentum
- technologically possible versus the sociologically probable

DISCUSSION QUESTIONS

1. How can sociology inform our understanding of environmental problems and solutions?
2. Has your experience been similar to mine: do people, books, and professors and instructors seem more interested in talking about environmental problems than solutions? If so, why do you think this is?
3. Do old distinctions between the social and natural sciences still hold when facing today's environmental problems? What about disciplines: do we still need them? Why or why not?
4. What actions of yours clearly cost the environment? Why do you still do them? What would it take for those behaviors to change?

SUGGESTED ADDITIONAL READINGS

Dunlap, R., and B. Marshall. 2007. "Environmental Sociology." In *21st Century Sociology: A Reference Handbook,* edited by C. D. Bryant and D. L. Peck, 2:329–340. Thousand Oaks, CA: Sage.

Freudenburg, W., and R. Wilkinson. 2008. "Equity and the Environment: A Pressing Need and a New Step Forward." In *Equity and the Environment,* edited by R. Wilkinson and W. Freudenburg, 1–18. *Research in Social Problems and Public Policy*, vol. 15. Binglet, UK: Emerald Group.

Orr, D. 2011. *Hope Is an Imperative: The Essential David Orr.* Washington, DC: Island Press.

RELEVANT INTERNET LINKS

- http://envirosoc.org/
  The "Environment and Technology" subsection of the American Sociological Association. This is an excellent resource for anyone interested in environmental sociology.
- http://vimeo.com/channels/186979
  Videos of the late William "Bill" Freudenburg describing a host of environmental sociological phenomena—anything from the "the history of modern environmental theory" to "the 'nature' of sprawl."

SUGGESTED VIDEOS

- *Earth Days* (2009)
  http://video.pbs.org/video/1463378089/. A documentary about the rise of the environmental movement in the United States and the first Earth Day in 1970.
- *The 11th Hour* (2008)
  Leonardo DiCaprio presents practical solutions for ecological problems as we run up against the limits of growth.
- *Living Downstream* (2010)
  After being diagnosed with cancer, acclaimed ecologist and author Sandra Steingraber investigates the links between cancer and environmental toxins.
- *Planet in Peril* (2007)
  Anderson Cooper, Dr. Sanjay Gupta, and Jeff Corwin take viewers around the globe, looking at today's threats to the world's environment.

PART I

LIVING IN A MATERIAL WORLD

2

Greenhouse Gases: Warmer Isn't Better

A friend once told me that you know when a person, catchphrase, or subject has become part of our collective consciousness when they've been immortalized on a bumper sticker. Well, I recently saw a bumper sticker that read, "**Greenhouse gases**: proof that you can have too much of a good thing." (Greenhouse gases are any gases in the atmosphere that absorb and emit radiation within the thermal infrared range.) True to my friend's words, the topic of human-induced **climate change**—a change in climate patterns due to human activity like burning fossil fuels—has become unavoidable. (The terms *climate change* and *global warming* are used interchangeably throughout the book.)

Contrary to what certain politicians and media personalities might be saying, scientific debate around climate change is coming to a close. To be sure, there still is a climate change debate within the peer-reviewed literature. Yet that debate is ultimately around questions such as "What are we to do about climate change?" and "Do we all bear equal responsibility for it, or do some individuals and nations deserve a greater share of the blame?" rather than "Is climate change happening?" Interestingly, whereas the peer-reviewed scientific literature is nearly unanimous in its support of the thesis that climate change is occurring and that it is *anthropogenic* (a.k.a. human induced) (Oreskes 2004), the general public holds a greater diversity of views (see ECOnnection 2.1).

So we are left with sociological questions. Some of these include, for example, "What might account for the aforementioned discrepancy between the views held among climate scientists and the general public?" "How did we get ourselves into this mess?" and "Why is it proving so hard to change course?"—though, I am sorry to say, a thorough treatment of these questions will have to wait for later sections of the book when we talk about pressures and drivers. In this chapter I address various societal impacts that we can expect from climate change—there are, unfortunately, many—and suggest potential solutions.

ECOnnection 2.1
The US Public's Knowledge of Climate Change

The Yale Project on Climate Change Communication (with funding help from the National Science Foundation) conducted a national survey on the public's understanding of climate change. The survey sought to measure general public understanding in the United States about how the climate system works and the causes, impacts, and potential solutions to global warming. The study found that 63 percent of Americans believe that climate change is occurring, though many do not understand why. The study found important gaps in knowledge and widespread misconceptions about climate change and the earth system. Below are just some of the findings contained in this report:

- 66 percent correctly understand that the greenhouse gases trap heat in the earth's atmosphere. Twenty-one percent incor-

rectly believe they make up the earth's protective ozone layer, while another 10 percent say they don't know.

- 50 percent of Americans understand that global warming is caused mostly by human activities.
- 45 percent understand that carbon dioxide (CO_2) traps heat from the earth's surface.
- Respondents also recognized their own limited understanding of the issues, with many expressing a desire to know more. Only 1 in 10 say that they are "very well informed" about climate change, and 75 percent say they would like to know more. Likewise, 75 percent say that schools should teach our children about climate change, and 68 percent would welcome a national program to teach Americans about the issue.

Adopted from Leiserowitz, Smith, and Marlon (2010).

Fast Facts

A portion of the sun's short-wave radiation that enters the atmosphere is absorbed by the earth's surfaces, where it is then transferred into long-wave radiation (namely, heat) and reradiated back into space. Some of this energy, however, is absorbed by the planet's atmosphere, thanks to greenhouse gases like CO_2, a process known as the **greenhouse effect**.

Not only are atmospheric levels of greenhouse gases rising, but the *rate of increase is growing.* In the 1970s and 1980s, global emissions of CO_2 from burning fossil fuels increased at a rate of 2 percent annually. Since 2000 the annual rate of increase of the world's CO_2 emissions is now 3 percent. At this rate of increase, global CO_2 emissions will *double* every 25 years (Hamilton 2010:4).

Present levels of atmospheric CO_2 have never been higher in the past 420,000 years (Kirkham 2011).

Humans emit more than 20 billion tons of CO_2 into the atmosphere, while natural emissions (coming from plants breathing out CO_2 and outgassing from the ocean) equal about 776 billion tons of CO_2 per year. Natural sources, however, absorb *more* than they emit—roughly 788 billion tons annually. Yet this difference is not enough to compensate for all that humans pump into the atmosphere (IPCC 2007).

A comparison between satellite data from 1970 to 1996 found a steady decline in the amount of energy escaping to space at the wavelengths that greenhouse gases absorb. Since there was no indication that there was less solar energy coming in, this is *direct experimental evidence* for a significant increase in the earth's greenhouse effect (Harries et al. 2001). This evidence has since been independently corroborated by other studies (e.g., Chen et al. 2007; Griggs and Harries 2004).

More than 80 percent of the trapped energy that is the result of the increased greenhouse effect goes in warming the oceans (which isn't terribly surprising, given that oceans cover 71 percent of the earth's surface). The world's oceans, like its land and atmosphere, have been steadily warming over the past half century. For an example of this differential heating of oceans and land, recall the last time you walked on a dry beach on a sunny day. The sand gets warmer faster than the ocean. That is because water is a slow conductor of heat and thus needs to absorb more energy than the sand (or land) for its temperature to increase. Similarly, once warmed, water takes longer to lose its heat than sand (or land).

Three billion years ago, the earth's atmosphere contained very low levels of oxygen but a great deal of CO_2. At the time, the world was teeming with bacteria, many of which survived by breaking down sugars and chemicals present in their environment—a process known as fermentation. These fermenting bacteria produced methane and CO_2— two greenhouse gases—as waste products. Over time these bacteria evolved to use sunlight to split the strong bonds of hydrogen and oxygen found in water. The waste produced was oxygen, which over many millions of years began accumulating and changed the composition of the earth's atmosphere (which today contains roughly 78 percent nitrogen, 20 percent oxygen, 1 percent argon, around 1 percent water vapor, and 0.039 percent CO_2). This atmosphere killed off many species ill adapted to an oxygen-rich environment. But it also led to the emergence of new life forms, such as, eventually, humans. In sum, the history of life *itself* is an intricate story of the coevolution between life, the earth, and the atmosphere (see Clark and York 2005).

Implications

While all are impacted by changing ecological conditions, some are clearly more threatened than others. We are still learning how climate change impacts human societies. Yet although the image emerging lacks high resolution, it is clear that climate change is going to be of major sociological consequence. The forthcoming discussion is organized around the following themes to speak of some of these consequences: urban areas; food security; children, women, and the elderly; and climate change refugees.

? ?

ETHICAL QUESTION 2.1

The Most Threatened Are the Least Responsible

Many of the urban centers that face the largest increase in threats due to climate change—and with the least capacity to deal with these threats—are in nations least responsible for global warming, as their national greenhouse gas emissions per capita are among the lowest in the world. As illustrated in Figure 2.1, whereas countries in Western Europe, North America, the UK, the Mediterranean, and Australia, Japan, and New Zealand account for only 19.7 percent of the world's population, they are far and away the lead contributors of total global greenhouse gas emissions (with a 16.1t CO_2 eq/cap national average). The rest of the world, meanwhile, as a result of being less affluent, has less capacity to adequately respond to the hazards of climate change. Is this fair? Seeing as they bear a significant share of blame, do affluent nations have a responsibility to help the rest of the world adapt to climate change?

FIGURE 2.1 Regional Per Capita Greenhouse Gas Emissions Relative to Population.

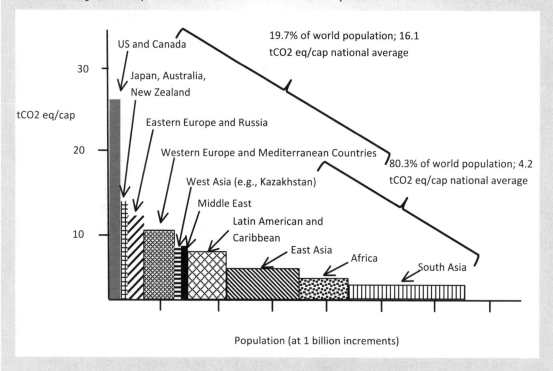

Adapted from IPCC (2007).

Urban Areas

As the number of people living in cities continues to grow—more than half of the world's population now resides in an urban area—so too will the number of urban residents vulnerable to climate change (see Ethical Question 2.1). Climate change–related risks facing those residing in urban centers are a function not only of actual events but also of the capacity (or lack thereof) of organizations, social networks, and governments (local and national) to respond to and withstand environmental threats. For example, the quality of housing and infrastructure-based services (like water and sewage), which are typically taken for granted in affluent nations, will considerably shape a society's ability to withstand certain hazards.

Within **informal settlements** (unplanned groups of housing that are constructed on land illegally or are not in compliance with current building regulations, or both), houses rarely comply with official safety standards and are often crowded and poorly maintained, making for a deadly witch's brew of sorts in a future where drastic weather swings become increasingly the norm. There is also very little coordination between neighbors when building these structures and altering the landscape, which increases the entire neighborhood's vulnerability to climate change. In the low-lying outskirts of Buenos Aires, for example, because neighbors lack any significant level of social cohesion, homes are built in an entirely uncoordinated fashion. Some of these homes are elevated. And throughout the settlement, ground has been moved without any thought given to drainage. Thus, when it rains some homes are hit particularly hard either because they are low lying or due to landscape alterations that place them in the path of most of the runoff (Barros 2006).

The vast majority of the world's poor also live without air-conditioning or adequate insulation, making heat waves lethal to the very young and old and the ill (Luber and McGeehin 2008). Exacerbating matters further is the fact that in many cities in low-income countries, a sizable proportion of the poor live in tenements and central districts with excessively high densities, precisely where the urban **heat island effect** is at its most pronounced. This effect describes the well-documented phenomenon of how built-up areas are warmer than nearby rural areas. Because concrete, tarmac, and other common construction materials absorb heat readily, the annual average air temperature of a city with at least 1 million people is between 1.8–5.4°F (1–3°C) warmer than the area outside of the city. In the evening, as this solar energy is released back into the atmosphere, the difference in temperature between city and countryside can be as high as 22°F (12°C) (see Image 2.1). (My grandmother has told me stories of going to bed as a child in the winter with a heated brick under the covers. It's the same principle.) Heat islands increase summertime peak energy demands, air-conditioning costs, greenhouse gas emissions, and heat-related illness and mortality. And as the mean atmospheric temperature continues to rise, the effect will become only more pronounced in the years ahead.

Countries with adequate resources and institutions, infrastructure, services, and regulations in place to protect public health will be able to adapt rapidly to a changing climate. There are many measures implemented in affluent nations that (often unknowingly) enhance a city's adaptive capabilities to climate change: integrated health-care services with emergency services; sufficient sewer and drainage capacity to serve

IMAGE 2.1 Urban Heat Island Effect

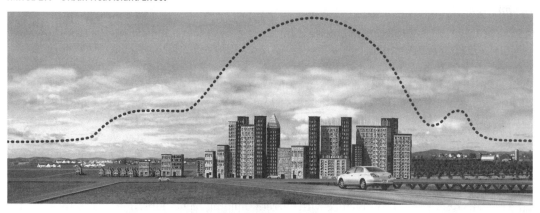

The dotted line represents the mean late-afternoon summer temperatures for the average city (with at least 1 million inhabitants) and surrounding landscapes. Research indicates that cities are between 1.8 and 5.4°F (1 and 3°C) warmer than the countryside immediately surrounding them, whereas temperature increases recorded in suburban residential districts show a slightly less pronounced heat-island effect. *Source:* NASA.

not only daily requirements but also less frequent (but high-capacity) storm events; structures that conform to building codes and health and safety regulations and that are serviced by piped water, sewers, all-weather roads, and electricity twenty-four hours a day; and institutions that can respond rapidly to high-impact weather events, from utility companies to repair downed power lines to the National Guard (as in the United States) for the more severe events (Bartlett et al. 2009). A summary of some urban and associated health impacts linked to climate change confronting populations within low-income nations are listed in Table 2.1.

A growing proportion of the world's population is also residing in what are known as **low-elevation coastal zones** (LECZ), a trend occurring most rapidly in least-developed countries. This refers to areas within ten meters of mean sea level (which represents about 2 percent of the world's land area). The coastal cities most at risk are in low-income countries (Revi 2008). More than 600 million people (or 10 percent of the world's population) are estimated to live within these low-elevation zones. Of these, 360 million reside in urban areas (13 percent of the world's urban population). In China alone, approximately 144 million people reside in an LECZ. The country with the greatest proportion of its population living in an LECZ is the Bahamas, where 88 percent of the country lives (elevation-wise) within ten meters of sea level (McGranahan, Balk, and Anderson 2007).

Some of the fastest urban expansion in low-income nations is also taking place in floodplains, along mountain slopes, and in other zones prone to flooding, sea surges, or other weather-related hazards (Bartlett et al. 2009). Individuals living in these risky sites are typically poor, as those with means can afford to live someplace safer. Consequently, not only are the sites themselves poorly suited for settlement, but the houses are often structurally deficient and thus do not provide adequate protection from more intense and frequent weather-related threats (see Case Study 2.1).

TABLE 2.1 Climate Change Impacts, Urban and Health

CHANGE	URBAN IMPACTS	HEALTH IMPACTS
Temperature	Increased energy demand for heating/cooling; worsening of air quality	Increased vulnerability to respiratory diseases; young and elderly particularly at risk
Precipitation	Increased risk of flooding; increased risk of landslides; distress migration	Increase in waterborne and water-washed diseases; food shortages and malnutrition
Sea-level rise	Coastal flooding; salinization of water sources	Loss of land and property; health problems from salinated water (especially children)
Extreme rainfall / tropical cyclones	More intense flooding; higher risk of landslides; disruption to livelihoods and city economies	Higher levels of mortality and morbidity; loss of income and assets
Drought	Water shortages; higher food prices; disruption of hydro-electricity	Higher prevalence of waterborne and water-washed diseases; food shortages
Heat- or cold-waves	Short-term changes in energy demand	Mortality from extreme heat or cold
Abrupt climate change	Rapid and extreme sea-level rise / rapid and extreme temperature change	Significant effects on morbidity and mortality (especially in most vulnerable groups)
Population movements	Movements from stressed rural habitats	Increased population; increased stress on infrastructure and resources
Biological changes	Extended vector habitats	Increased risk of diseases such as malaria and dengue

Source: Adapted from Bartlett et al. (2009).

Food Security

According to the Food and Agriculture Organization (FAO) of the United Nations (UN), the world's poor will likely be (if not already) the first affected by global warming as they are food insecure to begin with. Future climate changes will only exacerbate this vulnerability through an increased risk of crop failure, new patterns of pests and diseases, lack of appropriate seeds and planting material for the changing micro and macro climates, and through the loss of livestock (FAO 2008; see also ECOnnection 2.2). It is worth noting, so it can be immediately set aside, the claim that CO_2 emissions are good

CASE STUDY 2.1

Flooding in Santa Fe,
Argentina

The city of Santa Fe, Argentina (with about 400,000 inhabitants), has been slowly expanding onto the Río Salado floodplain. A major flood in 2003—the worst since the city was founded in 1573 (BBC 2003)—forced the evacuation of some 100,000 people. In the end, 24 people had officially died (local estimates where considerably higher), and 28,000 houses were damaged or destroyed (Bartlett et al. 2009). The floods were also said to be responsible for a dramatic increase in hepatitis and gastrointestinal illnesses (BBC 2003). Some reasons cited for the flood include several days of heavy rainfall (causing many of the area's major rivers to rise as much as fifty centimeters in twelve hours), deforestation, and land-use changes around the city. The city was largely unprepared for the event, just as it was for additional major flooding in 2006 and 2007.

Urban expansion into floodplains over the past fifty years is a major reason for the city's heightened vulnerability to flooding. It has even been reported that the local government encourages settlement into these high-risk areas by supplying the homes with piped water and electricity in exchange for political support. Levees and other infrastructure to defend the city were never completed due to insufficient resources. Likewise, although studies have highlighted the need to increase the capacity of bridges to ease evacuation pressures, these improvements lack the funding to be undertaken. Pumps and drainage infrastructure throughout the city have also been cited as being in a state of disrepair (Bartlett et al. 2009).

for humanity because they will turn the world into a lush oasis—CO_2, after all, is "plant food." Let's remember that plants rely on more than just CO_2 to survive. Any so-called CO_2 fertilizer effect will therefore be limited, as ecosystems become increasingly overwhelmed by the negative effects of heat damage and drought. To put it simply: plants can't metabolize CO_2 when stressed by a lack of water and excessive heat. Or to put it more simply still: they can't grow when they're dying.

With models used in the analyses that informed the *Fourth Assessment Report* by the **Intergovernmental Panel on Climate Change** (IPCC) (IPCC 2007), Battisti and Naylor (2009) conclude there is a greater than 90 percent chance that average growing-season temperatures by this century's end will exceed any single growing-season average recorded between 1900 and 2006 for most of the tropics and subtropics (see Case Study 2.2). (The IPCC was established by two UN organizations, the United Nations Environment Programme [UNEP] and the World Meteorological Organization, in 1988 to provide scientific assessments on issues relating to climate change. With the IPCC as the internationally accepted authority on the subject, the world's governments look to it as the official advisory body on climate change.) More than 3 billion currently live at these latitudes (and undoubtedly this number will increase in the decades ahead), many of whom live in **abject poverty** (a severe state of poverty) and depend on

ECOnnection 2.2

Climate Change Linked to Food-Related Vulnerabilities for Certain Populations

The FAO has highlighted certain populations that warrant special attention due to their heightened food-related vulnerabilities attributable to climate change. These populations include:

- low-income groups in drought- and flood-prone areas with poor food-distribution infrastructure and limited access to emergency response
- low- to middle-income groups in flood-prone areas that may lose homes, stored food, personal possessions, and means of obtaining an income;
- farmers whose land risks becoming submerged or damaged due to sea-level rise or saltwater intrusions
- farmers who lack capital to adjust to changing temperature and rainfall conditions
- farmers at risk from high winds

- low-income livestock keepers in drylands where changes in rainfall patterns will affect forage availability and quality
- low-income livestock keepers who, due to heat waves, will lose animals from excessive heat
- fishers whose infrastructure for fishing activities (e.g., port, landing, and storage facilities, fish ponds, and processing areas) becomes submerged or damaged by sea-level rise, flooding, or other extreme weather events
- fishing communities whose livelihoods depend on the presence of healthy coral reefs for food and protection from natural disasters
- fishers and aqua farmers whose catch suffers from shifts in fish distribution and the productivity of aquatic ecosystems due to changes in ocean currents and temperatures, increased discharge of freshwater into oceans, or both

Adopted from FAO (2008).

agriculture for their survival. While the wealthiest of the world's farmers will have the resources to adopt new technologies and techniques suited for future agroecological conditions, those living at a subsistence level likely will not. The biggest losers from climate change could well be those who depend most on agriculture, aqua culture, and pastoral animal husbandry and who have the least alternative sources of income, namely, the poor.

Children, Women, and the Elderly

The roles of women in less developed countries are as diverse as they are important. A classic piece from 1991 on women's work in tribal India highlights the following major areas of work in poor rural areas that are overwhelmingly performed by women: food procurement, such as food gathering and production; the protection of life and property, including the procurement of water, energy (e.g., fire wood, charcoal, and so on), and

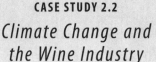

CASE STUDY 2.2
Climate Change and
the Wine Industry

Few crops are as vulnerable to temperature and extreme weather events as wine grapes. And with the prime agroecological conditions go the spoils: for example, there was a fifteenfold price difference in 2006 between cabernet sauvignon grapes grown in Napa Valley (US$4,100/ton), California, and those raised in California's warmer Central Valley (US$260/ton). The difference in average temperature between the regions: 5°F (or roughly 2.8°C) (Hertsgaard 2010).

In France there is worry that the famed Champagne region will become too hot to produce premium-quality champagne. And regarding the famed reds from the Châteauneuf-du-Pape region in southeastern

France: their prized white soil, once cherished for its ability to hold heat, may become the region's downfall. Thanks to climate change, the premium wine grape production area in the United States could shrink by as much as 81 percent by this century's end (White et al. 2006). The real killer for the industry is not so much the rise in average temperatures but an increased frequency of excessively hot days, which could "eliminate wine grape production in many areas of the United States." Adding further insult to injury, US "grape and wine production will likely be restricted to a narrow West Coast region and the Northwest and Northeast, areas currently facing challenges related to excess moisture" (ibid.:11217).

fodder; and childbearing and rearing, including the maintenance of health standards for the household, like securing clean water and collecting medicinal plants (Menon 1991). Note how climate change has the ability to touch on all these areas. Floods, droughts, wildfires, and higher or colder than average temperatures all impact the lives of those responsible for the well-being of the household, which continues to be (especially in less affluent nations) women (see Figure 2.2). It is again one more case of climate change having a disproportional impact on a population that is neither to blame for its existence nor capable of responding to its effects due to a lack of resources (Dankelman 2010; see ECOnnection 2.3).

During extreme events like flooding, high winds, landslides, and tsunamis in poor countries, the loss of life is disproportionately higher among children, women, and the elderly (Neumayer and Plumper 2007). A study of a severe flood in 1993 that devastated the Sarlahi district in Nepal found the death rate for children aged two to nine to be more than twice that of adult men (among preschool girls the rate was five times greater). When aggregated according to class, death rates among poorer households were found to be six times more than those of higher-income households (Pradhan et al. 2007). Rising temperatures are also expanding the range of tropical diseases, with children the most susceptible. Diseases like malaria also increase the severity of other maladies, in some cases more than doubling the overall mortality of young children (Bartlett et al. 2009). The young and the old, as already mentioned, are also at the greatest risk

FIGURE 2.2 Women and Their Vulnerability to Climate Change

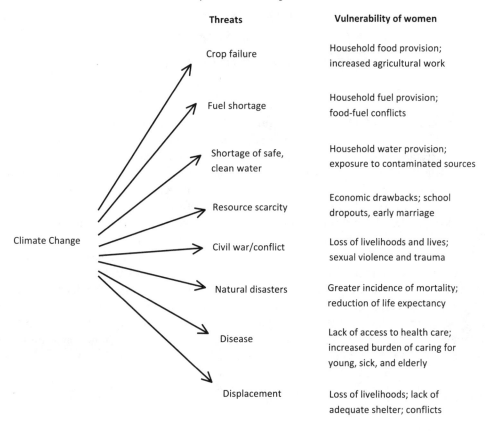

Threats	Vulnerability of women
Crop failure	Household food provision; increased agricultural work
Fuel shortage	Household fuel provision; food-fuel conflicts
Shortage of safe, clean water	Household water provision; exposure to contaminated sources
Resource scarcity	Economic drawbacks; school dropouts, early marriage
Civil war/conflict	Loss of livelihoods and lives; sexual violence and trauma
Natural disasters	Greater incidence of mortality; reduction of life expectancy
Disease	Lack of access to health care; increased burden of caring for young, sick, and elderly
Displacement	Loss of livelihoods; lack of adequate shelter; conflicts

Source: Adapted from WEDO (2008).

from heat waves. A study looking at the relationship between temperature and mortality in São Paulo, Brazil, found that every degree increase above 20°C was associated with a 2.6 percent increase in overall mortality in children under fifteen and in adults over sixty-five (Gouveia, Hajat, and Armstrong 2003).

Climate Change Refugees

Climate change will fundamentally alter the lives of millions who will eventually be forced in years ahead to leave their villages and cities in search of refuge, fresh water, food, employment, and the like. The **climate change refugees** crisis is expected to surpass all known refugee crises in terms of the number of people affected (Oliver-Smith 2009). (The term *climate change refugees* refers to populations that have been displaced due to climate change.) The issue will likely be most pronounced in poorer countries, where the adaptive capacity of people, cities, and nations to the effects of climate change is low (see Case Study 2.3). In more affluent countries, a refugee crisis may be largely avoided through successful steps at adapting to climate change, like fortified coastal protections or changes in agricultural production and water-supply management (and by having the capability to tightly patrol and effectively close one's borders). The term

ECOnnection 2.3
Testimony from Satou Diouf
(Female from the Gadiag
Village, Senegal)

We the women are responsible for feeding our families. The bush has now become a desert shrub in my area and there is nowhere to go to fetch wood. It is prohibited to cut acacia trees. If caught, one has to pay a fine. Every morning, we go to the bush with our bassinette to fetch cow dung for cooking. Unfortunately, during the dry season, it is rare to find foraging livestock. Therefore, we don't have a choice but to go against the Department of Water and Forests and cut acacia trees. One day, unable to find enough wood after a long search, I used some branches to cook. Since the wood was not enough, I cut my plastic bassinette in pieces to fuel the fire. My bassinette was gone before I finished cooking. Then I took the wooden bench where I was seated and cut it to feed the fire. That was not enough. I also had to use my bed sheet for the fire so the food could cook. After serving the food, my mother-in-law refused to eat. She said she didn't think food cooked with plastic bassinette and bed sheet was edible. I told her that if she doesn't eat, the children would eat her portion. Still, she refused. Since that day, I have been crying whenever I think of that incident. My children who don't understand why my eyes are always watery keep asking me why I cry, and I tell them that I am not crying; that's the way my eyes have become!

Quoted in WEDO (2008:26).

adaptation is useful here, as it refers to actions taken to adjust socioecological systems in response to existing or predicted climatic effects to reduce harmful effects. It is worth wondering, however, how many of these displaced people in the future will be seeking refuge in countries like the United States and will they will be granted access (Biermann and Boas 2010).

At present, the developing world hosts the vast majority of the world's refugees: four-fifths, to be exact. According to the UN, the forty-nine poorest nations provided asylum to almost 2 million refugees in 2010 (UNHCR 2010). This raises a question: what opportunities await refugees if they are seeking refuge in countries that can't even supply sufficient opportunities to their own residents?

In addition to lacking financial resources, refugees are also usually poorly integrated into the community and lack connections to influential people, institutions, and organizations, having left behind all their social networks when they moved (Lamba and Krahn 2003). In most cases, it takes years for refugees to insert themselves into local communities, at which point they may begin to participate in community organizations and local government. Research also indicates that climate change–induced population displacement is not gender neutral, especially when it comes to factors driving migration (Hunter and David 2011). For instance, research looking at migration from West African nations due to climate stress suggests that a recent rash of deaths of young male mi-

---

CASE STUDY 2.3

Climate Refugees from Indonesia and Bangladesh

Two countries viewed as prime candidates for climate change–induced migration are Indonesia and Bangladesh.

- Indonesia: Roughly 85 percent of this island nation of about 300 million people live within just a few miles of the coast. The steep inland terrain makes much of the noncoastal parts of the country poorly suited for large-scale resettlements. Some of the population could move inland temporarily to escape tidal surges and tropical storms. The more likely scenario, however, has a sizable population leaving the island entirely as sea levels rise.

- Bangladesh: This is a country of 160 million people living essentially at sea level. The country has already been hit by serious storms. Hurricane Sidr, for example, devastated the nation in 2007, killing, officially, 3,447 people, though some estimates place the death toll closer to 10,000. These storms are expected to increase in both intensity and frequency in the future. This, coupled with even a modest sea-level rise, risks making much of the country potentially uninhabitable. From this country alone, the world could see an additional 100 million refugees.

Based on Climate Refugees (2010).

---

grants trying to reach Europe by boat is in part due to gendered cultural variables (Terry 2009). As the main economic providers of their households, many of these men felt compelled to seek out incomes for their families, even if that meant placing themselves in harm's way by migrating by small boats to other countries. Environmental "push" factors have also been shown to impact women. In Nepal's Chitwan Valley, for example, outmigration among women has been linked to environmental deterioration. Specifically, as collection times increase for fodder and firewood for the Chitwan Valley's women residents, so too increases their likelihood of migration (Bohra-Mishra and Massey 2011).

Population displacement due to climate change has also been linked to conflict (Hartmann 2010; Reuveny 2007). Some contributing factors to climate change–induced conflict include the following:

- Competition: The arrival of climate change refugees into an area can increase the competition over already scarce resources, especially in nations where property rights are underdeveloped.
- Ethnic tension: When climate migrants and residents belong to different ethnic groups, climate-induced migration may promote tension. This will be a particular problem in regions and countries with long-standing ethnic disputes between migrants and residents.

FIGURE 2.3 Comparing the Costs of Climate Action versus Climate Inaction

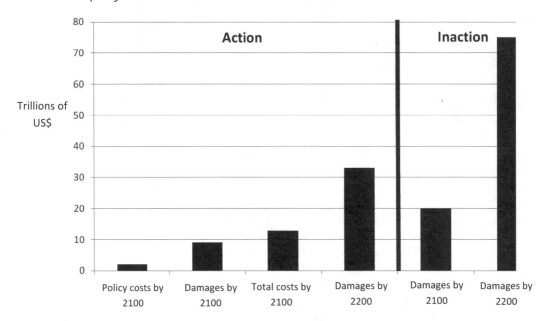

Although critics of taking immediate action to combat climate change like to cite the costs of this strategy, research indicates that we simply cannot afford to not take action. The costs of mitigating and adapting to climate change today are minuscule when compared to the costs of doing nothing, particularly after factoring in for predicated damages. *Source:* Adapted from Kemfert (2005) and Watkiss et al. (2005).

- Fault lines: Conflict may also follow previously established socioeconomic fault lines, such as between migrant pastoralists and resident farmers competing over land or migrants and residents competing over jobs.
- Weak states: Political instability and civil strife in receiving countries will also increase the likelihood of conflict, as weak states are less capable of keeping the peace if tensions were to arise between migrants and residents for any of the above reasons.

Solutions

Let's say we lived on a planet whose sun was expanding and consequently warming at an alarming rate. If nothing was done, future generations would experience wildly different (in a bad way) climate patterns. Under this scenario I am willing to bet—just as if an asteroid were on a collision course with the earth—there would be considerable social and political will to take action. That action would likely include not only adapting to post–tipping point climate patterns but also **mitigation** strategies (that is, lessening our greenhouse gas footprint), knowing the role emissions play in contributing to the greenhouse effect. (As opposed to adaptation, mitigation refers to making reductions in the concentration of greenhouse gases by reducing their sources, increasing absorption capacity, or both.) My point is that we know the earth's atmospheric temperature is rising, and we know these warming trends are going to have devastating social effects.

Does it really matter who—or what—we assign blame to for all of this? With that in mind, let's turn to some solutions to the problems of greenhouse gas emissions and climate change more generally.

The Cost of Action versus Inaction

One major excuse for not taking action to combat climate change is that such action is cost prohibitive. A number of analyses, however, find just the opposite to be true. According to reports commissioned by the German government (Kemfert 2005) and the European Union (EU) (Watkiss et al. 2005), the total cost of climate action (cost plus damages) in 2100 is roughly US$12 trillion, whereas the cost of inaction (damages alone) is approximately US$20 trillion (see Figure 2.3). The discrepancy is even more pronounced when costs are extrapolated out to the year 2200: damages if nothing is done total US$75 trillion versus US$33 trillion if reasonable steps are taken today. The steps prescribed in these reports include emissions trading, ecological taxes, and an international kerosene tax in addition to financial incentives that favor climate-friendly renewable-energy technologies.

Seventeen Pragmatic Behavioral Changes

Energy consumed by households accounts for roughly 38 percent of all CO_2 emissions in the United States (or approximately 8 percent of global emissions). A study by Thomas Dietz and others (2009) explored ways in which those emissions can be reduced through behavioral changes. Their findings are encouraging, explaining that a 20 percent emissions reduction can be achieved in the US household sector within ten years through some well-targeted policies aimed at changing behaviors. To put this into some perspective, the reduction that Dietz and colleagues are expecting is slightly *larger* than the total national emissions of France and *greater* than cutting to zero all emissions in the United States from the pollution-intensive sectors of petroleum refining and iron, steel, and aluminum manufacturing.

To get to this level of household-emissions reduction, the authors analyzed seventeen types of household activities that rely upon existing technology, are low in cost or bring attractive returns on investment, and do not require appreciable changes to one's lifestyle. They then estimated the potential emissions reduction (PER) in terms of CO_2 after ten years from each action (in other words, the total reduction that would be achieved if every household in the United States adopted it). Next they estimated plasticity into their study, which, according to the authors, "introduces a behavioral realism" (ibid.:18453). This represents an assessment of the percentage of current nonadapters who could be enticed to make the behavioral change. Table 2.2 shows the seventeen behavioral changes along with their associated PER, behavioral plasticity, adjusted PER after accounting for behavioral plasticity (a.k.a. "reasonably achievable emissions reduction," or RAER), and RAER as a percentage of total US household-sector emissions. As illustrated in the table, the four lowest-hanging fruits are (1) the adoption of fuel-efficient vehicles, (2) weatherization, (3) the adoption of high-efficiency appliances, and (4) the use of more efficient home heating and cooling systems. Combined, these four steps are estimated to result in a 12 percent reduction in CO_2 emissions in the United States.

TABLE 2.2 Achievable Carbon Emission Reductions Resulting from Household Actions

BEHAVIORAL CHANGE	PER (MTC)	BEHAVIORAL PLASTICITY (%)	RAER (MTC)	RAER AS PERCENTAGE OF TOTAL US HOUSEHOLD SECTOR EMISSIONS
Weatherization	25.2	90	21.2	3.39
HVAC (central heating, ventilation, and air-conditioning systems) and equipment	12.2	80	10.7	1.72
Low flow showerheads	1.4	80	1.1	0.18
Efficient water heater	6.7	80	5.4	0.86
Appliances	14.7	80	11.7	1.87
Low rolling resistance tires	7.4	80	6.5	1.05
Fuel efficient vehicle	56.3	50	31.4	5.02
Laundry temperature	0.5	35	0.2	0.04
Water heater temperature	2.9	35	1.0	0.17
Standby electricity	9.2	35	3.2	0.52
Thermostat setbacks	10.1	35	4.5	0.71
Line drying	6.0	35	2.2	0.35
Change HVAC air filers	8.7	30	3.7	0.59
Tune up AC (air conditioner)	3.0	30	1.4	0.22
Routine auto maintenance	8.6	30	4.1	0.66
Driving behavior	24.1	25	7.7	1.23
Carpooling	36.1	15	6.4	1.02
Totals	233	--	123	20

Source: Adapted from Dietz et al. (2009).

FIGURE 2.4 Stabilization Triangle

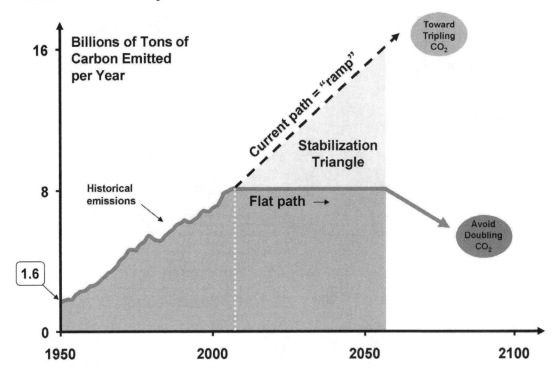

The stabilization triangle refers to the total carbon savings that must be achieved to hold CO_2 emissions at a constant level and avoid the predicted tripling of output by 2060. *Source:* Remik Ziemlinski, the Carbon Mitigation Initiative, Princeton University.

Stabilization Triangle and Wedges

Carbon emissions from the burning of fossil fuels are projected to double in the next fifty years. This business-as-usual scenario will lead to a tripling of atmospheric CO_2 from preindustrial levels. But let's say we wanted to keep emissions essentially flat over the next fifty years, followed by a decrease in CO_2 emissions as technologies improve and become cheaper (see Figure 2.4). In the United States, such a strategy would require cutting the projected carbon output by some 9 billion tons per year by 2060; globally, 225 billion tons might need to be cut annually. The amount that would need to be cut to level off CO_2 emissions has been called the "stabilization triangle." Let's say, then, that each billion tons of CO_2 avoided represent a "wedge." (At the global level, each wedge represents 25 billion tons, as the entire stabilization triangle involves cutting CO_2 output by some 225 billion tons per year by 2060.) Nine wedges like this in the United States would stabilize CO_2 output (and nine at 25 billion tons a piece would stabilize levels worldwide). So the question is: can we do it? It looks like we can.

Wedges can take different forms. The behavioral changes outlined in the earlier-mentioned study by Dietz and colleagues (ibid.) could certainly represent one such wedge. Another wedge or two could involve zero-emission technologies like wind and solar power. Still other wedges might come from building carbon-storage capacity of

FIGURE 2.5 Stabilization Triangle, Now versus Then

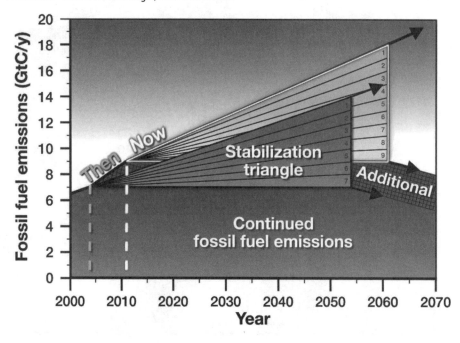

If we had acted in 2004, when the stabilization triangle was first introduced, we would have needed only seven wedges. But in 2011, nine wedges were required to fill the stabilization triangle. The effect is compounding. *Source:* Remik Ziemlinski, the Carbon Mitigation Initiative, Princeton University.

sinks (a natural or artificial reservoir—like a forest—that holds and stores greenhouses gases for an indefinite period, thus preventing their accumulation in the atmosphere). There may also be a wedge by moving toward carbon capture and storage coal plants, though this technology, as discussed further in Chapter 9, is still in its infancy (Carbon Mitigation Initiative 2011). One thing is certain: we cannot afford to wait. Princeton University professor and codirector of the Carbon Mitigation Initiative Robert Socolow—who along with Steve Pacala (see Pacala and Socolow 2004) came up with the "stabilization triangle" concept—recently noted that in 2011 nine wedges were required to fill the stabilization triangle (Socolow 2011). Yet only *seven* would have been needed if we had acted when the stabilization triangle was first introduced back in 2004 (see Figure 2.5). Our collective unwillingness to take climate change seriously also means we could expect an extra half-degree Celsius rise in the average surface temperature of the planet even if we were to come up with all nine wedges today due to the atmosphere having stabilized at a higher total emissions level (indicated in Figure 2.5 by "Additional" to the right of the wedges). And if we wait still longer to act, even more wedges will be required (which means an even higher-average surface temperature after stabilization).

Green Building

The energy consumed in the US building sector constitutes about half (48 percent) of all energy used in the country. Globally, that percentage is even higher—76 percent. In light of these figures, any serious attempt to reduce greenhouse gas emissions must include changes to the building sector. Yet buildings are not as flexible as, say, behaviors. Whereas I could conceivably be enticed to drastically change my ways in an attempt to radically reduce my CO_2 footprint, it is often not as easy (or cost-effective in the short term) to turn an old, poorly insulated, leaky building into a paragon of ecoefficiency. Yet when building new, there is now little excuse not to go "green." The cost to build highly efficient buildings increases total costs between 0 and 2 percent. Yet this investment yields a total life-cycle savings of 20 percent (Lovins and Cohen 2011:99).

There are still other ways it pays to go green when it comes to our buildings, beyond the obvious saving in energy costs. Green building, to put it bluntly, also makes people happy. In buildings that optimize the use of daylight, students perform better (Heschong, Wright, and Okura 2002), while employees express greater satisfaction and display greater productivity (L. Whitehead et al. 2010). Consumers have also been shown to buy more in stores using natural lighting, a fact that business owners may like to hear but one that has obvious broader ecological consequences. As employers on average pay one hundred times more for people as they do for energy, a "mere" 1 percent increase in productivity would go a long way toward offsetting the costs of green building (Lovins and Cohen 2011:100).

Taking a step back, let's talk briefly about the built urban environment. Cities are now home to more than half of the world's population. They also consume more than 75 percent of the world's energy and account for 80 percent of global greenhouse gas emissions (Hoffmann 2011:104). If New York worked to reduce its carbon emissions 30 percent over the next twenty years, the city would see substantial savings from this efforts in terms of energy consumed and emissions released into the atmosphere. Perhaps less recognized, however, are benefits to the labor market that would follow as tens of thousands of new jobs would be created to retrofit, caulk, seal, and insulate the city's buildings (Lovins and Cohen 2011:118).

More than 80 percent of all commercial buildings in the United States are greater than ten years old and therefore represent a considerable opportunity for reducing energy savings and carbon emissions. It has been calculated that if all commercial space built as of 2010 were included in a ten-year retrofit program, the savings in energy expenses could exceed US$41.1 billion annually (Bayani 2010). The cost to carry out such a plan: US$22.5 billion for each year of the ten-year period. Not only does that represent a sound investment—after all, taxpayers would be getting almost twice as much as what they put in—but that US$22.5 billion spent annually to retrofit the nation's commercial buildings would create a lot of good-paying jobs. For roughly the same price it costs the United States to air-condition its military bases and embassies in Iraq and Afghanistan annually (US$20.2 billion) (NPR 2011), it could work toward green-retrofitting every commercial building in the United States.

In June 2011, the Carbon Disclosure Project—a UK-based organization that publicizes the greenhouse gas emissions of major corporations—released its first-ever global report on city governments. The report details how many of the world's largest urban centers are tackling greenhouse gas emissions. For example, some 57 percent of reporting cities claim to have adopted citywide greenhouse gas reduction targets. The most commonly mentioned reduction activities are subsidies and other financial incentives to improve building efficiencies. Yet some cities are showing clear leadership by supporting

ECOnnection 2.4

Examples of Geoengineering, Mitigation, and Adaptation

GEOENGINEERING (CO₂ REMOVAL)

Ocean fertilization: Iron filings would be dumped into the ocean to spur phytoplankton blooms that draw CO_2 from the atmosphere (a saltwater version of forestation). Some downsides: we do not know what this would do to ocean life (it could likely have a negative effect), and blooms could release methane (another greenhouse gas).

GEOENGINEERING (SOLAR-RADIATION MANAGEMENT)

Space mirrors: Hundreds of thousands of thin reflective disks fired into low earth orbit could lower the amount of solar energy that enters the earth's atmosphere. Some downsides: cost aside, the rocket fuel burned to place these little mirrors in orbit would inject massive quantities of black soot into the atmosphere, which would absorb sunlight, trap heat, and thus exacerbate global warming.

MITIGATION

Carbon tax: Tax carbon emissions and therefore reward "green" behavior at both the industry and the household levels. Some downsides: energy-efficient technologies—from hybrid cars to high-efficiency furnaces—are more likely to be adopted by high-income households, meaning such a tax could fall disproportionately on those least able to afford it.

ADAPTATION

Genetically engineered (GE) food: Crops are currently being engineered to withstand changes to climate (e.g., drought tolerance). Some downsides: these seeds would likely be patented, meaning those most vulnerable (the poor) would likely not have access to these technologies; these plants may require additional inputs like fertilizer (which has its own significant CO_2 footprint) that could push the cost of production even higher; and there is always the risk that the crops will cross-breed with conventional or traditional (non-GE) plant varieties.

renewable energy initiatives and engaging in major infrastructure overhauls that involve making improvements in public transportation, cycling lanes and paths, and pedestrian areas. London, for example, hopes to have one hundred thousand electric vehicles on its streets by 2020. Seoul, South Korea, hopes to retrofit ten thousand buildings by 2030. And Austin, the capital of Texas, is aiming for zero waste by 2040 (Riffle 2011).

Geoengineering

Geoengineering (also known as climate engineering) is a term often used "to describe activities specifically and deliberately designed to effect a change in the global climate with the aim of minimizing or reversing anthropogenic climate change" (House of Commons 2010a:11). Geoengineering increasingly accompanies mitigation (strategies seeking to reduce our collective greenhouse gas footprint) and adaptation (strategies seeking to make communities, regions, and nations more resilient to the effects of climate change) in discussions about societal responses to global warming. Methods typically involve either CO_2 removal from the atmosphere or solar-radiation management, whereby the amount of solar energy that penetrates the earth's atmosphere is reduced (see ECOnnection 2.4). The idea of literally engineering the climate is nothing new, as scientists have been seriously discussing the possibility for well over a decade. What has changed in recent years, however, is that it is no longer just scientists who are talking about it. A watershed moment occurred in 2006 with an editorial essay by Nobel Prize–winning atmospheric scientist Paul Crutzen (2006). In this essay, Crutzen calls for serious consideration of geoengineering. With the idea now out in the open—as evidenced by the very fact that I am mentioning it here—talk of climate engineering has expanded beyond the scientific community, becoming a popular focal point of discussion and sometimes heated debate.

Late in 2010, during its meeting of the UN **Convention on Biological Diversity** (CBD) in Nagoya, Japan, the UN voted to impose a moratorium on geoengineering projects and experiments. (The Convention on Biological Diversity—an international legally binding treaty that entered into force in 1993—has three main goals: conservation of biological diversity, sustainable use of biological resources, and fair and equitable sharing of benefits arising from genetic resources.) The moratorium means all signatories to the CBD—a group of nations that, it is worth noting, does not include the United States—must ensure that climate-engineering projects do not take place until risks to the environment as well as social, cultural, and economic impacts have been properly assessed. This builds on a UN moratorium on ocean fertilization (adopted in 2008). Yet if we go by the definition provided at the beginning of this subsection, we are already geoengineering the climate, through "activities specifically and deliberately designed to effect a change in the global climate with the aim of minimizing or reversing anthropogenic climate change" (House of Commons 2010a:11). Based on this characterization, wouldn't the widely adopted practice of planting thousands of trees with the express purpose of "breathing in" CO_2 also be a case of geoengineering (see ECOnnection 2.5)?

Yet, in the end, does geoengineering really *solve* anything, or do these "solutions" better represent temporary technological Band-Aids? By totally ignoring the root cause(s) of climate change, what's to stop unrestrained emissions from rearing their ugly head again sometime in the future when we can no longer engineer away the warming effects of an atmosphere dense with greenhouse gases? I also worry that these "solutions" will make us complacent about the impact our actions have on the environment. Geoengineering, it could be argued, merely reinforces the unfounded belief that technology will continually ride in at the eleventh hour and save us.

Carbon Markets and Offsets

Cap and trade programs seek to halt (the "cap"), and eventually reduce, greenhouse gas emissions due to human activity. Cap and trade systems are regulatory programs that cap harmful greenhouse gas emissions by limiting them through a permitting system and distribute the allotted emissions to different participants (what are known as allowances, permits, or credits) who then trade them. The goal of the "cap" is to prevent further increases in net emissions. Cap and trade systems in principle therefore seek

ECOnnection 2.5
Biochar

The standard approach to removing carbon from the atmosphere is to grow plants (typically trees) that sequester CO_2 in their biomass or in soil organic matter. **Sequestering CO2—** the act of removing CO_2 from the atmosphere and holding it in a sink—through reforestation is in fact one of the more popular ways to "offset" carbon emissions. This sequestration can be taken a step further, however, by heating the plant biomass without oxygen, producing biomass-derived charcoal or what is known simply as "**biochar.**" Biochar is another name for charcoal derived from a thermochemical decomposition of organic material at heightened temperatures in the absence of oxygen. In some places, it has long been used to improve soil fertility and sequester carbon. Biochar oil and gas by-products can also be utilized as biofuels.

Fossil fuels are known as carbon positive, which is to say they add more carbon to the atmosphere. Sequestering carbon through typi-

cal biomass systems is, over the long term, largely carbon neutral, as much of the carbon captured will eventually be returned to the atmosphere as plants are burned for energy or through the inevitable process of decomposition. Biochar systems, however, can be carbon *negative* because they retain a substantial portion of the carbon fixed by plants. The precise length of time that the carbon remains locked up in biochar is still under debate, with claims ranging from millennia to "only" centuries. Calculations indicate that emission reductions can be up to 84 percent greater if biochar is put back into the soil instead of being burned to offset fossil-fuel use (burning, of course, would release some of the sequestered carbon into the atmosphere). Mixing it into the soil also reduces the need for fertilizer (leading to reduced emissions from fertilizer production) while increasing soil microbial life, which in turn leads to still greater carbon-storage capacity in the soil (Lehmann 2007).

absolute rather than just relative emissions efficiency. Those firms that find it most economical to reduce emissions can do so. The resulting **carbon credits** can then be sold to those who cannot yet modify operations to achieve emission reductions. Being market based, cap and trade schemes have found a receptive global audience, versus more top-down approaches that spell out specifically what firms can and cannot emit. Under cap and trade, firms still have a choice to pollute at higher levels. But to do so they will need to purchase allowances. Polluters therefore have an incentive to eventually clean up their acts.

Let's say, for example, that for a given year Firm X has ten carbon allowances, representing one thousand metric tons of greenhouse gas. Yet thanks to recently adopting certain greener technologies, they are able to reduce their annual greenhouse gas emissions to seven hundred metric tons. This firm will therefore have three emissions allowances, representing three hundred metric tons of greenhouse gas, which it can sell on the market.

The **Kyoto Protocol**—a UN treaty signed in 1997 that requires its signatories to reduce greenhouse gas emissions—is perhaps the most famous cap and trade scheme. But it's not the only one. Although refusing to sign on to Kyoto, the United States does house examples of successful cap and trade programs, as individuals, companies, and states are voluntarily making agreements to reduce emissions or purchase credits (or both) from others who have done so successfully. One example of this is the Chicago Climate Exchange, which launched in 2003. Before ceasing operations in 2010, it was North America's only voluntary, legally binding cap and trade system for emission sources and offset projects. Major chemical companies, electrical companies, and food processors who are involved in this exchange agreed to a 6 percent emissions reduction from their 2003 baseline levels by 2010. Those exceeding their limits can purchase credits from others who have successfully cut their emissions. Another example is the Regional Greenhouse Gas Initiative (RGGI). According to RGGI's website, this initiative involves ten northeastern and mid-Atlantic states that have capped and will reduce CO_2 emissions from the power sector by a not insignificant 10 percent by 2018.

Cap and trade schemes have been hotly contested, by those on both the political Left and Right. For the Right, cap and trade programs go too far. Take the recent announcement, by its Republication governor Chris Christie, that New Jersey will be leaving the RGGI. According to Governor Christie in a May 2011 press conference, "RGGI does nothing more than tax electricity, tax our citizens, tax our businesses—with no discernible or measurable impact on our environment" (quoted in Newman 2011). For those on the Left, cap and trade programs don't go far enough. The argument goes something like this: how can we fix a problem using the same business-as-usual (market-driven) mentality that caused global warming in the first place?!

Different from cap and trade, though still a "market" approach to climate change mitigation, **carbon offsets** are also gaining in popularity. Carbon offsetting is just as it sounds, in that it involves individuals and organizations buying carbon credits to "offset" some of their own carbon footprint. One popular offset organization is Carbonfund—a not-for-profit organization based in Silver Spring, Maryland, that provides carbon offsetting options to individuals, businesses, and organizations. Clicking on their "carbon calculator" on their website, I find that I can offset the carbon footprint for my four-person household for US$222.16 annually. Adding that to my "shopping cart," I am then asked to enter my credit card information. Carbonfund claims to allow consumers to live a "carbon-neutral" lifestyle (or even a carbon-*negative* lifestyle if one purchased sufficient offsets).

Carbon offsets have also had a mixed reception. On its face, sequestering (also referred to as "retiring") carbon from the carbon cycle—that is, fixing it from the atmosphere and storing it for long periods of time—seems an admirable goal. Yet rarely do carbon offsets challenge the underlying factors responsible for climate change. In fact, many contend they have just the opposite effect, by providing "moral cover" for consumers of fossil fuels (Bachram 2004). Irrespective of their claims of actually retiring carbon, carbon offsets also raise serious social justice issues. For example, lands previously used by local peoples are being enclosed and the people evicted, sometimes forcibly. This was famously the case in Uganda when a Norwegian company leased lands for a carbon-offset project that led to the eviction of eight thousand people in thirteen villages (ibid.). Unfortunately, residents of African nations have faced activities like this more than once (see, for example, Jindal, Swallow, and Kerr 2008).

IMPORTANT CONCEPTS

- adaptation and mitigation
- climate change refugees
- costs of action versus inaction
- human-induced climate change
- stabilization triangle
- vulnerable populations

DISCUSSION QUESTIONS

1. Why do some continue to deny the existence of anthropogenic climate change? (This question is investigated further in Chapter 13.)
2. What are your thoughts on geoengineering: can we effectively engineer ourselves out of this mess and thus avoid making any substantial changes to the status quo?
3. How is climate change a social justice issue?
4. What are some of the more pronounced impacts of climate change for those in low-income countries? And for those residing in high-income countries?

SUGGESTED ADDITIONAL READINGS

ACCORD. 2011. *Conflict Trends: Environment, Climate Change, and Conflict.* Umhlanga Rocks, South Africa: The African Centre for the Constructive Resolution of Disputes. Retrieved August 24, 2012 (http://www.accord.org.za/downloads/ct/ct_2011_2.pdf).

Lancet and University of College London Institute for Global Health Commission. 2009. "Managing the Health Effects of Climate Change." *Lancet.com* 373 (May 16). Retrieved August 24, 2012 (http://grist.files.wordpress.com/2009/05/ucl-lancet-climate-change.pdf).

Lovins, L. H. 2009. "The Economic Case for Climate Protection." *Innovations* 4(4):245–287.

RELEVANT INTERNET LINKS

- http://www.aaas.org/news/press_room/climate_change/
  The American Association for the Advancement of Science's (AAAS) Global Climate-Change Resources link.
- http://www.nature.org/greenliving/carboncalculator/index.htm
  Calculate your carbon footprint.
- http://www.skepticalscience.com/
  Excellent resource for debunking climate change skeptics.
- http://www.skepticalscience.com/docs/Debunking_Handbook.pdf
  Free download of the book *The Debunking Handbook* (2011), which is a guide for debunking misinformation (including misinformation about global warming).

SUGGESTED VIDEOS

- *The Age of Stupid* (2008)
  Academy Award–nominated film set in the bleak future of 2055 that provocatively looks back to how we ignored environmental problems (most notably climate change) in the first decade of this century.
- *Climate Refugees* (2010)
  Investigates the global mass migrations caused by climate change.
- *Earth* (2009)
  James Earl Jones narrates this documentary that shows how climate change has negatively impacted species across the planet by following polar bears, African elephants, and humpback whales over a one-year period as they cope with the changing environment.
- *Global Warming: Rising Storm* (2007)
  Look at the anthropogenic factors driving climate change.
- *The Story of Cap and Trade* (2009)
  http://www.storyofstuff.org/movies-all/story-of-cap-trade/. Introduces viewers to the energy traders and Wall Street financiers at the heart of the cap and trade scheme and reveals the complexity of current cap and trade proposals.
- *Sun Come Up* (2011)
  Academy Award–nominated film that follows the relocation of the Carteret Islanders who live on a remote island chain in the South Pacific Ocean—some of the world's first climate change refugees.

3

Waste: Our Sinks Are Almost Sunk

The trash can is a remarkable artifact, sociologically speaking. To begin, it's the "rabbit hole"—to draw momentarily on one of my daughter's favorite stories (*Alice in Wonderland*)—into the postconsumer world we all know exists but that few from the middle class and above have actually experienced. Whether the rubbish cans in your classroom, the Dumpster next to your friend's apartment complex, or the sixty-gallon waste bin in the alley behind your parents' house: stuff goes in and? . . . That's just it; it goes in and then "poof"—gone!

We moderns really want our waste to just disappear. The trash can, toilet, and kitchen sink are all designed to get our waste out of sight almost as quickly as we're able to generate it. Of course, it wasn't always this way. For our ancestors, there was no hidden world when it came to our waste. As recently as a century ago, waste for many of the world's urban dwellers was largely a household issue. As evidenced in Image 3.1, showing a New York sanitation worker in 1907 disposing of municipal waste by burning it right on the street, it wasn't until well into the twentieth century that the **municipal solid waste** (MSW) rabbit hole as we know it today started taking shape (MSW, generally speaking, refers to all solid waste originating from homes, industries, businesses, demolition, land clearing, and construction).

Yet the rabbit hole is filling up (see ECOnnection 3.1). This is a problem. And like all environmental problems, there are multiple entry points into the subject. Importantly, I do not see waste as just a problem of *management*. If "merely" a management issue, the problem of waste would disappear once we figured out how to utilize resources more efficiently during the production process and improve our disposal techniques (Clapp 2002). I don't buy that it's just a management issue, for reasons discussed shortly.

Fast Facts

MSW consists of items like product packaging, grass clippings, furniture, clothing, bottles, food scraps, newspapers, appliances, and batteries. Not included in this category are materials that may also end up in landfills, such as construction and demolition materials, municipal wastewater treatment sludge, and nonhazardous industrial wastes. The global production of MSW increased roughly 250 percent from 1972 to 2009, from 400 megatons to 1,001 megatons (see Table 3.1).

IMAGE 3.1 Garbage Burning at East Broadway and Gouverneur Street, New York City, 1907

Source: Library of Congress.

In the United States, paper and paperboard make up the largest share (prior to recycling) of MSW generated (28.2 percent), followed by food waste (14.1 percent), yard trimmings (13.7 percent), and plastics (12.3 percent). Rubber, leather, textiles, metals, wood, glass, and "other" combine to make up the remaining 31 percent (EPA 2009).

MSW management varies widely by country. Germany, for instance, imposed a ban on traditional landfills in 2005. This country of 83 million inhabitants operates with fewer than 300 landfills, and the only thing they accept is waste after recycling and incinerating (by comparison, Canada has a population of 34 million and more than 10,000 landfills). By 2020, all of Germany's landfills are expected to be out of operation, as the country plans to make use of all garbage and the energy produced by it. At the other extreme in the EU is Bulgaria, which landfills almost all of its MSW (see Figure 3.1).

The average nuclear power plant generates approximately 20 metric tons of used nuclear fuel annually. Worldwide, the nuclear industry produces a total of about 8,800 metric tons of used fuel per year. If all the world's used fuel assemblies were stacked end to end and side by side, they would cover a football field roughly a yard deep (depending on reactor type, a fuel assembly may contain up to 264 fuel rods and have dimensions of five to nine inches square by about twelve feet long).

ECOnnection 3.1

Some Statistics on Waste Sinks

As of January 2010, England and Wales contained 497 operationally permitted **landfills,** with a total of 614 million cubic meters of available landfill capacity. (Landfill is a method of solid waste disposal where refuse is buried between layers of dirt.) This equates to fewer than eight years of landfill life left at nonhazardous waste sites (Defra 2011). The United States has a little more breathing room. It will take another twenty years before its landfills reach their capacity (Hutchinson 2008).

Yet landfills are only one way we dispose of waste. We also dispose of rubbish by way of, for example, water, which, as discussed further in Chapter 5, is a waste sink we can ill afford to burden any further. According to the United Nations, humans require no less than 20–50 liters (5.3–12.2 gallons) of safe freshwater daily to ensure their basic needs for drinking, cooking, and cleaning. Yet slightly fewer than 1 billion people worldwide do not have access to even this small amount (United Nations n.d.). (The average American, if you're wondering, consumes roughly 670 gallons of water a day [National Geographic n.d.].) Worldwide, 1.5 billion adults and an additional 1 billion children live without even basic water sanitation. This helps explains why diarrhea—often little more than an inconvenience to most in affluent nations—is the leading cause of illness and death in the world, as approximately 88 percent of these deaths are the result of inadequate water sanitation (United Nations n.d.).

Between 30 and 40 percent of all food in developed and developing countries ends up as waste (Godfray et al. 2010). What varies between the most- and least-affluent nations is where in the food system those losses take place. Whereas the majority of food in developed nations is lost in retail, food service, and the home, in the developing world losses are attributable largely to factors like insufficient storage facilities on and off the farm. In India, for example, between 35 to 40 percent of fresh produce is lost annually, as neither wholesalers nor retail stores have adequate cold storage facilities (ibid.).

Waste has multiple links to climate change. First, everything we discard is **embodied energy** and thus already-emitted greenhouse gases. (Embodied energy refers to the sum total of the energy utilized throughout an entire product life cycle.) When we discard, say, a chair or an uneaten apple, we are therefore wasting more than just a chair or an apple but everything that went into making and transporting that object. Landfilling, the most common waste-management practice, also contributes to climate change. The trucks used to haul waste to landfills emit greenhouse gases (though the same can be said for vehicles that haul material for recycling). Landfills also release significant quantities of methane (CH_4) into the atmosphere from the **anaerobic decomposition** (the breaking down of biodegradable material by microorganisms in an oxygen-free environment) of organic materials—a process known as fermentation. (And CH_4 is twenty-one

TABLE 3.1 Solid Waste Generation (in Megatons) by Region and Globally, Selected Years

REGION	1972	1980	1990	2009
East Asia	25	45	100	170
Europe	150	125	170	202
Latin America	35	50	72	110
Middle East	5	25	45	75
North Africa	2	5	20	25
North America	110	125	165	243
Pacific Rim	40	50	52	74
Sub-Sahara	5	10	20	50
Southeast Asia	10	17	28	52
World	400	500	660	1,001

Source: Adapted from Defra (2011) and EPA (2009).

FIGURE 3.1 Municipal Solid Waste Management in the European Union, 2009

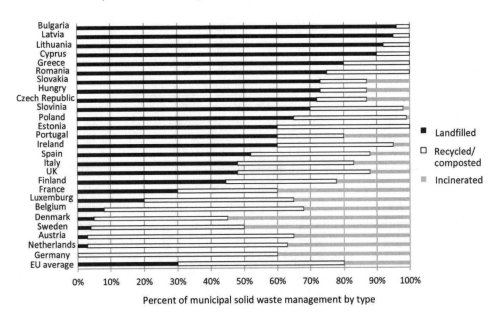

How waste is managed in the European Union varies tremendously, with some countries landfilling almost all of their waste (e.g., Bulgaria), while others (e.g., Germany) landfill practically nothing. *Source:* Adapted from Defra (2011).

times more potent at trapping heat in the atmosphere as carbon dioxide.) Landfills are the third-largest human source of CH_4 emissions in the United States. Encouragingly, this "landfill methane" is beginning to be harnessed in some countries for energy generation—what's known as biogas production. Landfills also act as carbon sinks. Lacking oxygen, organisms that feed upon waste and respire CO_2 are not present a few meters below a landfill's surface. Items such as grass clippings, then, which drew in carbon from the atmosphere to grow, will have their carbon sequestered when buried in a landfill. The carbon sequestering potential of landfills, however, does not offset its methane emissions (EPA 2011).

US consumers alone disposed of roughly 30.08 billion plastic water bottles in 2006, which collectively consumed enough oil during manufacturing to fuel 1 million of the nation's vehicles each year (Food and Water Watch 2009). Then there's all the energy required to pump, process, transport, and refrigerate all that packaged water. That's enough oil to run another 3 million cars annually (ibid.). And what happens to those hundreds of billions of plastic bottles discarded annually worldwide? About 86 percent of the empty plastic water bottles in the United States are landfilled (Arnold and Larsen 2006). My best guess, then, is that tens (if not hundreds) of billions of plastic bottles globally land in the garbage every year.

Implications

The very concept of waste is a social construction. There is no waste in the so-called natural world; everything released, emitted, secreted, and discarded is *food* for something else. *Waste* refers to what we (read: *humans*) have no use for. Thompson, in his book *Rubbish Theory* (1979), points out the fluidity of the term *rubbish*. Even something once deemed "waste" can regain societal value. Take *scrap*, a term that reclassifies objects of waste as having real economic (and thus societal) value. *Collector's item* is another term that varies considerably over time and can rescue an object from being identified as trash.

Pollution is another interesting term, referring to a specific type of waste. Pollution is, quite simply, matter that is out of place. Or, to be still more specific, it refers to waste that is out of place. A few years back, I examined societal understandings of odor pollution as they related to large-scale hog farms in Iowa (Carolan 2008c). To do this, I interviewed people working in and living near hog CAFOs (confined animal-feeding operations). One thing I found was that the odors emanating from these facilities were not in and of themselves defined as "pollution" by those I spoke to. Only when "out of place" were the odors classified as such. Thus, for example, no one said the inside of the highly odorous hog facilities was "polluted," as everyone expected the place to smell terrible. There the odors were "in place." Conversely, when *those same odors* were detected in a neighbor's kitchen while eating breakfast, they were classified as pollution, where they were viewed as clearly "out of place." Extending this thinking, we tend not to see a landfill as polluted, as the space by definition is meant to be filled with trash. The same holds for, say, sewage treatment plants, even though they are spaces where human excrement concentrates. Yet take those same artifacts—trash and human fecal matter—and place them where they are "out of place," and presto: pollution! There are, in short, many ways to talk about waste sociologically. Rather than aim to be comprehensive, the goal of this section is give the reader a sense of this diversity.

Energy Waste and the Life-Cycle Analysis

Traditional approaches to environmental impacts have tended to focus on a single firm or "link" in the **commodity chain** (a term that refers to the collective networks encompassing the beginning and end of a product's life cycle) and on one or two pollutants. Doing this, however, can lead to **"footprint shifting,"** where ecological efficiencies might be achieved at one stage of a product's life cycle only to increase environmental impacts in another. Examining the entire life cycle of a product also allows "hot spots"—links where impacts are high and where reductions can be achieved at minimal cost and effort—to be identified. The life-cycle analysis (LCA) is a useful tool when attempting to assess overall ecological footprints of practices (like landfilling and recycling) and competing commodities (such as disposable versus reusable coffee cups). By doing this, though, much to the chagrin of my students, we frequently learn that what's best from the perspective of environmental sustainability is rarely black and white.

Take the disposable-paper versus reusable-ceramic versus disposable-foam coffee-cup debate. The winner is obvious: the reusable ceramic coffee cup, right? It depends. In fact, under certain circumstances, either disposable cup may well be the "greener" choice (at least in terms of energy consumption) over the ceramic mug. Confused? Let me explain.

Everything, obviously, takes energy and resources to be made. Reusable cups, as they have to be made to be reusable (and thus withstand the abuses of dishwashing, drying, and so on), consume more energy than disposable varieties when being produced—quite a bit more, in fact. The average ceramic mug requires, at least according to one LCA (Institute for Lifecycle Energy Analysis 2002), 25.5 times more energy to make than the average paper cup—14 megajoules (MJ) versus 0.55 MJ per cup. The embedded energy disparity is even greater with foam cups, 14 MJ compared to 0.20 MJ per cup—a difference of 700 percent. Does that therefore mean it takes roughly 26 use cycles for the ceramic mug to reach its break-even point with the paper cup and 700 use cycles before it matches the embedded energy of a foam mug? Not quite. Remember, those reusable ceramic mugs need to be washed.

This is where the calculations get a little more uncertain, as washing techniques and frequencies vary considerably from case to case. Dishwashers generally require less energy than hand washing, as the newest models are made to make particularly efficient use of hot water (hot water usage is the most energy-intensive part of washing dishes). Moreover, not all households run their dishwasher using the "hot water" or "high temperature" setting. The same, however, cannot be said of commercial settings. Industrial-grade dishwashers (like those found at Starbucks) always use hot water to guarantee their dishes and mugs are fully sanitized. Factoring in for dishwashing after each ceramic mug use, its actual break-even point was calculated at 39 uses when compared to the paper cup and 1,006 uses when compared to the foam cup (see Figure 3.2).

There are a couple of take-home points to be derived from such analyses. First, if we choose to go with a reusable mug, we had better make sure we are going to reuse it. I know someone, for example, who buys a new ceramic mug monthly. From an energy conservation standpoint, that's a bad move. Similarly, we need to ask whether the setting

FIGURE 3.2 Uses of Ceramic Cup to Reach Energy-Breakeven Point Relative to Alternatives

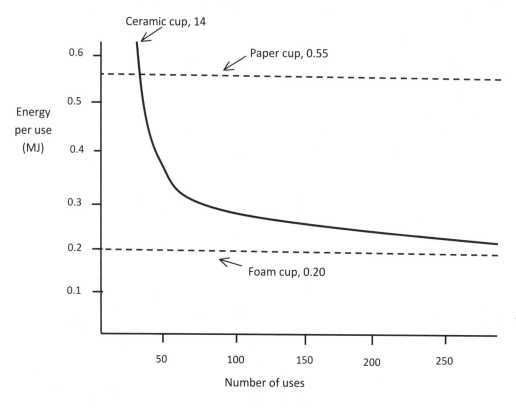

Ceramic cups require on average 14 megajoules (MJ) to produce (and additional energy to clean after every use). For paper and foam cups, those figures are 0.55 and 0.20 MJ, respectively. Recognizing this, it is important to maximize one's reuse of a ceramic cup before disposing of it for a new one. Those prone to losing or breaking reusable mugs might want to rethink how they transport coffee. *Source:* Adapted from Institute for Lifecycle Energy Analysis (2002).

will allow a reusable ceramic mug to survive for a couple dozen (or 1,006!) uses. Friends who work in coffee shops have confirmed my suspicions: ceramic mugs do not stand up nearly as well in commercial applications as they do at home, where they tend to be better cared for. If a ceramic mug at your local coffee shop survives, say, only 20 use cycles, you might be better off, from an energy-saving perspective, never using them. There are also clear energy (not to mention water) savings if we can avoid washing our reusable mugs after each use. Or, if you really want to cut energy waste, try reusing disposal paper cups.

That's just energy use. Air pollution and landfill impacts tell a somewhat different story. Clearly, while 1,001 foam coffee cups might be "equal," in terms of energy consumed, to 1,001 ceramic-mug use cycles, those foams cups will have a significantly greater landfill footprint than a single ceramic mug used 1,001 times. That's what I meant earlier when I said LCAs rarely cast the world in black-and-white terms. We have to ultimately choose for ourselves what to value (see Ethical Question 3.1). What's worse: landfill impacts, air pollution, water consumption, energy use . . . ?

? ETHICAL QUESTION 3.1 ?

What Ought to Be Most Valued?

LCAs show that being an informed "green" consumer is less about being able to choose between "good" and "evil" products than it is about choosing between, say, the lesser of the two (or three, four, . . .) evils. All products come with some environmental footprint. And if it comes down to deciding between impacting, for instance, water, air, soil, or energy resources, the consumer must somehow rank these resources when deciding which product ought to be purchased. Then there are all the other *social* variables missed in LCAs, which insert into the equation an even more diverse array of ethical questions. For example, when striving for both social justice and ecological sustainability, should we select bananas grown by smaller farmers in cooperatives in the Caribbean or those grown on plantations in Central America but by unionized and politically empowered workers? Should we place ecological concerns above social ones when forced to privilege one set of concerns over others, which is something we often have to do as consumers? If you're having a problem answering these questions, you should. That's my point.

Recycling

Judging by increasing recycling rates from around the world, the practice of recycling appears to be catching on. Nevertheless, these rates continue to vary tremendously across regions (as detailed earlier in Figure 3.1) as well as within countries. And, interestingly, a nation's level of affluence seems at best marginally correlated with recycling levels. San Francisco (United States) and Adelaide (Australia), for example, each report recycling rates of 70 percent. In Rotterdam (Netherlands), citizens recycle at a rate of 30 percent, whereas in Houston (the United States) only 2.6 percent of the city's MSW is recycled. These rates are comparable to what you would find in less affluent nations. Nairobi (Kenya) and Delhi (India) report recycling rates of 24 and 34 percent, respectively. At the higher end, with rates equal to or surpassing those found in San Francisco, Quezon City (Philippines) and Bamako (Mali) recycle 67 percent and 85 percent of their MSW, respectively (Hutchinson 2008; United Nations 2010).

LCAs have been very helpful in providing empirical support to what most environmentalists have been saying for decades: that recycling, to put it plainly, is good for the environment. These LCAs calculate the energy consumed from the moment the recycling trucks stop at your place of residence until this "waste" is processed into brand-new products. This figure is then compared with the amount of energy required to send the same goods to landfills or incinerators and to make new consumer goods from scratch. We find, for example, that aluminum requires 96 percent less energy to make from recycled cans than when processed using bauxite. Recycled plastic bottles use 76 percent less energy, newsprint about 45 percent less, and recycled glass about 21 percent less than when processed from raw (unrecycled) materials. Across the board, recycled goods come out on top, as the energy used to extract and process raw materials is an order of magnitude higher than what is used to recover the same material through re-cycling (Morris 2005).

An additional point to keep in mind when assessing the economics of recycling: the revenue generated from recycling need not actually surpass its costs to be a good in-vestment for a city. This might at first sound counterintuitive—after all, how could a money-losing venture be a good investment? You must keep in mind that landfilling costs money, too. Let's say it costs US$175 a ton to collect and process mixed recy-clables—a figure not too far off from what a lot of US cities pay. Let's further suppose that those recyclables can be sold on the open market for US$120 a ton, which repre-sents still another sensible assumption. This does not necessarily mean, however, that recycling is a money loser. What matters is the cost of taking that material to a landfill. If it is more than $50 a ton, then a recycling program is still a good investment. Looking toward the future, the price of mixed recyclables is expected to climb. This will be due, in large part, to the rising cost of energy, which is increasing the price of raw materials, recognizing that the extraction and processing of these materials are energy intensive. Another variable driving up the price of recyclables is the growing demand of consumer goods in places like China (Hutchinson 2008). As all of this happens, more municipal-ities will find "value" in recycling.

Yet at what, or more specifically *whose*, expense? That is a question asked by those not yet ready to embrace recycling unconditionally. There is a body of compelling evi-dence indicating that, in some instances at least, the ecological gains of recycling may be coming at the expense of social justice (see, for example, Pellow, Schnailberg, and Weinburg 2000). To enhance efficiencies, a number of cities mix rubbish with recy-clables during pickup. The rationale: to cut expenses by eliminating what are perceived as unnecessary redundancies—like two trucks making separate trips to each house—when handling MSW. The contents of each garbage and recycle truck are then sorted. This is bringing workers—those responsible for manually sorting through everything set out for curbside pickup—into closer contact with environmental hazards, like **bio-hazards** (environmental threats resulting from biological agents or conditions, like used needles) and other toxic substances (United Nations 2010).

Once separated, recycled waste itself can be hazardous. Plastic waste, for instance, often contains residues from its original contents, like toxic cleaners, pesticides, and herbicides. And in recycling operations in less affluent nations especially, workers may not be given protective clothing to safeguard against exposure to these potentially toxic chemicals (Clapp 2002). Yet the problems are not limited to the developing world. Tens of millions of pounds of electronic waste (televisions, computers, and the like) in the United States get funneled annually into its prison system for recycling. The prisoners break the components down (which, according to some reports, involves smashing with hammers) and then pack them up for shipment to processors. This practice, however, exposes inmates to lead, phosphorus, cadmium, barium, and mercury, all of which are toxic (Perry 2005). The organization responsible for overseeing this program, Federal Prison Industries (a government-owned corporation created in 1934 that produces goods and services from the labor of inmates), is now the focus of a US Justice Depart-ment investigation for exposing prisoners to unnecessary health risks (Leonard 2010).

Let's go back for a moment to the ecological gains associated with recycling. While proponents of recycling proudly tout the practice as "green," the more critically minded

ECOnnection 3.2
Is Recycling Accelerating Resource Consumption and Waste?

Some contend that although recycling leads to a reduction of natural resource withdrawals (as virgin materials are replaced with recycled ones), the gains come at the expense of more ecologically sound forms of waste disposal (Pellow et al. 2000). For one thing, recycling has forced many reuse (the second R of environmentalism) programs out of the marketplace. Whereas the first and second Rs of environmentalism—reduce and reuse—unmistakably lead to a slowing of consumption, waste recycling, arguably, has just the opposite effect.

Although it is difficult to assess this hypothesis empirically, an argument could be made that recycling helps assuage any guilt we might have about our consumption habits—"Well, since we recycle we shouldn't feel as bad about over-consumption." I see this reasoning at work most clearly with our continued love affair with the plastic water bottle, even though by now we are all aware of at least some of its ecological costs. If recycling was not an option, I wonder if there would be greater interest in putting a stop to their use.

should be asking in response, "Relative to what?" The empirical evidence is indisputable: recycling is clearly a "win" for the environment relative to landfilling. But what if we were comparing recycling to the act of not consuming the item in the first place? Recycling is a big ecological loser in this head-to-head comparison. Remember the so-called three Rs of environmentalism: reduce, reuse, and recycle. Recycling is last in this hierarchy, for good reason (see ECOnnection 3.2).

Food Waste

The food waste generated in the United States could pull approximately 200 million people out of hunger. If you were to include all the feed that went into producing the meat and dairy thrown away annually by consumers, retailers, and food services in the United States and United Kingdom, the number increases to 1.5 billion people (Stuart 2009). Up to 50 percent of all food in the United States is wasted, costing the American economy at least US$100 billion annually (Jones 2005). US per capita food waste has increased by 50 percent since 1974, to more than 1,400 kcal per person per day, or 150 trillion kcal per year. British consumers discard approximately 7 million tons of food; that's a third of all the food they purchase. At a retail cost of around £10.2 billion (US$19.5 billion), this waste has a CO_2 equivalent of 18 million tons—an amount equal to the annual emissions of one-fifth of Britain's total car fleet (Desrochers and Shimizu 2008). Canadians, as further evidence of the endemic nature of food waste in the world, toss out about CAN$27 billion worth of food annually (Gooch, Felfel, and Marenick 2010).

There are a number of factors responsible for all this food waste. Some might be classified as cultural. The Chinese, for example, have a long-held practice of providing more than their guests can eat, as hosts seek to "gain face" (Smil 2004:107). Rising costs for waste disposal caused one Shanghai branch of the roast-duck restaurant Quanjude to offer its customers a 10 percent discount if they would finish their food, as many of its customers were eating less than half of what they ordered (Smil 2004). Another variable is aesthetics, or what could be referred to as the cultural expectations about how we think particular foods ought to look. The state of Queensland, Australia, disposes of more than 100,000 tons of bananas annually because the fruits fail to meet national cosmetic retail standards (Hurst 2010). Globally, the amount of bananas wasted due to failing to meet such aesthetic standards represent between 20 and 40 percent of the annual harvest (Stuart 2009). A particularly memorable story came from Bristol, England, involving a fruit seller who was breaking the law by selling kiwi that were two grams below the sixty-two-gram minimum prescribed by EU law (Daily Mail Reporter 2008). Fortunately, after the story broke EU officials decided to clear the law from the books.

Tristram Stuart (2009:103–111) tells a story of a large British carrot farmer who supplies the supermarket chain Asda. Annually, 25–30 percent of his crop fails to meet the chain's aesthetic standards. "Asda insists," the farmer explains, "that all carrots should be straight so the consumer can peel the full length in one easy stroke" (ibid.:104). Any—and only—oversized carrots go to food processors, which account for about a third of those unwanted by Asda. Small carrots require too much labor to handle, so food processors usually avoid using them. What's left, the remaining two-thirds of that originally rejected by Asda, is fed to livestock.

The power wielded by food processors and supermarkets through **market concentration** (the dominance of a particular market by a few large firms) in these sectors also encourages food waste. Supermarkets in particular have considerable leverage over those "earlier" in the food chain. This leverage comes from **buyer power**—an effect that results when a market has numerous sellers but only one buyer (or a few). Buyer power means that whereas supermarkets can select from a range of processors and farmers to work with, the inverse is less often the case, giving the former tremendous leverage over the latter when it comes to setting the terms of the contract. In some cases, processors and farmers supply only one supermarket chain, which effectively allows the buyer (the processor) to write the terms of the contract. This allows firms like Birds Eye, for example, to contractually forbid their growers from selling their peas to anyone else, even those rejected by the company for not meeting certain standards. In such a scenario, growers are left with no choice but either to feed their surplus to livestock or to recycle the vegetables back into the soil (ibid.:117). In this case, the cost of waste is pushed onto farmers.

Consumers also waste food—a lot of it. Yet in some instances, it's not entirely their fault, thanks to a nifty little marketing strategy by supermarkets called the buy-one-get-one (BOGO) free promotion. Grocers often reserve these campaigns for items on the brink of expiring, items that they would lose money on if they held onto them just a day or two longer. These schemes might be a great deal if you actually use the "free" one. The research indicates, however, that most do not (Gooch et al. 2010). In Britain, BOGO offers have come under intense scrutiny in recent years for their links to household waste (see, for example, Wainwright 2009). In the United States, conversely, BOGO schemes remain very popular. It is also worth noting that "sell by," "best by," and "use by" dates go largely unregulated around the world. In the case of the United States, for instance, the federal government regulates such statements only when they apply to infant formula. That means companies decide on these dates. Yet they have an incentive to make those freshness windows unduly short, which further encourages food waste.

Waste and Public Health

All waste represents a potential health hazard (see Case Study 3.1). Those of us living in affluent countries often do not think about waste in the context of public health. Although all societies put their waste "somewhere," the characteristics of this location can vary considerably from nation to nation. In countries like Australia, Japan, and the United States, that somewhere is often a combination of landfills, incinerators, and recycling facilities. In less affluent nations utilizing poor waste-management practices that "somewhere" is usually a lot closer, like nearby rivers and lakes, parks, along public roadways, or, as in slums, in huge heaps in the middle of the street, creating a toxic playground of sorts for neighborhood children (United Nations 2010). "**Collective coverage**," as it's called in the waste-management community, varies widely not only between developing nations but also within nations. Collective coverage is just a way to talk about the proportion of an area serviced by the municipal waste stream. This is particularly noticeable when "slum" and "nonslum" households are separated. As Table 3.2 details, some nations (like Colombia) have quite high coverage rates for all of their inhabitants. Many, however, have a long way to go.

Uncollected waste is a scourge for everyone involved. It clogs drains and sewers, causing flooding and thus the spread of infectious disease. Stagnant water—from, for example, backed-up storm drains—offers prime breeding habitat for mosquitoes and rodents, which can also lead to the spread of disease. Uncollected waste can make it more difficult to attract businesses and tourists. It can also disrupt a country's ability to provide basic utilities. In Costa Rica, for example, an electric utility company has problems maintaining power to their grid from a hydroelectric plant because plastic litter repeatedly clogs its turbines (United Nations 2010).

Even after it is collected, waste represents a potential public health hazard. One review recently looked at the health risks associated with domestic waste-composting facilities and their product (Domingo and Nadal 2009). Since MSW contains a number of chemical and biological agents, compost was found to be a potential biohazard. The contaminants were cited for creating varying levels of risk to plant workers at composting facilities as well as to the consumers of vegetable products grown in soils treated with the adulterated compost. There is also tentative evidence linking certain negative health effects to living near landfill sites, like low birth weight, birth defects, and certain types of cancers (Vrijheid 2000; see also Ethical Question 3.2).

E-waste

Those of us in affluent nations throw away an awful lot of electronic waste, or what is becoming commonly known as e-waste. How often do you get a new cell phone: every year; perhaps every two? My service provider currently incentivizes getting a new phone every year, offering a hefty new phone credit after owning the device for only twelve months. And what about your computer—how often do you replace it?

This e-waste—discarded computers, printers, mobile phones, pagers, digital photo and music devices, refrigerators, toys, and televisions—is expected to rise sharply in the

TABLE 3.2 Collective Coverage for Non-slum and Slum Households for Select Countries in Africa and the Middle East, and Latin America and the Caribbean

COUNTRY	PERCENT OF HOUSEHOLDS WITH A COLLECTION SERVICE	
	Non-slum	*Slum*
Region: Africa and the Middle East		
Benin	48	9
Egypt	90	65
Ethiopia	59	31
Ghana	45	28
Kenya	44	12
Senegal	75	50
Region: Latin America and the Caribbean		
Bolivia	91	65
Colombia	99	90
Dominica	83	66
Guatemala	72	17
Nicaragua	82	48
Peru	90	52

Collective coverage among select low- and middle-income countries varies considerably. Some countries (such as Columbia) have been quite successful at providing collection services to all strata of society, while others (like Benin) have had considerably less success. *Source:* Adapted from United Nations (2010).

decades ahead with the growth in sales of electronics in countries like China and India. A 2011 report from one Ghana-based organization found, remarkably, that of 215,000 tons of electronic waste imported into the country annually, 30 percent was *brand new* but deemed "obsolete" (Green Advocacy Ghana 2011). According to the United Nations Environment Programme, e-waste from computers by 2020 will increase by 500 percent from 2007 levels in India and by 400 and 200 percent in China and South Africa, respectively. They also predict e-waste from cell phones, over the same time period, to rise 700 percent in China and 1,800 percent in India. By 2020, e-waste from televisions will be 1.5 and 2 times higher in China and India, respectively, while in India e-waste from discarded refrigerators will double or triple (UNEP 2009).

CASE STUDY 3.1

Health-Care Waste in Afghanistan

Between September 21 and 23, 2008, 1.6 million children were immunized against polio in Kabul, Afghanistan. This mass vaccination produced tons of medical waste that was discarded into the local municipal waste stream, causing infectious injury to individuals scavenging landfills for reusable items. City officials claimed to have little experience and resources to separate and properly dispose of medical waste. As explained by the director of Kabul's waste-management department, "It is the responsibility of hospitals and the Ministry of Public Health to safely dispose of medical waste." Whereas most government hospitals burn medical waste, as ordered by the government, many private hospitals do not (and cannot because they lack incinerators and other equipment). At least two government hospitals in Kabul, however, have recently been cited for dumping medical waste into open dustbins where poor children scavenge for food and reusable items. Children involved in scavenging in Herat Province (in western Afghanistan), where medical waste is also improperly disposed of, have been infected by hepatitis B, syphilis, and HIV (IRIN 2008).

The majority of e-waste in developed countries is exported to less affluent nations to be "recycled" (see Case Study 3.2). China currently receives the largest share of the world's e-waste, even though, strangely enough, they have "officially" banned its importation. Recycling there takes many hazardous forms, such as incinerating materials over an open flame in order to recover valuable metals like gold. These practices release toxic gases while yielding very low metal recovery rates, especially compared to modern industrial facilities. Some of the toxic materials found in e-waste include barium, cadmium, lead, lithium, mercury, nickel, palladium, rhodium, and silver. Exposure to these materials has been linked to, among other things, birth defects and organ, nervous-system, and skeletal-system damage (Sterne 2007).

There is hope, however, that with the establishment of ambitious regulations and oversight, the processes for collecting and recycling e-waste in developing nations can be improved and produce a net gain for the people of these nations as well as for the environment. If this happens, the potential is there to generate decent employment while cutting greenhouse gas emissions and recovering a wide assortment of valuable metals, including silver, gold, palladium, copper, and indium, without negative impact upon public health (UNEP 2009). In truth, something like this *must* happen. In the United States, the average home has slightly less than three televisions (and 2.62 persons to watch them) (Nielsen 2009). The average number of computers owned per household in the United States in 2008 was 1.16 (looking only at households with a computer, that figure increases to 1.55) (US Department of Labor 2010). Once other populations—like the 2.5 billion people who live in India and China—begin emulating this type of consumption for electronic goods, we will quite literally be swimming in a sea of e-waste unless a just, sustainable recycling system is put into place.

ETHICAL QUESTION 3.2

Public Health and Value Judgments

As members of a social network—with its own norms, identity structures, and social conventions—epidemiologists' understanding of "evidence" often differs from those embedded within different social networks (e.g., community activists). Among professional epidemiologists, social norms strongly discourage the making of false positives—that is, concluding that there is a causal link between contaminant X and a cancer cluster when there is not one (also known as a **type I error**). This explains why higher confidence limits—of typically 90 percent or higher—are usually the norm within this professional field. Scientists have a reputation to uphold as a result of their membership in a larger professional community, which could be severely undermined if they were to proclaim a causal link when none exists. Such type I errors could be not only embarrassing but potentially damaging to one's membership within the community and resources therein embedded (e.g., access to grants). If such errors occurred with great frequency, it could in fact undermine the legitimacy of the entire profession.

On the other hand, community activists, as a result of their different network connections and interests, have equally compelling reasons to avoid false negatives (known as **type II errors**). For them, erring on the side of caution, if it means saving their lives and the lives of loved ones, is well worth making a false negative occasionally. This in part explains why proponents of what has been called "**popular epidemiology**" (a type of citizen science that involves laypeople) prefer a much lower confidence limit when examining causal relationships between pollutants and cancer clusters (P. Brown and Mikkelsen 1997).

Solutions

I have noticed when discussing the subject of waste in the classroom that the conversation inevitably turns to individuals. "We need to stop wasting so much!" a student told me when asked how we solve the problem of waste. Yes; we do waste too much. But why do we? Are we the only ones to blame for this? Solutions to waste must reflect the multifaceted nature of the problem, or, as I told my student, "Working only to change what we as consumers do to produce waste will not effectively solve much."

MSW Management Alternatives from Around the World

There is a tendency to think that what works in affluent countries when it comes to MSW management will work equally well for less affluent countries. Unfortunately, to quote from a recent United Nations document on the subject, "Nothing could be further from the truth" (2010:93). The average inhabitant of a developing nation generates a fraction of what their counterpart in an affluent nation generates (see Case Study 3.3). Thus, the twenty-five-ton garbage trucks that seem so necessary to MSW planners in countries like the United States are a needless expense in countries that do not generate sufficient waste (these vehicles can cost more than US$130,000 new). And let's also not

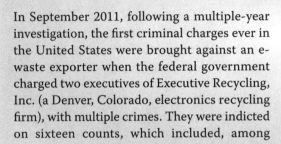

CASE STUDY 3.2

US Recycler Indicted for Exporting E-waste

In September 2011, following a multiple-year investigation, the first criminal charges ever in the United States were brought against an e-waste exporter when the federal government charged two executives of Executive Recycling, Inc. (a Denver, Colorado, electronics recycling firm), with multiple crimes. They were indicted on sixteen counts, which included, among other things, environmental crimes and exportation contrary to law (US law restricts the exportation of certain forms of e-waste to developing countries but does a poor job of keeping track of these exports). The charges were linked to shipments of e-waste going to less affluent countries, particularly China (ENS 2011).

forget: they weigh roughly twenty-five tons. Many roads (and bridges) in low-income nations just can't handle trucks of this size.

A popular trend, which started in China and has since spread outside of Asia to the Middle East, Africa, and Latin America, is a hybrid approach to waste transfer. This system involves setting up small, local transfer stations around the city to which people bring their trash. As labor costs in low- and middle-income countries are relatively low, this can be accomplished far more cost-effectively using handcarts and the like than with expensive trucks. The transfer stations also facilitate small-scale entrepreneurialism, as people are sought to collect and deposit trash from the neighborhood at these sites for those who choose not to do this themselves. Once at the transfer station, the city takes over and hauls the waste away. Once concentrated at one site, capital-intensive technologies like large trucks become more cost-effective. In countries utilizing this plan, the waste is collected daily and the transfer stations washed down to minimize odor and prevent rodent problems (Coffey 2005).

And what about all the food waste? Some commentators have argued that if food were more expensive—if its retail price more accurately reflected the actual costs that went into producing, processing, and transporting it—we would likely not waste so much of it (Stuart 2009). Perhaps. Yet there are other ways to disincentivize the act of wasting food, such as by charging people who do it. That's exactly what South Korea does. In 2005 they made it illegal to send food to the landfill (you won't actually go to jail for breaking this law, but you will be fined). South Koreans now must separate all food waste and place it in a special 100 percent compostable bag. The policy has been incredibly successful. The country has managed to remove more than 98 percent of food waste from its MSW stream, just the opposite of the United States, where just 2.6 percent of food waste is composted (ibid.:217).

Food waste could also be fed to livestock. Poultry and pigs thrive on organic waste (see Case Study 3.4). Under European laws, however, feeding food waste to pigs is banned. Conversely, in Japan, South Korea, and Taiwan, a percentage of the countries' food waste must be diverted to livestock. Japan disposes of roughly 20 million tons of

---

CASE STUDY 3.3

Garbage Collection in
Byala, Bulgaria

The village of Byala is located along the Black Sea in eastern Bulgaria. A popular tourist destination for Europeans over the summer months, it returns to a quiet fishing and agricultural community during the winter, with a population of just over two thousand. In 2002 rising fuel prices caused the town's sanitation department to exhaust its annual fuel budget before the year was even half over. A consultant was called in to assess the situation. During the audit, it was learned that 90 percent of the town's forty-liter trash containers were less than 20 percent full when collected three times a week—a terrible waste of fossil fuel, money, and greenhouse gas sinks. Based on this information, the town began varying its trash pickup to better reflect its needs. It now picks trash up only monthly during the slow nine months when the tourists are away, resuming the three-times-a-week service at the height of tourist season when trash is at its most abundant (United Nations 2010).

---

food waste a year (five times the amount that it gives annually as food aid to the world's poor). As prices for animal feed and fertilizers reached record highs in 2008, there was heightened demand for food pellets for pigs and poultry made from recycled leftovers. During this period, recycled feed was half the price of regular feed. Although only 1 percent of feedstock comes from recycled food, this percentage is growing. The majority of the food waste that is recycled into feed comes from convenience stores and restaurants, where strict health laws require food to be thrown away after one day (itself a problematic policy, as it accelerates the wasting of food). The discarded food is first taken to a plant, where it is sorted to remove skewers, plastic trays, and plastic wrap. From there it is turned into two kinds of dry feed—one high in fat and protein and another that is rich in carbohydrates—and a liquid feed made from pasteurized drinks and leftover vegetables.

Extended Producer Responsibility

"Waste isn't the fault of consumers—it's a design flaw," I once had a friend tell me. Although she was perhaps overstating matters a bit—clearly, as consumers we can do better when it comes to reducing our waste—I appreciate her point. As long as consumers continue to need (or think they need) the things supplied by the market, they have little choice but to waste. I realize that many consumers confuse "wants" for "needs," so the problem of waste must also be addressed from the angle of consumption (which is discussed in Part III of this book). But sometimes these needs are legitimate, like if someone needs a job and the job requires the purchase of a computer and printer. And even when those needs are not legitimate, the pragmatist in me realizes that people are going to continue to buy stuff, at least for the foreseeable future. So why not buy stuff that can be recycled and reused?

That's what my friend meant when she said waste is a design flaw. We're currently not making things that can be easily reused and recycled. This is where the concept of

CASE STUDY 3.4

Feeding Pigs Food Waste in Cairo, Egypt

Pigs and poultry can thrive on food waste. For a time, Cairo, Egypt, successfully utilized pigs for municipal organic waste management. That practice stopped, however, in May 2009, when the Egyptian government killed some three hundred thousand pigs as a preventative measure to keep swine flu from entering the country. It was not long, however, before Egyptian officials began regretting this decision. Prior to this action, the Zabaleen—a Christian community of garbage collectors living in the slums of Cairo—traveled door to door collecting organic waste. The animals consumed roughly 60 percent of the waste collected. The Zabaleen ate some of the animals (religion forbids the city's Muslims from eating pork). The rest were sent to market, where they generated additional income for their handlers (Stack 2009).

extended producer responsibility (EPR) comes in. Under EPR, manufacturers are held responsible for a product beyond the time of sale, thereby relieving consumers, governments, future generations, and the environment from the costs associated with landfilling and recycling hazardous materials. EPR is an attempt to internalize some of the costs of a product that have previously been externalized (not included in the retail price) onto society, taxpayers, the environment, and future generations. This cost externalization model not only is terribly unfair—by forcing people to pay for the consequences of actions not of their own doing—but also creates completely unsustainable actions and business models. Think about it in the context of waste. When, for example, companies manufacture computers, most are currently responsible for the product only from the moment it was manufactured through the life of its warranty. And not surprisingly, their design reflects these parameters. Consequently, they have no interest in designing products that can be either disposed of safely (e.g., that are not full of hazardous materials) or recycled and reused. Computer manufacturers currently don't care what the consumer does with their product when it reaches the end of its life. And why should they? Similarly, when the consumer disposes of their computer (and it is sent off to the landfill or to be recycled), they may pay a nominal disposal fee, but it is society, taxpayers, future generations, and the environment that are paying the real costs for this action. How is that fair?

EPR, as the title suggests, literally extends the producer's responsibility for a product throughout its life cycle, from cradle to grave. The concept was first used and defined in a report by Thomas Lindhqvist for the Swedish Ministry of the Environmental and Natural Resources in 1990 (see Lindhqvist and Lidgren 1990). EPR seeks to prioritize preventative measures (by asking questions like "How do we make things better so they don't become waste?") over end-of-pipe approaches (which involves such questions as "What should we do with the waste?"). EPR makes producers the primary actors responsible for the entire life cycle of their products. The logic behind this is simple: making producers responsible for having to recycle and reuse what they manufacture will lead them to redesign products for this end. When products are not designed to be recycled,

they often are not. We often mistake "**down-cycling**" (converting waste into new materials or products of lesser quality and decreased functionality) for recycling—carpet,
for example, not designed to be recycled is typically down-cycled to, for example, carpet
padding.

Maine was the first state in the United States to pass an EPR e-waste law in 2004, requiring manufacturers to be financially responsible for recycling specific electronics.
Under this law, while cities still ensure that collection sites are available and consumers
must bring their e-waste to these sites, the manufacturers pay for all recycling costs.
Since 2004 twenty-four states have enacted similar legislation. EPR has an even longer
track record in Europe, where the problem of landfill shortage is particularly acute.

One of the more visible examples of EPR is the recyclable printer cartridge. Every
printer cartridge I have purchased in recent years comes with a self-addressed, self-
sealing mailing bag with the postage prepaid. This is then used by the consumer to ship
their old cartridge off to be refilled. I have also noticed printer cartridge drop-off boxes
at some electronic stores. Hewlett-Packard's 2005 *Global Citizen Report* illustrates the
company's efforts to improve its design for recycling of their laser jet cartridges (see Figure 3.3). Figure 3.3 is representative of the industry as whole. Now that printer-cartridge
firms have an incentive to improve the recyclability of their products, they have reduced
the quantity of materials used in manufacturing, while those they do use have less environmental impact and more value at the end of their lives.

We also need to create incentives that entice firms—and electronic firms in particular
in light of what was just said about e-waste—to make products that can be repaired.
There is a reason it is often cheaper to buy a new appliance or piece of electronic equipment than it is to get that old one repaired: because they are not designed to be easily
repaired, which makes their repair expensive. I find it curious how much we as a society

FIGURE 3.3 Parts and Resins in Hewlett-Packard Monochrome Laser Jet Cartridges, 1992–2004

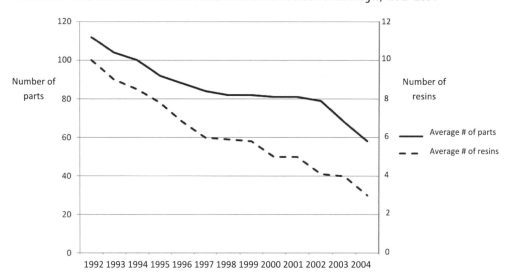

Readily recycled products often require fewer inputs. This not only can save companies money
but also conserves resources. *Source:* Adapted from Rossem, Tojo, and Lindhqvist (2006:16).

focus on the recycling aspect of the equation, on, in other words, the *end* of the life cycle. We talk about expanding recycling markets and improving recycling technology, which we hope will bring down its costs and help keep countries like the United States from shipping its e-waste overseas where labor is cheap and environmental and labor laws are weak. But if goods are not designed and manufactured to be recycled, what good does any of this do? And lest we forget: designing products that could actually be repaired or upgraded would effectively render this entire discussion about recycling moot. If we could just focus a fraction of those moneys and political energies on encouraging and regulating firms to make electronic products that can be refurbished, recycled, reused, and easily repaired, just think how far that would go toward reducing e-waste and stopping the types of recycling practices currently utilized in developing countries that are placing the health of individuals and the environment at risk.

IMPORTANT CONCEPTS

- e-waste
- extended producer responsibility (EPR)
- food waste
- life-cycle analysis (LCA)
- three Rs of environmentalism
- waste and public health

DISCUSSION QUESTIONS

1. It is often said that we've become a throwaway society. Why do you think this is?
2. When something of yours breaks, rips, or simply stops working, how often do you first try to get it repaired? What are some of the barriers to repair and reuse?
3. Do corporations bear any responsibility in this, or is waste a problem best addressed among consumers and through better municipal waste management practices?
4. Is necessity the mother of invention, to repeat an old and familiar saying, or is invention the mother of necessity?

SUGGESTED ADDITIONAL READINGS

Hutchinson, A. 2008. "Is Recycling Worth It? PM Investigates Its Economic and Environmental Impact." *Popular Mechanics*, November 13. Retrieved March 28, 2012 (http://www.popular mechanics.com/science/environment/recycling/4291566).

Leonard, A. 2010. *The Story of Stuff*. New York: Free Press.

Lovins, L. H. 2008. "Rethinking Production." In *State of the World 2008*, edited by Worldwatch Institute, 32–44. Washington, DC: Worldwatch Institute. Retrieved August 26, 2012 (http://www.worldwatch.org/files/pdf/SOW08_chapter_3.pdf).

Perry, T. 2005. "Recycling Behind Bars." *IEEE Spectrum*, June. Retrieved August 26, 2012 (http://spectrum.ieee.org/green-tech/conservation/recycling-behind-bars/2).

Wainwright, M. 2009. "Supermarket Offers and Food Waste Targeted in Government's Food Strategy." *Guardian*, August 10. Retrieved August 26, 2012 (http://www.guardian.co.uk /environment/2009/aug/10/food-security-climate-change).

RELEVANT INTERNET LINKS

- http://www.footprintnetwork.org/en/index.php/GFN/page/calculators/
  An ecological footprint calculator. Find out how large your "footprint" is.
- http://www.lovefoodhatewaste.com
  A useful resource for learning more about food waste and how you can cut down on
  the amount you produce.
- http://www.planetgreen.discovery.com/games-quizzes/ewaste-iq-quiz/
  Take this quiz and learn your e-waste IQ.
- http://www.youtube.com/watch?v=IKG8xRTFktg
  An instructional video on how to practice backyard composting.

SUGGESTED VIDEOS

- *Bag It!* (2011)
  A film that examines our love affair with plastic.
- *Garbage Warrior* (2008)
  Follows US architect Michael Reynolds who builds Earthship—entirely self-sustaining—
  homes from tires and beer cans.
- *Ghana: Digital Dumping Ground* (2009)
  http://www.pbs.org/frontlineworld/stories/ghana804/video/video_index.html. A fasci-
  nating story about the global e-waste trade.
- *Plastic Planet* (2009)
  An international look at our plastic problem.
- *The Story of Stuff* (2007)
  https//:www.thestoryofstuff.com/. An animated, widely viewed online documentary
  about the life cycle of material goods.
- *Texas Gold* (2008)
  A look at what it's like to live in the most polluted town in the United States.
- *Trashed* (2007)
  Takes a hard look at the amount of garbage we produce, where it goes, and the conse-
  quences it has on others and the environment.
- *Waste Land* (2010)
  Follows renowned artist Vik Muniz as he journeys from Brooklyn to his native Brazil
  and the world's largest garbage dump located just outside Rio de Janeiro. There he
  chronicles the lives of *catadores*—trash scavengers.
- *Waste Wars* (2011)
  http://vimeo.com/32400188. Documents a battle over access and control to garbage, as
  waste pickers and recyclers in Delhi, India, fight attempts to privatize trash collection.

Biodiversity: Society Wouldn't Exist Without It

It has been my experience that while everyone seems to believe biodiversity ought to be preserved, few can articulate the reasons we value it to the level we do. I discuss the subject every semester in my Global Environmental Issues class. And every semester upon asking why we ought to preserve biodiversity, I receive in return . . . silence. Sure; after an awkward stillness I hear from a few in the audience, but the silence always quickly reappears. It then becomes my turn to speak. I usually begin by making some grand statement pertaining to the value of biodiversity to society, talking about things like its links to quality of life, therapeutic applications, ability to limit infectious disease, and role in maintaining "services." In short, biodiversity supports a number of things that lead to happier and healthier humans. Human "health," as the term is defined here, and as the World Health Organization (WHO) has defined it since 1948, is "a state of complete physical, mental, and social well-being and not merely the absence of disease or infirmity" (WHO n.d.b). Let's touch briefly on each of the four benefits mentioned above:

Quality of life can be enhanced innumerably by biodiversity, as it boosts mental and spiritual health, provides opportunities for recreation, and enriches human knowledge.

Biodiversity is also responsible for supplying *therapeutic applications,* thanks to medicinal and genetic resources coming from plants and other organisms. The United Nations, for example, recently valued anticancer agents from marine organisms at roughly US$1 billion a year, while the global herbal medicine market was said to be worth at least US$43 billion annually (UNEP 2008:161).

Biodiversity places *limits on infectious disease* through biological controls that reign in **disease vectors** (an organism—such as a mosquito or tick—that carries disease-causing microorganisms from one host to another). For instance, when an ecosystem is biologically diverse, predation throughout the food chain is likely to keep populations of all species under control, including those linked to the spread of infectious disease.

The benefits of biodiversity-dependent *"services"* is incalculable, as many of these "values" cannot (and should not) be reduced to a monetary figure (see Table 4.1). This is not to say some haven't tried. Take the concept of **ecosystem services**: the processes by which the environment produces resources that we often take for granted (but we need

TABLE 4.1 Examples of Biodiversity-Dependent "Services" That We Value

Provisioning Services: Products obtained from biologically diverse ecosystems, including,
- Food and fiber
- Fuel
- Genetic resources
- Ornamental resources
- Fresh water

Regulating Services: Regulating benefits stemming from biologically diverse ecosystems, including,
- Air quality maintenance
- Climate regulation
- Water regulation
- Erosion control (and soil formation)
- Water purification
- Biological (e.g., pest) control
- Pollination
- Storm protection

Cultural Services: Nonmaterial benefits from ecosystems through spiritual enrichment, cognitive development, reflection, recreation, and aesthetic experiences, including,
- Cultural diversity
- Spiritual/religious values
- Knowledge systems
- Inspiration/aesthetic values
- Recreation
- Cultural heritage

Source: Adapted from Millennium Ecosystem Assessment (2005: 56-59) and Zhang et al. (2007: 254).

for our survival), such as clean air and water, timber, habitat for fisheries, and pollination of native and agricultural plants. A 1997 article published in *Nature* placed the value of seventeen ecosystem services at approximately US$33 trillion per year (compared to a gross world product at the time of around US$18 trillion) (Costanza et al. 1997). More recently, twelve atmospheric services vital to human well-being and all life on earth were valued at between one hundred and one thousand times the gross world product. This places the economic value of those twelve services—just twelve—somewhere between US$6,850 trillion and US$68,500 trillion annually (Thornes et al. 2010:243). Yet we can't—nor would we want to—put a price tag on everything that's provided by ecosystems (note especially those "services" located nearer the bottom of Table 4.1).

Fast Facts

In 2010 more than 1.7 million of the world's species had been identified. Yet this is just the beginning, since many of the world's species have yet to be discovered. Some estimates place total species diversity of earth at close to 10 billion (Wilson [1992] 1999). Others place the number closer to 30 billion (IUCN 2006).

Deep-sea exploration is pushing species totals even higher. Until recently, scientists believed this place too hostile for life. Turns out, the deep seabed might be the most diverse of all marine environments, with biodiversity levels comparable to those found in tropical rain forests and shallow-water coral reefs. Although only 0.0001 percent of the deep seabed has been subject to biological investigations, estimates place the number of species inhabiting it as high as 10 million. Deep-sea biodiversity is threatened by pollution, shipping, military activities, and climate change. Yet fishing presents the greatest threat, especially with the recent emergence of technologies that enable vessels to exploit ever-greater depths (UNEP 2008).

We are losing species at an alarming rate, many before even being discovered. Famed biologist Edward O. Wilson ([1992] 1999) estimates the current rate of species extinction at roughly 27,000 annually, or 74 per day. Furthermore, according to Wilson, extinction rates today may be as great as one thousand times the historical background rate. This is another way of saying we are presently experiencing the greatest mass extinction of all time.

Less than 3 percent of the 250,000 plant varieties available to agriculture are currently in use (Vernooy and Song 2004).

From the more than 1.2 billion hectares of tropical rain-forest habitat that originally existed, less than 400 million remain (Spilsbury 2010).

Implications

As detailed in Table 4.2, a great number of events and activities (most of which are human induced) threaten biodiversity. And these threats will only grow in the decades ahead, especially as the world becomes warmer (thanks to climate change), more crowded (as a result of population growth and urbanization trends), and more affluent (particularly in Southeast Asia). Complicating matters further are the ways in which pressures upon biodiversity can act at different temporal and spatial scales. For instance, sediments from deforestation in the headwaters of the Orinoco River along the Venezuelan-Brazilian boarder negatively impact marine life in the Caribbean more than a thousand miles away by altering the nutrient availability and clarity of the waters (UNEP 2008).

The reasons for biodiversity decline will come up again later, as many of the pressures and drivers discussed in Table 4.2 are subjects of later chapters. What I am most interested in detailing at the moment are impacts. Yet before doing this, there is one small conceptual problem that requires attention: what precisely does *biodiversity* even mean? Only after working our way through this question can we begin having a conversation about the various consequences associated with biodiversity loss.

TABLE 4.2 Threats to Biodiversity

Residential & Commercial Development	Agriculture & Aquaculture
• Housing & Urban Areas • Commercial & Industrial Areas • Tourism & Recreation Areas	• Annual & Perennial Non-Timber Crops • Wood & Pulp Plantations • Livestock Farming & Ranching • Marine & Freshwater Aquaculture
Energy Production & Mining • Oil & Gas Drilling • Mining & Quarrying • Renewable Energy	**Transportation & Service Corridors** • Roads & Railroads • Utility & Service Lines • Shipping Lanes • Flight Paths • Air and Space Transport
Biological Resource Use • Hunting & Collecting Terrestrial Animals • Gathering Terrestrial Plants • Logging & Wood Harvesting • Fishing & Harvesting Aquatic Resources	**Human Intrusions & Disturbance** • Recreational Activities • War, Civil Unrest & Military Exercises • Work & Other Activities
Natural System Modifications • Fire & Fire Suppression • Dams & Water Management/Use • Other Ecosystem Modifications	**Invasive & Problematic Species & Genes** • Invasive Non-native/Alien Species • Problematic Native Species • Introduced Genetic Material
Pollution • Household Sewage & Urban Waste Water • Industrial & Military Effluents • Agricultural & Forestry Effluents • Garbage & Solid Waste • Airborne Pollutants • Excess Heat, Sound, or Light That Disturbs Wildlife and/or Ecosystems	**Geological Events** • Volcanoes • Earthquakes/Tsunamis • Avalanches/Landslides
Climate Change & Severe Weather • Habitat Shifting & Alteration • Droughts • Temperature Extremes • Storms & Flooding	

Source: Adapted from Conservation Measures Partnership.

Biodiversity versus "Biodiversity"

Early definitions of biodiversity tended to focus almost entirely on species diversity, in which case biodiversity was simply another way of saying "species richness" (see, for example, Lovejoy 1980). More recently, the definition of the term has expanded to include, along with species richness, genetic diversity (within and across species) and ecological diversity (which includes ecosystem services and habitat) (see, for example, Hunter and Gibbs 2007). Yet the problem doesn't lie just in deciding which criteria to include in our definition. It also lies in the inherent ambiguity of the criteria themselves. Take the concept—or, I should say, *concepts*—of species.

A review of the modern biological literature well over a decade ago found at least twenty-four different species concepts (Mayden 1997), a figure that has no doubt increased in recent years, given the expanding literature on the subject. The "**species problem**," as it has come to be known, refers to the inherent ambiguity surrounding the use and definition of the species concept (see, for example, Hey 2001). The three more widely utilized contemporary species concepts include the biological species concept (centering on the property of reproductive isolation), the ecological species concept (emphasizing speciation through ecological selection), and the phylogenetic species concept (focusing on the property of common descent). This all matters tremendously from a conservation standpoint, for ultimately which species concept we adopt affects the number of species we find.

It has been argued, for instance, that the biological species concept tends to overemphasize gene flow between populations and thus aggregates species together, while the phylogenetic species concept often splits such populations into distinct and thus potentially "new" species (Meijaard and Nijman 2003). This inflation/deflation of biodiversity levels based on which species concept is ultimately employed has been well documented. A team of researchers reanalyzed organisms utilizing a phylogenetic species concept that were earlier classified according to other species definitions (Agapow et al. 2004). The reanalysis yielded a species *increase* of 121 percent. Focusing on avian endemism in Mexico (birds that are found only in Mexico), another team applied two alternative species concepts: the phylogenetic species concept and the biological species concept (A. Peterson and Navarro-Siguenza 1999). Their findings indicate not only divergent levels of biodiversity based on which species concept was used but also divergent **biodiversity hot spots** (a biogeographic region with a significant reservoir of biodiversity that is under threat from humans), signifying where endemism is particularly concentrated. When the biological species concept was used, 101 bird species were found to be endemic to Mexico, with populations concentrated in the mountains of the western and southern portions of the country. Using the phylogenetic species concept, endemic species total rose to 249, with population concentrations in the mountains and lowlands of western Mexico.

Equally problematic is the concept of "ecosystem"—a phenomenon, as mentioned previously, recently folded into biodiversity definitions. Maps of biologically diverse hot spots typically include tropical rain forests, for reasons related not only to species richness but also to the important ecosystem services (such as climate regulation and nutrient cycling) they provide. Wetlands and marshes, however, are typically ignored in

ETHICAL QUESTION 4.1
The Power of Conservation Maps

A wealth of literature has emerged in the past twenty years examining the power embedded within maps (e.g., Edney 1997; Harley 1989; Wood 1993). Perhaps the best-known instance of this involves how modern maps embody the commercial and political interests of western European and North American nation-states. Most world maps place North at the "top," have zero degrees longitude running through Greenwich, England, and are centered on either western Europe, North America, or the North Atlantic. Maps can also reflect societal preferences for certain landscapes and ecosystems. For example, forests are far more frequently mapped than grasslands (Hazen and Anthamatten 2004). Yet even what's defined as "forest" is hotly contested. A mapped, legally defined "forest" may in fact not contain a single tree (Vandergeest 1996).

Similar to how world maps give readers the sense that political boundaries are natural and objectively given, conservation maps also tend to naturalize a static view of ecological and social systems. In other words, while the socioecological space being represented in conservation images is inherently fluid, once mapped these spaces take on a near-timeless, permanent quality. Maps also tend to minimize differences across geophysical space. Harris and Hazen (2006), for instance, examined a widely distributed map created by the UN Environment Programme that visually depicts the spatial distribution of internationally recognized "protected" areas. Such global perspectives, however, risk endorsing the view that conservation spaces are comparable across what are in reality widely divergent areas. They point out how places of conservation in the United States and United Kingdom are often appreciably different. For example, due to divergent historical trajectories, national parks in the United States reflect the wilderness ideal (an image of nature devoid of human presence), while in the United Kingdom they are often populated agricultural landscapes. Although such spaces are radically different "on the ground," these differences are washed away when viewed at the level of a global map.

these maps, even though they provide equally essential ecosystem services (such as nutrient cycling, erosion control, water purification, and storm protection; see Ethical Question 4.1).

And what about humans? Are we not a species who create and alter ecosystems? Shouldn't *we* factor into measures of biodiversity, other than only being viewed as yet another thing that negatively impacts it?

The Bombay Natural History Society (BNHS) noticed in the late 1970s that bird populations were on the decline in the Bharatpur Bird Sanctuary (what is today known as the Keoladeo National Park) in Rajasthan, India. An accusatory finger was eventually pointed at cattle and buffalo, which were entering the preserve in sufficient quantities and disrupting what was believed to be an otherwise balanced ecosystem. In an attempt to correct the problem of decreasing bird populations, Bharatpur was declared a national park in 1981. This act was quickly followed by a ban on all grazing activities within the park (nine people were killed in the resulting riots that ensued as the park was cleared of its earlier human inhabitants).

By the mid-1980s, something was amiss. Studies were beginning to indicate the seemingly impossible: bird diversity within the park had *declined further* since the ban on grazing (Vijayan 1987). By the early 1990s, it was irrefutable: biodiversity not only had declined since the grazing ban but was diving downward at an alarming rate. The absence of grazing animals, it turns out, had a disastrous effect on the ecology of the park. Weed species were taking over wetlands and choking canals, thereby reducing fish populations. As the open wetland habitat—a habitat that once attracted a tremendous mix of birds—was being overrun by a handful of fast-growing opportunistic plant species, avian species went elsewhere in search of more suitable places to nest. In 1991, in a stunning course reversal, the BNHS—originally the most vocal opponent on grazing in the park—concluded that, to avoid further weed takeover, grazing animals needed to be brought back. A report announcing this policy reversal admitted the shortsightedness of conservation polices that place humans apart from—rather than as a part of—biologically diverse ecosystems: "In the case of most wetlands in this country, man's [and woman's] interaction with them has become almost inseparable and hence, man [and woman] has to actively manage them" (Vijayan 1991:1).

Biodiversity: The Fuel Driving Ecosystem Services

Biodiversity loss is our loss. Biodiversity may not make the world go around, but it certainly makes the planet inhabitable. Here I speak in a little more detail about some of the services provided by biodiversity.

Agriculture

No amount of technology and innovation could substitute for the ecosystem services provided by biodiversity in the production of food and fiber production (see ECOnnection 4.1). Biodiversity makes soil habitable for plant growth, as it is central to the breakdown and recycling of nutrients within this life-giving medium. Biodiversity also makes pollination possible and is essential for pest control, without which productivity losses would be even greater. Biodiversity may well also hold the key to future food security in light of climate change, as plant breeders will have to look increasingly into the gene pool to come up with varieties suitable to withstand and ideally thrive under a variety of agroecological conditions.

Forests

As with agriculture, commercial forestry depends on biodiversity for nutrient recycling and pest control. Some forests also generate revenue from hunting, the collection of wild food (e.g., berries and fungi), the collection of firewood, and occasionally bird-watchers and nature photographers. Forests also offer spaces for recreation, itself a major revenue-generating activity. Last, there is an incalculable intrinsic value associated with these spaces, as they not only serve as sources of creativity and inspiration but also hold religious and cultural significance for populations around the world.

ECOnnection 4.1
The Irreplaceable Bee

Insect pollination is not only a critical ecosystem service but also an essential component of most agricultural systems. Roughly 84 percent of the nearly three hundred commercial crops are insect pollinated (90 percent of this service is performed by honeybees) (Allsopp, de Lange, and Veldtman 2008). Pollination by European honeybees is estimated to be between sixty to one hundred times more valuable than the honey they produce, which explains why farmers dependent upon their services sometimes refer to them as "flying $50 bills" (Maser 2009:69). Unable to discern insect friend from insect foe, pesticides have had a major impact upon all insect pollinators (Desneux, Decourtye, J.-M. Delpuech 2007). Looking at the deciduous fruit industry of the western Cape of South Africa, one study estimates the total annual value of insect pollination services and managed pollination to be US$358.4 million and US$312.1 million, respectively. Between US$28 million and US$122.8 million of this is provided by managed honeybee pollination services, out of which only US$1.8 million is currently being paid. As for wild pollinators, they provide us with between US$49.1 million and $310.9 million worth of free services (Allsopp et al. 2008).

Fisheries

Waterways provide a provisioning ecosystem service in the form of fish catch. The fish catch, however, is heavily dependent on a functioning biologically diverse ecosystem that supplies nutrients, prey species, habitats, and a desirable water quality (Bullock 2008). There is also an intensely cultural component to fishing, as many societies have deep historical roots in this practice.

Water

Biodiversity performs an irreplaceable service in terms of both recycling nutrients and ensuring desirable water quality for agricultural use, fisheries, and human consumption. A significant amount of research has emerged in recent years documenting that species-rich aquatic ecosystems are more efficient at removing excess nutrients (and even some pollutants) from water than those with fewer species (Canfield, Glazer, and Falkowski 2010).

Atmospheric Regulation

Forests and other vegetation—and to a lesser extent all organisms—modify climate (though humans look to be the most influential organism). Plants and trees do this by, among other things, affecting solar reflection, water-vapor release, wind patterns, and moisture loss. Forests, for example, help maintain a humid environment, as evidenced by the fact that half of all rainfall in the Amazon basin is produced locally from the forest-atmosphere cycle (Kozloff 2010).

Biocultural Diversity

As recently acknowledged by the United Nations Environment Programme, "Biodiversity also incorporates human cultural diversity, which can be affected by the same drivers as biodiversity, and which has impacts on the diversity of genes, other species, and ecosystems" (UNEP 2007:160). The term **biocultural diversity** speaks to an unmistakable (and increasingly well-documented) empirical fact: that cultural diversity does not merely parallel biological diversity but is profoundly interrelated with it (Maffi and Woodley 2010).

There is a subtle but noticeable disdain toward humans in many environmental texts in their noting only the ways in which humans threaten biodiversity. It is unquestionably true that we are the greatest threat to the earth's biodiversity. But this shouldn't lead to the conclusion that humans somehow represent an *inherent* risk to biological diversity. Granted, it's far easier to see the various ways in which we are mucking things up, as we read routinely about the latest species threatened or lost entirely at our own hands. Yet there is growing evidence pointing to how humans are also positively contributing to ecosystems and biodiversity levels.

There are two general approaches to biological conservation: *ex situ* and *in situ*. *Ex situ* conservation involves the sampling, transferring, and storage of a species in a place other than the original location in which it was found, like a zoo or seed bank. The other option is *in situ* conservation, which involves the management of a species at the location of discovery. The *ex situ* model is often what comes to mind (at least for most in the developed world) when people think of biodiversity conservation, which is understandable in light of the more than fourteen hundred seed and gene banks and more than one thousand zoos worldwide.

The popularity of the *in situ* model, however, has grown considerably among conservationists in recent decades. Proponents of the *in situ* approach argue that it provides a more complete form of conservation, in that it makes room for, unlike *ex situ* approaches, socioecological dynamics. It is no coincidence that most of the world's biologically diverse hot spots are also its **cultural hot spots** (a biogeographic region with a significant reservoir of cultural diversity that is under threat of extinction) (Stepp et al. 2004). Research looking at indigenous populations in North America consistently notes a correlation between measures of biodiversity within a given region and its levels of cultural and linguistic diversity (Nabhan 1985; Smith 2001; Soleri and Cleveland 1993).

Virginia Nazarea has extensively studied sweet potato farmers in the Philippines. At one site they were beginning the processes of commercializing production, while at another they remained firmly at the level of subsistence agriculture. She had hypothesized that commercialization causes a narrowing of genetic and cultural diversity among sweet potatoes raised. Her hypothesis was confirmed. Yet she also observed something unexpected. There was a large disparity between the two sites in terms of the number of varieties known or remembered, compared to the biodiversity that actually existed. At the commercial site, farmers had knowledge about a far lower percentage of sweet potato varieties than at the other site, having forgotten many that still existed and were being planted elsewhere in the country. This suggests a faster erosion of cultural knowledge than genetic diversity itself. Reflecting upon this research, Nazarea writes how this

ECOnnection 4.2

Memory Banking

One way biocultural diversity is being conserved is through what are called "memory banks." The goal of these "banks" is to save more than just the plant or seed itself. Keeping a record of life history interviews of those with working knowledge of the plants in question helps ensure that further generations will know as much about these plants as those growing them today.

A well-known example of memory banking occurred in Cotacachi, Ecuador (Rhoades and Nazarea 2006). In this project, children were allocated approximately US$20 to interview their parents, grandparents, or other elders to record whatever they could tell of local plants. This money was sufficient to cover the expenses of school, as it was agreed beforehand that it would be used to pay for participants'

education, whether primary, secondary, or college (another goal of memory banking is to empower local communities). During the interview process, interviewees were asked a series of basic questions, like "What varieties did your grandparents grow?" and "How did farming change over time?" In addition to learning how to interview, record information, and store data in the project database, the children also collected culturally significant plants (in addition to leaves, seeds, and roots) and prepared them for display and storage. They also planted and maintained a biologically diverse garden and made public exhibitions of the plants and elders' knowledge during special days at the school. Between 1999 and 2004, fifteen students received free tuition in exchange for their involvement in the project.

finding signified that "in the context of agricultural development and market integration, knowledge may actually be the first to go" (2005:62).

Sociologists MacKenzie and Spinardi (1995) argued a while back that nuclear weapons are becoming "uninvented" due to global nuclear disarmament trends and nuclear test–ban treaties. It is their contention that "if design ceases, and if there is no new generation of designers to whom that tacit knowledge can be passed, then in an important (though qualified) sense nuclear weapons will have been uninvented" (ibid.:44). They are pointing, to put it simply, to the importance of putting knowledge to work. A lot of knowledge has to be acted out—literally *practiced*—for it to exist and be passed along to others. Try, for example, teaching someone to ride a bike with words alone—it just doesn't work. The same principle applies to our knowledge of biodiversity. This is why the term *biocultural* diversity is so apt, because the cultural knowledge tied to traditional crops is very much rooted in practice. Many traditional cultures are oral, meaning that much of this folk knowledge is thus not physically recorded (written down) anywhere. Once lost, there is therefore a good chance this knowledge—and with it a piece of biocultural diversity—is gone forever (see ECOnnection 4.2).

Biopiracy

Although we often think about biological loss in the context of, say, extinction, this is not the only way it is experienced. In some cases, while the object of concern still exists (perhaps even thrives), the loss felt is the result of the misappropriation of biocultural knowledge. Enter **biopiracy**: essentially the loss of biocultural diversity through legal—and sometimes illegal—means.

It is estimated that developing nations would be owed US$5 billion if they received royalties of 2 percent for their contributions in pharmaceutical research and another US$302 million for royalties in agricultural products (Anuradha 2001:28; Ismail and Fakir 2004:175–177). Biopiracy—or what's called bioprospecting by those doing it—occurs when folk knowledge and biological artifacts are conjointly exploited for commercial gain without just compensation to those responsible for discovering or originating it. Although it's easy to chalk biopiracy up to the greedy actions of powerful multinational corporations seeking to exploit the knowledge and resources of indigenous populations, it is important to understand certain sociolegal realities that make such activities possible in the first place.

To begin with, patent law makes it exceedingly difficult for indigenous populations to call biocultural knowledge their own. According to patent law, no patent can be issued where prior art exists due to the statutory requirement that patents are to be granted only for new inventions on the basis of novelty and nonobviousness. An invention is generally not regarded as new if it was patented or described in a printed publication. **Indigenous knowledge**—or local knowledge, which is knowledge unique to a given community, culture, or society—however, has tended to be an oral and embodied effect, acquired through years of literally *doing* and applying that knowledge. As such, it is rarely ever written down. Its transmission occurs through storytelling, not book reading. The knowledge of these indigenous societies can thus often be freely plundered for private gain, as evidenced by firms patenting and claiming as their own knowledge that had for centuries been part of the (indigenous) public domain.

One way indigenous groups are responding to this legal reality is by publishing their biocultural knowledge in large digital libraries, what are commonly known as Traditional Knowledge Data Libraries (TKDLs). Transforming this age-old embodied and oral knowledge into a written form turns it into something that patent law recognizes and which therefore constitutes prior art. Many countries—such as South Korea, Thailand, Mongolia, Cambodia, South Africa, Nigeria, Pakistan, Nepal, Sri Lanka, and Bangladesh—are following in the footsteps of India, who developed one of the first TKDLs in the late 1990s.

To what extent is biopiracy occurring? That's not easy to say, as a number of national laws, international agreements, and legally binding treaties make biopiracy illegal. So whatever is occurring is taking place under the radar. The most consequential legal structure to emerge to reduce biopiracy is the Convention of Biological Diversity (CBD), which was adopted at the Earth Summit of Rio de Janeiro in 1992. Its objectives are threefold: the conservation of biodiversity, the sustainable use of biodiversity, and the equitable sharing of benefits arising from the use of genetic resources.

Agreements reached through the CBD, however, do not apply to materials collected before 1992. Thus, any material in a gene or seed bank before 1992 can still be exploited for commercial ends without any money going back to the source country as compensation. Take the case involving a disease-resistant peanut from Brazil. The peanut was first picked in 1952 by Alan Beetle. It was not until 1987, however, that Beetle's sample would be utilized for commercial ends. In 1987 the tomato spotted wilt virus (TSWV) was first detected in US peanuts. This virus severely injures or kills any peanut plant

ECOnnection 4.3
Synthetic Biology and Biopiracy

Synthetic biology is an emerging field (often likened to a marriage between biology and engineering) that can involve anything from the design and construction of new biological functions and systems not found in nature to the reconstitution of "wet" biological materials (DNA, RNA, and so on) from "dry" genetic databases. The field has profound implications when it comes to the issue of biopiracy. For example, the CBD does not take into account the digital transmission of biological materials. Yet hundreds of thousands of DNA sequences are being downloaded daily from genomic databases (such as GenBank). Consequently, whereas an individual accessing a gene bank is required to sign a legally binding Material Transfer Agreement, that same person can obtain digital DNA sequences from a genomic database with anonymity.

Biopiracy has conventionally referred to the physical removal of a material from a country or community. Synthetic biology avoids this by allowing for the DNA of an organism to be sequenced *in situ*, which is, at present, perfectly legal. This information is then taken to a DNA synthesizer, where it is "rebuilt." Although they like to talk about "inventing" DNA from scratch, synthetic biologists typically start with naturally occurring derivatives of genetic code when looking to build novel organisms. This technology effectively allows firms to ignore benefit-sharing laws, like those prescribed under the CBD.

that it infects. It quickly spread throughout Georgia, Florida, Alabama, and South Carolina, seriously threatening the US peanut industry. Beetle's sample peanut was known to be resistant to TSWV and was quickly sought out for this trait by breeders. A number of peanut varieties have since been bred to be resistant to TSWV using this nut from Brazil. In fact, the germplasm from this nut is estimated to add at least US$200 million annually to the US economy (Edmonds Institute 2006). Brazil, conversely, receives nothing. Nevertheless, as a recent report on the subject adds, "no laws were transgressed." Rather, this example speaks to a perfectly legal case of "pre-CBD biopiracy" (ibid.:3).

Even with CBD, however, biopiracy remains a problem (see ECOnnection 4.3). Let's look briefly at two recent well-publicized cases of biopiracy, involving Bt brinjal from India and herbal teas from South Africa.

Bt brinjal is a genetically modified strain of brinjal (eggplant) created by India's largest seed company, Mahyco, which also happens to be a subsidiary of the multinational company Monsanto. Bt brinjal has been engineered to be resistant to lepidopteran insects, particularly the brinjal fruit and shoot borer. According to the National Biodiversity Authority (NBA) of India, the development of Bt brinjal is a case of biopiracy, which means Monsanto and Mahyco could face criminal proceedings. The NBA charges these alleged biopirates with accessing nine Indian varieties of brinjal to develop their genetically modified eggplant without prior permission from the NBA or relevant national and local boards. This is a violation of the country's Biological Diversity Act (enacted in 2002), which provides for the conservation of biological diversity and calls for fair and equitable sharing of the benefits that arise out of the use of biocultural resources (it is also illegal under the CBD). By using the local brinjal varieties without permission, Monsanto and Mahyco weakened India's sovereign control over its resources while denying economic and social benefits to local communities under the benefit-sharing requirements of the Biological Diversity Act (Jebaraj 2011).

Example two: biopirated tea. Global food giant Nestlé is facing allegations of biopiracy after applying for patents based on two South African plants (used in the making of herbal teas) without first receiving permission from the South African government. This puts Nestlé in direct violation of South African law as well as the CBD. The controversy centers on two South African plants, rooibos and honeybush, commonly used to make herbal teas with well-known—and long-known—medicinal benefits. A Nestlé subsidiary has filed five international patent applications seeking to claim ownership over some of those medicinal benefits, such as using the plants to treat hair and skin conditions and for anti-inflammatory treatments. At issue is benefit sharing: namely, Nestlé believes it does not need to share any future profits that might be derived from these patents. Yet according to the South African Biodiversity Act (enacted in 2004), firms must obtain a permit from the government if they intend to use the country's genetic resources for research or patenting. And these permits can be obtained *only* in exchange for a benefit-sharing agreement (ICTSD 2010).

Solutions

As biodiversity is threatened by multiple practices, pressures, and events, solutions directed at the problem of biodiversity loss must be equally multiple and diverse. I offer here two strategies that have had some success at enhancing biodiversity levels. In the space that remains, I discuss the practice of community conservation and agrobiodiversity conservation. As later chapters get at many of the anthropogenic drivers of biodiversity loss, do not think these are our only two solutions. Many others lie ahead, beyond those noted in this chapter.

Community Conservation

The modern conservation movement emerged in Europe in the nineteenth century. The "wilderness" model, around which so many of the world's national parks are built, came shortly thereafter out of the United States. Although these top-down—which is to say they are typically implemented and overseen by the state—conservation methods have had their successes, they are not without their problems.

For one thing, conservation has historically been viewed as separate from development. Indeed, in some camps they are antithetical to each other. The social costs of these conventional models of conservation have been great. Removing, sometimes forcibly, indigenous populations—like the Native Americans in the United States and the Parakuyo and Massai pastoralists in Tanzania—from lands they have lived on for centuries for purposes of "saving nature" is morally repugnant. But also, looking beyond the morality of these acts, the science refutes the ecological soundness of such policies. As the earlier case involving the Bharatpur Bird Sanctuary in India shows us, there may be better ways of conserving biodiversity than by removing people from the equation.

A paradigm shift of sorts is taking place in conservation and developmental circles. On the one hand, it is becoming clear that developmental policies that overlook conservation

ETHICAL QUESTION 4.2

Sustainability: For Whom and Toward What End?

The term *sustainability* reminds me a lot of the term *nature:* we seem to talk endlessly about both but struggle when forced to offer a clear definition of either. *Social sustainability, environmental sustainability,* and *economic sustainability* are hotly contested terms. *What* they mean depends on *who* you ask. What do we mean, for example, when talking about social sustainability? Does this mean, say, improving social justice or reducing inequality or something else entirely? Or environmental sustainability: do we mean zeroing out all ecological impact or just minimizing impact—and if it is the latter, is everyone expected to reduce equally, or might those with the largest ecological footprints be asked to reduce more? Or economic sustainability: does this mean simply that households and firms need to be profitable, or does it also suggest a desire to reduce, for example, economic inequality?

What do you, the reader, think about when the term *sustainability* comes to mind? If you're anything like my students, ecological sustainability likely comes to mind before social sustainability (and this is even among *sociology* students). Can you think of instances where an ecologically sustainable practice might not be socially sustainable?

are unsustainable in the long run and ultimately offer no relief to threats to biodiversity. On the other hand, conservationists are beginning to understand that they can no longer afford to ignore the impoverishment they may be causing when they exclude human populations from habitats they are seeking to conserve. In fact, what we've learned is that those indigenous populations that conservationists have been so busy evicting over the past century may hold the key to truly sustainable development (Brockington and Schmidt-Soltau 2004; see Ethical Question Box 4.2).

This is where community conservation comes into the picture (see ECOnnection 4.4). As generally practiced, community conservation is place based and highly participatory. There are different "flavors" of community conservation, as there are many different ways to define community involvement when it comes to conservation. This variability is captured in Table 4.3. As illustrated in the table, levels of community involvement can run the spectrum: from low, where an agency is in charge, to high, where independent community-centered groups develop their own initiatives as a result of a crisis or problem.

Arguably the most publicized community conservation success story comes out of Tanzania. It involves two woodland reserves, both of which were being poorly conserved under previous management regimes. In 1994 and 1995, communities located near the edge of the forests secured the return of control over woodlands they had previously informally managed for generations.

As one of the few remaining tracts of the Miombo woodlands in the Babati District, the Duru-Haitemba woodlands were targeted to be turned into a forest reserve as early

ECOnnection 4.4

Socioecological Benefits Known to Arise from Community Conservation

FIRST BENEFIT: STRENGTHENS COMMUNITIES

- builds local skills, interests, and capacities
- builds a sense of stewardship and community capacity for environmental problem solving that will remain with the community
- builds community cohesion
- increases the likelihood that the community will be able to solve future problems on their own.

SECOND BENEFIT: APPROACHES ARE TAILORED TO LOCAL NEEDS

- As opposed to top-down approaches, which tend to serve nonlocal interests, community conservation can be highly responsive to unique community and environmental needs by incorporating local knowledge, and strategies and solutions will likely be well suited to local socioecological dynamics.

THIRD BENEFIT: POSITIVE OUTCOMES FOR INDIVIDUALS

- enhances knowledge of and relationship with surrounding ecosystems

- working with others can have therapeutic benefits
- building social ties with others enhances individual well-being.

FOURTH BENEFIT: INCREASED LIKELIHOOD OF LOCAL ACCEPTANCE AND SUSTAINABLE OUTCOMES

- increased likelihood of successful implementation when actions and decisions are viewed by those involved as responsible and appropriate
- as local populations rely upon having a healthy surrounding ecosystem they have an incentive to be sure they get conservation strategies right.

FIFTH BENEFIT: EFFICIENT USE OF RESOURCES

- enforcement and monitoring are often done cost-effectively, as informal social norms, trust, and a shared commitment to success are linked positively to compliance.

Adapted from Trotman (2008) and Wily (1999).

as 1985. (The Miombo woodlands stretch in a broad belt across south-central Africa, extending from Angola to Tanzania.) The intention was to protect the forest against further deforestation by future expanding settlement through the deployment of government forest guards. By taking control, local governments were promised a steady source of revenue through the issuing of licenses for timber and pole-wood extraction, which would be granted to people living adjacent to the forest (Wily 1999).

TABLE 4.3   Citizen Involvement in Conservation Decision Making

	Low (full control by agency in charge)		High (full control by stakeholders)	
PROCESS	**Information Sharing**: Builds awareness by telling people what is planned	**Consultation**: Identifies problems, offers solutions, and obtains feedback to broaden knowledge base allowing for better top-down decisions	**Co-Directed**: Involves and actively engages stakeholders to contribute ideas and opinions when deciding best way to move forward	**Independent Community Initiatives**: Groups are enabled to act, in terms of process as well as outcome
ACTIVITY OF CITIZEN GROUP	**Passive**: Receptors of information	**Marginally Engaged**: Pre-determined phase is devoted to seeking public input	**Equal Players**: Involvement throughout entire processes	**Directing**: Groups set agenda and determine direction and outcome of project
OUTCOME	**Information Dissemination**	**Weak Participation**	**Strong Participation**	**Determination**

Citizen involvement can take many different forms. Some options offer little more than a façade of "involvement" (as illustrated by the "low" end toward the left of Table 4.3), while others (far-right or "high" end of the table) put communities firmly in the driver seat. *Source:* Adapted from Forgie et al. (2001) and Trotman (2008).

The plan met significant opposition among local people whose livelihood was dependent upon that tract of forest. There were also concerns about the plan's feasibility. As experience has shown, it is unrealistic to expect low-paid forest guards (many of whom are recruited from the same rural areas they are expected to police) to monitor the forest's border from villagers in need of forest products for basic subsistence. By the early 1990s, an agreement was reached to find a more acceptable management strategy. The solution ultimately settled on involved allowing and assisting each of the eight villages that border the woodlands to take full rights and responsibility for its conservation.

The results have been unmistakable. The forests show visible signs of gain, as most of the earlier unregulated in-forest settlement, charcoal burning, and illicit timber harvesting have ceased. The size of the woodland has actually increased. In the Duru-Haitemba Forest (which had previously suffered the most damage), the return of understory shrubbery, grasses, and bees points to improved forest health. In other parts of the forest, increases in wildlife biodiversity are being recorded. Hundreds of young village men have volunteered to patrol the protected areas, at zero cost to the government, due to a vested interest in the health of the forest (ibid.; see Case Study 4.1).

Agrobiodiversity Conservation

Agrobiodiversity—all forms of life directly relevant to agriculture, including crops and livestock but also many other organisms, such as soil fauna, weeds, pests, and predators—is the result of natural and human selection processes, involving farmers, herders, and

CASE STUDY 4.1
Participatory Forest Management in Kenya

Kenya has widely embraced participatory forest management (a variation of community conservation). Because of its track record, it is believed that this approach not only effectively achieves sustainable forest management goals but also simultaneously involves stakeholders, who have a vested interest in this end, as their livelihoods depend on it (Schreckenberg and Luttrell 2009). Participatory forest management is supported under the Forest Act of 2005. This act provides for the establishment, development, and sustainable management of forest resources for the socioeconomic development of the country. The avenues through which Kenyans in general, and Kenyan forest communities in particular, can directly or indirectly participate in the management and monitoring of their forests include the following: as members of community forest associations, as representatives appointed to the forest conservation committees, as representatives appointed to the Board of the Kenya Forest Service, and as individuals. The Forest Act of 2005 also allows forest communities to constitute up to 50 percent of the representation in the forest conservation committee that oversees the management of a recognized forest. The law further provides for community representation on the Board of the Kenya Forest Service.

fishers over millennia. The future of food security, it is widely believed (Lenne and Wood 2011), hinges on agrodiversity. Agrobiodiversity gives us options when responding to whatever threats to food production we can expect to face in the future. Phenomena that can fall under the category of agrobiodiversity include: harvested crop varieties, livestock breeds, fish species, and nondomesticated (wild) animals used for food; nonharvested species in production ecosystems that support food provision (like soil microbiota, pollinators, and other organisms such as earthworms); and nonharvested species in the wider environment that support food production ecosystems (such as species in a waterway that encourage the process of water purification) (FAO 2004; see ECOnnection 4.5).

Agrobiodiversity is not only viewed as representing one of the keys to future food security, but is also widely seen as central to any sustainable model of food production. There is compelling evidence showing how, through the implementation of agroecology farming techniques (an approach relying heavily on ecological principles rather than commercial inputs, also discussed further in Chapter 8), agrobiodiversity can help increase crop productivity—potentially even outproducing conventional agriculture. Agrobiodiversity is also seen as a central ingredient to the effective control of disease and pest outbreaks without the use of harmful chemical inputs (Altieri [1987] 1995; Gliessman 1998).

The promotion of agrobiodiversity can take many forms. Simply allowing farmers to save seed from one year to be planted the next is a good place to start, particularly since patents and other controls like so-called **terminator technology** (genetically engineered

ECOnnection 4.5
Crop Wild Relatives

The gene pool for a crop is composed of commercial varieties (varieties bred for commercial purposes), landraces (varieties developed by farmers through acts of seed saving), and **crop wild relatives**. Crop wild relatives are the wild ancestors of crop plants and other species closely related to crops. Their conservation has received less attention than either commercial varieties or landraces, even though they are likely to play a significant role in securing future food security. For example, as a source of immense genetic diversity, crop wild relatives will likely become an increasingly important resource for plant breeders looking to produce crops that can overcome imminent challenges, from the adverse impacts of climate change to increasing scarcity of water and other agro inputs. The global value in 1997 of crop varieties bred from crop wild relatives was placed at US$115 billion per year, a figure that would have only increased in recent years (Hopkins and Maxted 2011).

seed that produce sterile plants) are making this increasingly difficult (Carolan 2010a). Memory banks, as mentioned earlier, also help promote agrobiodiversity by ensuring that future generations have a working knowledge of this species diversity (see Case Study 4.2).

Agrobiodiversity can also be promoted and enhanced through such activities as home gardens. Research on Vietnam home gardens shows a tension between commercialization, conservation, and household economic security (Trinh et al. 2003). At one site located in the tropical Mekong Delta, home gardens were large and highly commercialized. At this site, 88 percent of all that the gardens produced went to market, providing, on average, 54 percent of the household income. The fact that the gardens had been essentially commercialized while remaining biologically diverse is encouraging, as it indicates that commercial gardens need not replicate the lack of biodiversity found on, say, large-scale farms. In the poorest site examined, where the majority of the regional economy is based on barter, trade, and sharing (particularly among family members and friends), home gardens contributed significantly to the food security of families surveyed—supplying households with roughly 75 percent of their food—while maintaining high levels of biodiversity. Important factors contributing to the persistence of biodiversity, even in the face of commercialization, were cultural needs. Cultural tastes and local ethnic cuisine compelled home gardeners to preserve certain species that were not easily acquired at local grocery stores and food markets. More than just a source of affordable food, these home gardens were thus also supplying households with ingredients necessary for the making of certain cultural dishes. And by doing this the home gardens helped ensure species—*and* cultural—survival.

Although humans pose the gravest threat to biodiversity, at the moment we are also its greatest potential ally. Once we accept our rightful identity as being part of

CASE STUDY 4.2

The Seed Bank That Makes Memories

The Seed Savers Exchange (SSE) is a US-based heritage seed bank in northeastern Iowa (see http://www.seedsavers.org/). Founded in 1975, the SSE is a nonprofit organization that both saves and sells heirloom fruit, vegetable, and flower seeds. On this 890-acre farm, which goes by the name of the "Heritage Farm," there are twenty-four thousand rare vegetable varieties (including about four thousand traditional varieties from eastern Europe and Russia), approximately seven hundred pre-1900 varieties of apples (which represents nearly every remaining pre-1900 variety left in existence out of the eight thousand that once existed), and a herd of the rare Ancient White Park cattle (which currently has an estimated global population below two thousand).

Although in part a gene and seed bank, the SSE is also much more, as visitors can also learn a tremendous amount about the seeds being saved, such as their history and how to grow the seeds and cook and prepare their bounty, and, if you come at the right time of year, you might even learn how the fruits and vegetables taste. You might even say the SSE is more than just a memory bank, as many visitors find the SSE also responsible for memory *making*. An example of this occurs at their Heirloom Tomato Tasting Workshop. During this event, participants get to not only taste more than forty different kinds of tomatoes but actively learn how to save the seeds of their favorite varieties for future planting (Carolan 2011a).

nature, rather than seeing ourselves apart from it, new possibilities open up. These links are particularly conspicuous between agricultural systems and ecological ones, given the former's grounding (pun intended) in the latter (Perfecto, Vandermeer, and Wright 2009). Agriculture, when done ecologically—which is why it's called agroecology—can go a long way toward preserving the ecological integrity of systems while helping to safeguarding biological (and cultural) diversity and enhancing long-term food security.

IMPORTANT CONCEPTS

- agrobiodiversity
- biocultural diversity
- biopiracy
- community conservation
- *ex situ* and *in situ* conservation
- memory banking
- participatory forest management

DISCUSSION QUESTIONS

1. What are the links between cultural and biological diversity?
2. Conventional agriculture has become a monoculture within a monoculture, where fields are populated by not just one crop but one variety of a single crop. What are some of the forces driving this specialization?
3. Can we rely entirely upon zoos and gene banks when it comes to preserving our biological heritage?
4. Why isn't community conservation more popular in a country like the United States?

SUGGESTED ADDITIONAL READINGS

Harvey, F. 2012. "Conserving Biodiversity Hotspots 'Could Bring World's Poor $500bn a Year': Study Puts Economic Value on the Indirect Ecosystem Services Provided by the World's Poorest People." *Guardian*, February 20. Retrieved August 26, 2012 (http://www .guardian.co.uk/environment/2012/jan/20/conserving-biodiversity-pooreconomic-value).

Puppala, J., M. Oommen, and A. Sridhar, eds. 2011. "Perspectives on Knowledge: Going Beyond Dichotomies." Special issue, *Common Voices* 7. Retrieved August 26, 2012 (http:// fes.org.in/common-voices-7.pdf).

Robbins, J. 2011. "Biodiversity in Turkey, at Risk yet Largely Ignored." *New York Times*, December 22. Retrieved August 26, 2012 (http://green.blogs.nytimes.com/2011/12/22/turkeys -biodiversity-at-risk-yet-largely-ignored/?ref=earth).

White, R. 1995. "Are You an Environmentalist, or Do You Work for a Living?" In *Uncommon Ground*, edited by W. Cronon, 185–204. New York: W. W. Norton.

RELEVANT INTERNET LINKS

- http://www.conservation.org/where/priority_areas/hotspots/Pages/hotspots_main.aspx/ Excellent resource to learn more about biodiversity hot spots.
- http://www.natureserve.org/index.jsp A rich resource for almost anything that has to do with conservation. Data banks, news, and scientific publications: it's all there.
- http://www.ted.com/talks/lang/en/e_o_wilson_on_saving_life_on_earth.html Video of well-known biologist E. O. Wilson talking about biodiversity and conservation.

SUGGESTED VIDEOS

- *The Cove* (2009) This Academy Award–winning documentary depicts the ritualistic slaughter of bottlenose dolphins in Taiji, Japan.
- *Dirt! The Movie* (2009) Looks at the importance of the essential resource dirt.
- *The End of the Line* (2010) Examines the subject of overfishing, suggesting the possibility of nearly fishless ocean by 2048 if sustainable fishing practices are not implemented soon.

- *Manufactured Landscapes* (2007)
  Documents changes to our landscapes across the globe due to industry and manufacturing.
- *Queen of the Sun* (2010)
  A film on the honeybee crisis and colony collapse disorder.
- *Sharkwater* (2006)
  A filmmaker undertakes a dangerous journey in an effort to save sharks from extinction.

5

Water: There's No Substitute

Economists, until recently, were fond of discussing what's known as the "water and diamonds paradox." The paradox, as summarized in an economics textbook from the 1990s, goes something like this: Why is it that "water, which has so much value in use, has no value in exchange, while diamonds, which have practically no value in use, are exchanged at high prices" (Ekelund and Hébert 1997:294)? This is clearly less the case today, as in some instances people are willing to pay more for a liter of bottled water than they are for a comparable amount of gasoline. Indeed, the paradox now is why are some willing to pay so much for this commodity when they can just as easily get it for free?! The reason water seems to defy economic reasoning is that its "value" cannot be neatly portrayed in exclusively monetary terms. Yet this is not to say that it defies reasoning itself—interjected, of course, with a little sociological imagination. In this chapter, I explore some of the consequences associated with humanity's growing need for this life-giving resource and, later, speak of some potential responses to ensure that this need never exceeds supply.

Fast Facts

The water cycle does not favor continents equally. Six countries—Brazil, Canada, China, Columbia, Indonesia, and Russia—account for half of the world's renewable freshwater (Myers and Kent 2005).

Approximately 70 percent of all the freshwater used by humans goes to agriculture, industry uses 22 percent, and the remaining 8 percent is utilized by municipalities and households (Sterling and Vintinner 2008).

A per capita freshwater supply of below one thousand cubic meters places countries in the category of "severe water stress" (Qadir et al. 2007). As documented in Table 5.1, a number of countries currently fall well within, or dangerously close to, this category. Projecting ahead to 2030, one word describes the situation for many countries: *thirsty.*

*The **water footprint** of countries,* as illustrated in Table 5.2, varies wildly. (A water footprint is an indicator of freshwater use that looks at both direct and indirect water use

TABLE 5.1 Renewable Water Resources (RWR) Per Capita for Select
Countries, 2005 and 2030 (Projected)

COUNTRY	2005 (M3/YR)	2030 (M3/YR)
Kuwait	7	5
United Arab Emirates	48	37
Saudi Arabia	94	56
Libya	94	56
Singapore	137	122
Jordan	157	104
Yemen	191	81
Israel	254	190
Oman	331	191
Algeria	435	324
Tunisia	458	372
Rwanda	604	387
Egypt	779	534
Morocco	919	682
Kenya	919	734
Lebanon	1170	938
Somalia	1257	553
Pakistan	1382	820
Syria	1410	915
Ethiopia	1483	865

Source: Adapted from Qadir et al. (2007).

of a consumer or producer.) The annual water footprint per capita in the United States, for example, is 2,483 cubic meters (roughly 655,939 gallons), compared to, say, China, which is 702 cubic meters (approximately 185,448 gallons) (although China's population is more than four times that of the United States). When it comes to domestic use, the variability is even greater. For example, the domestic water footprint per capita in the United States (217 cubic meters, or 57,325 gallons) is 13.5 times greater than the domestic water footprint per capita of Bangladesh (16 cubic meters, or 4,226 gallons).

Virtual water refers to water used during the growing, making, or manufacturing of a given commodity. As shown in Table 5.3, a lot of (virtual) water goes into the making of common commodities.

TABLE 5.2 Composition of Water Footprint (WF) for Select Countries

COUNTRY	POPULATION	WF, TOTAL (BILLION CUBIC METERS PER YEAR)	WF, PER CAPITA (METERS PER CAPITA PER YEAR)
Australia	19,071,705	26.56	1,393
Bangladesh	129,942,975	116.49	896
Brazil	169,109,675	233.59	1,381
Canada	30,649,675	62.80	2,049
China	1,257,521,250	883.39	702
Egypt	63,375,735	69.50	1,097
France	58,775,400	110.19	1,875
Germany	82,169,250	126.95	1,545
India	1,007,369,125	987.38	980
Indonesia	204,920,450	269.96	1,317
Italy	57,718,000	134.59	2,332
Japan	126,741,225	146.09	1,153
Jordan	4,813,708	6.27	1,303
Mexico	97,291,745	140.16	1,441
Netherlands	15,865,250	19.40	1,223
Pakistan	136,475,525	166.22	1,218
Russia	145,878,750	270.98	1,858
South Africa	42,387,403	39.47	931
Thailand	60,487,800	134.46	2,223
United Kingdom	58,669,403	73.07	1,245
USA	280,343,325	696.01	2,483
Global total/average	**5,994,251,631**	**7,452.00**	**1,243**

Source: Adapted from Hoekstra and Chapagain (2007).

Dams, as solutions to water-starved areas, are not without their problems. In addition to changing the ecology of a watershed and potentially negatively impacting human communities (as communities are displaced to make space for the reservoir), dams are often responsible for losing the very thing they are charged with storing: water. Dams lose on average 1.1 meters of depth per year due to evaporation. In hotter, dryer climates, the rate of evaporation can be much higher. The Aswan Dam on the Nile River, for instance, loses roughly 2.7 meters in depth annually (or 11 percent of the reservoir's

TABLE 5.3 Global Per Unit Average of Virtual Water Content for Select Commodities

COMMODITY	VIRTUAL WATER CONTENT (LITERS)
1 sheet of standard-sized printer paper (80 g/m2)	10
1 tomato (70 g)	13
1 potato (100 g)	25
1 microchip (2 g)	32
1 cup of tea (250 ml)	35
1 slice of bread (30 g)	40
1 orange (100 g)	50
1 apple (100 g)	70
1 glass of beer (250 ml)	75
1 slice of bread (30 g) with cheese (10 g)	90
1 glass of wine (125 ml)	120
1 egg (40 g)	135
1 cup of coffee (125 ml)	140
1 glass of orange juice (200 ml)	170
1 bag of potato crisps (200 g)	185
1 glass of apple juice (200 ml)	190
1 glass of milk (200 ml)	200
1 cotton T-shirt (250 g)	2000
1 hamburger (150 g)	2400
1 pair of shoes (bovine leather)	8000

Source: Based on Hoekstra and Chapagain (2007).

capacity) (Toulmin 2009). Or take Lake Mead, the largest reservoir in the United States, roughly thirty miles southeast of Las Vegas, Nevada, which formed behind Hoover Dam. Without changes in water allocation from the Colorado River system—which feeds the reservoir—there is a 50 percent chance it will go dry by 2021 (Barnett and Pierce 2008). Losses in dam storage can also impact a country's ability to generate power. A major drought in Kenya in 2000, for example, lost the country 400 megawatts due to under-utilized generators, costing the economy an estimated US$660 million over a six-month span (Toulmin 2009).

Climate change is expected to drastically alter the water cycle. As mean atmospheric temperature rises, the water-holding capacity of the air increases exponentially. In the future we can therefore expect an atmosphere saturated with moisture, which will only serve to intensify storms and other weather events. A higher atmospheric temperature also means more energy to drive intense weather events. More water, falling at greater rates of intensity, means more floods and soil erosion for some regions. Elsewhere rain will become an increasingly rare event, which, coupled with increased temperatures, will hasten the drying up of rivers, lakes, and reservoirs (ibid.).

People living in the slums often pay five to ten times more per liter of water than those residing in affluent neighborhoods in the same city (United Nations 2006). This statistic is particularly sad, given the impressive returns.on investments that can be realized when a country invests in its water infrastructure. According to the United Nations (2009), safe drinking water, proper sanitation, and efficient irrigation systems contribute to a country's economic growth while also saving it money. Each US$1 spent toward these ends returns somewhere between US$3 and US$34—a return of between 300 and 3,400 percent!—depending on the region and technology that is being invested in (ibid.).

In poor sections of Mexico City, residents get water through the municipal system only once every seven to ten days. In the Mexican countryside, families can spend up to 30 percent of their daily disposable income for bottled water. Where bottled water is not an option—or where people cannot afford it—family members may have to walk up to an hour in order to reach the nearest freshwater supply (Smith and Marín 2005).

As watersheds are "developed" and become blanketed with impervious surfaces (streets, parking lots, tennis courts, rooftops, and so on), they lose their ability to absorb rainwater, resulting in more being lost to runoff. With increased runoff comes a heightened chance of flooding, soil erosion, and the overall disruption of a watershed's water cycle (see Table 5.4).

Implications

It is a bit surprising that sociologists have not been more interested in water. So much of our lives are touched, in some way, by this precious compound. Cities, nations, and entire civilizations all need water to survive, though not too much, either, as I am reminded of a small town in Iowa near where I grew up that was relocated after the so-called Great Flood of 1993 (sadly, there have been two other "Great Floods" in the state since then). Water also resonates with us culturally. Take the case of the Klamath Native American Tribes (in northern California and southern Oregon), who were deemed, in the landmark legal decision *United States of America and the Klamath Indian Tribe v. Ben Adair* (1983), to have rights to water on reservation lands dating back to "time immemorial" (the distant past beyond memory) to protect culturally essential activities like hunting and fishing.

This chapter aims to give the reader a taste of how water impacts our world. It has repeatedly been said that water promises to be to the twenty-first century what oil was to the twentieth century. If so, sociologists (and the social science more generally) ought

TABLE 5.4 Runoff versus Soil Infiltration for Every Three Inches of Rainfall on Select Surface Types

SURFACE TYPE	RUNOFF (INCHES)	INFILTRATION (INCHES)
Forest	0.6	2.4
Meadow	0.6	2.4
Cultivated agricultural field	1.0	2.0
Residental lawn	1.6	1.4
Parking lot, street, sidewalk	3.0	0.0

Source: Adapted from Marinelli (2011).

to play as central a role in its study in this century as petroleum geologists did for oil in the last.

Bottled Water

Have you had bottled water in the past twelve months? Chances are good you have. Whereas Europe continues to rank as the leading regional consumer of bottled water, the largest national markets are not European (see Table 5.4). North America has the distinction of holding the two largest national markets, in the United States and Mexico. Together these bottled water–consuming powerhouses accounted for 29 percent of the world's packaged water market in 2008. China also deserves mention, given its mind-boggling 15.6 percent growth in volume consumed between 2003 and 2008—at that rate, its consumption of bottled water will double in roughly four and a half years! Due to Europe's firmly established bottled-water markets—for decades they boasted the world's largest—growth in this region is considerably slower than in those where this product is relatively new. Indeed, as detailed in Table 5.5, some European countries—like France and Spain—have seen their bottled-water consumption contract in recent years.

When looked at in terms of per capita (versus total) consumption, the ranking breaks down differently. Under this scenario, Mexico and Italy handily place first and second, respectively. The average Mexican consumed roughly 59 gallons of bottled water in 2008. That same year, the average Italian, who earlier reigned supreme in this ranking, consumed 54 gallons. The United States comes in tenth in this ranking (at 28.5 gallons), having been recently surpassed by Hungary. It is also worth pointing out China's absence from this top-ten ordering. Yet with a population of 1.33 billion, if (or more accurately *when*) they make this list, the country would handily outconsume all others in terms of total volume of packaged water consumed.

This tremendous market growth in recent decades is all the more remarkable in light of the intense criticism bottled water—and the industry responsible for "making" it—has come under. As already mentioned, bottled water is exceedingly more expensive than what you get from a tap, even though as much as 40 percent of it comes from precisely

TABLE 5.5 Growth of Top-Ten Global Consumers of Bottled Water, 2003 and 2008

RANK IN 2008	COUNTRY	2003 CONSUMPTION*	2008 CONSUMPTION*	ANNUAL GROWTH RATE
1	US	6,269.8	8,665.6	6.7%
2	Mexico	4,357.6	6,501.5	8.3%
3	China	2,523.6	5,207.7	15.6%
4	Brazil	2,842.0	3,775.7	5.8%
5	Italy	2,734.2	3,140.5	2.8%
6	Indonesia	1,834.7	2,899.5	9.6%
7	Germany	2,628.5	2,863.1	1.7%
8	France	2,352.9	2,218.4	-1.2%
9	Thailand	1,303.4	1,705.6	5.5%
10	Spain	1,346.8	1,291.3	-0.8%

* Millions of gallons consumed in total

Source: Adapted from Rodwan (2009).

this source (NRDC 1999). Questions have also been raised about the purity of the product. A report released in 2008 found mixtures of thirty-eight different pollutants, including bacteria, fertilizer, Tylenol, and industrial chemicals in ten popular US brands of bottled water (EWG 2008). The bottled-water industry apparently doesn't take kindly to those who advertise this fact. The City of Miami, Florida, learned this lesson the hard way. A few years back the city was threatened with a lawsuit by Nestlé Waters North America following an ad campaign touting the city's water as cheaper, purer, and safer than the bottled alternative. They were instructed to immediately cease and desist with the commercials (the ad campaign had already run its course when the threat was made).

Bottled water also uses precious resources (see ECOnnection 5.1). A single liter can require as many as three liters of freshwater to make (Azios 2008). As explained in the *Economist* (2008), the "five big food and beverage giants—Nestlé, Unilever, Coca-Cola, Anheuser-Busch and Danone—consume almost 575 billion liters of water a year, enough to satisfy the daily water needs of every person on the planet." Soda (and beer) also requires copious amounts of water to make. For example, while Coca-Cola improved its

ECOnnection 5.1

Soda and the Struggle for Fresh Water in India

A reporter for the newspaper *Toronto Star* recently wrote about a trip to Kala Dera, India, and a local conflict that arose over the 36 million liters of water that a single Coca-Cola plant uses annually (Westhead 2010). At another Coca-Cola plant, located in the water-stressed state of Rajasthan, approximately 500,000 liters of water are extracted daily. At still another, located in the highly impoverished village of Plachimada in the state of Kerala, between 500,000 and 1.5 million liters are extracted daily. All this is occurring at the expense of India's smallholder farmers, who struggle to obtain sufficient freshwater for their crops, and the rural poor, for whom access to clean water is a daily struggle (Nash 2007).

water efficiency by 6 percent between 2003 and 2004, its global average is still 2.72 liters per 1 liter of final soda product (*Economist* 2008).

Bottled water also risks contributing to political apathy. What I am talking about has been meticulously argued by Andrew Szasz, in his book *Shopping Our Way to Safety* (2007). Szasz develops a term for the type of individualized consumer "solutions" that things like bottled water are meant to represent. Szasz argues these consumer-focused solutions create an "inverted quarantine." Similar to a conventional quarantine, the inverted quarantine seeks to provide protection from a threat. Unlike a traditional quarantine, which works by isolating threats to a particular area, the inverted quarantine works by isolating the consumer in "a personal commodity bubble" (ibid.:97) from the threats, which are ubiquitous. We, as the title of the book aptly proclaims, try to shop our way to safety by, among other things, purchasing organic food, bottled water, and air purifiers for our homes.

But there are problems with this strategy. For one, all consumer-based "solutions" are biased toward those who can afford them. From the perspective of the working poor, this strategy might better be called "shopping *their* way to safety." In addition, in buying safety for themselves and their loved ones, the middle and upper class risk becoming politically indifferent to attempts at larger social change that could solve the problem for *all* segments of society. If, for example, bottled water were not available and the world's middle class and above had to drink from their tap, I wonder if greater willingness would not be expressed for public investment in clean and affordable water

Privatizing Water

Another way society is impacted by water is through recent attempts to privatize public water utilities under the guise of **neoliberalism**. According to David Harvey, "Neoliberalism is in the first instance a theory of political economic practices that proposes that human well-being can best be advanced by liberating individual entrepreneurial freedoms and skills within an institutional framework characterized by strong private property rights, free markets, and free trade" (2005:2) (neoliberalism is discussed further in Chapter 10). As opposed to liberalism, which prioritizes individual liberties, neoliberalism elevates free enterprise above all else, even if that means grossly impinging upon those allegedly sacred individual liberties, as we'll soon see. The rise of neoliberalism on the world economic stage can be seen in recent decades with the rapid push to hollow out the state by eliminating regulations and privatizing anything and everything: even water.

There is also an environmental argument, some contend, for privatizing water. **Market environmentalism**—emphasizing markets as a solution to environmental problems—is a way of packaging neoliberalism in "green" wrapping. The thinking goes something like this: by strengthening and expanding private property rights (to things like water) and relying more on markets for the allocation of resources, environmental goods will be more efficiently used, leading ultimately to less environmental degradation and a more sustainable use of resources.

Two influential international bodies heavily pushing the **water privatization** card are the World Bank and International Monetary Fund (IMF) (see ECOnnection 5.2). Put simply, water privatization means treating water like any other commodity and leaving questions of access and sanitation to market mechanisms. Yet doing this risks creating two water worlds: affluent nations that still overwhelmingly rely on publicly funded water services (and who would never dream of handing control of them over to profit-seeking corporations) and the rest of the world, who may have no choice but to get their water from a private water firm. Beyond obvious access questions—for example, what about slums and other areas where a profit could not be made by supplying its people with water?—the two-world scenario advantages affluent nations. We can see this occurring, for example, in the farming sector. The amount of money recovered by the US Bureau of Reclamation from irrigation projects averages at around 10 to 20 percent (the remaining 90 to 80 percent comes out of taxpayers' pockets). Irrigation subsidies for the semiarid states west of the Missouri River exceed US$500 million a year (Peterson 2009). US farmers, under the above scenario, would benefit tremendously if many of their global competitors had to get their water from a firm seeking full cost recovery plus a little more (the profit). It would give them a significant market advantage if they could obtain this valuable input for a fraction of the price it costs their competitors overseas.

In 1990 approximately 50 million people globally received their water from private water firms. By 2015 that number is predicted to hit 1.16 billion. To ensure this shift toward water privatization, developing countries are now unable to borrow from the World Bank or IMF without having in place a domestic water-privatization policy. It's fair to say that the majority of public-utility privatization deals that have occurred in the past decade in lower-income countries are the result of the direct participation of these global monetary institutions. As Michael Goldman, who has studied water-privatization deals extensively, explains, "That participation comes in the form of a threat, since every government official knows that the Bank/IMF capital spigots can always be shut off for those governments refusing to conform to their loan conditions. As overwhelming debt burdens have put tremendous pressure on borrowing-country governments and created dire social conditions in their countries . . . the Bank and IMF are using the carrot of debt relief to foist water policy reform on borrowing country governments" (2007:794).

ECOnnection 5.2
The IMF and World Bank

The World Bank and IMF are known collectively as the Bretton Woods Institutions, after the small community in rural New Hampshire where they were founded in July 1944. Each is charged, in different ways, with directing and supporting the structure of the world's economic and financial order. The World Bank's first loans were granted following World War II to help finance the reconstruction of Western Europe. As these nations recovered, the bank turned increasingly to the world's poorer countries to, in part, help them "develop" by folding them into the world economy and thus lure them away from communism (as this was at the height of the Cold War). The World Bank's stated mission is to promote economic and social progress in developing countries—though the bank believes the latter comes only *after* the former.

Whereas the World Bank is primarily a lending institution, the IMF's main role is to keep the international monetary system running smoothly. It does this by monitoring the world's currencies, making sure the unpredictable variations that helped to trigger (and unduly extended) the Great Depression in the 1930s do not happen again. Thus, although the IMF does provide loans, it is charged with more than just being a bank. Both institutions wield considerable power over international affairs, as their loans come with substantial conditions. Some of the "strings" that are attached to these loans have required countries to privatize their municipal water systems.

Unfortunately, the societal cost of privatization has been great. No profit-seeking firm can expect to expand their services to populations that cannot pay. So the water situation for the poor remains deplorable in many countries that were promised to be saved by these privatization schemes. Moreover, this aggressive push to privatize water utilities has caused donor spending on infrastructure to dry up, as it is now assumed that private firms will provide all the necessary capital to get the job done. In 2002, for example, World Bank lending for water and sanitation for sub-Saharan African countries was a quarter of what it was just five years earlier (Barlow 2007).

Evidence that water firms are failing in their contractual commitments to provide water for all can be seen by how some are vigorously redefining the language of their contracts. In the city of La Paz, Bolivia, for example, to connect a large slum to the water system, the privately owned utility argued that "connection" meant not only a "piped connection" but also "access to a standpipe or tanker." What's particularly distressing about this newly expanded definition is that it perpetuates the very conditions that water firms earlier used to make the case for water privatization, as developing countries were previously criticized for their inadequate water infrastructure that in some cases involved bringing temporary water tankers into neighborhoods (Goldman 2007). Ten years ago, water tankers in slums were pointed to and used by proponents of neoliberalism to justify water privatization. Today those same water tankers are now being used by private water firms because that's the only way those firms can earn a profit in some

TABLE 5.6 Top Virtual Water Exporting and Importing Countries (Annual Net Volume), 2007

TOP EXPORTING (BILLIONS OF CUBIC METERS)	TOP IMPORTING (BILLIONS OF CUBIC METERS)
Unites States (758.3)	Sri Lanka (428.5)
Canada (272.5)	Japan (297.4)
Thailand (233.3)	Netherlands (147.7)
Argentina (226.3)	Korea (112.6)
India (161.1)	China (101.9)
Australia (145.6)	Indonesia (101.7)

Source: Adapted from Hoekstra and Chapagain (2007).

neighborhoods. And the water supplied is often sold at a higher price than when provided by a public municipality in order to ensure profitability.

In other instances, firms are requiring residents of poor (unprofitable) communities to supply free labor to help build the connecting infrastructure. If free labor is the only way water firms can live up to their fiduciary obligations while ensuring a return for their shareholders, then, clearly, water privatization in those cases is a failure (ibid.). Perhaps this explains why the cost of one cubic meter of water charged by private vendors in some low-income countries is 136 times of what that same amount of water would cost in the United States (US$0.11 per cubic meter in the United States versus US$14.68 per meter) (UNESCO 2003). That may well be the lowest price that the market will bear in poorer nations. Socially and morally, however, such a price disparity between rich and poor countries is unacceptable.

In fairness to advocates of privatization, whatever we did in the twentieth century to deliver clean water to the world's poor didn't work either, or at least didn't work as well as many had hoped. Clearly, a new approach is needed, as we know for a fact that improving access to clean water can help eradicate extreme hunger and poverty. Among other things, access to water has direct positive effects on education and gender equity. Severe and repeated cases of diarrhea, often due to water-related diseases, contributes to malnutrition (as it reduces the body's ability to retain essential micro- and macronutrients), which impairs short- and long-term cognitive and physical development among children. Moreover, sick kids are more likely to miss school, thus further reducing their ability to take advantage of opportunities that could improve their lives. Because water is so difficult to access in some parts of the world—most notably Africa—millions of women and children must walk long distances daily just to obtain this needed resource for their families. There are reports of women and children in Africa spending close to 30 percent of their day fetching water (Marín et al. 2009). All this time walking for water is time that could be spent, for example, in school (Palaniappan 2009).

CASE STUDY 5.1

China's Growing Demand for Food and Thus Water

Per capita water requirements for food in China have increased by nearly 400 percent since 1961. This change is due primarily to increases in the consumption of animal products (Liu and Savenije 2008). China has an annual per capita water requirement for food of approximately nine hundred cubic meters per year—more than half of which is attributable to animal products. For a point of comparison, for the United States this figure is roughly eighteen hundred cubic meters per year, two-thirds of which is due to the use and consumption of animal products (ibid.). It will be interesting to see how China deals with this rapidly growing demand for water in light of the fact that already more than three hundred of its cities suffer from water shortages of various intensities (Khan, Hanjra, and Mu 2009).

Agriculture

For a variety of reasons, it does not make sense to import large quantities of water for purposes of raising water-intensive agricultural commodities, especially given that the commodities themselves can be imported. A sizable portion of a country's virtual water footprint (or embedded water) thus comes in the form of the agricultural commodities it imports. As of 2007, the top virtual water exporter was the United States, whereas Sri Lanka led all nations in the virtual water–importing category (see Table 5.6).

One thing that is as surprising and counterintuitive as it is disturbing is that a country's virtual water trade is not determined by its water situation. Virtual water, instead, often flows out of water-poor, land-rich countries into land-poor, water-rich countries. The evidence suggests that many countries import food not because they lack water but because they lack sufficient arable land that can be put to cultivation (Kumar and Singh 2005:759). In other words, water is not the limiting agricultural factor: fertile land is (see Case Study 5.1).

It would be careless of me to talk about water in the context of agriculture and not at least mention how agricultural practices can negatively impact water quality. Take the case of pesticides (more agriculture-related impacts on water supplies are discussed in Chapter 8). One study estimates that the annual costs of pesticides in drinking water for the United States, United Kingdom, and Germany are US$1,126,337,798, US$287,444,066, and US$180,522,199, respectively (Leach and Mumford 2008). In another analysis, looking just at the United States, this cost was placed at US$2 billion per year (Pimentel 2005). In a study that looks not only at the costs of pesticides but also at the costs of nitrate, phosphate, and cryptosporidium (protozoan pathogen) in water, agriculture's toll on freshwater sources in the United Kingdom was placed at US$515 million annually (Pretty and Waibel 2005; see Case Study 5.2).

Whereas agriculture continues to be a major water stakeholder—after all, approximately 70 percent of all the water used by humans globally goes to agriculture (Sterling

CASE STUDY 5.2
Coke, Pepsi, and Pesticides in India

In 2003 the Delhi-based environmental non-governmental organization the Centre for Science and Environment (CSE) released a stinging report announcing the presence of pesticides—at levels twenty-four times greater than allowed under EU standards—in a dozen popular beverages manufactured under the Coca-Cola and Pepsi labels. These drinks came from manufacturing and bottling plants located within India. The CSE used the report to underscore not only the problem of water scarcity in India but also the country's weak pesticide regulations. The CSE hoped that na-tionwide middle-class outrage—a population that believed their cherished Coke and Pepsi products to be safe—could be more successfully channeled to confront the problem of pesticide pollution than any fragmented peasant movement (Vedwan 2007:659–660). Yet the fact that products made under the Coke and Pepsi labels in India contained pesticide residues is not terribly surprising. Virtually *all* groundwater in India is tainted with pesticide residues, which means that many domestic beverages—from Indian-made milk to bottled tea—are too.

and Vintinner 2008)—it is not the only one. As the demands from other interests grow—like the growing thirst of cities—water conflicts will arise. These conflicting interests will not always be solved to the satisfaction of all stakeholders (see Case Study 5.3).

More than 75 percent of the population of developed countries resides in urban areas. This percentage is expected to increase to well over 80 percent by 2030. In less affluent nations, just below 50 percent of the population live in urban areas. Of this, more than 70 percent—or roughly 1 billion people—live in slumlike conditions. By 2030 the urban population of poorer nations is expected to increase to just below 60 percent as a proportion of their total population. Meanwhile, the number of **megacities**, that is, cities with more than 10 million residents, is expected to rise globally from forty-six to sixty-one between 2015 and 2030. Most of these megacities will be located in Asia and Africa (Jenerette and Larsen 2006). Balancing the competing water demands between city and the countryside—plus, we can't forget, those of industry and wildlife—in the twenty-first century promises to be a truly monumental task.

Climate Change

Freshwater systems are repeatedly cited as among the most vulnerable sectors to climate change. I will now briefly review, drawing from a variety of sources (Cooley 2009a; Kernan, Battarbee, and Moss 2010), how climate change impacts important components of the earth's freshwater systems. As the following points make clear, even though our future water woes are not insurmountable, aggressively pursuing policies to combat climate change would go a long way toward making those woes a little less daunting.

CASE STUDY 5.3

California's Recent Water Conflict

A recent controversy grabbed headlines in California—a state with a long history of water conflicts. With close to 40 million people and the most irrigation-intensive agriculture in the country, water is never far from the minds of state and city officials and those with strong agricultural ties. In late summer 2007, a federal judge ruled that the government must curtail water deliveries to the west side of the state by at least 80 percent. At the center of the lawsuit were two types of fish: salmon and the three-inch delta smelt. Their numbers have declined drastically in recent decades because, the lawsuit claimed, water projects had diverted too much water from their habitat.

The ruling had a noticeable impact on farms. With water flows drastically reduced, thousands of acres of crops were idled, and farm laborers were laid off. Some farmers responded by adopting drought-resistant crops, paying the higher costs of pumping scarce groundwater, or both. Then, in the winter of 2009–2010, the state entered one of its periodic wet cycles.

In light of the newly available freshwater, the case went back to court. The judge ruled that during wet cycles, farmers could be granted up to 85 percent of their contracted water deliveries (a major switch from the earlier ruling). Although this has made environmentalists happy, as it keeps the rivers flowing out to the sea and thus preserves habitat for the salmon and the delta smelt, farmers are still upset. If they're getting 85 percent of their water deliveries during one of the wettest seasons on record, they shudder to think about what to expect when the dry years return. They fear it will not be enough to keep farming profitable.

Adapted from Hanson (2011).

Surface Water

There is a remarkable similarity between climate models when it comes to predicting greater runoff in the tropics and higher latitudes and reduced runoff in many already dry, midlatitude regions such as the Mediterranean, South Africa, and the southwestern United States and northwestern Mexico. In regions with significant snowmelt, we can expect changes to the timing of runoff and rapidity of spring melt. In regards to the latter, this could lead to an increased risk of floods as that water overloads the capacity of the land to absorb it.

Groundwater

Demand for groundwater is expected to increase to offset reduced surface flows in some regions. Some sites will also see reductions in the rate at which they recharge, while others will experience increases in recharge rates. Warmer temperatures will also result in higher evaporation rates, which could lead to increasing rates of groundwater **salinization** (the buildup of salt in soil and groundwater). Sea-level rise will also increase the risk of saltwater intrusion in coastal aquifers.

Hydrologic Extremes

The frequency of intense flooding and drought conditions is expected to increase. Mid-continental regions, for example, are expected to be unusually dry during the summer. In all areas, climate models predict that when it does rain, the chance of an intense event will increase.

Water Quality

Warmer atmospheric temperatures are expected to result in increases in the temperature of lakes, reservoirs, and rivers, which in turn will increase algal and bacterial blooms and cause dissolved oxygen concentrations in those bodies of water to decrease. More intense weather events could also increase soil-erosion rates and negatively affect water quality. Similarly, significant flooding could increase the amount of pollutants and toxins that get washed into waterways.

Water Demand

There are a lot of unknowns that make it difficult to speak definitively on the subject of future water demand. Water demand could increase dramatically in the agricultural sector, though if drought-tolerant crops are grown and improvements in irrigation efficiencies achieved, these demands could be tempered. Similarly, demand in urban areas might increase radically as, say, warmer temperatures further stress lawns, gardens, and parks, thus increasing irrigation rates in metropolitan areas. However, if drought-tolerant grasses, bushes, and trees are planted or xeriscape lawns become more culturally accepted, these demands too could be reduced dramatically.

Solutions

There are so many problems, tensions, and conflicts that involve water that I couldn't begin to adequately summarize solutions to each. Consequently, to make this discussion manageable, the following text will be broken up into two subsections. In the first, I talk about changing how we think about water. Technological solutions will get us only so far. It is also important to keep in mind that not everyone can afford them. Technological fixes also involve trade-offs—**desalinization** (the removal of salt and other minerals from saline water), for example, is immensely energy intensive (see Case Study 5.4). This is why we need to revisit how we think about water. Specifically, it is worth discussing first whether water is something to which we all have a fundamental human right. I conclude the chapter by discussing citizen engagement around water, also known as water governance.

Water as a Human Right at the Right "Value"

There are only two international conventions that explicitly recognize the right to water: the UN Convention on the Rights of the Child of 1989 (article 24) and the UN

> ### CASE STUDY 5.4
> ## *Desalinization in Tampa Bay, Florida*
>
> The city of Tampa Bay (Florida) and the surrounding area was in trouble. They were over-pumping local groundwater resources. Something had to be done. Starting in the mid-1990s, water authorities in Florida began planning to build the largest desalination plant in the United States. Certain unique conditions to the area made such a plant feasible where elsewhere it was not: energy costs in the region were relatively low, colocating the plant next to a power plant further lowered the desalination plant's costs (from shared infrastructure, maintenance functions, and so forth), and the actual salinity of the source water was considerably lower than typical seawater. The plant became fully operational in December 2007, five years behind schedule and 40 percent over the original estimated cost. Moreover, the actual cost to desalinize also ended up being considerably higher than originally predicted, as energy prices had increased in the intervening years. More troubling news came in August and November 2007. Just prior to becoming fully operational, the plant was fined for violating its wastewater discharge permit by flushing too much cleaning solution into the sewer system. In January 2008, the plant was cited yet again for the same problem (Cooley 2009b). Although the plant now provides some 10 percent of the region's drinking water (Paschenko 2011), many are asking, in light of its total costs to taxpayers and the environment, if it was such a wise investment after all (and what happens if and when electricity prices climb still higher).

Convention on the Elimination of All Forms of Discrimination Against Women of 1979 (article 14). Prior to 1979, one must go back to the Geneva Convention of 1949 (article 26) to find any international legal document recognizing a human's right to water, though in this text that right extends only to prisoners of war. More recently, in 2002, General Comment No. 15 to the International Covenant on Economic, Social, and Cultural Rights, a major human rights treaty, was signed by 153 countries and recognizes that "the human right to water is indispensable for leading a life in human dignity" and "is a prerequisite for the realization of other human rights" (United Nations 2002). The treaty also notes the importance of sanitation in the fulfillment of these rights.

According to this document, the human right to water entitles everyone to "sufficient," "safe," "acceptable," "physically accessible," and "affordable" water for personal and domestic uses. Of course, the precise meaning of these terms is up for debate. As a limited resource, we cannot treat the right to clean water the same as, say, the right to clean air. Indeed, precisely so we can ensure access to everyone, we will likely need to impose a *limit* to the right to water, a practice not all that unusual, as we impose limits on rights all the time. Those living in the United States, for example, are protected by strong free-speech rights. Yet they still can't say anything they wish—like *bomb* in a crowded airplane. The scope of humans' right to water is normally limited, as it tends to refer to the fulfillment of basic needs, like those related to drinking, cooking, and other vital domestic needs (such as washing). It has proven very difficult, however, to translate this to a specific volume. Although it is generally agreed that an amount of three to five liters per day of clean water is the absolute minimum to allow for human survival, most understand that we can do better than just provide enough for mere survival. Research suggests that well-being improves significantly when these values increase to around twenty liters per day per person. That added water improves sanitary conditions considerably. For this reason, a number of international organizations, including the United Nations, proclaim humans have a right to between twenty and forty liters per day per person (Cunha 2009). Others arrive at much higher values, like fifty liters per day per person, in order to adequately satisfy our basic needs of drinking (five liters), sanitation services (twenty liters), bathing (fifteen liters), and food preparation (ten liters) (Gleick 1996).

To say water is a human right does not mean, however, that it must be delivered for free. Just like many argue humans have a right to food, they are not arguing that it ought to be provided at no cost. To accept the principle of a human right to water does, however, require that we treat water as a *social* as well as an economic good. This is where that aforementioned change in how we think about water comes into play.

Water doesn't fit into the "economic good" box as easily as other things. For one, the so-called law of supply and demand doesn't exist when talking about water. You can't choose what company's water you want piped into your house. That "choice" is made for you. Moreover, the price that is ultimately set is based on a lot more than just market mechanisms. There are also social and political factors that shape the cost of tap water, most notably subsidies (either for the water itself or for, say, the electricity that pumps the water).

There are two main competing visions about how to think about water as an economic good. The first, supported by traditional economic approaches, explains that water should be priced at whatever the market will bear. The second vision believes "value," especially when it comes to water, cannot and should not be left entirely to the free market to decide.

The first approach is problematic because it could (and likely would) disproportionately negatively impact rural populations and the urban poor who cannot pay-to-play in the life-sustaining game of water access. Water does seem to deserve the designate of a special economic good. It must be priced, but when going about establishing that price, we would do well to not let just the market decide. Others have laid out six characteristics of water that they believe justify us pricing it with a little more care than other economic goods (Cunha 2009; Rogers, Bhatia, and Huber 1998):

1. Water is essential: there is no life, economic production, or environment without it.
2. Water is nonsubstitutable: there is no alternative.
3. Water is finite: the water that currently circulates through the hydrological cycle is all there is.
4. Water is a system: water is part of a complex system and helps make possible innumerable ecosystem services.
5. Water is bulky: water's physical properties make long-distance transportation difficult.

Would the mere recognition of the human right to water actually improve conditions worldwide? Likely not. My point in talking about expanding our understanding of water as an economic good is a pragmatic realization that the imperatives to meet basic human water needs are more than just moral but rooted also in law and markets (Gleick 1996). We can change how people think about water all we want, but unless we likewise alter the social, economic, and political structures presently standing in the way of universal water access, millions will continue to go to bed at night in an unsanitary environment and thirsty.

Water Governance

Water resource management underwent a bit of a paradigm shift in the 1990s. Previously, the command-and-control—top-down, government-driven—model had proven modestly successful at regulating **point-source pollution** (pollution with an identifiable source). As recently as the 1970s, rivers were literally catching fire in affluent nations due to major pollution releases by industry. With the success of point-source pollution control measures, attention slowly turned to the impact of more diffuse pollution, called **nonpoint-source pollution**. From a governing standpoint, however, this shift complicates things for all but the most Orwellian of societies. The effective monitoring of pollution from nonpoint sources would require a level of government intrusion that most would be uncomfortable with (Wagenet and Pfeffer 2007). A new form of water governance has thus emerged: a broad social system of governance that operates at different levels of society while including, but not limiting itself to, the narrower perspective of government as the main decision-making political entity (UNESCO 2009). A number of attributes of effective water governance have been identified (Cunha 2009; UNESCO 2009):

- *Participation:* water users should have a voice in the decision-making process.
- *Transparency:* the decision-making process should be transparent and open for scrutiny.
- *Equity:* all stakeholders should have opportunities to meaningfully participate in the process.
- *Accountability:* governments, the private sector, and civil society organizations should all be accountable to the public.
- *Responsiveness:* institutions and processes should serve stakeholders and respond properly to their changes in demand and preferences (which is why participation is so important).
- *Ethics:* effective water governance should be grounded in society's ethical principles (such as the belief that water is a fundamental human right).

These new participatory models are appealing to governments and **nongovernmental organizations** (NGOs) on a number of levels. (An NGO refers to any legally constituted organization that operates independently from any government.) Many governments, especially those in less affluent nations, express a desire for decentralized forms of governance, as they are already overstretched in attempting to deliver and maintain rural services. As for NGOs, many operate by constructing a number of water

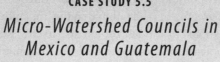

CASE STUDY 5.5

Micro-Watershed Councils in Mexico and Guatemala

Deforestation and climate change are increasing the risk of flash flooding in communities located in the high-altitude watersheds near the Tacana volcano in Mexico and Guatemala. The water cycle has become particularly vicious in recent years, as an increase in frequency of flash floods has further eroded the formally deep soils (which previously had tremendous capacity for water retention), thus further heightening the risk of flash flooding. With support from governmental and nongovernmental organizations, local communities are being empowered to form micro-watershed councils. These councils are leading watershed restoration projects. The projects are designed and implemented by the local councils. In addition to helping provide employment opportunities for community members, and thus also facilitating the meeting of development priorities, the micro-watershed councils are making local watersheds more secure and surrounding communities less vulnerable (IUCN 2010).

systems as part of a project but then leave the project area after several months or years to start new projects. Community-rooted governance projects have in some instances became a convenient method for shifting responsibility from the state and firms to end users (Harvey and Reed 2006). And in light of future threats related to climate change, these locally based models can help bolster watershed resiliency, at least at the micro level, given the level of local expertise involved (see Case Study 5.5).

Most problems with such open models of water governance do not occur immediately. Problems, when they do occur, often appear later, after the initial excitement fades. A review of the literature came up with the following commonly cited reasons for the breakdown of community management systems (Cunha, 2009; Rogers and Hall, 2003):

- Participation often relies on voluntary inputs from community members that can erode over the long term, as there are often no long-term incentives to keep the activity going.
- Key individuals leave the community or die and are not easily replaced.
- The community organization charged with managing the water supply loses the trust and respect of the general community (perhaps due to a lack of transparency and accountability).
- Potential free riders (such as community members who fail to contribute maintenance fees), or simply those who do not pay because they cannot afford to, can lead to disillusionment among committee members.
- If government steps entirely away from the project, community members could feel like they have been abandoned and become unmotivated.
- Communities are too poor to replace major capital items when they break down, which can be particularly problematic when or if government abdicates its responsibilities.

Too often public participation is viewed as something just needing to be "checked off" on a list of steps said to lead to successful environmental management. Yet when engaged meaningfully, public participation can produce long-term and sustainable results (Wagenet and Pfeffer 2007). It does, however, take a lot of work to make community-level governance projects work. Yet given the scope and severity of the problems at hand and the general excitement people tend to display when empowered to be involved in solution-oriented activities (Taylor, Taylor, and Taylor 2012), I have no doubt we can muster the energy and resources toward this end.

IMPORTANT CONCEPTS

- inverted quarantine
- neoliberalism
- virtual water
- water as a right
- water governance
- water privatization

DISCUSSION QUESTIONS

1. Do you drink bottled water? If so, why (knowing its life-cycle impact upon the environment)? Other than an outright ban, what policies would need to be implemented for you to stop your bottled-water consumption?
2. Do you believe humans have a fundamental right to water? If so, what's the best way to go about ensuring that right is satisfied—the market, government, community-based governance, or perhaps something else?
3. What are some of the downsides of letting markets allocate water? And some benefits?
4. If you were made more aware of your water footprint, would your consumption patterns change? Why or why not? What are some of the barriers to change, and how could those barriers be overcome?

SUGGESTED ADDITIONAL READINGS

Azios, T. 2008. "The Battle over Bottled vs. Tap Water." *Christian Science Monitor,* January 17. Retrieved August 26, 2012 (http://www.csmonitor.com/Environment/2008/0117/p15s03-sten.html).

Barlow, M. 2007. *Blue Covenant: The Global Water Crisis and the Coming Battle for the Right to Water.* New York: New Press.

Black, R. 2010. "Water Map Shows Billions at Risk of Water Insecurity." *BBC News,* September 29. Retrieved August 26, 2012 (http://www.bbc.co.uk/news/science-environment-11435522).

Pearce, F. 2008. "Water Scarcity: The Real Food Crisis." *Yale Environment 360,* June 3. Retrieved August 26, 2012 (http://e360.yale.edu/feature/water_scarcity_the_real_food_crisis/1825/).

Velasquez-Manoff, M. 2009. "Could Water Scarcity Cause International Conflict?" *Christian Science Monitor,* October 26. Retrieved August 26, 2012 (http://www.csmonitor.com/Environment/Bright-Green/2009/1026/could-water-scarcity-cause-international-conflict).

RELEVANT INTERNET LINKS

- http://environment.nationalgeographic.com/environment/freshwater/water-foot
  print-calculator/
  A water-footprint calculator.
- http://waterdata.usgs.gov/nwis
  Provides real-time data from selected surface-water, groundwater, and water-quality
  sites from around the United States, among other things.
- http://www.waterfootprint.org/?page=cal/waterfootprintcalculator_national
  A national water-footprint calculator. Find out the average per capita water footprint
  of any country, in addition to other information (like the percentage of a country's
  footprint that falls outside the country, a.k.a. "virtual").
- http://www.wateruseitwisely.com/kids/
  A website full of useful information (and even some games) directed at water conservation.

SUGGESTED VIDEOS

- *Blue Gold: World Water Wars* (2008)
  Examines the problems created by the privatization and commoditization of water.
- *FLOW: For the Love of Water* (2008)
  Documents efforts by multinational firms to privatize the world's water supply and the
  consequences of this practice.
- *Last Call at the Oasis* (2011)
  This documentary illuminates the essential role water plays in our lives, exposes the
  defects in the current system and shows communities already struggling under the
  status quo. The film features activist Erin Brockovich, water experts Peter Gleick,
  Jay Famiglietti, and Robert Glennon, and a variety of social entrepreneurs in search of
  revolutionary solutions.
- *Tapped* (2010)
  Documents the push by corporations to privatize water and then sell it back to us in
  plastic bottles that end up polluting our oceans.

PART II

AT THE INTERSECTION OF ECOLOGY AND SOCIETY

6

Population: A Problem of Quantity or Quality?

If I were writing this book forty years ago, I might have focused entirely on the subject of population growth. This was a period when people spoke of "the population bomb" and "a population explosion," when we were told that earth was like a spaceship with a near–maxed out seating capacity. It was also around this time when a group of scientists commissioned by the Club of Rome—a global think tank founded in 1968 with a history of examining a variety of international issues—looked at **exponential growth** (essentially, growth at a constant rate) in resource use, population, and economic activity and announced that we should see significant resource scarcities before the new millennium.

Although perhaps this anxiety was a bit misplaced—after all, the global population growth rate has considerably lowered since—I understand why the subject grabbed the attention it did. We have to remember that some forty years ago, world population was growing at an unprecedented (and since unprecedented) level. It was, quite frankly, a scary rate of growth, which explains the alarming talk of "bombs" and "explosions" when discussing world population levels.

In the previous century, countries could be fairly easily classified into one of two categories: affluent/developed or less affluent/developing. The former had high population growth rates, the latter low. With **birthrates** (or the ratio of live births per 1,000 of the population per year) now declining in the latter category, including much of Asia, Latin America, and the Middle East, the high population growth rates prevalent forty years ago are now restricted to the countries in sub-Saharan Africa plus a few others (like Liberia, Afghanistan, and the Palestinian territories). A number of less affluent countries in fact have birthrates that, a couple of decades ago, would have been found only in high-income countries. The Chinese have infamously slashed their birthrates, thanks in part to their **one-child policy**, by penalizing families that have more than one child. But strides toward this end have also been made due to recent socioeconomic attainments. To quote Nobel economist Amartya Sen, "While China gets too much credit for its authoritarian measures, it gets far too little credit for other supportive policies it has followed that have helped to cut down the birth rate" (1994:22). Some countries that would certainly not be considered affluent yet have fertility rates below that found in the United Kingdom (with a rate of 1.92) include Iran (1.89), Kazakhstan (1.87), Tunisia (1.71), Thailand (1.65), Serbia (1.39), and Taiwan (1.15) (CIA 2010).

How environmental sociologists talk about population growth, however, tends to be different from how others—such as, say, Paul Ehrlich (author of *The Population Bomb* [1968])—have grappled with the subject. For environmental sociologists, it is not population growth per se that is the central focus of concern but rather the *relationships* between population and resource consumption, use, and waste, recognizing too that these relationships are fundamentally mediated by social structures. Focusing too much on population growth itself also risks sidetracking us from understanding the *reasons behind* those growth rates. From a pragmatic environmentalist standpoint, what good does it do to bemoan excessive population growth if it means being distracted from uncovering its underlying drivers?

This is not to suggest that population growth itself is not worth talking about. It is important, however, not to rest too much of the blame at the feet of those parts of the world with higher than average fertility rates. Lest we forget, the average US citizen's ecological footprint is 30 times greater than that of the average citizen of India and 100 times as much as the average person in the world's poorest countries (Miller and Spoolman 2010). When we talk about population, we need to also have an honest discussion about *which* populations are having the biggest ecological impact, as not all people are equal in this regard. Nevertheless, current growth rates, while down from just a couple of decades ago, are not making things any easier. The stark reality is that the more people there are on earth, the more competition there will be for its already scarce resources, which only complicates matters as we strive to find ways to improve the livelihood of the world's poorest billion, a population who, quite frankly, are *not consuming enough*, as they live at subsistence levels.

Fast Facts

The world's population is just over 7 billion (for the latest figure see http://www.census.gov/main/www/popclock.html). We are all but certain to see a world population of at least 9 billion people by 2050.

If everyone in the world had the same size ecological footprint as the average US citizen, the earth could sustain only 1.4 billion people. At even more modest levels of per capita global consumption, such as what is practiced by the average citizen of Jordan or Thailand, the earth's *current* population could not be sustained (Worldwatch Institute 2010). Although calculations like this are far from perfect, the empirical evidence is clear: more than 9 billion people cannot all consume resources at levels comparable to the average citizen of affluent nations.

The average life-cycle carbon impact of a child born in the United States is more than 160 times that of a child born in Bangladesh (Oregon State University 2009).

Future world population growth will mirror closely population growth in cities. The number of urban dwellers will reach some 6.2 billion people by 2050 (compared to roughly 3.5 billion today). About 95 percent of this growth will be concentrated in developing countries. Asia will see the majority of this growth, accounting for 55 percent of it, followed by countries in Africa (30 percent) and in Latin America and the Caribbean (8 percent) (Martine 2009).

Although fertility rates in sub-Saharan Africa tend to be high, the countries of this region also have very high child mortality rates. In 2002 17 percent of children died before reaching the age of five. As of 2007, that rate had "improved" to 15 percent (one of the leading causes of death among children in this region is malaria) (UNICEF 2011). Conflict, AIDS/HIV, and extreme poverty have combined to drastically reduce life expectancy in this part of the world (to in some cases close to forty years of age!) (WHO 2012).

Implications

I understand the appeal of setting the responsibility for our ecological ills at the feet of population growth. Reducing environmental problems to demographics—thinking fewer people equals fewer environmental problems—is much easier than trying to deal with the root causes of global environmental impacts. And it's an attractive argument, especially for those living in affluent nations who can employ it to elude any moral responsibility for reducing their ecological footprints. To paraphrase sentiments I hear often from those looking to make ecological scapegoats out of rapidly growing lower-income countries: "We can just keep doing what we're doing; no reason to change our actions: *they* are the ones—those in poor countries with the high-fertility rates—that need to change!" Yet this argument fails to hold up to empirical scrutiny. In discussing the impacts of population, this section looks at whether today's environmental ills are primarily the result of population growth per se or a product of a process that's a bit more complex (see ECOnnection 6.1).

Greenhouse Gases

Table 6.1 compares different regions and countries with regard to their share of world population growth and CO_2 emissions growth between 1980 and 2005. It is clear from this table that population growth alone cannot account for raising CO_2 emissions. We see, for example, that sub-Saharan Africa accounted for very little of the growth in CO_2 emissions between 1980 and 2005, while accounting for 18.5 percent of global population growth during this period. At the other extreme, while accounting for 3.4 percent of population growth, the United States is responsible for 12.6 percent of the growth of CO_2 emissions between 1980 and 2005. In light of these facts, we need to realize that the actual impact of future fertility rate reductions on greenhouse gas emissions will likely not be proportional, especially if those declines are occurring in countries in sub-Saharan Africa (see Ethical Question 6.1).

Urban Sprawl

Urban sprawl—the spreading of urban development into areas adjoining cities—can occur with or without population growth. The causes of urbanization are multiple. People may migrate from rural to urban areas for employment opportunities or for

ECOnnection 6.1

From IPAT to STIRPAT

A widely applied accounting model to examine the relationship between human activities and the environment is the IPAT. First proposed in the early 1970s (see, for example, Ehrlich and Holden 1971), the IPAT model specifies that environmental *i*mpacts are the product of *p*opulation size, *a*ffluence (in terms of per capita consumption or production), and *t*echnology (defined as impact per unit of consumption or production). Each variable is assumed to have proportional effects on the environment. When calculating environmental impacts, in other words, IPAT reminds us that we cannot divorce talk about population from variables pertaining to levels of affluence and technology impacts.

Although a valuable accounting equation, the IPAT model remains a relatively crude instrument for social scientists, as it does not allow for the testing of hypotheses (York, Rosa, and Dietz 2003). To overcome this limitation,

Dietz and Rosa (1994) advanced a new model, one that allows for the calculation of probabilities and hence an evaluation of competing hypotheses and theories. This alternative model is called STIRPAT: *st*ochastic *i*mpacts by *r*egression on *p*opulation, *a*ffluence, and *t*echnology (Rosa and Dietz 1998). One of the most notable contributions of the STIRPAT program has been its ability to show that basic material conditions like demographic and economic factors to a very significant degree shape the size of national-level ecological footprints. In practical policy terms, STIRPAT tells us that there is no "magic bullet" that will solve environmental problems and that we must deal with deeper driving forces, which include population but also things like economic growth. (Thanks to Richard York for helping me distill an otherwise extensive literature into a couple of sentences.)

TABLE 6.1 Share of Population and CO_2 Emissions Growth for Select Regions/Countries, 1980–2005

REGION/NATION	SHARE OF POPULATION GROWTH (%)	SHARE OF EMISSIONS GROWTH (%)
Northern Africa	3.0	2.5
Sub-Saharan Africa	18.5	2.4
China	15.3	44.5
India	21.7	9.9
US	3.4	12.6
South Korea	0.5	3.7
Japan	0.5	3.6

Source: Adapted from Satterthwaite (2009).

ETHICAL QUESTION 6.1

Do Countries Have a Right to Their "Fair Share" of CO_2 Emissions?

A sizable proportion of future growth in the world's population will undoubtedly come from low-income households residing in low-income nations, individuals who, unfortunately, will likely remain in a state of poverty for the foreseeable future (Satterthwaite 2009). For these very poor nations, there will continue to be very little connection between future population growth and greenhouse gas emissions. Yet some countries—most notably India and China—will undoubtedly see their standard of living and populations (and thus their CO_2 footprint) increase between now and 2050. India's population is expected to surpass China's, currently the most populous country in the world, by 2030, when it becomes home to some 1.53 billion people. For these countries, we can expect to see a positive correlation between population, affluence, and greenhouse gas emissions. Yet this situation calls forth an ethical question: are countries entitled to a certain "fair share" of greenhouse gas emissions? And if so, what should that level be? More to the point: if an impoverished country's per capita greenhouse gas emissions levels are drastically less than, say, those of the United States, do they have a right to *increase* those emissions up to a point? Or should we treat emission increases in the developing world the same as we would treat increases occurring in wealthy nations?

something as fundamental as food. In the wake of the food crisis in 2008, Kenyan president Mwai Kibaki predicted that over the next two decades, the urban population of Africa will increase rapidly, as agricultural land becomes further degraded, causing millions to abandon their rural dwellings as they seek opportunity in cities.

Half of the earth's population are urbanities and occupy an area equivalent to between 0.4 and 2.7 percent of its surface, with the larger number reflecting the entirety of space within the perimeter of cities and the smaller number measuring only the built-up areas (Martine 2009). We must remember, however, that urban footprints are not the same as ecological footprints—the latter, to date, is always larger than the former. (I cannot tell you how many times I have had someone try to "prove" to me that the earth is nowhere near its carrying capacity by pointing to all the open space still available in the world.) Yet even the space taken up by actual human settlements is becoming an increasing concern. We know, for example, that urban land areas are sprawling faster than ever due to absolute increases in numbers of people living in cities combined with the decreasing average densities of urban space (Angel, Sheppard, and Civco 2005). The combined tendencies of declining density with unprecedented absolute increases in urban populations could greatly intensify urban sprawl in the future (Martine 2009). It has been estimated that the total population of cities in developing countries will double between 2000 and 2030, yet their built-up areas will triple. This calculation is not surprising, as cities in low-income countries are currently more than four times as densely

TABLE 6.2 Cities with 10 Million Inhabitants or More, 1950, 2000, and 2015 (Projected)

1950		2000		2015	
City	**Population**	**City**	**Population**	**City**	**Population**
New York-Newark	12.3	Tokyo	34.4	Tokyo	35.5
Tokyo	11.3	Mexico City	18.1	Mumbai	21.9
		New York-Newark	17.8	Mexico City	21.6
		São Paulo	17.1	São Paulo	20.5
		Mumbai	16.1	New York-Newark	19.9
		Shanghai	13.2	Delhi	18.6
		Calcutta	13.1	Shanghai	17.2
		Delhi	12.4	Calcutta	17.0
		Buenos Aires	11.8	Dhaka	16.8
		Los Angeles-Long Beach-Santa Ana	11.8	Jakarta	16.8
		Osaka-Kobe	11.2	Lagos	16.1
		Jakarta	11.1	Karachi	15.2
		Rio de Janeiro	10.8	Buenos Aires	13.4
		Cairo	10.4	Cairo	13.1
		Dhaka	10.2	Los Angeles-Long Beach-Santa Ana	13.1
		Moscow	10.1	Manila	12.9
		Karachi	10.0	Beijing	12.9
		Manila	10.0	Rio de Janeiro	12.8
				Osaka-Kobe	11.3
				Istanbul	11.2
				Moscow	11.0
				Guangzhou, Guangdong	10.4

Source: Adapted from United Nations (2006).

populated as cities in affluent countries. These cities can't get much more densely concentrated than they already are, meaning for many their only choice is to sprawl out. In high-income nations, urban populations are expected to increase by 20 percent, while their built-up areas will increase two and a half times (Dodman 2009).

Just how big are cities expected to get? There is a reason the adjective *mega* is used to describe today's largest cities. In 1950 there were two cities with 10 million or more inhabitants. By 2005 that number had increased to twenty. Two more cities are expected to be added to this list by 2015. All but five of these megacities will be located in developing countries (see Table 6.2).

I am less worried about the growth of cities per se. Rather, we should be looking at the *type* of growth occurring in these spaces. Just as there is growth that can be labeled as "smart," there are also forms that seem not so smart, like, for example, urban sprawl. Ecological impacts can vary widely depending upon which path of urban development is followed. Recent research, for example, has shown that metropolitan regions ranking high on a quantitative index of sprawl experience a greater number of ozone exceedances

FIGURE 6.1 Annual Average Growth Rates for Global Crop Yields versus Growth Rate for World Population, Select Years

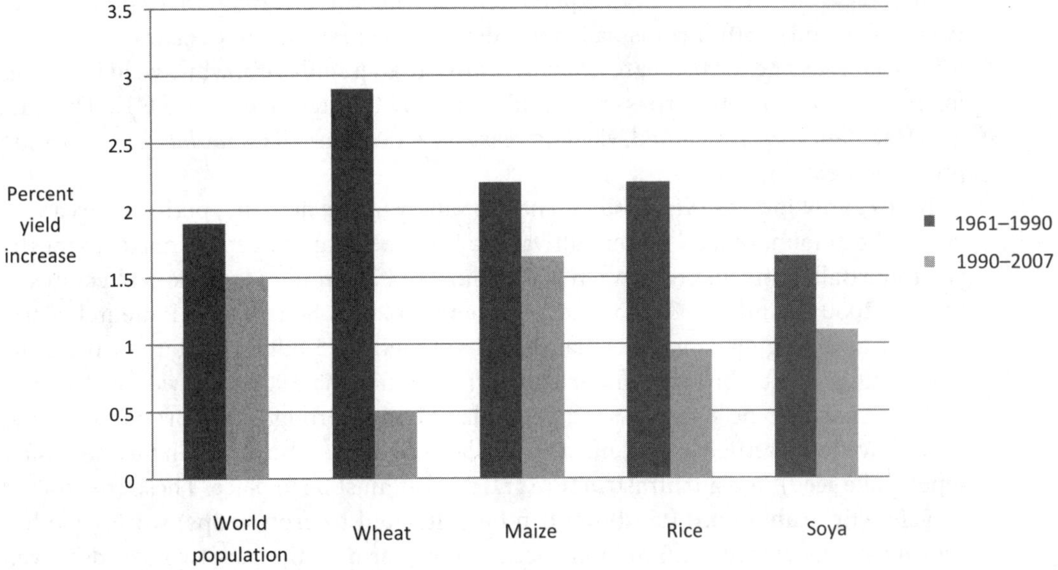

Growth rates in crop-yield increases were able to largely able keep up with—and in some cases surpass—world population growth (illustrated by the bars on the left of the figure) between 1961 and 1990. Since then, however, growth rates in yield increases (except for corn) have slowed and are no longer keeping up with population growth. *Source:* Adapted from *Economist* (2011b).

(concentrations that exceed what is allowed by the federal government) than more spatially compact metropolitan regions. Importantly, this relationship held even after controlling for population size, average ozone seasonal temperatures, and regional emissions of nitrogen oxides and **volatile organic compounds** (compounds that evaporate from housekeeping, maintenance, and building products made with organic chemicals) (Stone 2008). In fact, most of the negative environmental indicators often attributed to urbanization are actually the result of urban sprawl. And it's not just environmental health that suffers from urban sprawl; our health suffers, too. Even after controlling for demographic and behavioral variables—like gender, age, ethnicity, education, and diet—research has linked urban sprawl (at a level that's statistically significant) to such variables as fewer minutes walked daily, obesity, and hypertension (Ewing et al. 2003; Ewing, Brownson, and Berringan 2006).

Food

Many have a difficult time divorcing population growth from the subject of food security. It's a fair link to make. Each additional mouth that needs to be fed means additional competition for food. Fortunately, the links between population growth and food security are mediated by a number of social variables, which is cause for hope. But first, let's start with the bad news.

Annual average global crop-production growth is expected to slow from 2.2 percent (as recorded between 1997 and 2007) to 1.3 percent between now and 2030, slowing still further to 0.8 percent between 2030 and 2050. In developing countries, yield growth (the rate at which crop yields are expected to increase annually) looks like it will slow even faster, from 2.9 percent to 1.5 percent (between now and 2030) to 0.9 percent (between 2030 and 2050) (Bruinsma 2009). Also, for the first time in decades, crop yields for wheat, rice, and soybean are growing slower than population, while yield increases for corn are just barely surpassing population growth rates (see Figure 6.1). The data are clear: if all goes as planned, yield increases will take care of about *half* of the world's projected needs by 2050.

If we cannot increase yields sufficiently to satisfy future demand, perhaps we can increase the amount of land under cultivation. We are going to need, to make up for the yield shortfall, somewhere between 200 million and 750 million additional hectares of land by 2050 (Balmford, Green, and Scharlemann 2005; Schade and Pimentel 2010). There is an emerging consensus that there are roughly 1.5 billion hectares around the world that could be brought under cultivation (Bruinsma 2009). Yet we must realize that a lot needs to be accomplished before land can be brought into production: land rights have to be settled, credit must be available to farmers so they can buy necessary inputs (like seed), and an infrastructure and market must be in place. These constraints explain why **arable land** (land that can be cultivated to grow crops) worldwide has grown by a net average of 5 million hectares per year over the past two decades, even though there are tremendous pressures to expand faster (Rabobank 2010). As the easiest land to convert has already been plowed under, we can expect a slowdown in the annual growth of arable land, recognizing that what remains is increasingly marginal (which means it will require even more fertilizer and other inputs to be productive). Specifically, the annual growth of arable land is expected to slow from 0.30 percent between 1961 and 2005 to 0.10 percent between 2005 and 2050. This calculates out to an average annual net increase of arable area of 2.75 million hectares per year between 2005 and 2050, or a total of 120 million additional hectares (ibid.:14). This figure is well below the most optimistic estimates that claim we need 200 million additional hectares by midcentury to satisfy global food demand. Furthermore, the estimate ignores the fact that arable land in developed and transitional countries is *declining* (thanks most notably to urban sprawl) at an estimated rate of 0.23 percent a year (Bruinsma 2009).

In 1798 Thomas Malthus published his immensely influential *Essay on Population*. His argument, greatly oversimplified, was that growth in population will always outpace our ability to feed, shelter, and clothe people and that without some controls on population growth, it would ultimately be humanity's undoing. The future, in the eyes of Malthus, was bleak, especially for the poorest class, a position held to this day by so-called **neo-Malthusians**, who advocate for the control of population growth. Before we look upon the previous paragraphs as testament to Malthus's foresight, let's look more closely at why there is food scarcity in the world today.

According to the Noble Prize–winning economist Amartya Sen (1981), modern food crises are less related to the absence of food as to the inability to buy it. Examining the 1943 Bengal famine, which at its peak claimed the lives of more than fifty thousand Bengalese weekly (Fisher 1943), Sen describes how there was actually plenty of food to go around (he also looked at the 1974 Bangladesh famine and drew similar conclusions). The problem, in other words, was not a lack of food but a lack of *available* food, as those with the means to acquire it were engaging in acts of hoarding, knowing that its price would only go up. Whereas natural disasters may have been the main culprits in the past, extreme food insecurity today is more often than not the result of markets, governments, and civil society failing those at the margins of society.

This brings us to the subject of democracy. Sen argues that democracy creates an important political, social, and civil environment where famine is unlikely. Indeed, as Sen famously wrote, "No famine has ever taken place in the history of the world in a functioning democracy" (1981:16). Famines tend to affect only the poorest segment of a country's population. In nondemocratic states, those most likely to experience famine are likewise the least likely to have political access. Their famine-related suffering is therefore allowable to elites, as it does little to threaten their grip on power. What democracy provides is a voice to those living on the margins of society who would otherwise lack access to any levers of political influence. In nondemocratic states, famines can also go on without most of the public even aware of the suffering. A cornerstone of democracy is accountability, which is in part made possible through a free press. Without a free press, citizens would have a very difficult time holding politicians accountable for, among other things, failing to act expeditiously when the first signs of calamity (like a famine) arise. As we saw throughout the twentieth century, whether the massive Soviet and Chinese famines of midcentury or the Ethiopian famine of the mid-1980s, food can all too easily be grossly misallocated when governments are not held accountable (Ó Gráda 2007).

Feeding a Growing Nonhuman Animal Population

When discussing the relationship between population growth and food security, it is also important to be clear about what exactly we mean by the term *population*. When talking about the "mouths" that our food systems feed, we need to be clear that we are not talking just about those of the human variety. We feed a lot more than just humans with the food we produce. If we fed only humans, the task at hand would be considerably easier. According to the Food and Agriculture Organization (FAO) of the United Nations, world agriculture produces enough food to provide every woman, man, and child with some twenty-seven hundred calories a day. But we don't feed just humans. We also feed livestock, in the form of animal feed, and increasingly cars, in the form of biofuels.

If current trends continue, we are going to have to produce twice as much animal protein by 2050 just to keep up with demand. This means that by 2050, livestock will be consuming enough food to feed 4 billion people (the world's population in the early 1970s). In other words, if the world continues to eat meat at the rates that we are expecting—and since most of the animals that provide that meat are going to have to eat an enormous amount of grain—the world's effective population in 2050 will be 13.5 billion (9.5 billion, the projected human population, plus 4 billion, as that is how many people could be fed with the grain that is expected to be diverted to livestock) (Tudge 2010). Why these trends matter from a food-security perspective is because collectively, cattle, pigs and poultry *already* consume roughly half the world's wheat, 90 percent of the world's corn, 93 percent of the world's soybeans, and close to all the world's barley not used for brewing and distilling (ibid.). In case you're wondering: if the whole world were to consume meat at the same per capita rate as the average American, total grain output could sustain a global population of roughly only 2.6 billion people (Carolan 2011b).

Feeding a Growing Automobile Population

In addition to having to feed a growing nonhuman animal population, we are also feeding a growing *automobile* population. World ethanol (biofuels derived from cellulose) production has increased 500 percent in the past ten years, from roughly 17 billion liters in 2000 to just below 87 billion liters in 2010. And although total output is far behind ethanol's current levels, biodiesel (vegetable oil– or animal fat–based biofuels) production has grown rapidly in the past decade, from less than 1 billion liters in 2000 to approximately 20 billion in 2010.

Mandates for blending biofuels into vehicle fuels have been enacted in at least forty-one states and provinces and twenty-four countries and require blending 10–15 percent ethanol with gasoline or 2–5 percent biodiesel with diesel fuel. For example, Brazil, Indonesia, and the European Union expect to meet 10 percent of their energy demands by 2020 with biofuels, while the United States hopes to satisfy 30 percent of their energy needs by 2020 with these fuels (ethanol currently accounts for 8 percent of the fuel used for vehicles in the United States while consuming almost 40 percent of its maize crop) (*Economist* 2011b). It has been estimated that if all such targets were met, 10 percent of the world's cereal output would be diverted from food to fuels, pushing food prices up anywhere from 15 to 40 percent. Similarly, if all US corn otherwise destined for ethanol plants were instead used as food, global edible corn supplies would increase approximately 14 percent (ibid.). A recent survey by the National Academy of Sciences estimated that recent international biofuel growth accounted for 20–40 percent of the global price increases seen in 2007–2008, when prices of many food crops doubled (National Research Council 2011). In another study, it was calculated that from 2006 to 2011, US ethanol expansion cost the Mexican economy between US$1.5 and 3 billion due to ethanol-related corn-price increases (Wise 2012).

Solutions

It would be wrong to attribute all the world's ecological problems to population growth. Yet as far as long-term sustainability is concerned, it is hard to deny the virtues of a less populated planet, as long as those growth rates are brought down in an ethical, just, and equitable manner. With that, I offer the following piece of encouraging news: there is evidence that population growth rates will come down for countries as their levels of prosperity grow—which is known as the **demographic transition model**.

The demographic transition model illustrates the move from a state of high birth- and death rates to low birth- and death rates, the time between representing a period of rapid population growth (see Figure 6.2). A brief summary of the model is in order. Preindustrial (stage 1) countries have high birth- and death rates and consequentially fairly stable populations. In the earliest stage of industrialization (stage 2), death rates fall with improvements in food supply, sanitation, and health, while birthrates remain high due to lagging **pronatal social norms** (which refers to individual attitudes and societal expectations that promote high fertility rates). In late industrialization (stage 3), death rates continue to fall, while birthrates also begin to drop. Once a certain level of affluence is achieved (stage 4), however, birthrates begin flattening out to match death rates, causing the country's population to stabilize. Children in highly urbanized affluent

FIGURE 6.2 Demographic Transition Model

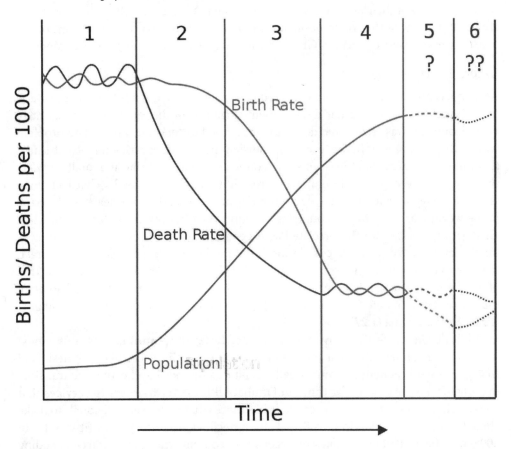

The dashed lines signify recently hypothesized stages.

countries are also more likely to be viewed as a "cost" to families much earlier than they are in rural, low-income nations, where they can help tend livestock and work the fields at a relatively young age. More recently, adding to the original four stages, there is growing discussion about a fifth stage to represent countries that have below-replacement fertility rates (below 2.1 children per women). As their resident population ages, some European (e.g., Germany) and Asian (e.g., Japan) countries actually have higher death rates than birthrates. More recent still is the addition of a possible sixth stage. First suggested in a 1999 issue of the journal *Nature* (Myrskyla, Kphler, and Billari 2009), this stage shows that very high levels of economic and social development promote (in some countries at least) a rebound in fertility (notable exceptions being Germany and Japan). There is still considerable debate around the existence of this newly suggested stage.

The demographic transition model does not attempt to forecast what will happen. It's simply a statistical representation of what has occurred for countries that have already undergone the transition—countries like the United States, Japan, and those in western Europe. It is therefore entirely fair to ask, "What makes us so sure those countries in stages 2 and 3 will move to stage 4 (or beyond) anytime in the foreseeable future?" If history is any guide, this demographic transition is anything but guaranteed;

after all, many nations on the UN's list of least-developed countries (LDCs) have essentially been stuck at their present level of development for decades (the LDCs constitute about 12 percent of the world population but account for less than 2 percent of the world's gross domestic product [GDP] and about 1 percent of global trade in goods).

Socioeconomic Development

Although economic development helps reduce fertility rates, it is not the panacea it was once thought to be. A popular development slogan from the 1970s, which has since been debunked, was "economic development is the best contraceptive." The problem with putting all our eggs in the "economic development" basket is that it misses the fact that population growth, at least in some countries, is so great that it actually *hinders* the very thing so many are hoping will forestall it: economic growth. That fact alone should be taken as evidence that we cannot rely on progrowth strategies alone in many of the world's fastest-growing countries to bring down fertility rates. Moreover, while GDP per capita is negatively correlated with a country's fertility rate (as the former goes up, the latter goes down), the correlation is not perfect. Quite a few countries, in fact, manage to maintain very low fertility rates with GDP per capita levels well below that of, for example, the highly affluent United States (with its 2.06 fertility rate). Some of those countries include Costa Rica (1.92), Vietnam (1.89), Uruguay (1.87), Romania (1.30), and Lithuania (1.27).

While declines in fertility have been facilitated by **family planning** programs—most infamously in China with their one-child policy but also in places like Indonesia and Malaysia—these reductions were equally facilitated by social and economic transformations. Family planning, for those unfamiliar with the term, refers to services that could include educational, social, or medical services that empower individuals to make choices around reproduction. In Brazil sharp declines in fertility rates (it was 1.8 in 2008) have been attributed mainly to larger socioeconomic transformations—including urbanization—that have encouraged people to limit family size (OECD 2010b). The old paradigm—out of which came the slogan "economic development is the best contraceptive"—was not necessarily wrong, just shortsighted. What really matters is the *type* of development. Remember, a country can have an impressive GDP per capita, but if all that wealth is concentrated in the hands of a few, the average citizen is essentially no better off than if he or she lived in any of the LDCs. What is required is *socio*economic development. This means improvements in literacy and rates of school enrollment, gender equity and women empowerment, heath care, and social institutions (e.g., education) while also meeting the needs of individuals in terms of sexual and reproductive health. Economic development alone—a point discussed in greater detail in Chapter 12—is insufficient on many levels (see Case Study 6.1).

When talking about "development," the following fact should never be far from our minds: although socioeconomic enhancements tend to motivate people to reduce their fertility rates, they also tend to increase consumption levels. One solution then for reducing consumption and emissions in the short term would be to further reduce fertility rates in affluent countries to compensate for the increased consumption and emissions in other countries as they climb out of poverty. Reducing fertility rates among those whose offspring would have a sizable ecological footprint would clearly go a long way toward reducing the stress that ecosystems are currently being placed under. Yet I also

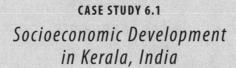

Socioeconomic Development
in Kerala, India

Kerala, an Indian state located on the south-west coast of the country, has made remarkable socioeconomic strides over the past couple decades. Kerala's fertility rate is actually lower than China's, even with the latter's coercive one-child policy. The reason, undoubtedly, is tied to Kerala's impressive strides in areas relating to basic education, health care, and gender equality (see Table 6.3). And it has done this with a mediocre, by global standards, GDP per capita. If it were a country, its GDP per capita would be lower than that of, for instance, Peru, South Africa, and Turkey. When it comes to reducing fertility rates, Kerala's developmental trajectory disputes the need for oppressive population-control policies like forced sterilization or the criminalization of having multiple children. It should also serve as a reminder of the shortsightedness of approaches that place too much emphasis on economic development to the detriment of social improvements and overall welfare enhancement.

TABLE 6.3 Well-Being Indicators for Indian State of Kerala Compared to Entire Indian Country

WELL-BEING INDICATORS	KERALA	INDIA
Birthrate (per 1,000)	14.6%	22.8%
Death rate (per 1,000)	6.6%	7.4%
Infant mortality rate (per 1,000)	12%	53%
Child mortality rate, 0–4 years (per 1,000)	3%	17%
Total fertility rate (children per women)	1.7%	2.9%
Life expectancy at birth (age at death)		
a) male	71.4	62.6
b) female	76.3	64.2
c) total	74	63.5
Literacy rate (per 100)		
a) male	94.2%	82.14%
b) female	87.86%	65.46%
c) total	90.92%	74.04%

Source: Adapted from India Planning Committee (2008).

ETHICAL QUESTION 6.2

Whose Behaviors
Should Change?

Are we asking those in the developing world to change their behaviors so those of us in rich nations do not have to change ours? If consumption was not occurring in affluent countries at the rates that they are, we likely would not be having this conversation about population growth. Residents of less affluent countries have told me how the finger wagging of countries like the United States (toward poor regions of the world with higher fertility rates) seems insincere; reminding me that rich countries are far from ecological sainthood, given their rampant consumerism and fertility rates that are actually *slightly up* since the 1970s. Is it fair—or even empirically justified—to continue framing "the population problem" as a developing country problem?

realize this is not a terribly realistic suggestion, as many affluent countries have actually started taking steps to *increase* their birthrates. These profertility policies are grounded in national interests triggered by demographic concerns about shrinking military and consumer might. It is therefore highly unlikely that a groundswell of popular support could be generated for fertility-reduction campaigns in these countries (see Ethical Question Box 6.2).

We also need to realize that even immediate reductions in fertility in less affluent nations will not rapidly stabilize the world's population. This is where the term **demographic inertia** comes into the picture. This is a term from demography based on the fact that a time lag is to be expected before the full effects of changes to a fertility rate are seen. (until the youngest cohort just prior to fertility rates' dropping essentially become too old to have children). Take China, for example. Although it reached a below-replacement level of fertility in the early 1990s, the nation will grow by an additional 320 million bodies before its population finally stabilizes and starts to decrease after 2035. In fact, the majority of population growth today is due less to present fertility patterns than to *past* fertility and mortality patterns (Martine 2009). There are, however, things that can slow demographic inertia, such as if the age at marriage or age at conception of first child were delayed a year or two (see Case Study 6.2).

Small changes in fertility rates can make a big difference over the long term. Figure 6.3 is based on demographic modeling by the United Nations (2004). The medium scenario indicates that world population will decline slightly and quickly stabilize in about a century—a very encouraging development. The high scenario, conversely, is calculated by making small deviations from the fertility path projected in the medium scenario, with devastating consequences. It assumes fertility levels that are 0.5 of a child above those projected in the medium scenario until 2050 and between 0.25 and 0.30 of a child higher between 2050 and 2300. Under this scenario, the future world population will continue to grow in rapid fashion, to around 15 billion by 2100 and 22 billion by 2200.

CASE STUDY 6.2
Family Planning
in Ethiopia

For every 100,000 live births in Ethiopia, 670 women will die from pregnancy-related problems. (For comparison, in the United States, which ranks thirty-ninth globally, that figure is 13; for Italy, which ranks first, it is 3.9.) As the country is predominantly rural, 94 percent of women deliver at home. In light of these abysmal figures, the Ethiopian government is looking to restructure its health-care system. Particular attention is being given to the problems faced by rural women, as some 83 percent of the population reside outside of cities. The government now trains and has on its payroll approximately thirty thousand trained health-extension workers, whose job it is to cover the countryside providing health services.

Access to affordable contraception is also a top priority. In 2005 less than 15 percent of women had access to contraception. Since then the Ethiopian government has implemented a plan for providing free birth control pills or a contraceptive injection with effects that last for three months. Yet these "short-term" birth control methods are still problematic, given that for some women, the nearest health center may be an eight-hour walk from where they reside. In light of such barriers to access, there is a move to make widely (and freely) available an implant that protects women from pregnancy for three years (Hegarty 2010).

FIGURE 6.3 World Population Estimates, High and Medium Models (projected through 2250)

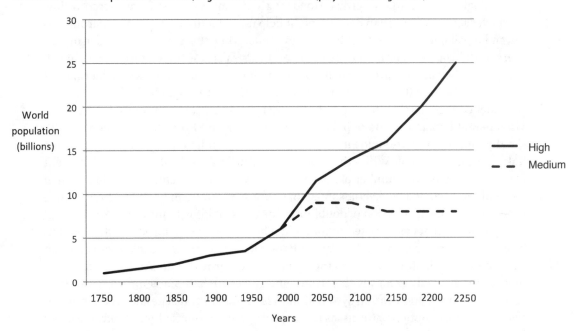

Source: Adapted from United Nations 2004.

The Future Role of Cities

If you are like some of my students, you might be thinking: "Cities as a *solution* to our environmental ills? You can't be serious! Didn't we just get done discussing the problems associated with urban sprawl?!" For reasons that are largely justified, cities have generally been viewed in a noticeably *un*ecological light. Otherwise well-intentioned approaches, like "ecological footprint" analyses, have further reinforced the idea that cities are fundamentally unsustainable, as they have a tendency to conflate "sustainability" with "self-sufficiency." To be sure, urban areas concentrate people, cars, industries, and the like, which naturally means they concentrate emissions, pollution, noise, and consumption. And historically, this concentration made cities—and continues to make many cities around the world—hazardous places to live. Yet those very things that often caused people to look upon urban areas as a "brown" blight on the landscape also give them distinct "green" ecological advantages.

Urban residents, for example, tend to possess substantially smaller carbon footprints than residents elsewhere in the same country. Per capita greenhouse gas emissions in New York City are less than 30 percent of those for the United States as a whole, those for London roughly half of the British average. The average resident of Rio de Janeiro has a greenhouse gas footprint that's less than a third the size for the average Brazilian, while the per capita greenhouse gas emission in Barcelona is 33.9 percent of that for Spain as a whole (Dodman 2009).

There are many reasons for this. The concentration of services and industries lessens the need to travel long distances. Dense cities generally have better public transportation services, in part because the concentration makes building an efficient transportation system more cost-effective. Residents of dense cites also generally live in smaller residential dwellings due to the scarcity and high cost of land. That said, not all cities possess this ecological profile. Many newly formed megacities in Asia suffer from overcrowding, in which case *reducing* urban density might help meet a number of social, environmental, and developmental needs (ibid.). For example, while the average urban density for cities in the United States, New Zealand, and Australia is estimated to be roughly 15 persons per hectare, the average density for low-income Asian cities is a staggering 204 persons per hectare (Chen, Jia, and Lau 2008; see Case Study 6.3).

Evidence suggests that the number of households in a country has a more direct environmental impact than its population per se (Dietz and Rosa 1994; Liu et al. 2003). Yet the number of households in a country and its population do not grow together. Take the case of Brazil. While the population grew at an annual rate of 1.41 percent from 1996 to 2006, the number of households grew at 3.21 percent. Brazil had a total of 54.6 million occupied households in 2006, up from 39.8 million in 1996. On a positive note, however, the proportion of double-income households with no kids (a.k.a. DINKs) living in apartments as opposed to individual houses is increasing across the country. The ecological silver lining of this trend is twofold. First, fewer households with children translate into reductions in the country's population growth rate. And second, apartment living not only comes with certain efficiencies (most notable in energy-critical areas like cooling and heating systems) but also tends to translate into reductions in household consumption patterns, as there is simply less room for household consumer items (Martine 2009).

CASE STUDY 6.3

The Rationale Behind China's New Mega-Megacity

The Pearl River Delta is in the Guangdong Province of the People's Republic of China where the Pearl River flows into the South China Sea. It is one of the most densely urbanized regions in China (indeed the world) and a key economic center for the country. China recently announced plans that will produce a 16,000 square-mile city—that's twenty-six times larger geographically than Greater London. The new city will include the existing cities of Zhuhai (1.5 million), Zhongshan (2.4 million), Jiangmen (3.8 million), Huizhou (3.9 million), Zhaoqing (3.9 million), Foshan (5.4 million), Dongguan (6.4 million), Shenzhen (8.9 million), and Guangzhou (11.7 million). That's roughly 48 million people! At its widest, the new city will be about 120 miles (from Zhaoqing to Huizhou). For some perspective, this is the same distance from Malibu to the eastern side of the Moreno Valley, which essen-

tially represents the Greater Los Angeles, California, metropolitan area (Economist 2011a).

China is currently working to connect the infrastructure (transportation, energy, water, and telecommunications) of the existing nine cities. Doing so will cost the government a projected US$200 billion. As the chief planner at the Guangdong Rural and Urban Planning Institute explains, "The idea is that when the cities are integrated, the residents can travel around freely and use the health care and other facilities in the different areas . . . and . . . help spread industry and jobs more evenly across the region and public services will also be distributed more fairly" (as quoted in Moore and Foster 2011).

How sustainable—ecologically *and* socially speaking—do you view this plan? By privileging cities in this manner, do we run the risk of (further) marginalizing rural populations?

The Case FOR a Population Explosion

Although empirically unsubstantiated, there is the argument out there that the best solution to the problems associated with population growth is . . . *more* population growth. Let me start my offering a more moderate position: that given by Ester Boserup.

Boserup (1965) famously turned Thomas Malthus on his head. Malthus's argument was essentially that agricultural methods (and more specifically the available food supply) determine population size. Boserup, instead, argued population determines agricultural methods and in turn food supply, suggesting that population pressures will sufficiently incentivize ways to feed those additional mouths. To put it simply: given the essential nature of food, people will always find ways to increase agricultural production by increasing their labor (or workforce), machinery, fertilizer applications, and other technologies.

Yet the "Boserup effect," as it has come to be known, is also sensitive to certain realities that can dampen the otherwise optimistic scenario painted by its namesake. Having written extensively on the relationship between gender and development (giving us some of the earliest scholarship on the subject), she was well aware of how inequality can limit the impact of the Boserup effect. Making the necessary investments to one's operation to keep agricultural output ahead of population takes money and credit, two things, unfortunately, that are not always available to the millions of small farmers in less developed countries (Carolan 2011b). Boserup was also well aware that the sheer *level* of population growth that some countries were experiencing—especially in the 1960s when formulating this argument—outstripped the capacity of their governments, economies, and agricultural sectors to keep ahead of growing needs. In sum: a Boserup effect might be discernible in some countries but certainly not all.

I would classify Boserup as a pragmatic optimist; her optimism, after all, was tempered by empirical reality. There is someone, however, who, rather famously, takes technological optimism to the extreme. That person is Julian Simon. For Simon (1981), people represent, as the title of the book detailing his position states, "the ultimate resource." Hence, the greater the population, the greater the collective brainpower and the faster we'll find answers to all the problems that currently trouble us. An increase of 100 million, 1 billion, 10 billion . . . : the more, the better. Each birth, Simon reasons, increases our chances of yielding another Einstein or Mozart (he fails to acknowledge that by this reasoning, it increases our chances of more Hitlers and Bin Ladens, too). Simon's position epitomizes what is known as **cornucopian**. Based on the Greek myth of a horn from a goat that suckled Zeus and became filled with fruit, a cornucopian is someone who believes unending progress, economic growth, and material abundance can be had with advancements in technology.

Yet there is an enormous gap in this reasoning. Had Einstein been born to a poor family in, say, Calcutta (the capital of India during the British Raj until 1911), I doubt we would be speaking of him today. My point is that we already have billions of these underutilized "resources" available to us *today*, minds and bodies that, if just given a chance, could do great things. If we only spent more time concentrating on educating, feeding, and generally improving the lives of the more than 1 billion people living in poverty around the world (Banerjee and Duflo 2011), we would *all* be better off.

Simon also assumes that our resources are infinitely substitutable, that when we get low on one resource, we'll find, through technology, brainpower, and hard work, something else to use in its stead. That's an awfully big assumption to make, given the stakes involved. If anything shows the folly of this assumption, it is climate change. Simon died in 1998, well before the definitive evidence came out as to its very real existence. It's hard enough to even think about what a substitute for things like clean water and air might look like. But with global climate change, how can we substitute an entire planet?

"Up Rather Than Out": If It Works for Cities, Can It Work for Farms?

I've already discussed some of the possible ecological benefits that urban density has over urban sprawl. Of course, to make something like this work—like China's proposed city of 48 million—will take an immense amount of coordination. Urban density is not going to solve anything without a sustainable supporting structure in place, like agriculture. The issue of food production takes center stage in Chapter 8, so I will limit my comments here. But the following question bears asking: how are we going to feed tomorrow's megacities in a way that's ecologically sound? One possibility is to turn agriculture, literally, on its head: **vertical farming**—the practice of farming "up," rather than "out."

Other than the "footprint" of the facility itself, vertical farms require no land. Contrary to what we think we know about plant physiology, plants do not require soil to survive. Hydroponics—from the Greek words *hydro* (water) and *ponos* (labor)—involves growing plants using mineral nutrient solutions in water, without soil. The practice has been around since the 1930s and is used in nurseries around the world for seed germination. More recent still is what is known as aeroponics, essentially an ultraefficient version of hydroponics where tiny nozzles spray a nutrient-rich mist onto the plant's roots (Roberto 2003). The National Aeronautics and Space Administration and the European Space Agency are at the forefront of aeroponic and hydroponic agriculture, working to make these systems entirely self-contained for long-distance space exploration (see, for example, Finetto, Lobascio, and Rapisarda 2010).

Another misconception about plant physiology: plants also do not need all the energy in sunlight to grow to maximum yield. Light-emitting diodes (LEDs) have recently been engineered just for plants, giving them only the parts of the spectrum of light that they need. On the horizon are organo-light-emitting diodes (OLEDs), which promise to offer an even more narrow spectrum of light, thus further reducing the energy demands of vertical farms (Cox 2009; Despommier 2010). Of course, in those regions of the world where sunlight is plentiful, vertical farms could take advantage of this free and abundant resource. Similarly, buildings could be powered using wind turbines and photovoltaic panels.

Despommier (2010), in his book *The Vertical Farm*, tells the story of a strawberry farmer who replaced his thirty-acre farm after it was destroyed by a hurricane with a one-acre vertical farm utilizing hydro-stackers (a hydroponic vertical gardening system). That single acre now yields as many strawberries as the thirty acres did prior to the hurricane. The farmer also reports that the remaining twenty-nine acres, those not replanted with strawberries, have returned to a more biologically diverse—or "wild"—state.

It is not my suggestion that vertical farms could entirely support tomorrow's megacities. Yet we've got to ask how tomorrow's megacities are going to be fed, particularly in light of the growing interest around concepts like regional food security and resiliency and rising energy prices. Recall the aforementioned megacity currently being assembled in China. It is projected to have the same population as what lived on the *entire plant* in the year 1000 BCE (roughly 50 million people). To feed them all will require some outside-the-box—perhaps even some vertical—thinking.

IMPORTANT CONCEPTS

- Amartya Sen on famines
- Boserup effect
- demographic transition model
- IPAT
- Julian Simon's ultimate resource
- socioeconomic development
- STIRPAT
- Thomas Malthus on population growth

DISCUSSION QUESTIONS

1. Is it fair to continue framing "the population problem" as a low-income country problem when the average US citizen's ecological footprint is thirty times greater than that of the average Indian and one hundred times greater than that of the average person in the world's poorest countries?

2. Having large families in low-income nations is perfectly rational for many living in those environments. What are some of the sociological forces underlying high fertility rates in developing countries?

3. Does a person have a fundamental human right to have as many children as he or she chooses?

4. Take the hit reality US television show *19 and Counting* (on TLC), of the family with nineteen children (and who have expressed a desire for more). Why is it socially acceptable for this family to have so many children (and then we glamorize it by putting it on television) but not for families in poorer nations?

5. What is the earth's carrying capacity (how many people can it hold)?

SUGGESTED ADDITIONAL READINGS

Bremner, J. 2012. "Population and Food Security: Africa's Challenge." Population Reference Bureau, USAID, February. Retrieved August 26, 2012 (http://www.prb.org/pdf12/population-food-security-africa.pdf).

Economist. 2011. "The 9-Billion People Question: A Special Report on Feeding the World." February 26. Retrieved August 26, 2012 (http://www.economist.com/surveys/download SurveyPDF.cfm?id=18205243&surveyCode=%254e%2541&submit=View+PDF).

Kangalawe, R., and J. Lyimo. 2010. "Population Dynamics, Rural Livelihoods, and Environmental Degradation: Some Experiences from Tanzania." *Environment, Development, and Sustainability* 12(6):985–997.

Ray, S., and I. Ray. 2011. "Impact of Population Growth on Environmental Degradation: Case of India." *Journal of Economics and Sustainable Development* 2(8). Retrieved August 26, 2012 (http://iiste.org/Journals/index.php/JEDS/article/view/627).

UNFPA. 2011. "The World at Seven Billion: Top Issues/Fact Sheet." United Nations Population Fund, July. Retrieved August 26, 2012 (http://www.unfpa.org/webdav/site/global/shared /documents/7%20Billion/7B_fact_sheets_en.pdf).

Urdal, H. 2005. "People vs. Malthus: Population Pressure, Environmental Degradation, and Armed Conflict Revisited." *Journal of Peace Research* 42(4):417–434.

RELEVANT INTERNET LINKS

- http://www.census.gov/main/www/popclock.html
  US and World Population Clocks, maintained by the US Census Bureau.
- http://populationpyramid.net/
  Population pyramids of the world and for every nation, based on UN data.
- http://www.prb.org/Journalists/Webcasts/2009/distilleddemographics1.aspx
  Link to the Population Reference Bureau's (PRB) "Distilled Demographics" video series. In the first video, *Deciphering Population Pyramids*, the PRB's senior demogra-

pher shows how population pyramids give us a snapshot of a country's demographic profile.

- http://rumkin.com/tools/population/
  Population statistics for every country.

SUGGESTED VIDEOS

- *Aftermath: Population Zero* (2008)
  http://topdocumentaryfilms.com/aftermath-population-zero/. This film speculates what the earth, animal life, and plant life might be like if humanity no longer existed, as well as the effect that humanity's disappearance would have on the artifacts of civilization.
- *Earth Days* (2009)
  http://video.pbs.org/video/1463378089/. A documentary about the rise of the environmental movement in the United States and the first Earth Day in 1970. It also nicely chronicles the late 1960s and 1970s, when talk of a "population bomb" was at its peak.
- *How Many People Can Live on Planet Earth?* (2011)
  http://documentaryvideos.org/bbc-documentary-about-earths-population/. A British Broadcasting Company (BBC) six-part series on the earth's population.
- *Mother: Caring Our Way Out of the Population Dilemma* (2011)
  Takes a feminist and humanist view of population growth.

Transportation: Beyond Air Pollution

It is understandable why discussions on transportation in my classes repeatedly veer to pollution, since roughly a third of US greenhouse gas emissions are transportation related (Maibach, Steg, and Anable 2009). Not surprisingly, then, the tone taken toward the subject has grown increasingly critical, as its global shape and character look increasingly like those found in the United States, where the car takes center stage. For those not familiar with the car craze in the United States, here are a couple of statistics. According to a recent national survey:

- 25 percent of all trips by automobile are made within a mile of the home;
- 40 percent of all trips by automobile are made within two miles of the home;
- 50 percent of the working population commutes five miles or less to work;
- more than 82 percent of trips five miles or less are made using the car (whereas about half of all car trips in the United Kingdom and Netherlands are less than five miles [ibid.]);
- 60 percent of the pollution created by automobile emissions happens in the first few minutes of operation—before pollution-control devices become fully effective—which means shorter car trips are more polluting on a per-mile basis than longer trips (LAB, n.d.).

Yet it is more than just its links to pollution that make transportation a fascinating subject for sociologists. We often think about transportation as a *response to* changes in how we organized society. In this scenario, we therefore drive because our urban environments require us to. Yet the data tell precisely the opposite story. Urban and community patterns, in other words, have taken the shape they have in part *because of* available transportation systems. The car, for example, made certain patterns of urbanization possible, patterns that, not surprisingly, are found today to be difficult to service under alternative transportation forms. Thus, although many urban environments leave us with little "choice" (I place the term in quotes as it really isn't one, as I'll later explain) but to drive, those very environments place this demand on us only because the car makes their existence possible. Although we often like to think of the car's rise as the outcome of consumer democracy—where you vote with your wallet—a careful analysis reveals the vote to have been rigged in its favor. After all, wouldn't you expect the automobile to win when the question is "What mode of transportation would you choose in a society that's specifically designed for the automobile?"

FIGURE 7.1 Idealized and Conceptual Diagrams of Traditional, Commuter, and Automobile Cities

Traditional city, e.g., prior to 1850 in Europe (horse carriage– and walking-based transportation)

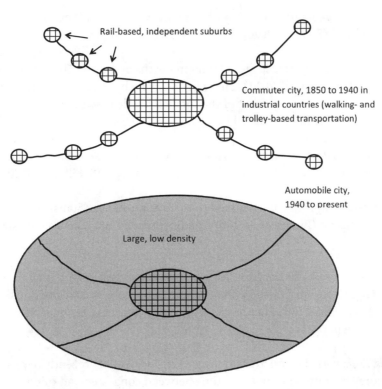

Rail-based, independent suburbs

Commuter city, 1850 to 1940 in industrial countries (walking- and trolley-based transportation)

Automobile city, 1940 to present

Large, low density

Source: Schiller et al. (2010).

Figure 7.1 offers idealized conceptual diagrams of three urban types that are meant to illustrate how the shape and character of cities have changed with available transportation systems. Cities prior to 1850 were highly dense and mixed-use (residential and commercial were mixed together). They reflected the fact that people got around with either their feet or by horse. As rail was established, suburbs began to form along the rail line. The city itself, however, while slowly beginning to grow outward, remained moderately to highly dense, as transportation within the city was limited. The car changed everything, ushering in an almost anything-goes model of urban sprawl. Those previously independent suburbs have since spread out, as has the inner city, making for all intents and purposes one large megacity. And without well-thought-out alternative transportation systems (like those discussed in the Solutions section of this chapter), many urban dwellers today have little choice but to take the car, even perhaps when going just a couple of blocks. I have a friend, for example, who must cross an eight-lane intersection when she wishes to walk to a local grocery store that's less than a mile away.

How can we expect people to abandon their cars if doing so comes at great risk to life and limb?

Fast Facts

More than 1 billion vehicles populate the world today (Sperling and Gordon 2009).

Globally, we drive more than 18 billion miles daily (1 billion of these miles are driven in the United States) (Schiller, Bruun, and Kenworthy 2010).

Road accidents are responsible for 1.3 million deaths and up to 50 million injuries per year globally (Douglas et al. 2011). These figures, which are expected to increase in the years ahead, account for 5 percent of the total global disease burden by 2030 at a cost of roughly US$2.5 *trillion* (Huff 2011).

Road accidents cost developing countries approximately US$100 billion annually (that's twice the amount of aid that's going into these economies) (Schiller et al. 2010).

Noise from road traffic has been linked to sleep disturbance (Stansfeld and Matheson 2003), hypertension (Bluhm et al. 2007), and hyperactivity in children (Stansfeld et al. 2009).

AAA's (formally known as the American Automobile Association) annually calculated "Your Driving Costs" places the average annual cost to own and operate a car in the United States at US$8,776. That breaks down to 58.5 cents per mile, based on 15,000 miles of driving per year.

The Texas Transportation Institute at Texas A&M University recently released a report that measures the difference in travel time between congested and free-flowing conditions (Lomax et al. 2011). Commuters in Chicago and Washington, DC, see on average seventy hours of their lives eaten up by rush-hour traffic every year, followed by those in Los Angeles (sixty-three hours) and Houston (fifty-eight hours). That's not how much time they spend in a car but the *additional time* spent in a car due to congestion. Slightly less than 4 billion gallons of fuels were wasted in 2009 in the United States from traffic congestion.

A 2005 report to the House of Commons estimated the total annual cost of congestion, pollution, and climate change attributable to cars and light vans to be between £9 billion and £46 billion. Additional direct costs associated with road maintenance and policing, which are easier to calculate, were placed at just under £4 billion annually. The costs associated with the depreciation of the asset value of the road network and the cost of investment capital needed to extend the network were £7 billion annually (House of Commons 2010b).

In the United States, transportation accounts for 32 percent of CO_2 energy-related emissions. Approximately 60 percent of these emissions are attributed to the burning of

TABLE 7.1 Annual Cost of Transportation-Related Health Outcomes in the US

HEALTH OUTCOME	COST (IN US$ BILLIONS)	ESTIMATE INCLUDES
Obesity and overweight	142	• Healthcare costs • Lost wages due to illness and disability • Future earnings lost because of premature death
Air pollution from traffic	50–80	• Healthcare costs • Future earnings lost because of premature death
Traffic crashes	180	• Healthcare costs • Lost wages due to injuries • Property damage • Travel delay • Legal/administrative costs • Pain and suffering • Loss of quality of life

Source: Adapted from American Public Health Association (2010).

gasoline, while 22, 12, and 2.8 percent comes from the burning of diesel fuel, jet fuel, and maritime fuels, respectively. CO_2 emissions from transportation have grown an average of 1.5 percent annually since 1990 (Black 2010).

Implications

This section focuses heavily on the automobile due to its ubiquity and oversize ecological footprint. The following represents a brief overview of some of the socioecological impacts associated primarily with this model of transportation. Our understanding of "transportation" broadens considerably when solutions are discussed.

Pollution and Public Health

It's ironic that the very technology to win praise a century ago from street cleaners, public health officials, and politicians because it delivered urban dwellers from a major environmental ill at the time—namely, horse manure that blanketed urban streets—would someday be responsible for far more severe public health threats. Although it is difficult to attach a specific dollar amount to transportation-related health outcomes (though some have tried; see Table 7.1), the car's deleterious effects to public health are obvious.

If we accept the argument that cars helped create urban conditions that eventually made them a necessity (which by definition discourages human-powered forms of transportation), then it is entirely fair to associate the cost of things like obesity to the automobile, as obesity has been closely linked to automobile-centered urban design (Dixon and Broom 2007). The data on this relationship are quite compelling. For example, each additional kilometer walked per day lowers an individual's likelihood of becoming obese by 4.8 percent, whereas each additional hour spent in a car per day is associated with a 6 percent increase (Frank, Andresen, and Schmid 2004). A recent study examining urban sprawl in US metropolitan areas between 1970 and 2000 estimates that had those areas held to their 1970 levels of urban density, their rates of obesity would be 13 percent lower than what they presently are (Zhaoa and Kaestnerb 2010). Other studies have been able to link obesity directly with car use (see, for example, Ewing et al. 2003; Frank, Andresen, and Schmid 2004).

Globally, more than 1.2 million people die each year on roads; another 20 to 50 million suffer nonfatal injuries. The risk of dying on the road is considerably higher in low- and middle-income countries, where fatality rates lie somewhere between 21.5 and 19.5 (per 100,000), respectively. In high-income countries, the rate is 10.3 (per 100,000). This disparity in fatality rates explains why more than 90 percent of the world's road fatalities occur in less affluent countries, even though they have only 48 percent of the world's registered vehicles. As Table 7.2 illustrates, road traffic injuries are a major cause of death for people ages five to forty-four (and among those ages fifteen to twenty-nine, it represents the number-one cause of death). While road traffic injuries are currently the tenth leading cause of death worldwide, the World Health Organization estimates that by 2030, that ranking will be fifth (WHO 2009).

Who are these people dying and getting injured on the world's roads? That again depends on whether the accidents are occurring in high-income or lower-income countries. In the United States and Canada, for instance, 65 percent of reported road deaths involve vehicle occupants. Conversely, in low-income and middle-income countries of the Western Pacific Region (one of the six regions according to the WHO), 70 percent of reported road fatalities are among what are known as "**vulnerable road users**." According to the WHO, this population includes pedestrians, cyclists, and users of motorized two-wheel vehicles (ibid.).

There is also growing evidence pointing to a positive association between exposure to road traffic and aircraft noise and hypertension (high blood pressure) and ischemic heart disease (reduced blood supply to the heart). Road traffic noise is known to increase the risk of ischemic heart disease, including myocardial infarction (heart attacks). And both road traffic noise and aircraft noise have been shown to increase the risk of high blood pressure (WHO 2011). A recent WHO report calculated **disability-adjusted life-years** (DALYs) due to noise pollution for all of Europe, recognizing that the majority of the noise comes from road traffic and airplanes. The WHO defines DALYs as "the sum of years of potential life lost due to premature mortality and the years of productive life lost due to disability" (WHO, n.d.a.). It was estimated that DALYs lost in Europe from environmental noise equated to 61,000 years for ischemic heart disease, 45,000 years for cognitive impairment of children, 903,000 years for sleep disturbance, 22,000 years for tinnitus, and 654,000 years for annoyance. In short, more than 1 million healthy life years are lost annually in Europe due to auto and airplane noise (WHO 2011; see Case Study 7.1).

Source: Adapted from WHO (2009).

TABLE 7.2 Worldwide Leading Causes of Death by Age

RANK	0–4 YEARS	5–14 YEARS	15–29 YEARS	30–44 YEARS	45–69 YEARS	70 AND ABOVE	AGGREGATE AVERAGE
1	Perinatal causes	Lower respiratory infections	Road traffic injuries	HIV/AIDS	Ischemic heart disease	Ischemic heart disease	Ischemic heart disease
2	Lower respiratory infections	Road traffic injuries	HIV/AIDS	Tuberculosis	Cerebro-vascular disease	Cerebro-vascular disease	Cerebro-vascular disease
3	Diarrhea	Malaria	Tuberculosis	Road traffic injuries	HIV/AIDS	Chronic pulmonary disease	Lower respiratory infections
4	Malaria	Drowning	Violence	Ischemic heart disease	Tuberculosis	Lower respiratory infections	Perinatal causes
5	Malaria	Meningitis	Self-inflicted injuries	Self-inflicted injuries	Chronic pulmonary disease	Trachea, bronchus, lung cancers	Chronic pulmonary disease
6	Congenital anomalies	Diarrhea	Lower respiratory infections	Violence	Trachea, bronchus, lung cancers	Diabetes	Diarrhea
7	HIV/AIDS	HIV/AIDS	Drowning	Lower respiratory infections	Cirrhosis of the liver	Heart disease	HIV/AIDS
8	Whooping cough	Tuberculosis	Fire	Cerebro-vascular disease	Road traffic injuries	Stomach cancer	Tuberculosis
9	Meningitis	Protein-energy malnutrition	War and conflict	Cirrhosis of the liver	Lower respiratory infections	Colon and rectum cancers	Trachea, bronchus, lung cancers
10	Tetanus	Fires	Maternal hemorrhage	Poisonings	Diabetes	Nephritis	Road traffic injuries
11	Protein-energy malnutrition	Measles	Ischemic heart disease	Maternal hemorrhage	Self-inflicted injuries	Alzheimer and other dementias	Diabetes
12	Syphilis	Leukemia	Poisonings	Fires	Stomach cancer	Tuberculosis	Malaria
13	Drowning	Congenital anomalies	Abortion	Nephritis	Liver cancer	Liver cancer	Heart disease
14	Road traffic injuries	Trypanosomiasis	Leukemia	Drowning	Breast cancer	Esophagus cancer	Self-inflicted injuries
15	Fires	Falls	Cerebro-vascular disease	Breast cancer	Heart disease	Cirrhosis of the liver	Stomach cancer
→	→	→	→	→		→	→
20	Epilepsy	Poisonings	Malaria	Trachea, bronchus, lung cancers	Mouth and oropharynx cancers	Road traffic injuries	Violence

CASE STUDY 7.1

China's Pollution Problem

A mere 1 percent of China's 560 million city dwellers breathe air considered safe by EU standards. The European Union has determined as unsafe any reading above 40 micrograms of particulate matter (fine dust, soot, and aerosol particles) less than 10 microns in diameter. (At this diameter, particles can pass through the throat and nose and enter the lungs. After being inhaled, they can affect the heart and lungs and cause serious health effects.) The United States has set the threshold at 50 micrograms. In 2006 Beijing's average was 141 micrograms (Kahn and Yardley 2007). In 2007 the World Bank released a study concluding that outdoor air pollution in China was causing 350,000 to 400,000 premature deaths a year (indoor pollution contributed to another 300,000 due to things like poorly ventilated coal- and woodstoves) (World Bank 2007). Although a sizable proportion of China's pollution comes from industrial sources, automobile emissions were shown to play a significant role. Indeed, as the country moves away from older "dirty" coal technology and toward "cleaner" renewables and nuclear technologies, the automobile's emission impact will only grow. It is estimated, for example, that half of the 2012 global growth in auto production will be due to rising demand in China (PWC 2011).

Habitat and Biodiversity

Habitat fragmentation—the emergence of discontinuities (or fragmentation) in an organism's preferred environment (or habitat)—is also a concern when looking at impacts associated with (primarily) the automobile. One of the more well-known examples involves the pygmy possum. The habitat of this threatened marsupial had become highly fragmented thanks to roads and other land-use changes. By constructing tunnels—or what are known in Australia as *talus tunnels* (tunnels of love), as they increase the rate of breeding in an area—to run under roadways, natural movements were restored. In the Netherlands, road mortality in the 1980s accounted for between 20 and 25 percent of total annual badger mortality. The installation of tunnels beneath many of the country's roadways caused national badger populations to increase some 65 percent while simultaneously reducing the animal's road mortality rates to 10 percent. A similar story, but involving panthers, comes from Florida. Roughly half of all panther deaths occurred on roads prior to the 1990s, as the result of collisions. The state has since built a number of underpasses that give animals (panthers included) safe passage beneath the busy four-lane divided interstate highway I-75 (Forman et al. 2002).

Habitat fragmentation has received a lot of attention over the past two decades. In the early 1990s, a five-year-old alpha female wolf, wearing a radio collar containing a satellite transmitter, began a remarkable two-year journey. She was tracked making an unexpectedly large circle, beginning far north, near Banff National Park in Alberta, Canada, then south into Montana, turning west through Idaho into Washington State, before heading north into British Columbia, finally ending up again near Banff. In other words, this wolf's habitat was literally thousands of times the size of Yellowstone National Park (Fraser 2009).

The term *islandization* is often used to talk about the disastrous effects that transportation systems (like multilane roads) can have on wildlife. It refers to the "chunking up" of habitats without **wildlife corridors** (like underpasses and tunnels between roadways) to connect them. Without this connectivity, the isolated plants and wildlife within an "island" risk going extinct. Island populations (an ecological term used to refer to largely isolated populations of species) are also susceptible to disease, overhunting, and major events like floods or fires. With climate change, the issue of connectivity becomes even more significant. As the ecological conditions of habitats change, wildlife are going to need to migrate in order to remain in optimal environments. Without wildlife corridors to facilitate this movement, the future of many species is at risk.

How to connect these islands depends upon the situation and the species in question. Some animals, like badgers and possum, are more comfortable using tunnels under roadways. Other animals, such as deer, cross at higher rates when given the opportunity to go over the road, in which case a wildlife overpass may be the preferred option. To enhance their effectiveness, vegetation has proven to be an important component to overpasses, as it reduces noise and creates a visual wall between the animals and traffic (O'Brian 2006).

Community

There is also compelling evidence pointing to the car's adverse impact on communities. Robert Putman's famous book *Bowling Alone* (2001) is often cited for single-handedly bringing this link into popular light, through the conceptual lens of "social capital" (see ECOnnection 7.1). Putman's extensive research led him to conclude that "the car and the commute . . . are demonstrably bad for community life." He continues by noting that "each additional ten minutes in daily commuting time cuts involvement in community affairs by 10 percent—fewer public meetings attended, fewer committees chaired, fewer petitions signed, fewer church services attended, less volunteering, and so on." In sum, though not quite as powerful an influence on civic involvement as education, commuting time "is more important than almost any other demographic factor" (ibid.:213).

Research generally supports Putman's conclusions. For example, Freeman (2001) shows that high dependence on the automobile is positively associated with weakened neighborhood social ties. Other studies suggest that the emotional and intellectual development of children is enhanced in more walkable, mixed-use communities, most likely due to a combination of increased opportunities for physical activity, independence, and community cohesion (Gilbert and O'Brien 2005; Litman 2010). Automobile reliance is found to have a strong negative impact on whether an individual visits friends or participates in out-of-home sports and cultural activities, and a positive effect on in-home and potentially asocial amusements such as watching television.

One of the more extensive studies looking at the links between the automobile and community health comes out of Harvard University's Department of Government (see Williamson 2002). Based on some thirty thousand interviews from forty different US

ECOnnection 7.1

Social Capital

Social capital formalizes what we all intuitively know: that who we know matters as much as what we know. A growing literature over the past two decades shows that social capital—social networks and the norms of trust and reciprocity that come with frequent social interaction—is central to community well-being. Norms of trust and reciprocity enhance social interaction much the same way cash enhances trade, namely, by allowing action to be taken without having to separately negotiate the terms of every exchange. But how? "Dense" social networks make it easier for individuals (and the community as a whole) to discover who should not be trusted. They also create a significant incentive to live up to people's trust expectations, as failing to do so will result in an immediate loss in reputation across the community as a whole. More generally, social capital makes working with others easier, enhances information flow across the community, encourages cooperative behavior, and reduces the likelihood of unproductive "defensive" behaviors (like locking doors, avoiding going out for walks at night, and so forth) (Sander 2002). Yet social capital can also have a dark side, as it can result in community exclusion, group think, and a general distrust of outsiders if levels of **"bridging" social capital** (networks between groups) are not present at concentrations comparable to **"bonding" social capital** forms (networks within groups).

geographical settings, this research paints an unflattering picture of the car as a vehicle (pun intended) of civic disengagement. Findings to come out of this research include:

- The lower the percentage of solo commuters in one's ZIP code, the more likely an individual is to belong to a political organization, attend a partisan political meeting, attend a demonstration, sign a petition, or vote.
- Living in a high-density area is a positive predictor of membership in a political organization, attendance at demonstrations, and signing a petition (even after controlling for central-city residence status and an individual's interest in politics).
- Residence in a very high density area is associated with membership in a local reform group.
- Residents of neighborhoods built before 1950 (which is a strong predictor of being a walkable neighborhood) are significantly more likely to belong to a political organization, attend a partisan political event, attend a march or demonstration, vote in a national election, or attend a public meeting (even after controlling for central-city residence status).
- A long commute is a very strong predictor of a reduced number of friends and attendance at public meetings and a modestly strong predictor of reduced social trust and reduced membership in groups.
- Neighborhood-level (ZIP code) commuting time is a very strong predictor of reduced social trust and even a stronger predictor than individual commuting time (if your neighbors are stuck in traffic every day, the fact that your commute is short isn't going to do much to increase your social interaction with them).

ECOnnection 7.2

Community Severance

Community severance is an important social impact associated with transportation (Geurs, Boon, and Van Wee 2009). It can be defined as a real or perceived barrier to people's movement through an area that is created by the transportation infrastructure (like roads or rails) or traffic. Whereas physical severance is the most obvious type, there are also psychological and social forms. An example of the former might be having a fear of crossing busy roads, whereas an example of the latter could be when one's friendships do not go beyond the barrier in question, thus creating less of a social need to traverse any particular physical structure. Groups most adversely affected by severance include those without cars, those with restricted mobility—most notably the disabled and elderly—and schoolchildren (Markovich and Lucas 2011).

- Commuting time is inversely associated with an individual's subjective levels of personal happiness as well as their levels of happiness toward their community.

Pointing to these findings, the author of the study explains that "there is good reason, from a civic point of view, to encourage forms of community design that reduce commuting time and to encourage the preservation and increased livability of both our older neighborhoods and our central cities." He goes on to point out that "the biggest payoff, at least from a political participation point of view, appears to be in getting Americans out of their cars" (Williamson 2002:243).

Precisely *how* we do this, however, he does not say. What we do know is that many current urban planning practices tend to reduce community interaction by favoring vehicular mobility over alternative modes such as walking, cycling, and public transit. Traffic engineers generally evaluate transportation systems based on things like vehicle traffic speeds and road capacity, even if this practice degrades the pedestrian environment and reduces community cohesion (Litman 2010; see ECOnnection 7.2).

Solutions

There is no going back. Having organized society over the past century around the automobile, we cannot pretend that those structures—whether made of concrete and reinforcing steel bars or of long-held habits and routines—are of no sociological consequence (Cohen 2012). There are, however, a number of ways forward that reduce the impacts addressed in the previous section, as I'll now explain.

Dense, Livable, Intermodal Cities

I've already talked a little about the potential ecological benefits associated with the high-density city, particularly in affluent nations, where the financial resources are available to maximize those benefits. We already know that population density is negatively

FIGURE 7.2 Urban Density and Transport-Related Energy Consumption, Select Cities

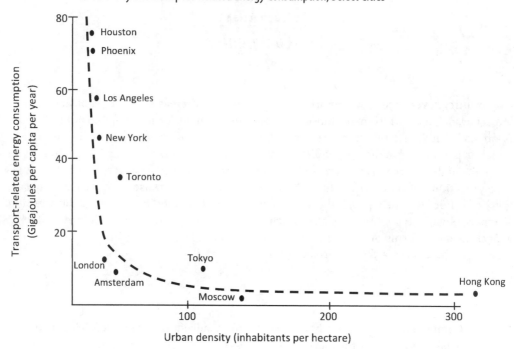

The dotted line represents the regression line when all cities are plotted (a regression line comes as close to all points as possible through a scatterplot of two variables). With more than 7 million inhabitants packed onto an island of roughly 426 square miles, residents of Hong Kong never have to travel very far to get anywhere—a reality that also makes public transportation highly attractive from an urban planning standpoint. The city of Houston, conversely, spreads 2.1 million inhabitants over 656 square miles. This lower density not only means Houstonians have to travel on average farther than residents of Hong Kong, but they do so (in most instances) using an inefficient mode of transportation: the automobile. This level of urban sprawl makes the car nearly the only option for many of the inhabitants of this iconic Texas city. *Source:* UNEP/GRID-Arendal.

associated with transportation-related energy consumption at the per capita level (see Figure 7.2). Dense cities come with reduced travel distances for the average inhabitant to things like work and social visits. Urban density also reduces the transactions costs for building a viable public transportation system, as the network can service more people per unit of track than is possible in sprawled-out cities.

One of the ecological benefits associated with mass public transit lies in its vehicle per passenger fuel efficiencies, especially when maxed to capacity. Table 7.3 documents the energy efficiency of various passenger modes, in terms of miles per gallon (mpg) and per-passenger mpg (for average and maximum capacity). The Toyota Prius's respectable 238 mpg per passenger (when fully loaded up with five occupants) pales in comparison to intercity rail, high-speed rail, the London Underground, or light rail, which, when fully loaded with passengers, register 560 mpg per passenger, 767 mpg per passenger, 1,125 mpg per passenger, and 2,460 mpg per passenger, respectively.

There are also social benefits that come when one abandons the solo commute for something less isolating (see Case Study 7.2). Recent research indicates that public

TABLE 7.3 Energy Efficiency of Various Passenger Modes (Land, Air, and Water)

MODE (EXAMPLE)	MPG	AVERAGE NO. PASSENGERS (MPG PER PERSON)	MAXIMUM NO. PASSENGERS (MPG PER PERSON)
Scooter (50cc engine)	75	1 (75)	2 (150)
Medium motorcycle (Suzuki GS500)	60	1 (60)	2 (120)
Hybrid auto (Toyota Prius)	47.6	1.5 (72)	5 (238)
Very small auto, highway (Smart Car)	41	1.5 (62)	2 (82)
Very small auto, city (Smart Car)	33	1.2 (40)	2 (66)
SUV, highway (Fort Explorer, V8)	21.6	2 (43)	7 (151)
SUV, city (Fort Explorer, V8)	14.1	1.2 (17)	7 (98)
40-foot diesel transit bus	3.1	25 (78)	90 (279)
40-foot trolley bus	9.77	30 (293)	77 (752)
Light rail	13.6	65 (887)	180 (2,460)
London Underground	7.4	19 (141)	152 (1,125)
Intercity rail (Swedish Railways Regina)	3.35	34 (114)	167 (560)
High-speed rail (LGV Atlantique; runs from Paris to western France)	1.58	291 (460)	485 (767)
Private small airplane (Cessna 172)	12.6	1 (12.6)	4 (50.4)
Regional turboprop (DHC 8-300)	1.19	35 (41.7)	137 (58.9)
Short/medium-range airliner (Boeing 737; average flight, 607 miles)	0.43	96 (41.3)	137 (58.9)
Medium/long-range airliner (Airbus 320, average flight, 1,358 miles)	0.447	109 (48.7)	156 (69.7)
Very-long-distance airliner (Boeing 777-200ER, average flight, 6,818 miles)	0.252	211 (53.1)	301 (75.8)
Passenger-only ferry (Vancouver SeaBus)	0.25	140 (35)	400 (100)
Passenger and car ferry (BC Ferries Spirit Class)	0.0246	1,000 (24.6)	2,100 (51.7)
Transoceanic luxury ship (Queen Mary 2-25 knots)	0.00753	2,000 (15)	3,090 (23.2)

Vehicles are typically designed to carry more than just one passenger. Indeed, some—like transoceanic luxury ships—can accommodate thousands. It is therefore inaccurate (and unfair) to compare modes of transportation by their miles per gallon without also factoring in for the number of people each can accommodate at any given time (or on average). Table 7.3 shows the miles per gallon if only one person rode each mode of transportation in addition to the miles per gallon per person according to both average capacity and maximum capacity per mode. *Source:* Adapted from Schiller et al. (2010).

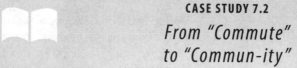

CASE STUDY 7.2

From "Commute" to "Commun-ity"

Bus riders on Victoria Island have transformed their hourlong work commute to and from Victoria into an exercise in community building. Everyday riders on the No. 61 play games, buy and sell goods (like free-range eggs and crafts), have sing-alongs, and plan social events with each other. "It's a small town unto itself," one rider quips. Treats and snacks occasionally get handed out, especially during the holidays, when home-baked goods are shared. One rider keeps an e-mail distribution list of all the other riders. Riders even routinely hang out outside the bus. A recent Christmas dinner attracted forty riders and family members. As one rider explained, the commutes feel like good old-fashioned house visits, as the buses are climate controlled and comfortable: "You start to feel like it's your living room and that's created a social networking opportunity" (Hatherly 2008).

transportation, for instance, can increase social capital for individuals and neighborhoods as a whole (Currie and Stanley 2008). And among those unable to drive, such as the elderly and disabled, having alternatives to the car is central to improving their integration within a community as well as to providing access to such life-sustaining phenomena as food and health care (Banister and Bowling 2004).

Yet just having alternatives to the automobile is rarely enough to make people choose to leave their cars in the garage. Multimodality is great, as it means individuals have multiple modes to choose from. But without intermodality—the ability to make efficient connections between modes—those alternative choices are rarely as attractive for many as the car. For example, if you still have to walk ten blocks after getting off the nearest light-rail stop to get to your friend's house, you'll likely choose to take the automobile more often than not (see Case Study Box 7.5). Just what those connections will involve will vary from community to community, depending upon what those communities value (see Ethical Question Box 7.1). The overarching goal, however, is the same: to make alternative modes as attractive as—or ideally more attractive than—the car.

We are presently doing a lot to incentive driving. For example, many federal, state, and local government tax policies prioritize motor vehicle use. Fuel is exempt from general taxes in many jurisdictions. Land devoted to public roads and parking facilities is exempt from rent and taxes. And oil companies are given significant tax exemptions and subsidies (Litman 2010). Large taxpayer-funded roads represent a significant portion of land that cannot be taxed, while being of benefit primarily to private motorists. Similarly, private lands are typically taxed at a lower rate when paved over to make a parking lot (ibid.).

Let's talk more about free parking: if it were not in such abundance (especially in the United States), do you think we would have as much of an incentive to drive? And who pays for that "free" parking? We all do, as taxpayers, regardless of whether you use it. Many current zoning codes also favor automobile-oriented land-use patterns, which

CASE STUDY 7.3
Montreal's
BIXI

One successful bike-sharing scheme that began in 2009 is Montreal's BIXI—short for *bike* and *taxi*. City leaders have made clear goals to reduce greenhouse gas emissions and to make the city more livable. In addition to expanding the city's bike paths, the city made bikes more widely available to people of all socioeconomic backgrounds. The city also set out to provide bike-share docking stations all around the city. City leaders realized early on that bike-sharing schemes would be successful only if they were convenient, which meant docking stations needed to be on almost every block of the city. If people were forced to walk far to return a bike, they wouldn't use the service.

BIXI launched with three thousand bikes and docking stations located never more than a thousand feet apart. Many were located out-side subway stops to encourage people to take a bike (versus their car) to finish their trips. The bikes are designed with sealed components (e.g., brakes, chain, and so on) to make them resistant to abuse. And if not returned (stolen), the bikes are implanted with a radio frequency identification chip that tells the city planners their location. This technology also allows the bike's brakes to be locked remotely, which permanently disables it until returned.

BIXI has been a tremendous success. After just four months, BIXI had more than seventy-seven thousand resident users (this was also around the time that the millionth ride was logged). The program has proven so popular that the city added two thousand bikes and more than one hundred stations a full year ahead of schedule (Botsman and Rogers 2010).

include things like density restrictions, single-use zoning, and, yes, minimum parking requirements. To drive or not to drive? What at first blush looks like an individual choice starts looking more and more like a decision that was largely made for us long ago (see ECOnnection 7.3).

We also know, following the "fundamental law of highway congestion" first articulated back in the early 1960s (Downs 1962), that something different *must* be done. More roads, in the long term, only make traffic congestion worse (see Case Study 7.4). The fundamental law of highway congestion is this: any increase in road capacity will be met with a proportional (or greater) increase in traffic volume. In one recent study, a 10 percent increase in the interstate network within the typical urban country was met with a 10.3 percent increase in vehicle kilometers traveled on those roads (Duranton and Turner 2009). In this case, congestion actually *grew* with an increase in road capacity, as the additional lanes led to more people driving more frequently.

From Street Hierarchy to Interconnectivity

Urban planners have also been incentivizing the car—and disincentivizing alternatives—in how they have gone about laying out streets. Prior to the automobile, street systems maximized connectivity, as evidenced by the relatively high number of street intersections per square mile in older communities. Think about preautomobile city

ETHICAL QUESTION 7.1
Value Judgments Embedded in Transportation Policy

Value judgments are unavoidable in transportation policy. You can't value all transportation forms equally. If we decide we want dense, walkable cities, for example, we will need to stop giving priority to the automobile, recognizing that it creates an urban scale much too expansive (e.g., sprawl) for our feet. Below are some of the thorny questions embedded in any comprehensive transportation policy:

- Whose trips do we prioritize—individual citizens or freight interests?
- Which trips do we prioritize—work commutes, long-distance freight, local goods distribution, or leisure?

- Which transportation services—whether entire modes (e.g., light rail) or components of specific modes (e.g., free parking)—should be supported with public funding, and which should be left to individuals and private-sector interests?
- Should mobility be thought of as a right, recognizing that those unable to drive—most notably the elderly and disabled—can be dangerously isolated in communities where the car is the only transportation option?

Adapted from Schiller et al. (2010).

 ## ECOnnection 7.3
High-Occupancy Vehicle Lanes

High-occupancy vehicle (HOV) lanes are for automobiles, at least in the United States, carrying two or more passengers. (It says something about our transportation values when a car with *two* people is considered "high occupancy.") The goal of HOV lanes is to encourage ride sharing and thus reduce the total automobile volume on roads. There are a couple of inherent problems with ride sharing, however, that disincentivize its use. For one, the total commute time must be significant to overcome the time lost while waiting for the carpool to arrive and during travel when picking up and dropping off fellow carpoolers. In many cases,

these additional "costs" more than offset the savings from traveling in the HOV lane. There are also what might be called "inconveniences"—different schedules, the need to run errands during the trip, and so on—that further make ride sharing unattractive to commuters.

So, do they work? Between 50 to 80 percent of HOV lanes are used by members of the same households. Other significant users are friends on an outing or a date. In other words, HOV lanes are overwhelmingly used by people who would have "carpooled" anyway.

Schiller et al. (2010).

CASE STUDY 7.4
"Daylighting" the Cheonggyecheon Stream in South Korea

For more than fifty years, concrete (in the form of a major freeway) entombed a three-mile stretch of the Cheonggyecheon Stream that ran through the heart of Seoul, South Korea. It was finally liberated in 2001, when the former chief executive officer (CEO) of Hyundai Engineering and Construction, Lee Myung-bak, was elected mayor of Seoul. One campaign promise was to remove the freeway and restore the Cheonggyecheon stream. This practice of uncovering previously concealed natural amenities (like streams) is known as **"daylighting"** within the urban planning community. Four years (and US$384 million) later, the Cheonggyecheon was flowing freely through the heart of downtown Seoul (see Image 7.1).

The project has enhanced the quality of life, public health, and social interaction of those living downtown (though it has increased the property values near the stream, pushing some poorer families out). Roughly ninety thousand pedestrians visit the stream banks on an average day. Biodiversity along the Cheonggyecheon has increased, with the number of fish, bird, and insect species expanding from 4 to 25, 6 to 36, and 15 to 192, respectively. Air pollution along the corridor has decreased, now that the tens of thousands of cars are gone. Small-particle air pollution along the corridor dropped to forty-eight micrograms per cubic meter from seventy-four. Moreover, summer temperatures are now routinely five degrees cooler near the stream than in nearby areas (due to a reduced-heat island effect). Finally, even with the loss of a major freeway, traffic speeds in the areas have actually *increased* thanks to transportation changes such as expanded bus services, restrictions on cars, and higher parking fees.

Lonsdorf (2011); Revkin (2009).

IMAGE 7.1 Cheonggyecheon Stream in Seoul

Source: Ken Smith Landscape Architect, © 2010.

centers—as found in any European city—and note the narrowness of streets and the diverse ways that they interconnect. Connectivity in these spaces exists because these street systems provide multiple paths to reach surrounding major streets.

In the twentieth century, a concept known as **street hierarchy** came to dominate urban planning. Street hierarchy seeks to eliminate connections, funneling traffic "up" the hierarchy. Cul-de-sac streets are at the lowest level of the hierarchy, followed by primary or secondary "collector" streets. At this point, traffic is fed onto arterial streets (also occasionally called a boulevard), eventually ending up on intercity highways, which rest atop the hierarchy. This system has become a ubiquitous feature of the landscape in most "modern" cities (see Case Study 7.5).

A more interconnected street model is often criticized for the fact that it actually seeks to slow traffic down (a tough selling point in countries like the United States). Yet we must keep in mind that by resisting congestion, these systems also *save* us a tremendous amount of time that is otherwise lost in bumper-to-bumper traffic. Moreover, we are learning that as speeds slow down in a transportation system, the *scale* of the urban landscape is reduced too, thus making speed less important. In other words, communities that have slowed down no longer need the range and speed provided by the automobile—a truly remarkable discovery.

An excellent example of this comes to us from Home Depot. Store location and size formula for this company depend heavily on two factors: the income range of families living in the "service area" and the number of trips per day through the nearest intersection to the proposed site. "Service area" is an estimation of what's a reasonable distance people would drive to get to the store. Thus, the more taxpayers spend on hierarchical car-oriented infrastructure, the larger the "service area"—and thus the store and parking lot—will be. Yet, given the aforementioned fundamental law of congestion, forces are exerting themselves on today's auto-oriented system in such a way that is making congestion inevitable. In response, Home Depot has recently altered the formula used to calculate store location and size, leading the firm to build smaller stores more frequently spaced across the urban landscape (Condon 2010). They realize traffic congestion is essentially *shrinking* the distance consumers are willing to cover in their cars. This is an interesting development. A major concern has been finding alternatives to the automobile that mimic its speed and range. Yet the Home Depot example contradicts this assumption, indicating that cities may actually scale down as we slow down. Quite a counterintuitive finding: that one strategy for decreasing the time we spend going from point A to point B is *to slow down*.

Some other benefits of slowing down: pedestrian safety. Research examining Longmont, Colorado, cataloged and entered into a database some twenty thousand police accident reports (Swift, Painter, and Goldstein 2006). Each accident location was mapped and described by several physical characteristics. To compare injury accidents per mile per year against other factors, several correlations were explored. The most significant relationship to injury accidents was street width. The authors of the study explain that "as street widths widen, accidents per mile per year increase exponentially, and the safest residential street width are the narrowest" (ibid.:1).

What about, for example, fire-equipment access? Even here, the data do not support the need for either wide roads or the street-hierarchy model. No difference was detected in fire-related fatalities or response times between communities with narrow streets

---

CASE STUDY 7.5

Breaking Through the Street Hierarchy

In Salem, Oregon, new development plans must include street assignments according to the street hierarchy before they can be approved. In 2003 the designers of a new sustainable community submitted plans without assigning streets according to this hierarchy. They argued that their plans sought to distribute traffic throughout the network rather than concentrate it in a few arterial streets. City planners, noting their hands were tied, demanded the inclusion of a street hierarchy as stipulated by the city code. The designers reluctantly identified the new community's street with shops and community facilities like libraries and schools as the arterial. This, in turn, caught the eye of school district officials, noting that their policy expressly prohibited elementary schools located on "arterial" streets. So the school was relocated to a less accessible cul-de-sac, with ample space for parents to drop off and pick up their children . . . in their cars.

Condon (2010).

---

and those with wider ones (Swift et al. 2006). Any costs that come with narrower streets are more than offset by increased housing density, which reduces overall travel distance, and the benefit of having multiple routes to choose from (Condon 2010).

Disincentivizing the Car

How might we go about making the car a less attractive form of transportation? I have already discussed the importance of making the alternatives more attractive; after all, we can't expect people to choose to leave their cars at home if the alternatives take appreciably more time, cost more money, and might even be dangerous. What has not been discussed, however, are ways to make the car more costly to drive, a move that would effectively make alternatives immediately more attractive. Before criticizing such a scheme, remember all the money we already spend to incentivize the car (which makes any such criticism seem more than a bit insincere and hollow). In light of all these incentivizing structures, I am not a bit surprised that the vast majority of individuals in affluent nations "choose" to drive (though this might be changing; see ECOnnection 7.4). Who wouldn't choose an activity when they're paying for only a fraction of its real costs?

One widely discussed policy mechanism is a gas tax (or a further increase in existing gas taxes). The economic models are pretty clear as to their efficacy: such a tax would encourage consumers to drive less, switch from two vehicles to one, or buy more fuel-efficient vehicles (Fullerton and Gan 2005). In addition to encouraging motorists to drive less, such taxes would signal to manufacturers to incorporate fuel-saving technologies in new vehicles (in response to consumers' choosing smaller, fuel-efficient vehicles) (Parry 2005). If implemented, however, we would need to make sure this tax wasn't regressive and therefore not unduly burdensome to those already socially and

ECOnnection 7.4

Have Cars Reached Their Peak?

As I've ready mentioned, car use globally will continue to climb—China is expected to have more cars than the United States in 2030 (Chamon, Mauro, and Okawa 2008). Yet digging deeper into the data reveals something surprising, indeed almost unbelievable. Years of government travel survey data are leading some (though these findings remain highly contested) to conclude that in high-income nations, car use is either flattening out or in *decline* (see, for example, Goodwin 2012; Schipper 2011). Furthermore, according to these studies, the trends predate 2008, so we can't just chalk them up to the global recession.

Why this might be happening is unclear. Rising fuel costs and road congestion would be the most obvious reasons. Yet other variables are no doubt also at work, some of which possibly include stagnating wages among the middle class, growing income inequality, and increasing vehicle operating costs (Cohen 2012). We also know that younger people today are less enamored with driving and car ownership than generations past. One survey found that 46 percent of American drivers ages eighteen to twenty-four said they would choose having access to the Internet over owning a car (Chozick 2012). In response, car manufacturers are taking major steps to reach out to new drivers. General Motors, for example, recently announced collaborating with MTV Scratch (a unit of Viacom that specializes in connecting with younger consumers) in an attempt to better understand the millennials' (individuals born between 1981 and 2000) market (ibid.).

economically vulnerable. The other population such a tax would immediately impact is commuters. Of course, the goal of such a tax would be to discourage precisely this type of behavior. We must remember, however, that while people commute for a variety of reasons, one is because they cannot afford to live near where they work. I see this variable at play in Fort Collins, Colorado, where my employer (Colorado State University) is located. I know that a number of the janitorial and office staff, who make appreciably less than tenure-track professors, reside in surrounding communities because of the lower housing prices. The fact that I do not commute—I can actually walk to work—is a luxury not everyone can afford.

An even more promising policy is **pay-as-you-drive auto insurance**, where one's insurance rate (but not coverage) is contingent upon, among other things, the amount of miles driven. Nobel Prize–winning economist William Vickrey once quipped, "The manner in which [auto insurance] premiums are computed and paid fails miserably to bring home to the automobile user the costs he [or she] imposes in a manner that will appropriately influence his [or her] decisions" (1968:464). Little has changed in the fifty or so years since Vickrey made these comments. The current lump-sum pricing of auto insurance remains inefficient and inequitable (Parry 2005). It is widely recognized that, just as an all-you-can-eat restaurant encourages more eating, all-you-can-drive insurance pricing encourages more driving, which also means more

CASE STUDY 7.6

The London Congestion Charge

By the late 1990s, more than 1 million people were entering into central London on any given workday. A study from 1998 concluded that the average driver spent almost 30 percent of his or her time stationary during peak traffic periods. In response, a "congestion charge" was proposed in 2000. In 2003 the City of London (which is a small area within Greater London, referring to its historic core) began charging motorists for driving or parking within Central London between 7 a.m. and 6:30 p.m. on weekdays. The standard charge is £10 (approximately US$16) per day.

The number of private vehicles coming into the zone has declined 27 percent, which translated into some sixty-five to seventy thousand fewer daily trips made into the area. Bus, taxi, and bicycle use into Central London, conversely, is up 21, 22, and 28 percent, respectively. The average traffic speed within the zone has increased by almost 17 percent. Traffic has also decreased just outside the zone. Finally, surveys of retailers within the zone indicate that the congestion charge has had no significant effect on total sales (Skousen 2011).

accidents, congestion, and greenhouse gas emissions. It is also terribly inequitable, in that miles driven is positively correlated with income. Low-mileage (and low-income) drivers therefore subsidize insurance costs for high-mileage (high-income) drivers (Bordoff and Noel 2008).

A study by the Brookings Institution calculates that if all motorists in the United States paid for auto insurance on a per-mile basis rather than in a lump sum, driving would decline by 8 percent nationwide, saving society the equivalent of about US$50 billion to $60 billion a year through reduced driving-related harms (ibid.). The study further estimates that this driving reduction would translate into a reduction in CO_2 emissions by 2 percent and oil consumption by about 4 percent. The authors note that it would take a $1-per-gallon increase in the gas tax to achieve the same reduction in driving. Yet unlike the gas tax, which would increase the cost of driving for everyone, roughly two-thirds of all US households would end up actually paying *less* for auto insurance (the average savings is estimated at US$270 per car).

Other strategies to make driving less attractive could include doing away with the ubiquitous free parking, which, as already mentioned, is a significant taxpayer-funded subsidy to motorists. We might also think about eliminating minimum parking requirements that are embedded in city planning codes around the world. Another option would be to increase the cost of registering vehicles, which could be placed on a sliding scale so as to not unfairly impact low-income households. There is also the strategy of literally charging people to access a given area with their car (see Case Study 7.6). Or we could base urban design more around interconnectivity, to reference a point made earlier, and thus allow narrower streets, more intersections, and slower average car speeds to take precedence over the street-hierarchy logic.

There are numerous empirical reasons for criticizing the automobile, from, for example, its negative impacts on the environment, public health, and community cohesion to its links to climate change and air and noise pollution more generally. The good news is that there is nothing about the automobile that makes it an inherently superior form of transportation. Millions around the world "choose" this form of mobility over others not because of some quality inherent to the automobile but because societies have done such a good job of organizing around the car. Organize societies around the alternatives, and consumer "choice" will happily follow (no sense of sacrifice required).

IMPORTANT CONCEPTS

- costs of transportation to public and environmental health and community cohesion
- "free" parking
- fundamental law of highway congestion
- habitat fragmentation
- peak car
- street hierarchy versus interconnectivity

DISCUSSION QUESTIONS

- How has the automobile altered how we plan and organize communities?
- In what ways does society incentivize trips with the automobile and disincentive alternative forms of transportation?
- Some argue people want to continue this love affair with the automobile, as evidenced by the fact of just how many people *choose* to drive—"shame on environmentalists for wanting to go against what people clearly want." How would you rebut this argument?
- What barriers keep you from choosing to leave your car at home and opting for alternative modes of transportation?
- Why might younger people today be less enamored with driving and car ownership than generations past?

SUGGESTED ADDITIONAL READINGS

Eicher, C., and I. Kawachi. 2011. "Social Capital and Community Design." In *Making Healthy Places,* edited by A. Dannenberg, H. Frumkin, and R. Jackson, 117–128. Washington, DC: Island Press.

Ewing, R., K. Bartholomew, and A. Nelson. 2011. "Compactness vs. Sprawl." In *Companion to Urban Design,* edited by T. Banerjee and A. Loukaitou-Sideris, 467–483. New York: Routledge.

Ewing, R., G. Meakins, G. Bjarnson, and M. Hilton. 2011. "Transportation and Land Use." In *Making Healthy Places,* edited by A. Dannenberg, H. Frumkin, and R. Jackson, 149–169. Washington, DC: Island Press.

Midgley, P. 2009. "The Role of Smart Bike-Sharing Systems in Urban Mobility." *Journeys* (May):23–31. Retrieved August 26, 2012 (http://www.ltaacademy.gov.sg/doc/LTA%20 JOURNEYS_IS02.pdf#page=23).

Newman, P., and J. Kenworthy. 2011. "Peak Car Use: Understanding the Demise of Automobile Dependence." *World Transport, Policy, and Practice* 17(2). Retrieved August 26, 2012 (http://www.eco-logica.co.uk/pdf/wtpp17.2.pdf).

RELEVANT INTERNET LINKS

- http://www.nature.org/greenliving/carboncalculator/index.htm
  Calculate your carbon footprint.
- http://www.organiclinker.com/food-miles.cfm
  Calculate the distance the food from your last meal has traveled (a.k.a. its food miles).
- http://planetgreen.discovery.com/games-quizzes/transportation-footprint-quiz/
  Calculate your transportation footprint.
- http://www.youtube.com/watch?v=dH9ygL1AAII
  Short video of the recently "daylighted" Cheonggyecheon River in Seoul, South Korea (mentioned in Case Study Box 7.4).
- http://www.youtube.com/watch?v=LRrl7LwNUtw
  Short video segment from *CBS Sunday Morning* on new urbanism—a movement in urban planning circles that seeks to create more mobile, livable communities.

SUGGESTED VIDEOS

- *The End of Suburbia* (2004)
  Documentary on how decades of cheap energy created cities and suburbs as we know them today.
- *Revenge of the Electric Car* (2011)
  Four different automobile visionaries race to capture the electric car market.
- *Subdivided* (2007)
  About life in contemporary suburbia, where individuals suffer from isolation and struggle to find and maintain community.
- *Taken for a Ride* (1996)
  http://www.youtube.com/watch?v=rAc4w11Yzys. An older but still excellent documentary about how American public mass transit was undermined and systematically destroyed during the first half of the twentieth century by General Motors and other firms.
- *Who Killed the Electric Car?* (2006)
  Details General Motors' efforts to hinder their own electric-car research and development.

8

Food: From Farm to Fork

Few things are as obviously social *and* ecological as food and agriculture. Clearly, we need food to survive. As for *what* constitutes "food"—that too is a social act. Take bugs: an example of how one culture's "pest" is another's "delicacy." As for agriculture, its links to the environment are obvious even to the uninitiated. *How* we produce food is also sociologically relevant, impacting society at all scales, from rural communities to entire nations. And how we've gone about feeding ourselves has changed drastically over the years.

One of the more consequential innovations in agriculture over the past two hundred years has been the substitution of capital for labor—known widely as the "**mechanical revolution**." Examples vary widely: from the cotton gin in 1793, which separated the cotton lint from the seed (and initially increased the demand for slave labor in US southern slave states) to the threshing machine in 1816, which separated grain from the stalk; the John Deere steel plow in 1837, which turned the soil cleanly, thereby minimizing the drag that bogged down earlier plows; and Cyrus McCormick's reaper in 1834, which cut grain. Later in the nineteenth century came the tractor, which, unlike the horses it replaced, did not require food, water, or sleep and allowed the land used previously to raise hay and oats to feed one's horses to instead be put toward the production of commodities for sale.

This capital intensification (and energy intensification) had clear impacts on the **structure of agriculture**, at least in countries where this transition is well under way. (The term *structure of agriculture* is shorthand to describe how farms, rural populations, and agribusiness firms are arranged to produce and distribute food and fiber.) Take, for example, the United States, where the requisite human hours to farm an acre of corn dropped rapidly throughout the first half of the twentieth century due in no small part to mechanization: from thirty-eight hours per acre in 1900 to thirty-three in 1920–1924, twenty-eight in 1930–1934, and twenty-five in 1940–1944 (and by 1955–1959, the figure had dropped to only ten hours of labor per acre). A study conducted by Iowa State College (now Iowa State University) in the 1930s concluded that a hired husker left between three and five bushels of corn per acre when the harvest occurred by hand. By comparison, a mechanical corn picker left two to three bushels. In addition, hired huskers charged on average US$2.00 per acre, whereas custom mechanical pickers charged roughly US$1.25 to US$1.50 per acre. It is not surprising, then, that by 1938, between

33 and 50 percent of the laborers previously hired to handpick corn were replaced by mechanical pickers (Colbert 2000). The mechanical revolution was favored early on in the rapidly expanding agricultural sector in the United States, especially in the Midwest and Great Plains, where land was plentiful but labor scarce (Pfeffer 1983).

Mechanization, in turn, also encourages specialization and scale increases at the farm level. Though not the only force driving the specialization trends illustrated in Table 8.1, the mechanization of agriculture undoubtedly contributed to the state's shrinking commodity basket. Iowa, depicted in the table, is representative of the commodity erosion occurring throughout much of the world where grains and livestock are raised for export and agroindustrial purposes (e.g., feed for livestock, biofuels, high fructose corn syrup, Chicken McNuggets, and so on). Why is mechanization at least partially responsible for this? It makes economic sense to spread the cost of these expensive capital investments over as much land as possible, which, from a labor standpoint, is relatively easy to do, as mechanization allows one or two individuals to work large tracts of land in a short amount of time.

This represents the barest of introductions into the incredibly nuanced and increasingly complex subject of food production (for more detail, see, for example, Carolan, 2011b, 2012). Just remember that food systems are not static; they're continually changing, as are their impacts. Although the impacts about to be discussed are significant, it is heartening to know it doesn't have to be this way. These systems did not just appear. As products of our (society's) own creation, we hold the collective capacity to re-create them.

Fast Facts

It is estimated that each resident of the United States requires approximately two thousand liters a year in oil equivalents to eat as they do (with animal products accounting for half of this figure). This represents about 19 percent of the total energy used annually in the country (Pimentel et al. 2008).

The annual external costs of agriculture in Germany, the United Kingdom, and the United States have been estimated at US$2 billion, US$3.8 billion, and US$34.7 billion, respectively (Pretty et al. 2001).

The cumulative weight of both solid and liquid animal waste in China is approximately 4 billion tons annually. This represents an amount 4.1 times greater than what the country produces in industrial waste. One twenty-five-hundred-head dairy farm produces as much excrement as a city with roughly 411,000 residents (EPA 2004).

A conservative estimate is that animal agriculture is responsible for approximately 18 percent of total greenhouse gas emissions annually (Stehfest et al. 2009), though other estimates, such as that from the Worldwatch Institute (Goodland and Anhang 2009), place the figure as high as 51 percent.

The thirty largest countries (economy-wise) spend roughly US$365 billion annually—that's *$1 billion* a day—on food and agricultural subsidies, with the majority going to

TABLE 8.1 Number of Commodities Produced for Sale in at Least One Percent (1%) of all Iowa Farms (1920 to 2007, Various)

1920 (%)	1935 (%)	1945 (%)	1954 (%)	1964 (%)	1978 (%)	1987 (%)	1997 (%)	2002 (%)	2007 (%)
Horses (95)	Cattle (94)	Cattle (92)	Corn (91)	Corn (87)	Corn (90)	Corn (79)	Corn (68)	Corn (58)	Corn (54)
Cattle (95)	Horse (93)	Chicken (91)	Cattle (89)	Cattle (81)	Soybeans (68)	Soybeans (65)	Soybeans (62)	Soybeans (54)	Soybeans (45)
Chicken (95)	Chicken (93)	Corn (91)	Oats (83)	Hogs (69)	Cattle (60)	Cattle (47)	Hay (42)	Hay (37)	Hay (28)
Corn (94)	Corn (93)	Horses (84)	Chicken (82)	Hay (62)	Hay (56)	Hay (46)	Cattle (42)	Cattle (35)	Cattle (32)
Hogs (89)	Hogs (83)	Hogs (81)	Hogs (79)	Soybeans (57)	Hogs (50)	Hogs (35)	Hogs (19)	Horses (13)	Horses (11)
Apples (84)	Hay (82)	Hay (80)	Hay (72)	Oats (57)	Oats (34)	Oats (25)	Oats (12)	Hogs (11)	Hogs (09)
Hay (82)	Potatoes (64)	Oats (74)	Horses (42)	Horses (48)	Horses (13)	Horses (10)	Horses (11)	Oats (08)	Oats (03)
Oats (81)	Apples (56)	Apples (41)	Soybeans (37)	Chicken (26)	Chicken (09)	Sheep (08)	Sheep (04)	Sheep (04)	Sheep (04)
Potatoes (62)	Oats (52)	Soybeans (40)	Potatoes (18)	Sheep (17)	Sheep (08)	Chicken (05)	Chicken (02)	Chicken (02)	Goats (02)
Cherries (57)	Cherries (34)	Grapes (23)	Sheep (16)	Potatoes (06)	Wheat (01)	Ducks (01)	Goats (01)		
Wheat (36)	Grapes (28)	Potatoes (23)	Ducks (05)	Wheat (03)	Goats (01)	Goats (01)			
Plums (29)	Plums (28)	Cherries (20)	Apples (05)	Sorghum (02)	Ducks (01)	Wheat (01)			
Grapes (28)	Sheep (21)	Peaches (16)	Cherries (04)	Rdclover (02)					
Ducks (18)	Peaches (16)	Sheep (16)	Peaches (04)	Apples (02)					
Geese (18)	Pears (16)	Plums (15)	Goats (04)	Ducks (02)					
Stwberry (17)	Mules (13)	Pears (13)	Grapes (03)	Goats (02)					
Pears (17)	Ducks (12)	Rdclover (10)	Pears (03)	Geese (01)					
Mules (14)	Wheat (12)	Mules (06)	Plums (03)						
Sheep (14)	Geese (11)	Stwberry (06)	Wheat (03)						
Timothy (10)	Sorghum (09)	Ducks (06)	Rdclover (03)						
Peaches (09)	Barley (09)	Wheat (04)	Geese (03)						
Bees (09)	Rdclover (09)	Timothy (04)	Popcorn (02)						
Barley (09)	Stwberry (08)	Geese (03)	Timothy (02)						
Raspbry (07)	Soybeans (08)	Swtpatoe (02)	Swtpatoe (02)						
Turkeys (07)	Raspbry (06)	Rye (02)	Swtcorn (02)						
Wtmelon (06)	Bees (05)	Popcorn (02)	Turkeys (01)						
Sorghum (06)	Timothy (05)	Swtcorn (02)							
Goosebry (03)	Turkeys (04)	Turkeys (01)							
Swt corn (02)	Rye (02)								
Apricots (02)	Sorghum (01)								
Tomatoes (02)									
Cabbage (01)									
Popcorn (01)									
Currents (01)									
n = 34	**n = 33**	**n = 29**	**n = 26**	**n = 17**	**n = 12**	**n = 12**	**n = 10**	**n = 9**	**n = 9**

Source: Based on data from the US Census of Agriculture, 1920–2007.

agribusinesses and very large landowners. In the European Union, for instance, the Dutch firm Campina (a Dutch dairy cooperative that merged with Royal Frieslands Foods in 2008) received €1.6 billion in agricultural subsidies between 1997 and 2009, whereas the Denmark-based firm Arla Foods Amba was paid just less than €1 billion between 1999 and 2009 (Carolan 2011b).

At the height of the global food crisis in 2008, millions of Haitians resorted to eating biscuits made out of mud, oil, and sugar (Katz 2008). At the same time, agribusinesses were reporting record profits. For example, during the first quarter of 2008, Cargill, ADM (Archer Daniels Midland), and Bunge saw their net earnings rise 86, 55, and 189 percent, respectively (McMichael 2009).

Global demand for phosphorus is expected to increase anywhere from 50 to 100 percent by 2050 as a result of increases in global meat consumption (grains [grown using copious amounts of fertilizer] are used for feed), food demand, and biofuel production (Cordell, Drangert, and White 2009). In light of predicted future demand, global supplies of phosphate are expected to peak in approximately thirty years (White and Cordell 2008).

Implications

At the risk of overgeneralizing, the impacts discussed in this section refer to those associated with what we might call the global **food system**, which can be defined as the entire array of activities—from input production and distribution to on-farm activities, marketing, processing, wholesale, and retail—that connect seed (and gene) to the mouths of consumers. To speak of a "system" is to make reference not just to certain agricultural practices but also (and equally) to regulatory, economic, and legal structures that reinforce the use of those practices (and even the ecological base that makes it all possible). Food production impacts more than our stomachs, touching our lives in a variety of ways.

Environmental Impacts

Where to begin? Let's start with water. As I have already discussed agriculture's link to water in Chapter 5, this discussion will be brief.

Commodities, it is important to know, have wildly different water requirements. Table 8.2 shows the virtual water content and calories-to-water ratios of different agricultural commodities. By far the thirstiest commodity is beef, requiring 12.56 cubic meters of water for every kilogram of live weight gain. Potatoes and other starchy roots, conversely, need a mere 0.23 cubic meters of water for every kilogram produced. As measured by the calories-to-water ratio, intensively raised beef again performs poorly, producing 161 kilocalories (kcal) for every cubic meter of water, while calorically dense sugar gives us 3,423 kilocalories per cubic meter of water.

Let's turn now to **irrigation efficiency**. Irrigation efficiency refers to the ratio of water that evaporates to what saturates the soil. The efficiency of traditional gravity irrigation, a method still widely used throughout the developing world (and particularly in low-income countries), is about 40 percent—meaning that 60 percent (more than half!) of the water applied is lost to evaporation. Sprinkler systems, conversely, have an

TABLE 8.2 Virtual Water Content and Calories to Water Ratio for Select Commodities

COMMODITY	VIRTUAL WATER CONTENT (M3/KG)	CALORIES TO WATER (KCAL/ M3)
Rice	1.31	2,770
Wheat	0.98	2,701
Corn	0.84	3,403
Potatoes & other starchy roots	0.23	3,107
Sugar cane	1.02	3,423
Soybeans	3.20	1,035
Beef	12.56	161
Pork	4.46	785
Poultry	2.39	715
Mutton	4.50	446
Fish	5.00	99
Eggs	3.55	410

Source: Adapted from Liu and Savenije (2008).

efficiency range of between 60 and 70 percent, whereas drip irrigation systems are between 80 and 90 percent efficient (Seckler 1996). Conventional understandings of irrigation efficiency refer to the minimal amount of water that can be applied to achieve maximum yield. Yet there are other ways to understand this concept. It could be defined as the maximization of crop production *per unit of applied water*. This admittedly means we stop striving for maximum yields, as the relationship between yields and applied water is linear only up to roughly 50 percent of **full irrigation** (which refers to the amount of water needed to achieve maximum yield). After this point, the yield curve takes on a curvilinear shape due to increased surface evaporation, runoff, and deep percolation, until turning downward from anaerobic root-zone conditions, disease, and the leaching of nutrients (English et al. 2002; see Figure 8.1). Conventional wisdom has farmers irrigating for maximum *yield*—the moment on the figure just prior to the curve turning downward. Yet if fresh water were to become additionally scarce, it might make more sense to strive for, say, 80 percent yields, especially if that could be achieved with half the water that would otherwise be needed to obtain the remaining 20 percent (and thus maximum) yield.

Another highly visible subject is agriculture-related **hypoxia**. Hypoxia refers to a state where oxygen concentrations in a body of water fall below the level necessary to sustain most animal life. The Gulf of Mexico is home to one of the Western Hemisphere's largest "**dead zones**"—the name given to bodies of water with low levels of dissolved oxygen. There are roughly 405 dead zones in the world today (Diaz and

FIGURE 8.1 General Relationships Between Yields and Total Amount of Water Applied

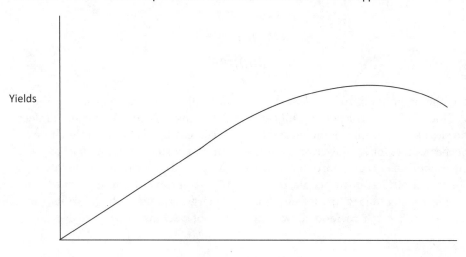

Yields

Amount of water applied

Rosenberg 2008). The one found in the Gulf of Mexico is the product of excess nitrogen coming down through the Mississippi River. The majority of this excess nitrogen (roughly two-thirds) comes from agriculture and, to a lesser extent, lawns. Nitrogen levels in the Raccoon River, for example, which is part of the watershed of the Mississippi River, forced Des Moines (Iowa) Water Works to build the world's largest nitrate-removal plant-treatment facility in 1991. Nitrate concentrations in this river have more than doubled in the past twenty-five years, a rate of increase that shows no sign of slowing (Hatfield, McMullen, and Jones 2009). After making its way into the Gulf, the nitrogen fuels the rapid growth of algae and plankton. When those·organisms die and sink to the bottom, they decay and in doing so rob the water of oxygen (see Case Study 8.1). Although we have known of this problem for some time, there are growing concerns that the size of the dead zone in the Gulf will expand in the years ahead, especially if biofuel and meat demands continue to drive corn prices upward (creating an incentive to expand the amount of land raising this commodity) (Potera 2008). It has consistently been about the size of New Jersey since the beginning of the new millennium, or about eight thousand square miles (give or take five hundred miles) (NOAA 2008).

Then there's agriculture's rather conspicuous links to climate change. The livestock sector, when emissions from land-use change are included in the calculation, accounts for 9 percent of CO_2 deriving from human-related activities (United Nations 2006). Animal agriculture is also responsible for roughly 37 percent of all human-induced methane emissions, which has an atmospheric warming potential that is twenty-three times that of CO_2 (ibid.). When calculating for all greenhouse gases, animal agriculture accounts for between 18 percent (Stehfest et al. 2009) and 51 percent (Goodland and Anhang 2009) of global emissions, depending on the study cited. It has been calculated that producing one kilogram of grain-fed beef generates as much CO_2 as driving 250 kilometers in an average European car or using a 100-watt (incandescent) bulb continuously for twenty days (Ogino et al. 2007:424).

CASE STUDY 8.1
Mobile Bay Jubilee

Jubilee is the name given to an event on the shores of Mobile Bay on Alabama's Gulf Coast when hordes of crab, shrimp, flounder, and eels leave deeper waters for shallower areas in the bay. The event often occurs more than once a year. The jubilee attracts many people, most of whom come looking to load up on free, abundant, and easy-to-catch seafood. It was not until the 1960s that a cause for the event was determined: hypoxia. During jubilees sea life becomes trapped between the shore and an advancing water mass low in dissolved oxygen (May 1973). Low levels of dissolved oxygen in the water can also cause marine life to become lethargic and slow, which further simplifies the task of catching these animals.

Last, it is important that I say a few words about agriculture's links to soil erosion. A report recently released by the Environmental Working Group (EWG) indicates that the topsoil in America's top corn-producing state—namely, Iowa—is disappearing at an alarming rate (Cox, Hug, and Bruzelius 2011). This finding is all the more disturbing after considering the many millions of dollars spent on conserving this precious resource, involving programs that pay farmers to construct buffer strips and in some cases to have them remove their most highly erodible land from production entirely (to pay them, in other words, to *not* farm the land). Soil scientists at Iowa State University analyzed eighteen thousand samples gathered between 2002 and 2010 on Iowa farmland. With these data it was learned that far more soil was ending up in the Mississippi River watershed than what the US Department of Agriculture (USDA) considers sustainable. According to the USDA, five tons of soil per acre per year can be lost without reducing soil productivity. According to the EWG, soil erosion rates in Iowa are as great as *twelve times* that amount. This translates into roughly sixty-four tons of topsoil per acre per year. One reason for the high rates of erosion cited in the report is a highly inequitable incentive structure that delivers maximum rewards to farmers who ramp up production while providing a pittance, in comparison, to encourage them to conserve topsoil. For example, between 1997 and 2009, the government paid farmers in the Corn Belt US$51.2 billion in subsidies to expand corn production (this figure does not include the tens of billions of dollars spent during the same period subsidizing the expansion of the corn-ethanol industry). At the same time, the government made available just US$7.0 billion to implement conservation practices (Carolan 2009).

Community Impacts

There is a rich, long literature looking at the impact of industrial agriculture on communities. The most famous of these studies, and one of the first, was conducted almost three-quarters of a century ago. Overseen by Walter Goldschmidt, a USDA anthropologist, and funded by the USDA, the study looks at two California communities in the early 1940s: Arvin, where large, absentee-owned, non-family-operated farms were

ECOnnection 8.1

Negative Impacts of Industrialized Farms

Social scientists report the following negative impacts that industrialized farms have upon community well-being:

SOCIOECONOMIC WELL-BEING
- greater income inequality, higher rates of poverty, or both
- higher rates of unemployment
- reduced employment opportunities

SOCIAL FABRIC
- decline in local population
- social class structure becomes poorer (due to, for instance, increases in hired labor)

SOCIAL DISRUPTION
- increases in crime rates and civil suits
- general increase in social conflict
- greater childbearing among teenagers
- increased stress and social-psychological problems
- swine CAFOs located in census blocks with high poverty and minority populations
- deterioration of relationships between farming neighbors
- more stressful neighborly relations

- deterioration in community organizations; less involvement in social life
- decrease in local-level political decision making (as outside interests gain influence)
- reduction in the quality of public services
- decreased retail trade and fewer, less diverse retail firms
- reduced enjoyment of outdoor experience (especially when living near CAFO)
- neighbors of hog CAFOs report upper-respiratory, digestive-tract disorders and eye problems
- residences closest to hog CAFOs experience declining values relative to those more distant

Social scientists report the following negative impacts that industrialized farms have upon the health of the environment:
- depletion of water and other energy resources
- increase in Safe Drinking Water Act violations
- air-quality problems
- increased risks of nutrient overload in soils

Based on a review of literature by Lobao and Stofferahn (2008) and Stofferahn (2006).

more numerous, and Dinuba, where locally owned, family-operated farms were the norm (the names of both towns are pseudonyms). The researchers concluded that industrial agriculture had, overall, a negative impact on a variety of community quality-of-life indicators (Goldschmidt 1978). For example, relative to Dinuba, Arvin's population had a smaller middle class, a higher proportion of hired workers, lower mean family incomes, higher rates of poverty, poorer-quality schools, and fewer churches, civic organizations, and retail establishments. Residents of Arvin also had less local control over public decisions due to disproportional political influence by outside agribusiness interests. Goldschmidt's research was rediscovered in the 1970s, perhaps in response to rapid changes to agriculture during this time. Research since the 1970s has over-whelmingly supported the Goldschmidt thesis (Lobao and Stofferahn 2008; see ECOn-nection 8.1).

It is important to clarify that "industrial agriculture" in this tradition often goes be-yond the size of an operation, looking also at indicators of farm organization. Accord-ing to this literature, features like absenteeism (when land is leased and the owners live outside the community), contract farming, dependency on hired labor, and operation by farm managers (as opposed to owner-operator situations) place a greater burden on communities than when surrounding farms (even large ones) lack these character-istics. Large-scale, family-owned farms, for example, tend to still purchase their inputs, farm equipment, and services locally; volunteer their time at local organizations (church groups, school fund-raisers, and the like); and regularly interact with their neighbors.

Research has also looked at the impact of large-scale livestock-feeding operations—a.k.a. confined animal-feeding operations (CAFOs)—on community well-being and public health. Neighbors of CAFOs have been found to have higher levels of respiratory and digestive disturbances (Radon et al. 2007). They also have abnormally high rates of psychological disorders, such as anxiety, depression, and sleep disturbances (Bokowa 2010; Carolan 2008c). Children living on or near hog farms have abnormally high rates of asthma (Chrischilles et al. 2004). These rates are known to increase proportionally with the size of the operation (Donham et al. 2007). North Carolina school administra-tors report rates of asthma among the student population at levels well above the state average in schools within three miles of one or more large hog-feeding facilities (Mirabelli et al. 2006). Post-traumatic stress disorder has also been reported among res-idents living near CAFOs (Donham et al. 2007:318). This can result from such things as a reduction in one's quality of life or property values—for example, one study calcu-lated an average reduction in property prices of US$144 per hectare within 3.2 kilome-ters of a CAFO (Seipel et al. 1998). Researchers have also documented that a significant level of social tension—specifically between producers and their neighbors—can emerge when CAFOs are sighted within a community (Constance and Tuinstra 2005).

Malnutrition and the Green Revolution

The **green revolution** refers to a series of strategies developed during the mid- to late twentieth century to combat starvation by expanding the global production of staple food crops through crop breeding. Was the green revolution a success? It depends. For example, we unequivocally grow more calories today globally than we did a half century ago. So as a food calorie revolution, the green revolution was an unqualified success. But calories do not a nutritious diet make, as evidenced by the green revolution's links to **micronutrient malnutrition**—a condition defined as a diet lacking in sufficient quantities of micronutrients (Carolan 2011b; Weis 2007).

Micronutrient malnutrition plagues billions around the world. As stated in a report prepared by the United Nations Children's Fund (UNICEF), World Health Organization, and United Nations World Food Programme (WFP): "Deficiencies of micronutrients are a major global health problem. More than 2 billion people in the world today are estimated to be deficient in key vitamins and minerals, particularly vitamin A, iodine, iron and zinc. Most of these people live in low income countries and are typically deficient in more than one micronutrient" (UNICEF, WTO, and WFP 2007:1).

Children are a particularly sensitive population to micronutrient malnutrition due to having higher nutritional requirements per kilogram of body weight. Almost two-thirds of all deaths of children globally are attributable to nutritional deficiencies (Caballero 2002). A consensus is emerging that the growth lost in early years due to malnutrition is, at best, only partially regained during childhood and adolescence with dietary improvements (Alderman, Behrman, and Hoddinott 2003). One study, examining children who were between twelve and twenty-four months in age at the peak of the drought in rural Zimbabwe in 1994–1995 had average heights well below that of comparable children not impacted by this event when measured at ages sixty to seventy-two months (Hoddinott and Kinsey 2001). Another study notes that among children in rural Zimbabwe who were exposed to the 1982–1984 droughts, average heights at late adolescence were reduced by 2.3 centimeters compared to children not exposed to this nutritional shock (Alderman, Hoddinott, and Kinsey 2006).

There is no disputing that the green revolution has occurred at the expense of dietary diversity. Crops bred for traits associated with improved yields or to withstand mechanization have displaced traditional crops that are high in iron and other micronutrients. In South Asia, for example, although cereal production has increased more than fourfold since 1970, production of pulses (a high-protein legume) has dropped 20 percent (Gupta and Seth 2007; Welsh and Graham 1999). There is a well-documented relationship between green revolution cropping systems and a decline in the density of iron in the diets of people in South Asia (Seshadri 2001; Welsh and Graham 2002). But this is not merely a matter of what's being raised. *How* the cereals of the green revolution are processed and consumed has also impacted the dietary health of millions. Cereals, and rice in particular, are consumed primarily after milling—a process that removes micronutrients. Pulses, conversely, are traditionally consumed whole after cooking, allowing for the consumption of a more complete nutritional profile. Whole cereal grains also contain relatively high levels of antinutrients, which are known to lower the absorption of micronutrients, and lower levels of substances that promote the bioavailability of micronutrients (Welsh and Graham 1999).

Fortunately, micronutrient malnutrition has received greater attention in recent years. As evidence of this, note the rise of what is known as **biofortification**—the breeding (and increasingly genetic engineering) of plants with the aim of higher micronutrient content. "Golden rice" is rice that has been genetically engineered to contain high levels of vitamin A and is a well-known example of biofortification. Yet as a solution to a diet deficient in beta-carotene, golden rice seems to sidestep larger sociological questions. Vitamin A is fat soluble, which means its uptake within the body is dependent upon a certain amount of fat in the diet. In less developed parts of the world, however, levels of dietary fat are often insufficient. And simply increasing a population's daily intake of rice, by itself, provides none of this dietary fat. Of greater concern, however, is the fact that the production of golden rice glosses entirely over the deeper question: namely, why is vitamin A deficiency a growing problem throughout the developing world to begin with? Because the green revolution has helped to radically alter dietary patterns in some parts of the world, which, for some populations, has led to diets dangerously low in vitamin A.

Biofortification strategies also do nothing to increase dietary diversity. They may, in fact, have just the opposite effect. Simply packing more nutrients in a handful of staple crops risks further shrinking the diets of those in the developing world, which have already seen their diets become dangerously narrow by the green revolution with its **monocultures** (an agricultural practice of producing a single plant species over a wide area for a number of consecutive years). There is also the concern that fortification programs will draw attention away from the more important issue of food access. As Tripp notes, biofortification schemes embrace, whether implicitly or explicitly, a "technical fix" attitude that "can tempt governments to believe they don't have to worry about nutrition because the plant breeders are handling this" (2001:258).

The "Treadmills" of Agriculture

In the 1950s, agricultural economist Willard Cochrane (1958) introduced the concept of the "agricultural treadmill." According to Cochrane, farmers are under tremendous economic pressure to adopt new technologies and increase the size of their operations. The logic behind the argument is straightforward. Those first to adopt a technology (especially those that increase yields or a farm's efficiency) initially experience windfall profits from increased output—like in the case of hybrid corn, which immediately upon adoption doubled a farmer's yield. Soon other farmers, seeing the relative advantage of the technology and wanting to capture additional profits, choose also to adopt. Yet the cumulative effect of the heightened output eventually exerts downward pressure on prices, as the market becomes flooded. It's important to realize that new agricultural technologies rarely do anything to directly increase consumer demand. At this point, those who have yet to adopt the technology now *must* adopt it, if they wish to remain competitive in the market.

A consequence of being caught on the agricultural treadmill is the continual pressure to adopt the latest technologies and inputs while at the same time increasing the size of one's farming operation. This, however, increases one's operating costs, which in turn requires farmers to continually seek out ways to increase their output. Yet there are other input-specific treadmills also at work here. The "pesticide treadmill" is perhaps the best known of these additional treadmills and was first discussed back in the 1970s (van den Bosch 1978). This is the phenomenon where insects evolve to become resistant to pesticides, which leads to more applications, higher concentrations, and new chemicals, which leads to still further resistance, and so on. Studies going back to as early as the 1970s note that despite large increases in pesticide use during the 1960s and 1970s, crop losses due to insect pests were actually *on the rise* (Pimentel et al. 1978), a trend that continues to this day (Pretty 2004). Whether we're discussing pesticides or fungicides (see ECOnnection 8.2), evolution has proven a formidable foe to agrichemical companies.

Another input-specific treadmill involves the use of synthetic fertilizers—also known as the fertilizer treadmill. Synthetic fertilizer can easily lead to a "need" for more fertilizer over time. This treadmill is particularly acute when tilth, which are levels of organic matter, and microorganism activity are diminished due to poor soil-management practices and a general "mining" of one's land—problems that are all too common on farmland where synthetic fertilizers are used. Under such a scenario, the only option becomes ever increasing the applications of fertilizer in order to maintain one's yield.

Last, there is the seed treadmill. A number of protections, as discussed in Chapter 4, are utilized by the seed industry that either discourage or outright prevent farmers from

ECOnnection 8.2

Yes! We Have No Bananas

The banana that Americans first came to know was called the Gros Michel banana—also known as "Big Mike." If you went to the store between 1906 and 1960, Big Mike was the banana for sale. It was ubiquitous in grocery stores around the world. Big Mike met with a tragic end, however. Panama disease—a fungus resistant to fungicide—wiped it from the face of the global marketplace. A hurried search for a viable replacement led to the discovery of the Cavendish cultivar, which was resistant to the disease. (A "cultivar" refers to a race or variety of a plant created or selected intentionally and maintained through cultivation.) Now it looks like a new strain of Panama disease is attacking the Cavendish in Asia, which, if it were to spread to other continents, could cause the Cavendish to go the way of the Big Mike.

Banana firms have developed their industry entirely around not only a single product but a single cultivar—talk about specialization! The industry has been likened to a pipe from many countries to local supermarkets. But this pipe fits only one variety of the world's one thousand banana varieties, which makes changing to a new variety very difficult and expensive.

The looming Panama disease threat has led to calls for the banana industry to move away from the monoculture (or, more accurately, monovarietal) model that it has been using for more than a hundred years. Growing multiple varieties will ensure that no single disease will be able to wipe out the entire industry, bringing resiliency to the industry. There are, however, hurdles to this. Many varieties, for example, cannot withstand the transportation and handling requirements of long-distance shipping. Other hurdles are more cultural. Take "baby bananas." These taste best when eaten in a far browner state than a traditional Cavendish. Yet most people are accustomed to the signature yellow color that the Cavendish (and Big Mike before) gives, which indicates ripeness before it goes brown. It will take some work to get people used to eating a banana that looks, through a Cavendish lens, noticeably overripe.

Koeppel (2007).

saving their seeds and replanting them the following season. Moreover, as also discussed in Chapter 4, the knowledge of how to save and replant seeds is another resource that farmers lose when they cease practicing seed saving. This creates a dependency upon seed firms. In the United States, for example, the rate of saving corn seed fell from approximately 100 percent at the turn of last century to less than 5 percent by 1960, while rates for soybean saving dropped from 63 percent in 1960 to 10 percent in 2001 (Howard 2009).

Solutions

In 2002 then UN secretary-general Kofi Annan asked an appointed panel of experts how a green revolution could be achieved in Africa. After more than a year of study, the group had their answer. Foremost, they questioned the one-size-fits-all approach to food security taken by the green revolution: "The diverse African situation implies that no single magic 'technological bullet' is available for radically improving African agriculture." The panel's strategic recommendations explain that "African agriculture is more likely to experience numerous 'rainbow evolutions' that differ in nature and extent among the many systems, rather than one Green Revolution as in Asia" (InterAcademy Council 2003:xviii).

I've found the term *rainbow evolutions* useful when talking to students and the public about issues pertaining to food security. The term alters the scope of the discussion by, first, directing attention away from single magic-bullet thinking—hence the term *rainbow*. Second, it emphasizes—which is why the word *evolutions* is so apt—how agricultural development cannot be divorced from the social, economic, and agroecological conditions of place. And as every place is different and unique, the term reminds us that solutions cannot be overly generalized. The following are some potential "colors" of this ever-changing rainbow.

Agroecology

Small, diverse farms—also known as **polycultures**—that raise grains, fruits, vegetables, and livestock have been shown to outproduce, in terms of harvestable products per unit area, large, specialized (monoculture) operations. Yield advantages of small, diverse farms can range from 20 to 60 percent (Altieri and Nicholls 2008). One study found that 1.73 hectares of corn in Mexico are required to produce as much food as a 1-hectare plot planted with a mixture of corn, squash, and beans. Moreover, the 1-hectare poly-culture plot produces twice as much dry matter (the part of the plant that is not harvested). The nutrients of that dry matter are then recycled back into the soil, replenishing it (Gliessman 1998:10). In Brazil polycultures containing 12,500 maize plants per hectare and 150,000 soybean plants per hectare exhibited a 28 percent yield advantage over soybean monocultures (Altieri 1999:200).

Agroecological principles also lie at the center of many organic farms, which explains, when managed properly, their favorable comparison to conventional farms. Examining approximately three hundred studies from around the world, Badgley and colleagues (2007) conclude that organic agriculture has the potential to feed the world. They further conclude, after comparing yields between organic and conventional systems, that **organic systems** have the potential to produce yields comparable to if not *better than* conventional operations (see ECOnnection 8.3). As defined by the USDA, an organic system "is an ecological production management system that promotes and enhances biodiversity, biological cycles and soil biological activity . . . based on minimal use of off-farm inputs and on management practices that restore, maintain and enhance eco-logical harmony" (USDA, n.d.).

The inverse relationship between farm size and productivity is the result of a more efficient use of land, water, biodiversity, and other agricultural resources by small farmers. Polycultures minimize losses not only due to weeds, insects, and diseases—by keeping ecological internal controls intact—but also by more efficiently utilizing water, light, and nutrients (Altieri and Nicholls 2008). Small farms are also overwhelmingly owner operated, which, as discussed earlier, benefits rural communities and their economies.

Small, diverse operations are also more likely to be resilient to environmental events, pests, and disease. One reason for this is because polycultures tend to display more

ECOnnection 8.3
Agroecology: Growing More Than Food and Fiber

When we think about agriculture, we tend to view it as being solely about food and fiber production. This is a terribly narrow (and perhaps even dangerous) view of all that is provided by this sector. Agriculture is important to us in such additional ways as:

DIET
- enhancement of nutritional quality and the cycling of trace elements
- food security

PUBLIC HEALTH
- protection of the health of farmworkers and consumers
- suppression of vectors of human disease (e.g., mosquitoes, snails, ticks)

ENVIRONMENTAL SUSTAINABILITY
- preservation of biodiversity
- protection of wildlife
- preservation of our productive capacity against erosion, salinization, acidification, and compaction

- maintenance of an ecological community of natural enemies of pests and diseases of crops
- protection of the general environment against runoff, eutrophication, volatilization of nitrites, and dust in the atmosphere
- protection of water resources and quality

RURAL DEVELOPMENT
- supporting employment, farm income, and rural life
- support for the economic independence of women

NATIONAL DEVELOPMENT AND SOVEREIGNTY
- contribute to the international balance of payments
- defense of national sovereignty against possible dumping or political blackmail backed up by economic blockade
- food sovereignty

Based on Carolan (2011b) and Levins (2006).

consistent yields than monocultures during extreme weather events (ibid.). In India, for example, the number of varieties a farmer grows increases with the variability of conditions (e.g., atmospheric, agronomic, pest ecology, and more). Thus, the low terraces, which are wetter and prone to flooding, are planted with indigenous long-growing rice varieties. The upper terraces, in contrast, dry out more rapidly after the rains, so they are planted with drought-resistant, fast-growing varieties. In total, a small Indian rice farmer can plant up to ten different rice varieties (Holdrege and Talbott 2008).

Small-farm efficiency can also be attained with surprisingly little investment, especially when compared to the massive capital expenditures required of industrial farms. In Peru, for example, several NGOs and government agencies have created initiatives to restore abandoned terraces and build new ones by offering peasant communities low-interest loans or seeds and other inputs. Terraces reduce the losses associated with frost

ECOnnection 8.4

La Via Campesina *and the Plight of Rural Women*

A notable feature of *La Via Campesina* involves its striving for greater gender equality. At an organizational level, the movement has a man and a woman representative from each region. The movement has released a number of public statements about its views on the injustices women face around the world. I will therefore let *La Via Campesina* speak for itself on the subject. The following statement is taken from a document titled "Declaration of Maputo" (Maputo is the capital and largest city of Mozambique):

> All the forms of violence that women face in our societies—among them physical, economic, social, cultural and macho violence, and violence based on differences of power—are also present in rural communities, and as a result, in our organizations.... We recognize the intimate relationships between capitalism, patriarchy, machismo and neo-liberalism, in detriment to the women peasants and farmers of the world. All of us together, women and men of *La Via Campesina*, make a responsible commitment to build new and better human relationships among us, as a necessary part of the construction of the new societies to which we aspire.... We recognize the central role of women in agriculture for food self-sufficiency, and the special relationship of women with the land, with life and with seeds. In addition, we women have been and are a guiding part of the construction of *La Via Campesina* from its beginning. If we do not eradicate violence towards women within our movement, we will not advance in our struggles, and if we do not create new gender relations, we will not be able to build a new society. (La Via Campesina 2008)

and drought, minimize soil erosion, improve water efficiency, and increase crop yields between 45 and 65 percent compared to crops raised on sloping land (Altieri and Nicholls 2008:476).

La Via Campesina *and Other Peasant-Based Movements*

La Via Campesina is viewed by many as the world's most important transnational social movement (Desmarais 2008; McMichael 2006; Martínez-Torres and Rosset 2010), a fact that surprises a great many in countries like the United States, where most have never heard of the organization. As explained on their website (http://www.viacampesina .org/en/): "La Via Campesina is the international movement which brings together millions of peasants, small and medium-size farmers, landless people, women farmers, indigenous people, migrants and agricultural workers from around the world. It defends small-scale sustainable agriculture as a way to promote social justice and dignity. It strongly opposes corporate driven agriculture and transnational companies that are destroying people and nature."

The movement, which collectively represents about 200 *million* farmers, is founded on the belief that for too long, rural and food policies have been developed in the absence

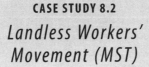

CASE STUDY 8.2
Landless Workers' Movement (MST)

The Landless Workers' Movement in Brazil (also known as the MST, after its Portuguese title, Movimento dos Trabalhadores Rurais Sem Terra), which includes members throughout Latin America, is an estimated 1.5 million strong (MST n.d.). The energy of the movement is due to the perceived unjust distribution of land throughout the region and especially in Brazil, where 3 percent of the population own and control two-thirds of the country's arable land.

Under Brazilian law, a landowner risks losing title to his or her land by letting it lie idle, especially after someone else settles it and begins using it productively. Under such a scenario, the latter party could challenge the landholder's title to the land in court. The MST has sought to utilize this law to the advantage of landless peasants. To give their movement further legitimacy, they also point to a passage in Brazil's constitution that states that land should serve a "larger *social* function," which they interpret to mean that it should not be viewed through solely an economic lens. Members of the MST thus seek to identify and occupy idle land and make it agriculturally productive, arguing that such actions meet the constitutional requirement of a "social function." While doing this, the MST is also pushing for broader land reform throughout the region (Carolan 2011b).

of those most affected: namely, rural peoples, including women (Martínez-Torres and Rosset 2010; see ECOnnection 8.3). The class-profile of *La Via Campesina* is remarkably diverse: landless peasants, tenant farmers, sharecroppers, and rural workers largely in Latin America and Asia; small and part-time farmers in Europe, North America, Japan, and South Korea; peasant farmers and pastoralists in Africa; small family farms in Mexico and Brazil; middle-class (and some affluent) farmers in India; and poor urban (and urban-fringe) dwellers in countries like Brazil and South Africa (Borras 2008).

A quick word about the term *peasant*, as it has historically signified a less than flattering identity. *La Via Campesina*, and other peasant movements (see Case Study 8.2), seeks to recast the term *peasant* as an identity to be embraced. Delegates from the United Kingdom, when seeking to first name the movement, initially resisted the term *La Via Campesina*—which literally translates into "Peasant Way"—out of concern for the derogatory connotations attached to the term *peasant*. The delegate instead preferred the term *farmer*. Many outside the UK delegation, however, favored the term *peasant*, noting that *farmer* also had connotations that failed to capture the character of the movement and most of its participants (Desmarais 2008). A compromise was reached: keep the name *La Via Campesina* but do not translate it into English. It has also been noted that the title *La Via Campesina* pays homage to Latin America's founding role in the movement.

La Via Campesina is responsible for elevating the term *food sovereignty* in the public consciousness. The term was first used publicly by the movement during the World Food Summit in 1996. As detailed in Table 8.3, food sovereignty speaks to a way of life

TABLE 8.3 View of Dominant versus Food Sovereignty Models

ISSUE	DOMINANT MODEL VIEW	FOOD SOVEREIGNTY MODEL VIEW
Free Trade	Everything ought to be governed by the market	Food should be exempt from trade agreements, as it is fundamentally different from, say, cars
Production Priorities	Agro-exports	National and local markets
Subsidies	Claims to favor market logics yet relies heavily on government subsidies for the largest farms	Subsidies okay if they level the playing field and do not unduly harm small scale farms in developing economies
Food	A commodity to be traded (fundamentally no different from any other commodity)	A unique commodity that everyone has a right to
Agriculture	Increasingly an occupation for those with access to significant amounts of credit, capital, land, and labor	A livelihood that should be available to all
Hunger	A technological/production problem	A problem of access (of food and of land to produce food)
Food Security	Achieve through trade and by adopting Green Revolution principles	Improved by enabling the hungriest to produce food and by embracing Rainbow Evolution policies
Seeds	Can be privatized (like land); a commodity with no cultural significance	A common heritage of humankind that everyone has a right to; an artifact that allows for the reproduction of culture
Overproduction	Is good (leads to cheap food)	Is bad (erodes food security around the world)
Peasantry	A holdover from feudalism (which no one wishes to return to); a pejorative term	"People of the land"; a proud identity for hundreds of millions around the world

Source: Adapted from Desmarais (2008) and Martínez-Torres and Rosset (2010).

that is in many ways diametrically opposed to the dominant view that presently dictates conventional food and agricultural policy.

The World Forum on Food Sovereignty was held in the village Nyéléni in Mali, Africa, in February 2007. The meeting brought together six hundred delegates from five continents to reaffirm the right to food sovereignty and to begin an international drive to reverse the worldwide decline in local community food production. The forum was organized through an alliance of diverse social movements: Friends of the Earth International, *La Via Campesina*, the World March of Women, the Network of Farmers' and Producers' Organizations of West Africa, the World Forum of Fish Harvesters and Fish Workers, and the World Forum of Fisher Peoples. The group wrote the "Declaration of Nyéléni," in which you'll find the following lengthy definition of food sovereignty. I quote the definition in full to give the reader an idea of just how expansive the concept is:

> Food sovereignty is the right of peoples to healthy and culturally appropriate food produced through ecologically sound and sustainable methods, and their right to define their own food and agriculture systems. It puts the aspirations and needs of those who produce, distribute and consume food at the heart of food systems and policies rather than the demands of markets and corporations. It defends the interests and inclusion of the next generation. It offers a strategy to resist and dismantle the current corporate trade and food regime, and directions for food, farming, pastoral and fisheries systems determined by local producers and users. Food sovereignty prioritizes local and national economies and markets and empowers peasant and family farmer-driven agriculture, artisanal-fishing, pastoralist-led grazing, and food production, distribution and consumption based on environmental, social and economic sustainability. Food sovereignty promotes transparent trade that guarantees just incomes to all peoples as well as the rights of consumers to control their food and nutrition. It ensures that the rights to use and manage lands, territories, waters, seeds, livestock and biodiversity are in the hands of those of us who produce food. Food sovereignty implies new social relations free of oppression and inequality between men and women, peoples, racial groups, social and economic classes and generations. (IPC n.d.)

Urban Gardens

Approximately 70 percent of the world's population is expected to live in urban areas in 2050 (today that figure is closer to 50 percent) (Rabobank Group 2010). Whereas rural poverty is rife in the developing world, the number of urban poor in these countries is expected to rise rapidly in the decades to come. In these rapidly urbanizing nations, the poor are moving to the city at a faster rate than the population as a whole (Ravallion, Chen, and Sangraula 2007). If current trends continue, the world's slum population—those living in irregular settlements, without access to suitable food, water, shelter, and sanitation—will increase 50 percent between now and 2020 (Mougeot 2005:1).

Most urban poor in low-income nations spend the majority of their incomes on food. An estimated 60 percent of all household income generated by the poor in Asia goes toward purchasing food, compared to Canada and the United States, where the figure is closer to 10 percent (Carolan 2011b). Food insecurity among the urban poor is further exacerbated by diets composed heavily of tradable commodities (versus traditional foods) and a lack of space to grow their own food (Redwood 2010).

Although it is easy to brush urban agriculture aside as a nonviable strategy for developing food security, the role that urban agriculture *currently plays* in keeping millions from falling over the edge into abject hunger and poverty is quite surprising. This fact was brought to light in a recently published study (Zezza and Tasciotti 2010). In it, urban centers located in fifteen developing countries in Africa, Asia, Eastern Europe, and Latin America were examined for the role played by urban agriculture in promoting food and economic security and diet diversity among the urban poor.

Participation in urban agriculture among poor households in the countries studied was as high as 81 percent. Urban agriculture was also shown to be of major economic significance, making up more than 50 percent of the income for poor households in certain countries. Two-thirds of the countries analyzed were shown to have a correlation between active participation in agricultural activities and greater household dietary diversity, even after controlling for economic welfare and other household characteristics. There was also a link—albeit not as robust as the others—between urban agriculture participation and the consumption of fruits and vegetables.

Before ending this chapter, I need to stress one important point (which I've given evidence to in previous chapters): do not think for a moment that our food problems lie only in production. This is *good* news, as the thought of having to further industrialize food production is not an attractive one, given the associated costs to the environment (e.g., climate change and soil erosion), community well-being (recall the Goldschmidt thesis), and public health (e.g., pesticide exposure). For one thing, hunger is ultimately a problem of access and distribution. The Food and Agricultural Organization (FAO 2002), for example, calculates that world agriculture produces enough food to provide everyone in the world with at least 2,720 kcal per person per day. As detailed in Chapter 6, discussing Amartya Sen's work on famines, producing more food does not do the world's hungry any good if they cannot afford or more generally do not have access to it. We also waste, as detailed in Chapter 3, an outrageous amount of food. Why continue pushing for higher yields and greater agricultural output if we are going to continue to throw a significant chunk of those productivity gains away? Some food for thought . . .

IMPORTANT CONCEPTS

- agroecology
- food sovereignty
- Goldschmidt thesis
- green revolution
- peasant-based movements
- rainbow evolutions
- the "treadmills" of agriculture

DISCUSSION QUESTIONS

1. It seems as though labor abuses and injustices take a backseat to issues of environmental sustainability when thinking and talking about food. Why do you think that is? How can

we make all those involved in the growing, manufacturing and processing, transportation, preparing, and selling of food more visible?

2. What are some of the links between the green revolution and micronutrient malnutrition?
3. In many respects, people from developing countries are at the forefront of challenging the dominant global food system (like *La Via Campesina* and the Landless Workers Movement). Why is that? What threats does this system pose to them?
4. Summarize the Goldschmidt thesis. Based upon that literature, what policies would you recommend with the aim of enhancing rural community vitality and well-being?

SUGGESTED ADDITIONAL READINGS

Bell, B., and T. Field. 2010. "Miami Rice: The Business of Disaster in Haiti." *Grain.org,* October. Retrieved August 27, 2012 (http://www.grain.org/bulletin_board/entries/4212-miami-rice -the-business-of-disaster-in-haiti).

Cochrane, L. 2011. "Food Security or Food Sovereignty? The Case of Land Grabs." *Journal of Humanitarian Assistance,* July 5. Retrieved August 27, 2012 (http://sites.tufts.edu/jha /archives/1241).

Hertsgaard, M. 2012. "How to Feed the World After Climate Change: Genetically Modified Seeds Aren't Enough—We Have to Change the Entire Agricultural System." *Slate,* April 6. Retrieved August 27, 2012 (http://www.slate.com/articles/technology/future_tense/2012/04 /heat_resistant_seeds_ecological_agriculture_growing_food_after_climate_change_.html).

Neuman, W. 2011. "High Prices Sow Seeds of Erosion." *New York Times,* April 12. Retrieved August 27, 2012 (http://www.nytimes.com/2011/04/13/business/13erosion.html).

Rosenthal, R. 2011. "Rush to Use Crops as Fuel Raises Food Prices and Hunger Fears." *New York Times,* April 6. Retrieved August 27, 2012 (http://www.nytimes.com/2011/04/07/science /earth/07cassava.html).

RELEVANT INTERNET LINKS

- http://www.fcrn.org.uk/
  Web address for the Food Climate Research Network. An excellent resource for those looking for cutting-edge research dealing with the food system's impact on the environment (in addition to many other agrifood-related issues).
- http://www.organiclinker.com/food-miles.cfm
  Calculate the distance the food from your last meal has traveled (a.k.a. its food miles).
- http://www.viacampesina.org/en/
  The website address for *La Via Campesina.*
- http://vimeo.com/27473286
  Excellent short video about the movement *La Via Campesina.*

SUGGESTED VIDEOS

- *Bananas!* (2009)
  Explore the real cost of our cheap bananas.
- *Big River* (2010)
  A sequel of sorts to *King Corn* that investigates the socioecological impacts of the main characters' acre of corn.

- *A Chemical Reaction: The Story of a True Green Revolution* (2009)
  Looks at the health risks and side effects of synthetic lawn pesticide and herbicide use and what a small town did to be the first place in North America to ban the use of these chemicals.
- *Colony* (2009)
  Explores how colony-collapse disorder threatens our entire food system.
- *Food, Inc.* (2008)
  Eric Schlosser (author of *Fast Food Nation*), Michael Pollan (author of *The Omnivore's Dilemma*), and others discuss the dangerous state of our food system.
- *Fresh* (2009)
  Documents people—farmers, thinkers, and entrepreneurs—who are reinventing our food system.
- *The Garden* (2008)
  Chronicles the rise and fall of the largest community garden in the United States.
- *The Harvest* (2011)
  Follows three of the close to half-million migrant child farm laborers in the United States.
- *Ingredients* (2009)
  Traces the roots of the local food movement while telling stories of the chefs, farmers, and activists who seek to transform our food system.
- *King Corn* (2008)
  Two friends learn about the food system by moving to Iowa and growing an acre of corn.
- *Meat the Truth* (2008)
  Explains the large greenhouse gas footprint of the livestock sector.
- *Planeat* (2011)
  About the impacts of meat and dairy on the planet and our health.
- *Save the Farm* (2011)
  A popular organic farm in the middle of South Central Los Angeles is threatened by land developers, and community members take action.
- *The World According to Monsanto* (2008)
  Documentary about the influence Monsanto has had on our food system.

9

Energy Production:
Our Sun-ny Prospects

You've likely heard the news that, in 2009, China became the world's number-one consumer of energy, overtaking the United States, which had previously been on top for close to a century. China consumed 2.252 billion tons of oil equivalent in 2009, which was about 4 percent more than the United States' 2.170 billion tons (the oil-equivalent metric represents all forms of energy consumed, including crude oil, nuclear power, coal, natural gas, and renewable sources like hydropower and biofuel) (Swartz and Oster 2010). And 2009 proved not to be a fluke, as China has managed to hold on to that top spot, increasing its energy consumption by an additional 5.9 percent in 2010 (Yang 2011).

Many in the United States expressed a collective sigh of relief in 2009, not so much because they were happy that China is, quite literally, killing hundreds of thousands of its people annually with its pollution (World Bank 2007), but because they could finally point an indignant finger at someone other than themselves on the subject of energy consumption—how dare *they* do this?! (I remember watching a couple of political pundits on television act precisely this way.) I still hear these expressions, even though they are dangerously misplaced. Although China might consume more energy in *absolute* terms, it comes nowhere close to outconsuming the United States on a *per capita* basis. So, in fairness, China's title as "Top Energy Consuming Nation" is just a consequence of demographics. They have, remember, *more than four times* the population of the United States, a fact that also helps put into some perspective why China is investing heavily in its energy sector (see Case Study 9.1). If the United States had China's population, it would easily hold the title, outconsuming China by a factor of four.

The cloud of energy, however, has a silver lining. (It's there; we just can't see it at the moment, thanks to the layer of coal dust and other fine particulates that presently cover it.) While our thirst for energy is growing, as long as the sun exists we'll have plenty available to quench it, as electricity can be readily generated from solar, wind, geothermal, tidal, wave, and biomass. (The sun, thanks to its energy and gravitation pull, is the source of all these renewables.) At the moment, however, it's a case of where the

CASE STUDY 9.1
Three Gorges Dam

Three Gorges is the world's most notorious dam. The dam's body was completed in 2006 and is located in China along the Yangtze River. Three Gorges Dam generates significant quantities of electricity, roughly eight times that of the US Hoover Dam. But at what cost, beyond the roughly US$24 billion spent to build it?

The massive project, with its 1,045 km² (403 mi²) wide reservoir, broke the record books for number of people displaced (more than 1.2 million) and number of cities (13), towns (140), and villages (1,350) flooded. The reservoir also submerged roughly 100 archaeological sites, some dating back more than 12,000 years. Those displaced were allocated plots of land and small stipends as compensation. The dam itself also creates an impassable barrier to one endangered mammal (the Yangtze finless porpoise) and two that are threatened (the Chinese river dolphin and the Chinese paddlefish). The Chinese government recently went so far as to admit that two foreseen consequences are actually *worse* than anticipated: deteriorating water quality and erosion. Toxic algal blooms regularly blight the river's many tributaries due to reduced water flow and nutrients from land-use changes. Landslides are also a frequent occurrence, some of which are due to tremors and small earthquakes caused by the tremendous weight of the *reservoir itself* (which lays on two major faults lines). To mitigate these problems, China has embarked on a ten-year effort that will cost $26.45 billion—more than the cost of the entire dam!

Adapted from Hvistendahl (2008) and Science (2011).

"possible" and "probable" do not yet line up, though they could, as I address later in the Solutions section.

Fast Facts

More than 6,185 million tons (Mt) of coal were produced worldwide in 2010. The top coal-producing nation was China, with 3,162Mt, followed by the United States (932Mt), India (538Mt), Australia (353Mt), Russia (248Mt), South Africa (244 Mt), Indonesia (173Mt), and Kazakhstan (105Mt). According to the World Coal Association (n.d.), proven global coal reserves exceed 847 billion tons, an amount, at current rates of production, that would last about 118 years (compared to proven oil and gas reserves that are equivalent to around 46 and 59 years at current production levels).

Nuclear power plants supplied 13.5 percent of the world's electricity in 2010. Countries generating the largest percentage of their electricity in 2010 from nuclear energy included France (74.1 percent), Slovakia (51.8 percent), Belgium (51.1 percent), Ukraine (48.1 percent), and Hungary (42 percent). It is the United States, however, that leads the world in electricity generated from nuclear power (NEI n.d.). As of October 2011, the United States had 104 reactors (compared to France's 58), which collectively produced 807.1 billion kWh (compared to France's 410.1 billion kWh). Looking into the future, nuclear power will play a major role in China's energy portfolio. The country has 27 reactors under construction, another 51 planned to soon be under construction, and 120 additional reactors in the proposal phase. These figures collectively are greater than *all other countries combined* (WNA n.d.).

With less than 5 percent of the world's population, the United States is responsible for roughly 25 percent of global oil consumption, while holding just above 1 percent of the world's oil reserves. More than 53 percent of the world's oil reserves are held by just four countries: Saudi Arabia (17.68 percent), Venezuela (14.35 percent), Canada (11.91 percent), and Iran (9.31 percent). Rounding off the top ten are Iraq (7.82 percent), Kuwait (6.9 percent), United Arab Emirates (6.65 percent), Russia (4.08 percent), Libya (3.16 percent), and Nigeria (2.53 percent) (EIA 2011).

*Oil (37 percent), coal (25 percent), and gas (23 percent) collectively make up 85 percent of world *energy usage* (a more expansive term than *electricity use*), followed by nuclear (6 percent), biomass (4 percent), and hydro (3 percent). Constituting slightly more than 1 percent of energy use globally are solar heat, wind, geothermal, biofuels, and solar photovoltaic.

Implications

Earlier chapters have covered many of the most significant socioecological implications of past and current energy use, with climate change chief among them. A substantial amount of time has also been spent describing the consequences of our collective addiction to oil and the car in particular. Yet the subject of energy *production* has yet to be given its due, particularly in regard to sources other than oil.

"Clean" Coal

The aforementioned vastness of global coal reserves makes it deserving of closer scrutiny. Coal is the most carbon intensive of all fossil fuels, which is why it has been called "the real global warming culprit" (Perrow 2010:66). Coal is about as far from "green" as you can get when all available energy sources are lined up. Yet I doubt we'll abandon it anytime soon, primarily because of its great abundance in countries like China and the United States—numbers one and two, respectively, in terms of coal production *and* energy consumption. Thank goodness for **clean coal**, right?

What "clean coal" means depends on *who* you ask. According to the industry-sponsored American Coalition for Clean Coal Electricity (n.d.), "Clean coal technology refers to technologies that improve the environmental performance of coal-based electricity plants. These technologies include equipment that increases the operational efficiency of power plants, as well as technologies that reduce emissions." Broadly speaking, then, clean coal, according to the coal industry and its wide net of proponents, refers to any coal-burning technology that is an improvement over what we used to have. That definition of *clean* might work for my six-year-old daughter, who after washing her dinner plate (which remains covered in food) tells me how dirty it used to be prior to dipping it in the sink. The first time she did that, I remember going to the sink and showing her "what clean really means." Perhaps someone ought to do that to the coal industry.

Outside the coal-lobbying industry, however, clean coal typically means something more befitting of the name. That something typically involves capturing and storing the CO_2 produced by coal-fired power plants, thereby preventing this greenhouse gas from being emitted into the atmosphere and contributing to climate change. Unfortunately, while carbon-capture technology has been shown to work on a small scale, it has yet to be successfully scaled up. For example, the British government recently announced that its plans for the nation's first clean coal plant have collapsed over the newly projected £1.5 billion cost (depending upon the exchange rate, between US$2 and US$3 billion). That figure is £0.5 billion more than what was originally projected (Mason 2011).

Besides the large expense, carbon capture of clean coal still comes with a significant ecological footprint. Conventional coal plants are terribly inefficient to begin with, operating at around 32 to 38 percent efficiency. A few years ago, the US National Academy of Sciences (2008) released a report explaining how 98 percent of the coal-generated energy that goes into lighting an incandescent bulb is wasted. For every one hundred units of energy that enter the conventional coal plant, sixty-three units are lost (as heat) during the combustion process, two units are lost during the transmission of energy over power lines, and an additional thirty-seven units are lost (as heat) during the actual lighting of the bulb. Capturing CO_2 *further reduces* plant efficiency while increasing water use. A study released by the Massachusetts Institute of Technology (MIT 2007) estimates that carbon capture reduces efficiency to such a level that 27 percent *more coal* would have to be burned than in a conventional coal plant to produce the equivalent electricity.

Then there is the realization that regardless of how "clean" the combustion process becomes, there are components of coal's life cycle that will likely forever remain unclean, ungreen, and unsustainable. Millions of acres of habitat across the United States have been radically altered over the past 150 years by **strip-mining** (a practice involving the removal of soil and rock overlying the mineral deposit). Sixty percent of all coal mined in the United States comes from strip mines. Included in that total are 750,000 to 1 million acres of hardwood forests, thousands of miles of waterways, and hundreds of mountaintops (Biggers 2008; see ECOnnection 9.1). In China coal mining has degraded an estimated 3.2 million hectares (or roughly 7,907,372 acres), according to a 2004 estimate (so undoubtedly the total is considerably higher today) (GPI n.d.).

An attempt has been made to inventory material and energy inputs and emissions in not only the coal-combustion stage but also in the raw-material extraction and material-disposal stages (Babbitt and Lindner 2005). This life-cycle analysis found that while the combustion stage contributes the most to CO_2 air emissions, the extraction stage contributes the largest quantities of volatile organic compounds and methane (more than 98 percent of life cycle), as well as the most total dissolved solids to water (more than 76 percent). Meanwhile, the disposal stage has its own environmental impacts, contributing substantially to particulate air matter (PM10) pollution and emissions of total dissolved solids to water while contaminating land with a variety of metals. And let's not forget about the toll of coal mining on public health. A study published in the *American Journal of Public Health* found that residents of coal-mining communities have a 70 percent increased risk for developing kidney disease and a 64 percent increased risk for

ECOnnection 9.1
Mountaintop Removal Mining

Mountaintop removal mining involves clearing upper-elevation forests (typically at the summit of mountains), stripping the ground of topsoil, and utilizing explosives to break up rocks to expose underlying (yet relatively shallow) coal seams. The practice is widespread throughout the central Appalachian region of the United States, particularly in eastern Kentucky, West Virginia, and southwestern Virginia. A recently published paper in *Science* outlines the extensive environmental and public health consequences associated with this practice of coal extraction (Palmer et al. 2010). Those consequences include the following:

- ecological losses and downstream impacts: for example, burial of headwater streams leading to the permanent loss of ecosystems, declines in stream biodiversity, and elevated water concentrations of sulfate, calcium, and magnesium
- human health impacts: for example, contaminated groundwater and elevated levels of airborne and hazardous dust
- mitigation problems: reclaimed land (after a mine is closed) has lower organic content, low water-infiltration rates

(which increases the risk of flash flooding), and low nutrient content

Mountaintop mining is considerably more economical than traditional coal mining, as it is less labor intensive. Approximately 250 percent more coal can be extracted per worker using this technique than in traditional underground mines (NMA n.d.). It is no coincidence that the recent expansion of mountaintop mining has coincided with the loss of thousands of jobs over the past twenty years in the US coal industry. The industry claims the lost jobs are due to increasing government regulations when the data indicate *they* are the ones to blame. Proponents of the practice often cast critics as looking to damage the economic livelihood of mining communities (perpetuating the false "jobs versus the environment" argument). This criticism ignores the fact that mountaintop mining is doing *precisely that* by replacing labor with dynamite and heavy equipment, and in the end (as all mines eventually close) leaving communities with a devastated natural resource base and no alternative opportunities for employment (Bell and York 2010).

developing chronic pulmonary disease (such as emphysema), and they are 30 percent more likely to report hypertension (Hendryx and Ahern 2008).

Hydraulic Fracturing (a.k.a. Fracking)

Natural-gas production is expected to increase rapidly in the decades ahead in countries with rich natural-gas reserves. China, Canada, and the United States are expected to see their natural-gas domestic production levels rise from 3 to 6 trillion cubic feet, 5 to 8 trillion cubic feet, and 20 to 26 trillion cubic feet, respectively (EIA 2011). The United States has been called the "Saudi Arabia of natural gas," thanks in no small part to shale gas (this is where **fracking** comes into play—see below for a definition). The US Department of Energy estimates that shale-gas reserves, in conjunction with other domestic

FIGURE 9.1 Greenhouse Gas Emissions of Coal versus Natural Gases of Various Types

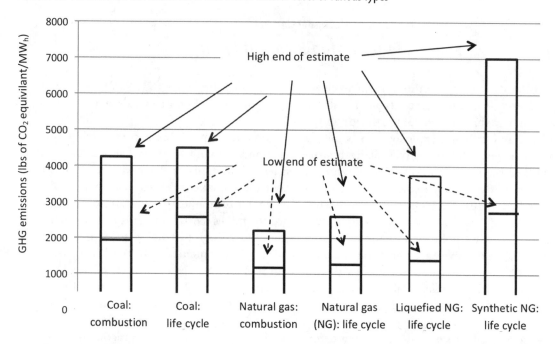

Source: Adopted from Jaramillo et al. (2007).

sources of natural gas, will provide the United States with enough natural gas to last for more than a century (Trzupek 2011). And as new technologies are developed—and existing ones become less expensive to utilize—those reserve estimates will no doubt continue to climb.

It widely known that combustion of natural gas in power plants produces substantially less—approximately half—CO_2 than that emitted by coal-fired power plants when equal amounts of energy are generated. The results of a life-cycle analysis comparing natural gas with coal are clear: the former emits fewer greenhouse gases, regardless of whether the combustion stage or the entire life cycle are compared (Jaramillo, Griffin, and Matthews 2007; see Figure 9.1). Even liquefying natural gas to transport it great distances results in fewer overall emissions compared to coal. Only synthetic natural gas (produced by the gasification of coal) has higher overall emissions than coal power plants.

Between 1995 and 2005, US production of natural gas held steady at roughly 2 trillion cubic feet per month. In 2006 shale-gas exploration (and fracking) began taking off (Trzupek 2011). In 2009 63 billion cubic meters of gas were produced from deep shale formations. That figure doubled by 2010. By 2035 fracking is estimated to account for just less than 50 percent of US gas production (Perkins 2011).

Fracking works like this: a well is sunk several thousand feet into the shale formation, after which "laterals" are then drilled that fan out from the main vertical well. "Fracking" takes place when large amounts of water, sand, and a secret chemical mixture (it's considered proprietary knowledge) are injected into the well. The pressure from this mixture fractures the shale, which in turn releases the natural gas. Once the fracking process is done, the well goes into production, though some wells may require multiple "frackings."

Fracking has come under increasing scrutiny, as many home owners in areas where the practice is common say it has tainted their drinking water, either with methane or with the wastewater produced by the process. And the research is beginning to back up those claims. A study published in the *Proceedings of the National Academy of Sciences* looked at sixty drinking-water wells in northeastern Pennsylvania and nearby areas in New York State (Osborn et al. 2011). Dissolved methane concentrations in water from the thirty-four wells located more than 1 kilometer from fracking operations were tested to have, on average, about 1.1 milligrams of dissolved methane per liter. In water taken from twenty-six wells within 1 kilometer of at least one fracking site, methane concentrations averaged 19.2 milligrams. Isotopic analyses of the carbon in the methane show it to have the same signature as that being recovered from nearby shale operations, thus implicating the fracking process. Other gases were also detected, which too were unique to the active gas-drilling areas. Ethane, another component of natural gas, and additional hydrocarbons were detected in 81 percent of water wells near fracking operations but in only 9 percent of water wells farther away. Propane and butane were also more likely to be detected in wells closest to drilling areas (see Case Study 9.2).

Nuclear Power

A recent publication from the Nuclear Energy Agency (2010) proclaims that nuclear power "could provide around 25 percent of global electricity with almost no CO_2 emissions." But it's not just industry types who are singing the praises of nuclear power; many environmentalists are too. Patrick Moore, the cofounder of Greenpeace who has famously become a nuclear power advocate, recently noted in a bulletin for the International Atomic Energy Agency that "nuclear energy is the only non-greenhouse-gas-emitting power source that can effectively replace fossil fuels while satisfying the world's increasing demand for energy" (IAEA n.d.). These claims, while factually accurate, mask deeper, less "green," truths, which life-cycle analyses help make visible.

Some life-cycle analyses show nuclear power emitting up to *twenty-five times more* CO_2 emissions than wind energy once uranium refining and transportation, reactor construction, and waste disposal are considered. A typical nuclear plant uses roughly 900 miles of electrical cables, 170,000 tons of concrete, 32,000 tons of steel, 1,363 tons of copper, and 205,464 tons of other materials, many of which, like aluminum, are carbon intensive (Sovacool 2008). As for the other end of the life cycle, some estimates place the total energy required for decommissioning a nuclear plant to be as much as 50 percent more than the energy needed for its construction (Fleming 2007).

Figure 9.2 illustrates top-end and mean (signified by the X and the corresponding number) emissions from a review of life-cycle analyses on nuclear power (Sovacool 2008). Proponents are correct when they say the operation phase has a relatively small CO_2 footprint. Yet nuclear plants and nuclear fuel do not just appear. Nor do they disappear at the end of their life cycle. After factoring in for the entire life cycle of nuclear power a very different ecological footprint image emerges. Of the life-cycle studies reviewed, the mean total CO_2 estimate was 66.08g CO_2e/kWh (the highest was 288g CO_2e/kWh). This is still far better than, say, coal's CO_2 life cycle, which is around 1,000g CO_2e/kWh (Gagnon, Belanger, and Uchiyama 2002). Yet if compared to the minuscule

CASE STUDY 9.2

Fracking Takes Its Toll on Home Owners in Pennsylvania

Dimock is located in northern Pennsylvania and has a population of (roughly) fourteen hundred people. Craig and Julie Sautner moved to Dimock in March 2008. Not long after arriving, they were approached by the Houston-based Cabot Oil and Gas and asked whether they would consider leasing the mineral rights to their three and a half acres of land. They were told that the drilling would have zero impact on their land. Others in the town said they had been told by Cabot Oil and Gas that if they didn't agree to lease their mineral rights, their land would be mined anyway, noting that under Pennsylvania law a well drilled on a leased piece of property can legally capture gas from any adjoining neighboring (unleased) properties. Upon signing the lease, they were given a onetime payout of US$2,500 per acre plus some royalties on each producing well.

The wells were drilled in August 2008. Within a month, the Sautners' well water had turned brown and become so corrosive that it scarred dishes in their dishwasher (likely from the sand used during the fracking process).

After pointing this out to Cabot Oil and Gas, a water-filtration system was eventually installed in their basement. Although it resolved the discoloration and corrosive problem, the Sautners soon learned, after a visit from the Pennsylvania Department of Environmental Protection (DEP), that their water held dangerously high levels of methane, iron, and aluminum. In the words of Craig Sautner, "It was so bad sometimes that my daughter would be in the shower in the morning, and she'd have to get out of the shower and lay on the floor" due to the effects of the fumes, while "my son had sores up and down his legs from the water."

By October 2009, the DEP acknowledged that a major contamination of the aquifer had occurred and instructed all homes to avoid contact with its water. Residents now rely upon weekly water deliveries (paid for by Cabot Oil and Gas). Though they would like to move, the value of their land has plummeted. "Our land is worthless," Craig Sautner sourly notes.

Adapted from Bateman (2010).

CO_2 life-cycle footprint of wind power, which is estimated at around 9 g CO_2e/kWh, nuclear power comes in a distant second (Pehnt 2006).

Nuclear power is also very expensive. Even with massive government subsidies, nuclear power remains uneconomical. One recent estimate calculates existing US subsidies to nuclear power to be more than 33 percent of the value of the power produced. And although the industry promises that the newest generation of nuclear plants will be cheaper to build and operate, the facts say otherwise. New plants under construction in Finland, for example, were originally estimated to cost €3 billion are already €2.7 billion over budget and four years behind schedule (Taylor and Van Doren 2011). Beyond all that, the technology carries with it inherent risk, not just of the meltdown variety but others related to weapons proliferation and the threat of terrorists targeting nuclear facilities. These realities further increase its costs, as expensive steps have to be taken

FIGURE 9.2 Range and Mean of CO_2 During the Life Cycle of Nuclear Power

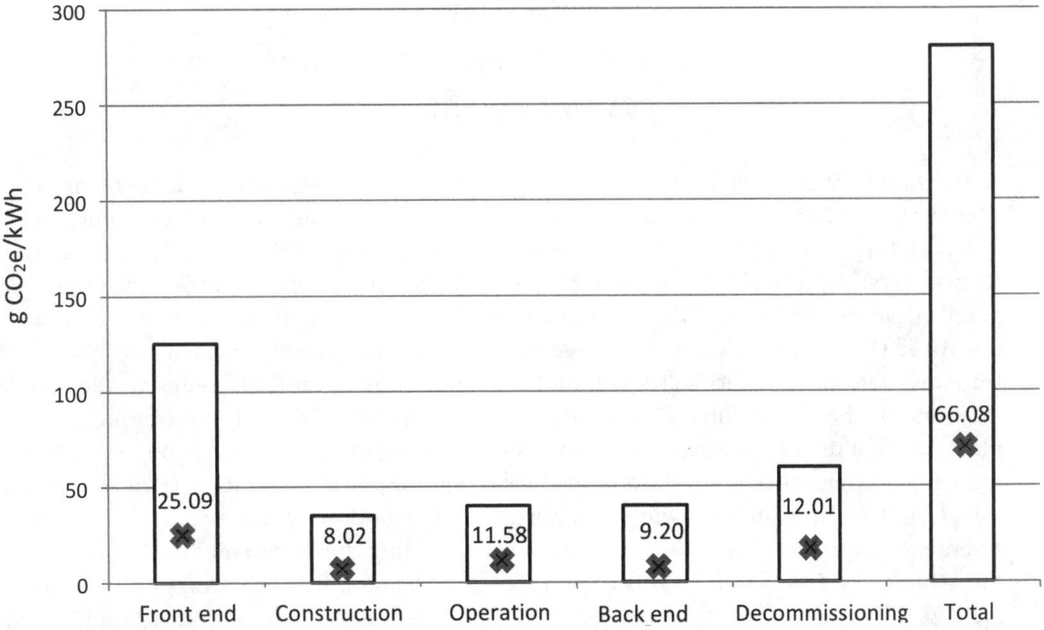

The mean is signified by the X and the corresponding number, in g CO2e/kWh. *Source:* Adapted from So-vacool (2008).

to secure not only nuclear facilities but also the transportation of nuclear waste (see Case Study 9.3).

Solutions

Ten years ago I couldn't have been as optimistic as I am today about energy generation. We have known for a long time that, theoretically, there's more potential renewable energy on this planet than we know what to do with. A popular statistic along these lines is that every hour, the energy equivalent to what all of humankind uses in an entire year strikes the earth's surface in the form of solar energy (Gilding 2011). Of course, we're a long way from capturing even a sizable fraction of this renewable energy. The point is that we can do it. It's now a matter of turning the technologically *possible* into the socially, economically, and politically *probable*.

Efficiency and Curtailment

For decades, the principal solution to the energy problem was conservation and sacrifice. President Jimmy Carter in the late 1970s famously appeared on national television calling for energy conservation while wearing a sweater and sitting in front of a fireplace, a visual image that then presidential candidate Ronald Reagan later exploited when he argued that "energy conservation is being too cold in the winter and too warm in the summer" (as quoted in Kempton et al. 1985:131). And to a significant degree, the mantra of "sacrifice" continues to be widely evoked among environmentalists. For example, of

CASE STUDY 9.3

Fukushima Nuclear Disaster as "Normal Accident"

A magnitude 9 earthquake struck Japan on March 11, 2011, which was quickly followed by a devastating tsunami that rose to a peak of forty meters. Together, these events left 20,000 people dead or missing and 125,000 buildings destroyed (Watts 2011). They also triggered a third disaster: the multiple meltdowns of three reactors at the Fukushima Daiichi nuclear plant, which ultimately released more radiation than any accident since the meltdown at Chernobyl in 1986 (though a growing number of scientists say that the total release at Fukushima is worse than even this event [McNeill 2011]).

Charles Perrow's (1984) *Normal Accidents* helps us think through events like the Fukushima nuclear disaster. Rather than ascribe the event to isolated equipment malfunction, operator error, or random acts of nature, Perrow makes the case that technological failures like what happened in Japan are the product of complex interacting systems. In this particular case, the root cause of failure lies in the tremendous complexity of nuclear plants. These "high-risk systems," as Perrow calls them, are inherently prone to failure regardless of how well they are managed or regulated. We therefore have two choices. One option is to radically redesign the systems to marginally reduce their complexity, by, say, moving the spent storage pools away from the site of power generation (Pidgeon 2011). The other option, which is also the surest way of avoiding these **"normal accidents,"** would be to abandon the technology entirely in favor of something less prone to catastrophic malfunction. A normal accident speaks of a failure that is inevitable, given the manner in which particular human and technological systems are organized. Extending this concept, might we call some of today's most pressing environmental problems—most notably global climate change—normal accidents?

the seventy-seven "essential" skills touted to stop climate change in *The Life Earth Global Warming Survival Handbook* (Rothschild 2007), just three deal with efficiency-increasing actions. What's curious about these solutions is that comparisons of energy saved by curtailment versus those saved by increased efficiency show that the latter generally win out (Gardner and Stern 2008). While "turning out lights when leaving the room" continues to be parroted to our children, the evidence indicates that our focus might be better spent elsewhere.

I will be the first to admit that our energy problem will not be solved through efficiency gains alone (see Chapter 10, where the rebound effect and Jevons paradox are discussed). Yet as a pragmatic environmentalist, I think it is a mistake to ignore the low-hanging fruits that are sociotechnological solutions, so long as they do not get in the way of deeper socioecological change. If you had a very high temperature from an infection, you would treat the fever as well as the infection, wouldn't you? For the moment, let's talk about ways we can tinker with our consumption of energy at the margins and save the discussion of systemic change for later chapters.

Take the compact fluorescent (CFL) lightbulb. The average life of a CFL is between eight and fifteen times that of the traditional incandescent bulb but uses only 20 to 33 percent of the power of an equivalent incandescent—a truly remarkable gain in efficiency over the old lighting technology. Let's compare CFL and incandescent bulbs over a twelve-year period. During that time, you can either purchase fifteen incandescent bulbs and 1500 kWh of electricity and spend roughly US$225 (£150) or buy one CFL and 300 kWh of electricity at a cost of about US$45 (£30). Yet the savings of CFLs pale when compared to the savings that could be had elsewhere through efficiency enhancements. Individuals, at home and in nonbusiness travel, consume roughly 38 percent of all the energy in the United States—that's more than the industrial (32.5 percent), commercial and service (17.8 percent), and nonhousehold transportation (11.7 percent) sectors. The majority of this energy is consumed for just two purposes: to drive our cars, trucks, and sport utility vehicles (SUVs) (38.6 percent) and to heat and cool our homes (25 percent). Compare this to lighting, which uses noticeably less energy. Only 6.1 percent of all household energy consumed in the United States annually is attributed to lighting (which is why I was earlier dismissive of the impact of "turn off the lights" campaigns) (Gardner and Stern 2008).

One problem is that the average person does not fully understand how their actions use (or save) energy. In a national survey, 505 participants were asked to report their perceptions of energy consumption and savings for various household, transportation, and recycling activities (Attari et al. 2010). The vast majority of respondents ranked curtailment (like turning off lights and driving less) above efficiency improvements (such as installing more efficient appliances and windows). When asked to indicate the most effective thing they could do to conserve energy, only 11.7 percent of participants mentioned efficiency improvements, whereas 55.2 percent mentioned curtailment (this does not add up to 100 because some gave very general answers like "recycle" and "conserve energy"). Moreover, when asked about certain activities, participants repeatedly underestimated energy use and savings, especially when it came to energy-intensive activities. The results of this exercise are illustrated in Figure 9.3. Although respondents' answers were close to accurate for less energy-intensive technologies and behavior, they *grossly underestimated* the energy consumption of appliances such as clothes washers, central air-conditioning systems, clothes dryers, and dishwashers. Take the case of lowering the hot water temperature in one's washing machine. Participants on average reported a savings of less than 100 Wh. The actual savings is closer to 7,000 Wh.

Individuals also gave inaccurate answers when asked to compare consumption and savings related to transportation. For example, they significantly overestimated the savings attributable to reducing one's driving speed from 70 mph to 60 mph for 60 miles. Conversely, they drastically underestimated—by almost a factor of ten!—the energy savings derived from having their car tuned up twice a year. Pointing to these deficiencies in home owners' knowledge about energy consumption and savings, the study concludes that "the serious deficiencies highlighted by these results suggest that well-designed efforts to improve the public's understanding of energy use and savings could pay large dividends" (ibid.:16054).

Studies indicate that public understanding of energy use could be enhanced by merely changing how we talk about certain phenomena. Take, for example, how we (in the

FIGURE 9.3 Mean Perceptions of Energy Used or Saved versus Actual Energy Used or Saved

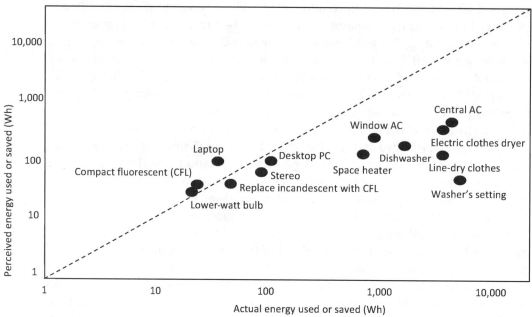

The diagonal dashed line represents perfect accuracy. *Source:* Adapted from Attari et al. (2010).

United States) talk about energy use as it pertains to automobiles: as a ratio of volume of consumption to a unit of distance—or specifically miles per gallon. Whereas people think that the amount of gas consumed by an automobile decreases as a linear function of a car's mpg, the actual relationship is curvilinear (see Figure 9.4). In one study, 171 participants from a national pool were given the following scenario: "A town maintains a fleet of vehicles for town employee use. It has two types of vehicles. Type A gets 15 miles per gallon. Type B gets 34 miles per gallon. The town has 100 Type A vehicles and 100 Type B vehicles. Each car in the fleet is driven 10,000 miles per year" (Larrick and Soll 2008:1594). They were then asked to select a plan for replacing vehicles with the end goal of reducing overall gas consumption. Seventy-eight participants were given the following two options (framed in mpg terms): replace the 100 vehicles that get 15 mpg with vehicles that get 19 mpg or replace the 100 vehicles that get 34 mpg with vehicles that get 44 mpg. Seventy-five percent chose the second option, which offers the largest gain in mpg *but not the greatest fuel savings.*

The remaining participants were given a policy choice framed in terms of gallons per 100 miles (gpm). This group was told that the town "translates miles per gallon into how many gallons are used per 100 miles. Type A vehicles use 6.67 gallons per 100 miles. Type B vehicles use 2.94 gallons per 100 miles." Then they were given the same choices as the other group, though these options were expressed in gpm, versus mpg, terms. The percentage choosing the more fuel-efficient option increased from 25 percent in the mpg frame to 64 percent in the gpm frame. Based on this, the authors of the study

FIGURE 9.4 Gallons of Gas Used per 10,000 Miles Driven

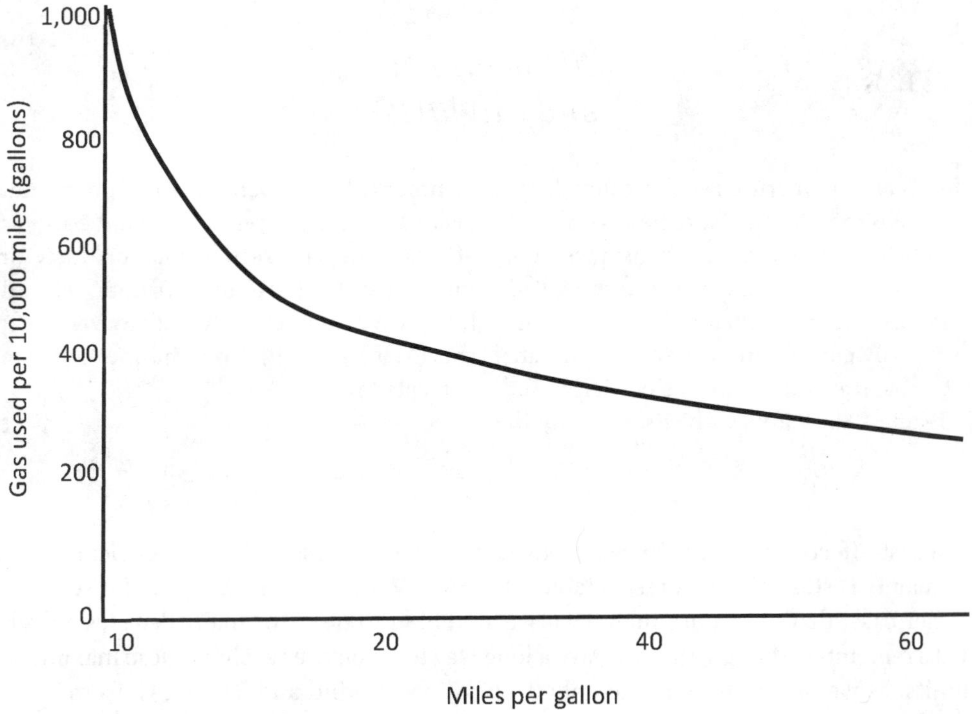

Source: Adapted from Larrick and Soll (2008).

conclude that whereas "mpg is useful for estimating the range of a car's gas tank, gpm allows consumers to understand exactly how much gas they are using on a given car trip or in a given year" (ibid.).

Renewables

The maximum amount of power consumed globally at any given moment is roughly 12.5 terawatts (TW). By 2030 that figure is expected to grow to 16.9 TW as population and living standards rise. It has been calculated, however, that if the planet were powered by wind, solar, geothermal, tidal, and hydroelectric power, with no fossil-fuel or biomass combustion (that's right, *none*), something rather interesting occurs. Global power consumption would presently be only 11.5 TW. How can the power-generating *method* impact consumption levels? The decline is due to the fact that, in most cases, electrification is a more efficient way to use energy. To take just one example: whereas roughly 18 percent of the energy in gasoline is used to move a vehicle (the vast majority is lost as heat), somewhere between 75 to 86 percent of the electricity delivered to an electric car is used to create motion (Jacobson and Delucchi 2009).

Earlier I mentioned how every hour the energy equivalent of what humankind uses in an entire year strikes the earth's surface as solar energy. Clearly, some of that solar radiation—such as that falling on open seas and atop remote mountains—cannot be captured

ECOnnection 9.2
Windmills and Bird Fatalities

Windmills are often criticized for killing large numbers of birds. Do they? It depends on what they are being compared to. For instance, it is estimated that 30,000 birds per year are killed by wind turbines in Denmark. A sizable number, especially considering windmills generate only 9 percent of the nation's electricity. But wait. Traffic kills 1 million birds annually in Denmark. If we abandon wind power due to avian fatalities, surely we should ban cars—after all, they are responsible for thirty times more bird deaths. And in Britain, 55 million birds are estimated to be killed every year by cats (MacKay 2009). Does this mean we should ban cats too?

in a cost-effective manner. Yet even with subtracting for these and wind-deficient areas, humanity is still left with a respectable 40 to 85 TW for wind and 580 TW for solar. In either case, that's far more than what we are going to need for many decades ahead. Let's remember, though, that we have a long way to go before reaching these maximum limits, as we presently generate only 0.02 TW from wind and 0.008 TW from solar (ibid.).

Critics of wind power contend that if we invest heavily in this renewable energy, the world will be blanketed with windmills, and even then wind power will constitute only a small portion of the total energy generated (see, for example, Cravens 2008). The latter criticism has already been shown to be blatantly incorrect—wind could be a substantial energy source. As for the former, the footprint of the 3.8 million turbines needed to supply more than half of the total future global energy demand would be less than fifty square kilometers, or roughly half the size of Denver, Colorado! Granted, we will need to make sure there is proper spacing between each turbine so as not to unduly impact bird and bat migratory routes, among other reasons (see ECOnnection 9.2). Let's also not forget that sticking with fossil fuels means energy demand by 2030 will increase further than if we were to rely only (or substantially) on renewables. This future fossil-fuel demand will need to be supplied with some thirteen thousand new coal plants, each of which comes with its own land footprint, especially after factoring in for mining and mountaintop removal (Jacobson and Delucchi 2009).

Another dishonest critique of wind power is the "wind doesn't blow all the time" argument. First, a smart mix of renewable energy sources will ensure that something is always blowing, shining, turning, and so forth, so electricity is constantly being generated. Second, while wind does not blow all the time, coal plants are not online all the time, either. The average US coal plant is offline 12.5 percent of the year for scheduled and unscheduled maintenance. Compare this to the average downtime for the newest generation of wind turbines: 2 percent on land and 4 percent at sea. Photovoltaic (solar) systems also fare well in this regard, with downtimes that factor out to about 2 percent of the year (Eccleston and March 2011).

Incentivizing Renewables and Household Efficiency

We can do so much more than what we currently are to shift from a fossil fuel to a renewable energy–based society. Governments of affluent nations are spending in the tens of millions of dollars annually in renewable research and development (R & D). But relative to other expenditures, this is a remarkably small sum. Annual global sales of cosmetics, for example, total US$33 billion. US taxpayers spend US$46 billion annually to fight the so-called war on drugs. UK taxpayers recently spent US$900 billion to bail out the banks. Or take the US$2,000 billion spent by the United States on the war in Iraq (MacKay 2009). Do these expenditures accurately reflect our priorities?

Currently, the cost of wind, geothermal, and hydroelectric electricity is less than seven cents a kilowatt-hour (¢/kWh). Although presently considerably higher, the price (¢/kWh) of wave- and solar-based electricity is expected to drop substantially by 2020 to about 10¢/kWh, whereas wind, wave, and hydro are expected to drop still further, to 4¢/kWh or less. These prices compare very well with fossil fuel–based electricity. The average cost in the United States of conventional (fossil-fuel) power generation and transmission is roughly 7¢/kWh, and it is expected to increase to 8¢/kWh in 2020 (Jacobson and Delucchi 2009).

A **carbon tax** is one widely discussed strategy to disincentivize the use of fossil fuels—especially coal—for electricity generation. The rationale behind such a tax is fairly simple. A carbon tax would make the market price of this fossil fuel more accurately reflect its true cost, for, as earlier discussed, electricity generated from this non-renewable is currently incorrectly priced (to use standard economic parlance), as many of its real costs (such as to the environment and public health) are presently not given their proper due. In other words, these costs are currently treated as an **externality** (a cost or benefit not transmitted through prices and incurred by a party who did not agree to the action causing the cost or benefit). It is also clear that coal-plant owners will only invest in technology like carbon capture and storage if they are convinced the price of carbon is going to remain high long enough to justify the additional expense associated with these facilities. A carbon tax would signal to investors that "cheap" (incorrectly priced) coal is a thing of the past and that investments in carbon capture make sense (and cents).

It is less clear, however, if a carbon tax would change consumer behavior. Households historically have not responded to rising energy prices by making sufficient energy-efficiency investments. Part of the reason for this is because, as stated earlier, people on average poorly estimate how their actions consume or save electricity. (I mentioned previously how individuals tend to overemphasize curtailment over efficiency improvements.) This is in part because efficiency improvements—such as installing new windows or buying new energy-efficient appliances—almost always require out-of-pocket costs, whereas curtailment (like turning lights off) cost nothing. A carbon tax could conceivably, by making energy more expensive in the short term (before renewables catch up), cause individuals to place even more emphasis on curtailment. As rising energy costs would no doubt be at the forefront of consumers' minds (the media love to remind people when these are increasing), this would very likely cause people to become even more vigilant to turn things off. Conversely, efficiency improvements might be seen as an expense that cannot be afforded at the moment. I see it all the time. As more

CASE STUDY 9.4

Carbonarium: A Nongovernmental Association in Hungary

Established in 2005, Carbonarium seeks to decrease its members' CO_2 emissions while increasing climate-change awareness among the general population in Hungary. Members are required to track their CO_2 emissions and compare them with others involved in the association, implement mitigation measures, and pay a membership fee based on their CO_2 footprint. The success of the association hinges on its ability to create a voluntary community among its members, which includes individuals as well as organizations. This shared sense of community in turn, it is believed, will instill within participants a sense of responsibility to reduce their energy consumption. As a result of this association, members report learning about their greenhouse gas footprint as well as about the most effective methods for reducing it. The organization also organizes low-carbon activities like bike tours. Such events not only build "community" but also educate participants on how best to achieve a low-carbon lifestyle (Heiskanen et al. 2010).

of one's paycheck is redirected toward paying for raising energy costs, the last thing many consumers want to do is to spend even more money on, say, heating and cooling their homes by investing in a high-efficiency furnace or so-called high-performance windows, even though those short-term costs will eventually pay for themselves (many times over) in the long run.

Subsidies could play a useful role in changing behaviors. Financial incentives—from subsidized loans to deferred-payment loans, rebates, and tax credits—to reduce initial out-of-pocket costs would help consumers overcome certain barriers to improving household efficiency. We also need to be aware of nonmonetary barriers, which could be overcome by utilities or governments providing free energy audits, lists of approved contractors, and help in securing low-cost financing and inspection of completed work (Gardner and Stern 2008). Community-based efforts that rely upon informal social networks to help spread information and knowledge on strategies for improving the energy efficiency of homes could also facilitate people in making efficiency improvements to their homes (McKenzie-Mohr 2011; see Case Study 9.4).

One very popular policy tool used at the production end is what is known as the **feed-in tariff**. A feed-in tariff "is an intervention by influencing the price . . . [where] the electric utilities are required by law or regulation to buy renewable electricity at fixed prices set normally at higher than the market price" (Bhattacharyya 2011:262). These price supports are long term but not permanent. Feed-in tariffs are used around the world to support renewables until they can compete head-on in the marketplace with fossil fuels.

TABLE 9.1 Generating Capacities for Wind Power by Region and Country, Gigawatts, 2008–2035 (Projected)

REGION/COUNTRY	2008	2015	2020	2025	2030	2035	ANNUAL % CHANGE, 2008–2035
OECD Americas	27	66	69	73	76	80	4.1
US	25	51	51	54	55	57	3.1
Canada	2	11	13	14	15	17	7.5
Mexico/Chile	0	5	5	5	6	7	16.8
OECD Europe	65	126	181	207	217	227	4.8
OECD Asia	4	13	18	20	21	23	6.4
Japan	2	4	5	8	8	8	5.6
South Korea	0	1	2	2	3	4	9.9
Australia/New Zealand	2	8	11	11	11	11	6.2
Total OECD	**97**	**204**	**267**	**300**	**315**	**330**	**4.7**
Non-OECD Europe/Eurasia	0	4	4	4	5	5	9.8
Russia	0	0	0	0	0	0	0.1
Other	0	4	4	4	5	5	10.0
Non-OECD Asia	23	77	117	143	165	185	8.1
China	12	62	99	119	139	156	9.9
India	10	14	16	20	22	24	3.3
Other	0	1	3	3	4	4	10.5
Middle East	0	1	1	1	1	2	11.3
Africa	0	4	5	5	6	6	10.3
Central/South America	1	3	3	3	4	4	7.7
Brazil	0	2	2	3	3	4	8.5
Other	0	1	1	1	1	1	5.0
Total Non-OECD	**24**	**88**	**130**	**157**	**181**	**203**	**8.2**
Total World	**121**	**293**	**398**	**456**	**496**	**533**	**5.7**

Source: Adapted from EIA (2011).

In the aftermath of the Fukushima nuclear disaster (discussed earlier in this chapter), for example, Japan passed legislation in late 2011 that models successful feed-in tariff schemes in Europe. The policy came into effect in July 2012 and will require utilities to purchase electricity generated by solar, wind, biomass, geothermal, and small-scale hydroelectric plants at set rates for twenty years. The government estimates that the incentives will produce more than 30 gigawatts of renewable energy capacity in Japan over the next decade, lifting renewables' share of Japan's energy mix from 9 percent to more than 20 percent (Murray 2011). Thanks to policies like these, global renewable energy capacity is expected to increase dramatically in the years ahead (see Table 9.1). As mentioned earlier, though, much more could—or, more accurately, *needs* to—be done to hasten our development of these capacities.

There is an old saying that has been evoked in different forms over the centuries—from such diverse sources as Christianity, Eastern philosophy, and even Shakespeare—about how the depths of darkness also house the most brilliant light. There are clearly many ways that this can be interpreted. The one that interests me here, for want of a better term, is the environmental sociological interpretation. Namely, there is value in delving into the problems that plague us, for only through an understanding of their roots are lasting (and real) solutions proposed. Thus far, we've covered a lot of terrain that has encompassed both problems and solutions. But I dare say we have yet to really roll up our sleeves and discuss what it is about how we organize society that makes environmental problems so prevalent. That changes in the proceeding chapters. The following section goes to depths yet to be explored in the hope of uncovering that light of understanding that we'll need to organize a truly sustainable society.

IMPORTANT CONCEPTS

- clean coal
- energy curtailment versus efficiency
- hydraulic fracturing (a.k.a. fracking)
- normal accident
- nuclear power life cycle

DISCUSSION QUESTIONS

1. The process of shifting away from certain energy sources and toward others will create winners and losers as, for instance, jobs move out of one region and into another. What becomes of the "losers" in a so-called green economy (like rural coal mining communities)?
2. I have had people tell me that even if "fracking" does negatively impact those living near wells, we shouldn't place their interests above those of society. Some contaminated wells are a small price to pay for cheap, domestically produced energy, they tell me. What's your response to such a position?
3. Why are governments not investing more in renewable R & D? Or should research into renewable energy be entirely left up to the private sector?

4. Have you replaced all your old-fashioned incandescent lightbulbs with newer, more efficient illuminants (like CFLs)? If not, why? What other easy steps to reduce your energy
   footprint have you yet to do? And why haven't you?

SUGGESTED ADDITIONAL READINGS

Biggers, J. 2008. "'Clean' Coal? Don't Try to Shovel That." *Washington Post,* March 2. Retrieved
August 30, 2012 (http://www.washingtonpost.com/wp-dyn/content/article/2008/02/29
/AR2008022903390.html).

Gardner, G., and P. Stern. 2008. "The Short List." *Environment Magazine* 50(5):12–25. Retrieved August 30, 2012 (http://www.environmentmagazine.org/Archives/Back%20Issues
/September-October%202008/gardner-stern-full.html).

Hvistendahl, M. 2008. "China's Three Gorges Dam: An Environmental Catastrophe." *Scientific
American,* March 25. Retrieved August 30, 2012 (http://www.scientificamerican.com/article
.cfm?id=chinas-three-gorges-dam-disaster).

MacKay, D. 2009 *Sustainable Energy: Without Hot Air.* Cambridge: UIT Press. Retrieved August 30, 2012 (http://www.withouthotair.com/download.html).

RELEVANT INTERNET LINKS

- http://www.eia.gov/countries/
  Address for the US Energy Information Administration. It offers a wealth of energy-
  related data for 217 countries.
- http://www.iaea.org
  Address for the International Atomic Energy Agency that's full of information relating
  to nuclear power.
- http://www.thewindpower.net/
  An extensive global wind-turbine and wind-farm database.

SUGGESTED VIDEOS

- *Aftermath: World Without Oil* (2010, series)
  Looks into the future and reveals what would happen if the world fundamentally
  changed.
- *Burning the Future: Coal in America* (2008)
  Appalachian residents battle a coal industry that's wreaking havoc on their health as
  well as the health of their surrounding environment.
- *Collapse* (2009)
  Explores the link between energy depletion and economic collapse.
- *Crude* (2009)
  Details the lawsuit between indigenous Amazon rain-forest dwellers who accuse oil
  giant Chevron of poisoning and destroying their rain forest.
- *A Crude Awakening: The Oil Crash* (2007)
  We're more dependent upon oil than you think.

- *Escape from Suburbia* (2007)
  A film that addresses solutions to peak energy, highlighting people who are challenging the status quo and striving for meaningful social change.
- *Fuel* (2010)
  More than eleven years in the making, the film documents the United States' addiction to fossil fuels and explores viable alternatives.
- *GasHole* (2011)
  Film about the history of oil and existing viable alternatives to fossil fuels.
- *Gasland* (2010)
  An exposé of the widespread water pollution resulting from hydraulic fracturing.
- *The Last Mountain* (2010)
  A remarkable exposé on the threats of coal mining and corporate greed on human, community, and environmental health.
- *The Power of Community: How Cuba Survived Peak Oil* (2006)
  An empowering look at how communities in Cuba decreased their dependence on fossil fuels.
- *The Spill* (2010)
  http://www.pbs.org/wgbh/papges/frontline/the-spill/. An investigation into the trail of problems—accidents, deaths, spills, and safety violations—that have long plagued the oil and energy company BP. Could the 2010 disaster in the Gulf of Mexico have been prevented?
- *Windfall* (2010)
  Highlights the benefits as well as the potential costs that come with large-scale wind-power generation.

PART III

ORGANIZING A SUSTAINABLE SOCIETY

10

Political Economy: Making Markets Fair and Sustainable

In his 1865 book, *The Coal Question* (in the chapter titled "Of the Economy of Fuel"), William Stanley Jevons highlights the paradox of how the rising efficiency of coal used in production was associated with rising coal consumption. The Jevons paradox is based on a not-so-paradoxical principle: any time the cost of consuming a resource is reduced, people will respond by consuming more of it. Its implications, however, are profound. It suggests that in our rush to save the environment and natural resources through efficiency gains, we may be unintentionally *hastening their demise*. A related term is *the rebound effect,* which occurs when gains in efficiency fail to lead to proportional reductions in consumption—for example, when a 20 percent gain in efficiency leads to a reduction in consumption or waste of only 10 percent. When a rebound effect is more than 100 percent of the efficiency gain, it is called a Jevons paradox (see Case Study 10.1).

The line between where a rebounded effect ends and a Jevons paradox begins, however, is quite murky. Take the efficiency gains of hybrid cars. By going farther on each unit of gasoline, they are making travel by car cheaper, even with rising gas prices. And whenever something becomes cheaper, we respond by doing more of it. Let's say the efficiency gains accrued by your purchasing a new hybrid car still outweigh the losses incurred by your increases in driving (perhaps you now take more road trips on weekends after buying this vehicle). What precisely do you do with those savings? If you're like most people, you take those savings and spend them on something else—a vacation to Hawaii, a new iPhone, or perhaps on another vehicle. The problem is that we tend to reinvest efficiency gains in additional consumption, which arguably nullifies the ecological gain of *any* gain in efficiency (Owen 2011).

The amount of energy, for example, required to produce each unit of the world's economic output—what is known as **"energy intensity"**—has fallen more or less steadily over the past half century. Global energy intensity is now more than 33 percent lower than it was in 1970 (World Bank 2008). Energy intensity in both the United States and the United Kingdom is approximately 40 percent lower today than in 1980 (Jackson 2009). Global **carbon intensity**—the amount of CO_2 emitted for each unit of economic

CASE STUDY 10.1
Compact Fluorescent Bulbs: Jevons Paradox or Rebound Effect?

I have a confession to make: I sometimes leave lights on in my house for extended periods of time. It all started when my wife and I switched out all our incandescents for compact fluorescent bulbs. The average life of a CFL is between eight and fifteen times that of incandescents, and they use 20 to 33 percent of the power of equivalent incandescents—a truly remarkable gain in efficiency over the old lighting technology. Or it would seem. The problem is that our lighting behaviors changed with the adoption of the technology. Before the changeover, my wife and I hated leaving lights on for long periods of time. This meant no night-light for our daughter. We were also very hesitant to leave lights on in the house when we went on extended trips. Not anymore. We now leave at least one light on all night for our two kids. And when we go on vacation, we always make sure at least one room is partially illuminated. We have the CFL bulbs to thank for this change in behavior. I cannot say whether this is a Jevons paradox or a rebound effect. I'd like to think the overall efficacy gained by switching over to CFLs outweighs our increased household bulb use (and as I think more about it, I am quite sure it does). Nevertheless, this remains a personal reminder of why efficiency gains alone should not be expected to solve all of our ecological ills.

output produced—declined by some 25 percent between 1980 and 2006. Every dollar spent in the United States in 1980 translated into 1 kilogram of CO_2 emitted, whereas in 2006 it equaled 770 grams (ibid.).

This is great—right? It would be, if subsequent increases in productivity were not occurring faster than the aforementioned efficiency gains. To put it simply: while we are producing each unit more efficiently, we are also producing so many more units that we've more than offset any gains in efficiency. Thus, even with those aforementioned admirable reductions in carbon and energy intensities, global CO_2 emissions have risen a staggering 105 percent (or 2 percent annually) since 1971. Worse still: total global CO_2 emissions are projected to rise by another 39 percent by 2030—or 1.4 percent annually (OECD 2010a).

It would seem we need to develop a language whereby we very clearly differentiate between two distinct types of efficiencies. There is, on the one hand, "relative efficiency," which refers to the well-documented decreasing (per unit) intensities. But there is also, and this is where *real* sustainability resides, "absolute efficiency," which refers to a reduction in *total* throughput and emissions. From a long-term sustainability perspective, what good is the former if we continue to increase our overall impact on the environment?

Don't get me wrong; it is not that we should entirely discount relative efficiency gains. We must not confuse them, however, for absolute efficiency gains, either. Otherwise, we risk what I like to call "**efficiency shifting**": namely, when money and resources

FIGURE 10.1 CO_2 Emissions, United States, 1980–2006

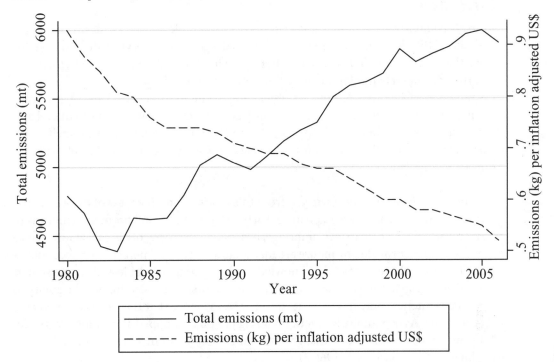

Source: Richard York, used with permission.

saved through energy efficiency (such as from placing solar panels on the roof of a manufacturing plant) merely get shifted and consumed on other goods and services (like
increases in the use of air travel for shipping or business-related travel). We see this
happen all the time. The money saved by home owners through energy savings is used,
for example, to buy more energy-using gadgets. Or note how the efficiency gains in the
internal combustion engine made during the latter half of the twentieth century led to
larger vehicles ultimately giving birth to the SUV boom in the late 1990s. Sociologist
Richard York (2010) recently examined trends in CO_2 emissions and the carbon intensity
of the global economy as well as for its top-five CO_2-emitting nations: China, the United
States, Russia, India, and Japan. These countries, in 2006, accounted for 55 percent of
total world emissions, 52 percent of world GDP, and 46 percent of world population.
York found that although each economy (and the global economy as a whole) is trending
toward improved *relative* efficiency gains in terms of CO_2 emissions (per inflation ad-
justment unit of GDP), their *overall* CO_2 footprints are growing at alarming rates. Figure
10.1 illustrates these trends for the United States.

This chapter, like those that follow, goes "deeper" than any that preceded it. It does
not take a professional sociologist, ecologist, economist, or otherwise to realize there is
something profoundly amiss with the current system, that the path we are presently on
is fundamentally unsustainable, and that *real* social change is much in need. What that
"system" is and how it might be changed are the subjects of this and the remaining chapters. I begin in this chapter by tentatively outlining those structures while also taking
time in the Solutions section to reorient ourselves toward more sustainable directions.

Fast Facts

Market economies, as presently conceived, are fairly simple beasts. Firms utilize people and capital (like buildings and machinery) to make goods and services that households think they need. Households, in turn, offer up their labor and capital (namely, their savings) to firms in exchange for incomes. Some of this income is spent on consumer goods; the rest is saved, invested, or both. In either case, the money filters back into firms, completing and reinvigorating the cycle. Credit has also increasingly been used to fuel and lubricate the system, particularly just prior to the recent global financial meltdown. These components collectively constitute what is known as the circular flow of the economy (Hall and Papell 2005).

Yet something is conspicuously absent from this macroeconomic view of the world: the productive material base—a.k.a. nature. Partha Dasgupta (2006), professor emeritus of economics at the University of Cambridge, has noted how many of his colleagues believe that the services provided by nature are marginal, at best 2 to 3 percent of an economy's output. Many believe instead that knowledge—because it is durable and can be shared collectively—can circumvent all ecological constraints, giving economies the ability to grow indefinitely. If only it were that simple. The evidence that this view is incorrect is all around us. As economist Kenneth Boulding famously quipped almost fifty years ago: "Anyone who believes exponential growth can go on forever in a finite world is either a madman or an economist" (1966:3).

Natural capital (assets that are indispensable for human survival and economic activity provided by the ecosystem) are not like your typical capital assets, like bridges, roads, buildings, and machinery. Like capital assets, ecosystems depreciate when misused or overused. But they also differ from reproducible capital assets in three important ways (P. Dasgupta 2006). First, depreciated natural capital is often either slow to recover (like a polluted lake) or irreparable (such as a species extinction). Second, it is often difficult to substitute one depleted or exhausted ecosystem or ecosystem service for another— it would be impossible, for example, to replace the pollination services provided by bees. And third, ecosystems can collapse abruptly, with little prior warning, a point famously detailed in Jared Diamond's best-selling book *Collapse* (2006).

Implications

Although environmental sociologists do not speak with one voice, they do share in the belief that business as usual is not an option. Not only portrayed as the ideal contraceptive, as discussed earlier when talking about population, economic growth is cast as *the* cure-all elixir to whatever social or environmental ill might be ailing us. Are progress, prosperity, and well-being strongly (positively) correlated with—and thus essentially reducible to—economic growth? And can economic growth go on indefinitely? These are empirical questions. In the chapters that remain, I look to see what the data have to say about economic growth, as to whether it's the cure, disease, or something in between.

In this chapter, I address a significant body of environmental sociology's theoretical core, particularly that which offers an explicit critique of the present system's unsustainable growth imperative. In doing this, I avoid ascribing to any totalizing narratives. Many of my colleagues, for example, feel strongly about chalking up most of the environment's (and humanity's) ills to capitalism. Although I agree with many of their central points, I don't find it particularly helpful to place blame without also offering pragmatic alternatives. Without well-thought-out alternatives, I am not convinced any of our problems would be solved by merely doing away with this admittedly problematic mode of production (capitalism). Moreover, echoing a point made in Chapter 1, I am not convinced that any one thing is responsible for the mess we're in—a point I intend to bolster in the remaining chapters. That being said, so as not to minimize their valuable contributions, these scholars are correct in highlighting the inherent problems associated with how we presently organize society and allocate its resources.

The Growth Imperative

Capitalism, as currently practiced, makes growth an imperative rather than an option. Any firm seeking to maintain rather than grow will be hastily eliminated from the market by its competitors. Going without economic growth for any length of time causes the entire global macroeconomic edifice to shake. Under this scenario, debts go unpaid, credit subsequently dries up, unemployment skyrockets, and the earlier-mentioned circular engine of growth begins to stall. And (infinite) growth *needs* (infinite) resources. By every aggregate measure, even with the aforementioned relative efficiencies, our impact upon the environment (our net throughput) is *increasing*. Global cement extraction just prior to the financial crisis was more than 125 percent greater than its 1990 level, iron ore roughly 100 percent higher, while bauxite, copper, and nickel extraction had increased more than 70 percent since 1990 (Jackson 2011). This cannot go on indefinitely.

The hope—the *only* hope—for the status quo lies in something called "**decoupling**," which refers to the ability for an economy to grow without corresponding increases in environmental pressure. Through decoupling, production processes are radically reconfigured and goods and services radically redesigned until economic output becomes entirely independent of material throughput. Right now, the two—economic output and material throughput—are tightly coupled: an increase in the former results in a more or less proportional increase in the latter. Only with decoupling can an economy grow indefinitely without worrying about breaching ecological limits.

There is a small catch. Decoupling is looking more and more like a pipe dream. We cannot even achieve efficiency gains fast enough to offset global CO_2 increases in production and consumption. CO_2 is widely considered one of the easiest decoupling challenges for the simple reason that energy can be produced with no CO_2, as explained in Chapter 9. Compare this to, say, making a laptop with only renewable resources, which is at present an insurmountable challenge. The fact remains, energy production is tightly coupled to material resources and subsequently CO_2 emissions. So when I come across a statistic like the average American today buys a new piece of clothing every 5.4 days, up from 10.7 days just twenty years ago, I get discouraged, as I know this growth in consumption comes with a growing ecological footprint (316 million pounds of used clothes were exported from the United States in 1991, and by 2004 that figure rose to 1.1 billion) (Schor 2010). What does the environmental sociology literature have to say about this?

Treadmill of Production

The "treadmill of production" is one of the core theoretical frameworks in environmental sociology. Its roots extend back to Allan Schnaiberg's classic *The Environment: From Surplus to Scarcity* (1980), where the concept is given its first thorough treatment. It is a macrolevel framework, in that it places particular attention on institutions and social structures. It is also a quasi-Marxist framework. As Foster (a leading ecological Marxist) puts it, without directly naming "the system" at the heart of today's ecological crisis, this literature has developed the treadmill concept to the point that it has become the functional equivalent of capitalism (2005:7–8).

According to treadmill-of-production scholars, modern capitalistic societies are driven by a never-ending commitment to growth, despite (and equally because of) its social and ecological costs. In pursuit of profit maximization, firms are continually seeking ways to expand production. With the support of government (and a complicit public), industrial production is allowed to expand, which in turn places still further demands on nature while creating growing amounts of waste. In other words, production begets more production, as all sectors of society depend on economic growth to solve the world's problems (e.g., unemployment, environmental degradation, and poverty and inequality), even though those very problems were caused, to various degrees, by growth itself. The following is a (nonsequential) breakdown of the treadmill logic (from Schnaiberg and Gould 1994):

- Increasing accumulation and concentration of wealth as fewer firms remain on the treadmill.
- Increasing movement of workers toward the private sector (as the public sector shrinks), thereby making it necessary to continually expand production in order to gain jobs and wages.
- Increasing allocations of wealth to firms that replace labor with capital, which generates more profits for wealth holders and creates pressures for all wealth holders to adopt similar practices if they wish to remain competitive. This places smaller firms, who do not have the capital to adopt these technologies, at a continual disadvantage. As smaller firms then fall off the treadmill, wealth (point 1) and market share become further concentrated.
- The net result of ever-increasing production is an ever-increasing need for greater ecological withdrawals (resource extraction and utilization) and additions (pollution).
- Societies become increasingly vulnerable to socioeconomic disorganization as their ecological resource base is undermined.

Internal Contradictions

Alongside capitalism's insatiable thirst for growth lie certain internal contradictions that threaten its very existence. Through the writings of Karl Marx, scholars have been able to identify some of these threats. Thus far, however, these contradictions have had just the opposite effect, speeding the treadmill up rather than slowing it down (or causing it to fall apart entirely). As highlighted in the previous section, capitalism has proven very wily, using problems of its making to hasten the circular engine of growth and expand its reach, an invisible hand (to evoke Adam Smith's famous metaphor) that now extends not only around the globe but "up" into the heavens with the privatization of space (Dickens and Ormrod 2007) all the way "down" to the genetic level (Carolan 2010a). The question remains: how long until these problems become so great (with climate change coming immediately to mind) that we can no longer turn to the market for our "solutions"?

Metabolic Rift

One such argument draws upon some of Marx's more obscure comments on matters of economic growth and natural resource exploitation and the "rift" these processes create. These writings were rediscovered largely thanks to sociologist John Bellamy Foster (1999), who brought them to the attention of the environmental sociology community. And so was born (or reborn) the metabolic rift thesis, as it has come to be known.

Mid-nineteenth-century environmental crises—from declining agricultural soil fertility to rising levels of sewage in cities—and the equally deplorable living conditions of urban workers were linked, according to Marx, to a disruption (a rift) in a previously sustainable socioecological metabolism. This rift, for Marx, is tied to the expansion of capitalist modes of production and urbanization—the latter made possible because of the rise of the former and in particular the displacement of small-scale agriculture. This process created a rift in ecological systems, leading to environmental degradation at points of production and consumption as people (and their waste) became concentrated in cities.

Inspired by the work of German chemist Justus von Liebig and his (later in life) ecological critique of "modern" agricultural methods, Marx derided the problem of "soil exhaustion" (what we today would call soil depletion). At one point in volume 1 of *Capital*, Marx writes that "all progress in capitalist agriculture is a progress in the art, not only of robbing the worker, but of robbing the soil" ([1863] 1976:638). Concerns over soil exhaustion became rather acute in Britain in the early 1800s, arising as an important issue slightly later in North America and continental Europe in parallel with their emerging capitalist economies. Early on, the problem of diminished soil fertility was resolved by mixing into the soil guano (dung) imported from Peru, which eventually was replaced with artificial fertilizers.

Soil exhaustion during this period has been linked to the expansion of capitalism, which drew people into the cities to work in factories. As such, land had to be farmed utilizing more inputs (to support a growing population) and soon thereafter with machinery so a shrinking rural population could continue to farm all available arable land. Disconnecting people from the land caused major disruptions in the soil nutrient cycle in the form of too few nutrients in the countryside and far too many concentrated in cities, often in the form of sewage. The summer of 1858 in London was famously known as the summer of the Big Stink, as the Thames's smell was so foul that lawmakers were forced to flee Parliament for the countryside. These disruptions reeked both ecological and social havoc, a point Marx witnessed firsthand in London, where "they can do nothing better with the excrement produced by 4½ million people than pollute the Thames with it, at monstrous expense" ([1863–1865] 1981:195). And what was the "solution" to this problem? Was it to repair the rift by bringing agricultural practices in line with ecological limits? No. Instead, the solution was to exacerbate the rift through

ECOnnection 10.1

Treadmill/Metabolic Rift:
Declining Global Fish Stocks

Expansion of the capitalist enterprise into oceans has created another "rift," signified by the depletion of fish stock (Clausen 2005; Clausen and York 2008). As natural limits are approached, new technology is required to improve productivity and (temporarily) resolve tensions. Initially, making boats faster (so they can cover more territory) and larger (so they can stay out longer) and equipping them with technology to fish deeper (so greater depths can be exploited) seemed to do the trick. For a while, these gains in "efficiency" helped to keep supply up and the retail price of fish down, even as global fish stocks shrank. These technological "advances," however, did nothing to resolve the ecological tensions between capitalism and the aquatic ecosystems that are home to the world's ocean fish stock. In fact, they had precisely the opposite effect, as they sped up the treadmill. And so still further technological fixes were required. Enter capitalist aquaculture—a practice whereby fish are essentially treated like livestock. Yet the ecological limits still remain. As the most profitable farmed fish are carnivorous (e.g., Atlantic salmon), aquaculture continues to depend on wild fish, as they constitute the primary ingredient of fishmeal and fish oil. A farmed Atlantic salmon, for example, consumes four pounds of fishmeal for each one pound of live weight gain.

The treadmill of capital-intensive aquaculture is now running so fast that only a privileged few can compete in the market. A prawn farm in Queensland, Australia, for example, with all appropriate equipment, ponds, buildings, and processing facilities (*not* including land costs), is estimated to cost between AU$100,000 and $150,000 per hectare of pond. And the cost of an intensive pond-culture system that grows fifty tons of barramundi (also known as Asian sea bass) is AU$780,000. As the market becomes dominated by economically efficient (and ecologically inefficient) models of aquaculture, the small-scale fisher will find it increasingly difficult to remain economically viable. This is unfortunate, as the livelihoods of roughly 27 million people in less affluent nations are dependent upon being able to sell the fish they catch (Weeratunge and Snyder 2009).

artificial fertilizers—a solution that also sped up the treadmill, as those inputs had to be manufactured and purchased. This move might have resolved the problem of soil exhaustion in the short term, but it did nothing to deal with the root of the rift, as evidenced by the fact that our food continues to be produced in a fundamentally unsustainable manner.

The consequences of this rift are all around us (see ECOnnection 10.1). The first European Nitrogen Assessment (ENA) was released in 2011. It documents that nitrogen pollution is costing each person in Europe around £130–£650 (€150–€740) annually. The ENA represents the first time that the multiple threats of nitrogen pollution, including its impact on climate change and biodiversity, have been valued in economic terms on a continental scale. The study, carried out by two hundred experts from twenty-one countries and eighty-nine organizations, calculates that the annual cost of damage caused by nitrogen throughout Europe is £60–£280 billion (€70–€320 billion), a figure that is more than double the income gained from using nitrogen fertilizers in European agriculture (Sutton et al. 2011).

The overarching critique of the metabolic-rift thesis is the notion that capitalism, by its very nature, is slowly (yet undeniably) destroying the very thing it needs to survive: its material productive base. Clark and York put it as follows: "'Metabolic rift' refers to an ecological rupture in the metabolism of a system. The natural processes and cycles (such as the soil nutrient cycle) are interrupted. The division between town and country is a particular geographical manifestation of the metabolic rift, in regards to the soil nutrient cycle. But the essence of a metabolic rift is *the rupture or interruption of a natural system*" (2005:399; emphasis in the original).

Another Contradiction of Capitalism

Capitalism, as I've already described, has proven most resourceful. Population growth has no doubt aided in its growth. There is also a geographical dimension to its success, most notably globalization. Yet, as Marx and Engels (1978) noted so long ago, these tendencies produce contradictions, which must be resolved in some form so as not to derail the circulation of capital. And therein lies capitalism's transformational engine, in these contradictions and tensions that it then "resolves." This has allowed capitalism to continue on the tracks without (yet?) a major derailing of its logics.

Marx and Engels predicted that eventually such tensions would become too much for capitalism: "The development of Modern Industry, therefore, cuts from under its feet the very foundation on which the bourgeoisie produces and appropriates productions. What the bourgeoisie, therefore, produces, above all, is its own grave-diggers" (Marx and Engels [1848] 1978:483). The first contradiction of capitalism, as described by Marx and Engels, is overproduction—that eventually there will simply be too much stuff and not enough people able to buy it all. Continually substituting labor for capital logic would suggest that capitalism will eventually reach a point where low salaries and unemployment (and underemployment) will make it impossible for consumption rates to increase indefinitely. Before we ever reach this point, however, capitalism may hit a wall that stops it in its tracks. That's James O'Connor's thesis at least, which he calls the second contradiction of capital. Whereas the contradiction discussed by Marx and Engels centers on a crisis of demand, for O'Connor capitalism will, over time, witness a crisis of supply. This underproduction will occur as industry and the state—both of which are directed by the logics of capital—fail to protect the conditions of production, namely, the environment. "Put simply," in the words of O'Connor, "the second contradiction states that when individual capitals attempt to defend or restore profits by cutting or externalizing costs, the unintended effect is to reduce the 'productivity' of the conditions of production" (1998:245) (see ECOnnection 10.2). Or more simply still: no more resources, no more capitalism.

Globalization of Environmental Goods and Bads

One myth that continues to be perpetuated is that economic growth is good for the environment. As argued by the Property and Environmental Research Center (the oldest pro–free market and private property institute in the United States), "Market forces also cause economic growth, which in turn leads to environmental improvements. Put

ECOnnection 10.2

*Capital Shaping Humans in Its
Image: A Third Contradiction?*

Sociologist Peter Dickens (2001, 2004) has applied Marx's writings in a rather unique way to speak about potential linkages between the biological and the social. For Dickens, "Capitalism, in conjunction with the various forms of biological predispositions . . . may over the long term have been shaping human biology in its own image" (2001:106). For evidence of this Dickens points to, among other things, epidemiological work suggesting the effects of the mother's environment are transmitted to her unborn child. The implication is that inadequate prenatal care—which can alter "normal" (in developmental terms) rates of metabolism, hormonal excretion, blood flow, and the like within the uterus—can potentially lead to individuals born physiologically disadvantaged compared to those with adequate resources and capital. Futuristic accounts of gene therapy to cure illnesses (like diabetes) and inconveniences (such as nearsightedness), if someday realized, will initially be quite expensive. How might access to these technologies shape (literally) class relations? In sum, if Dickens is correct, the working class is at risk of becoming not only socially but also *physiologically* underprivileged and disadvantaged.

simply, poor people are willing to sacrifice clean water and air, healthy forests, and wildlife habitat for economic growth" (http://www.perc.org/articles/article446.php). What this quote misses is that well-off people do this too. And when you factor in for scale of impact, the environmental footprint of the impoverished turns out to be minuscule compared to the ecological damage inflicted daily to maintain the standard of living the affluent have come to expect. This should already be perfectly clear, based on what has been discussed thus far in the book. But in case you still need a little more convincing, allow me to take on a cherished concept among growth enthusiasts: the Environmental Kuznets Curve (EKC).

Critiquing the Environmental Kuznets Curve

Simon Kuznets (1955) famously postulated (and he won a Nobel Prize in economics for his efforts in 1971) that a country's transition from preindustrial to industrial to postindustrial initially leads to increasing income inequality, followed by greater income equality, and overall increases in per capita incomes. In the past two decades, the model was extended to environmental pollutants, as early analyses seemed to indicate that although air and water pollution levels frequently increased with initial economic growth, they eventually declined as countries reached a certain level of affluence (S. Dasgupta et al. 2002). This apparent pattern has come to be known as the Environmental Kuznets Curve. The EKC simply states that growth is (eventually) good for the environment. Although initially positively correlated with pollution, at some point economic growth becomes negatively associated with pollution and positively correlated with environmental quality (see Figure 10.2).

FIGURE 10.2 Environmental Kuznets Curve

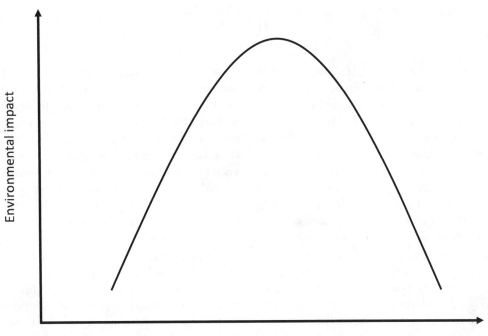

Economic development

There was some early empirical support for the EKC. Grossman and Krueger (1994), for example, examined urban air-pollution levels as well as water pollution for a number of countries. They found pollution indexes increased and then declined with economic affluence. In more recent years, however, the EKC has come under fire for mischaracterizing the extent of the environmental "efficiencies" that are said to be correlated with economic growth.

One criticism centers on what has come to be known as the Pollution Haven Hypothesis (PHH). Following the logic of comparative advantage, it is reasonable to assume that developing economies with weaker environmental regulations (and lax government enforcement of whatever regulations do exist) would attract polluting industries. Thus, the PHH posits that what we are seeing with the EKC is actually the result of polluting industry moving from developed to developing countries in search of governments more likely to turn a blind eye toward their activities. Though a reasonable hypothesis, it does not stand up well to empirical scrutiny. Studies have found "little" (Kearsley and Riddel 2010:905) to at best "some" (Eskelanda and Harrison 2003:1) evidence in support of the PHH. One major reason is that environmental costs are, for most industries, a relatively small share of overall operating costs. In other words, the benefit of being able to pollute does not typically outweigh other costs that would be incurred as a result of relocating to a haven (such as due to a poor infrastructure or undertrained labor force).

It is important to point out that the PHH speaks only to *emissions* associated with production, ignoring, for example, the mountains of toxic e-waste that end up being shipped annually to less developed countries to be "recycled." As mentioned in Chapter

Forest Transition Theory

In the early 1990s, Alexander Mather (1990, 1992) began writing about what became known as the Forest Transition Theory (FTT). Much like the EKC, the FTT speaks to a recurring pattern that countries seem to go through as they industrialize and urbanize. First, the theory posits, they go through a process of rapid deforestation while initially industrializing. At some point, however, after ascertaining a certain level of economic development, deforestation stops and reforestation begins.

Early formulations focused almost exclusively on Europe and North America. In the past ten years, greater focus has been placed on less affluent countries. The results have been mixed. A number of studies, for instance, illustrate how agricultural retreat and forest recovery in one area typically occur only at the expense of agricultural expansion and deforestation elsewhere (see, for example, Pfaff and Walker 2010). Evidence is also beginning to emerge suggesting that reforestation, in countries fortunate enough to undergo it, may be only a temporary phase, eventually giving way to still further drivers of deforestation. This appears to be happening in the eastern portion of the United States (Drummond and Loveland 2010). After a period of reforestation, recent prospects for additional forested land have diminished, as accelerated rates of forest cutting, low-density development in the countryside, and pressures placed on land due to biofuels are, once again, causing a net loss of forests in this region (see Figure 10.3).

Adapted from Drummond and Loveland (2010).

FIGURE 10.3 Forest Cover Changes in the Eastern United States

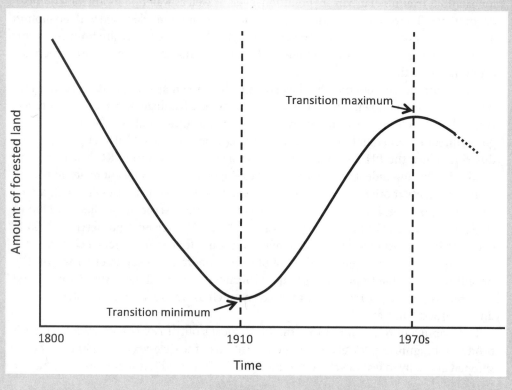

3, the evidence is mixed as to what actually gets recycled and what is landfilled or incinerated. My point is that the ecological footprint of a nation is more—*much* more—than its emissions. There is ample anecdotal evidence indicating that affluent nations are exporting their "environmental impact" (to reference the *y* axis in Figure 10.2) to other nations. We just have to look beyond industrial air emissions to find it. E-waste is just one well-publicized example of this. We also have to realize that residents of affluent nations might also pollute *differently* than their contemporaries in lower-income nations. An example of this is with air travel. Some 2 million people daily—or 730 million annually—fly in the United States (TSA 2010). In Indonesia, by comparison, which has roughly 75 percent of the population found in the United States, approximately 50 million flights are taken annually (Baskoro 2011). The EKC's most fatal flaw, however, resides in its mistaking *relative* efficiency for *absolute* efficiency. Technically speaking, as I tell my students, the EKC and its inverted-U curve is both right and wrong. It all depends upon how you define ecoefficiency (see ECOnnection 10.3). York, Rosa, and Dietz (2004), for example, found that the most affluent nations tend to be the most ecoefficient, as measured by ecological footprint per unit of GDP. However, these countries were also found to be guilty of having, in absolute terms, the largest ecological footprints.

World Systems Framework

Another body of literature highly critical of the EKC is the world-systems approach. This tradition in environmental sociology has produced a diverse array of sophisticated analyses to assess the relationship between world-system factors and environmental impacts. The relationship between affluent (a.k.a. "core") and less affluent (a.k.a. "periphery") nations, according to this literature, is an overwhelmingly exploitative one, as the former are able to extract far greater benefits from the present system than actors residing in the latter. Roberts and Grimes (1997), for example, have shown that an EKC for CO_2 emissions may be fundamentally unattainable for many periphery nations, as their position in the global economy has effectively fixed them into a particular emissions trajectory. As a result, they are locked out of being able to adopt many of the greener technologies used in affluent nations, for reasons tied to things like a lack of credit, capital, expertise, and the like. Other studies in this tradition have extensively documented the gross asymmetry between core nations, who consume the vast majority of the world's resources and produce a sizable chunk of its pollution, and those that are more peripheral, who experience the vast majority of the environmental *impacts* (Frey 1998; Jorgenson and Clark 2012).

Solutions

In light of the deeply embedded nature of the problems discussed throughout this book, I ask the reader for patience as solutions are rolled out over this and remaining chapters that take aim at their roots. The problems we face are complex, which is why I am certain that no proposed solution alone is sufficient. They are products of patterns of social organization, which though deeply flawed are not irreversible. I am not offering these solutions in an either-or spirit. Put them to work *collectively*—that's the source of my pragmatic optimism.

Total Cost Accounting

Many of the goods supplied by the environment are public in nature. A good is said to be public if it is nonrival and nonexcludable. Many ecological phenomena that we value, like biodiversity and clean air, exhibit these characteristics. Their nonrival character is evidenced by the fact that my use and enjoyment of these phenomena does not affect your use and enjoyment of them. For instance, my breathing as much clean air as I want does not affect your ability to stand next to me and enjoy the clean air too. They are also nonexcludable in the sense that it is usually rather difficult to prevent others from benefiting from their existence. Short of erecting domes around people or communities, how could you possibly make clean air excludable? Or take biodiversity, which is more problematic still from the standpoint of excludability. It benefits humanity in so many ways—from food security to the manufacturing of drugs, purifying of water, and the enriching of spirit—that excludability means more than just keeping people out of a bi-ologically diverse space.

As already discussed, the prevailing cost-price system is poorly equipped to account for damage to ecosystems and human communities. Climate change—the most significant market failure in history—is proof that current market mechanisms cannot be entrusted to protect long-term public and environmental health. Public goods tend to be underprovided—and underprotected—if left to the market, as costs are externalized and paid disproportionately by third parties, future generations, or society at large. This practice of socializing costs not only makes for a terribly unsustainable economic system, but is also incredibly unfair—a point I'll elaborate on in a moment. What, then, are our options if total cost accounting (or at least more honest cost accounting) is the goal?

One strategy that has been around for a while is known as "**Pigovian taxes**"—a tax levied on companies that pollute or create excess social costs (called negative externalities). English economist Arthur Cecil Pigou (1912) argued a century ago that the existence of externalities justifies government action. He advocated for pollution-avoidance charges and welfare-damage costs (a.k.a. taxes), which would be applied to any and all offending firms and activities. Such taxes would not only serve to disincentivize certain behaviors but also generate revenue to pay whatever costs were socialized (e.g., to clean up a polluted river) as well as any expenses associated with the administration and monitoring of firms.

The largest problem associated with Pigovian taxes involves getting the tax rate just right. If too low, the taxes will not sufficiently disincentive the behavior or provide sufficient revenue to pay for cleanup and enforcement; if too high, firms will be unduly burdened for costs that are not their own. Relatedly, information in these matters is always imperfect. For instance, when dealing with nonpoint-source pollution—like greenhouse gases—how can we be sure we're not overcharging some and undercharging others?

A notable challenge to the logic of Pigovian taxes came from economist Ronald Coase (1960), who argued that well-defined property rights to resources would nullify the need for government intervention and save society the inevitable efficiencies associated with antipollution taxes (noting the difficulty of getting tax rates just right). Coase's argument—or what is known today as the **Coase theorem**—alleges that when property rights are involved, parties naturally gravitate toward the most efficient and mutually beneficial outcome. Suppose a livestock producer holds the right to a stream (and thus the right—within limits—to pollute this stream) that a neighboring food processor draws its water from. Knowing precisely who owns what allows these individuals to negotiate an outcome that is suitable to both. The food processor has an incentive to pay the livestock producer to treat their wastewater, as long as that cost is less than the cost of treating their intake water. The livestock producer also has an incentive to accept payment, especially as they have an opportunity to profit from treating their waste. This is because the cost to the livestock producer of treating their concentrated manure will likely be less than the cost to the food processor for treating their more diluted intake water.

Unfortunately, real life is more complicated than idealized scenarios. What if there are thousands of competing firms with interests in this outcome? What does the negotiating process look like, and how do we ensure all parties' interests are heard? Moreover, who decides what's sufficiently "clean" when talking about treating water? I promise you that a brewery's definition is astronomically stricter than a steel refinery's. There is also space to justify species extinction under such an arrangement. As long as the negotiating parties agree on a particular definition of "clean water," what's to stop, say, an endangered bird that nests along the banks of the stream from going extinct if that definition does not suit the needs of wildlife? And what about future generations: are they also to be left entirely out of this negotiating process?

Pricing tangible and visible costs is one thing, which is difficult enough. Yet there are no markets for many of the things we value that are associated with ecosystems and communities. The market price for a pickup load of logs, for example, says absolutely nothing about the value they played in a previous life for things like flood control, water purification, habitat, and carbon sinking. As William Rees, founding member and past president of the Canadian Society for Ecological Economics, correctly points out, "This is why the consumer purchasing a board foot of lumber—or just about anything else—doesn't come close to paying the full social cost of production" (2009:470). So what are we to do? Again, Rees: "Such conclusions are not cause for despair but rather should liberate society from the dictates of oppressively wrong-headed economic models" (ibid.:471). Merely coming to the realization that the market can't solve all our problems is half the battle. Once we realize this, a world of possibilities opens up.

Fair (versus Free) Trade

If markets are insufficient, what, then, are our options? Let's take a step back and look closer at the precise type of capitalism that's driving today's global economy. It typically goes by the name of "neoliberalism." As David Harvey explains in *Brief History of Neoliberalism*, "Neoliberalism is in the first instance a theory of political economic practices that proposes that human well-being can best be advanced by liberating individual entrepreneurial freedoms and skills within an institutional framework characterized by strong private property rights, free markets, and free trade" (2005:2). As opposed to individual liberties (the holy grail in classic liberalism), neoliberalism sees salvation only through free enterprise—and a really no-holds-barred, dog-eat-dog approach to free enterprise at that (see ECOnnection 10.4).

What, then, is free enterprise? Or, better yet, taking another step back, what does "freedom" mean, as the term *free* comes up a lot when talking about markets (*free* markets,

ECOnnection 10.4
"Apolitical Ecologies" and Foucauldian Governance

The tendency to blame individuals for social and environmental problems is linked closely to the rise of neoliberalism and a shift toward neoliberal forms of what French philosopher Michel Foucault called "governance." Foucauldian governance, to admittedly oversimplify a highly nuanced concept, refers to the reduction of societal problems to an aggregate of individual ones. Doing this skillfully transfers responsibility for developing solutions from society as a whole onto individuals, making it up to individual consumers to do "the right thing." This move also supports the very system responsible for the problem in the first place. As good consumer-citizens, we are therefore taught to shop our way to safety, happiness, and sustainability by buying, in the case of environmental problems, ecofriendly products, high-efficiency gadgets, and carbon offsets.

Take the case of climate change. The most popular solutions are often individual ones, like *buying* hybrid cars, photovoltaic panels, and locally grown organic foods. Yet this disproportionately (and dangerously) places the focus on individual consumption choices rather than on creating policies that would enforce corporate accountability and lead to larger socioeconomic changes to the *system* responsible for the state we are in. In this sense, climate change can been seen as an **"apolitical ecology"**—a case where explanations do not fully account for the asymmetries in power that first created it materially and then later define it as a "problem" to be solved by the same system that gave birth to it (Robbins 2012). This move effectively absolves that system of any blame.

free enterprise, *free* trade, and so on). Like a small (but growing) cadre of economists (see, for instance, Sen 1984; Jackson 2009), I have found twentieth-century English philosopher Isaiah Berlin's dual understanding of freedom extremely useful for informing our understanding of all this free talk in economic parlance (Carolan 2011b).

Conventional understandings of free markets remain dangerously fixated on only one "side" of this dual understanding, as evidenced by the fact that free markets are rarely ever fair (see ECOnnection 10.5). That is because most of this talk is heavily infused with, to draw from Berlin, "freedom *from*" rhetoric—freedom *from* other countries' production-oriented subsidies, freedom *from* government regulation, freedom *from* the state, and so forth. Freedom *from* talk is especially pervasive in neoliberalism discourse. Isaiah Berlin describes this as "negative freedom," which refers to the "absence of interference" (1969:127). It seems as though when most people are asked about "freedom," negative freedom is the type most have in mind—a freedom where we are allowed to pursue actions unimpeded (see also Bell and Lowe 2000:287–289).

In addition to its negative component, freedom also has a positive side. "Positive freedom"—or freedom *to*—refers to the ability "to lead one prescribed form of life . . . that derives from the wish on the part of the individual to be his [or her] own master" (Berlin 1969:127). Without the active pursuit of positive freedom, most people would not—in-

ECOnnection 10.5
Fair Trade

Fair trade represents a producer-consumer relationship through a supply chain that attempts to distribute economic benefits more fairly between all stakeholders (Raynolds, Murray, and Wilkinson 2007). This is in contrast to the conventional supply-chain model, which primarily seeks the maximization of return somewhere in the middle of the food system. Fair trade makes trade fairer through a number of practices. Some of these practices include the following (taken from Nicholls and Opal 2005:6–7):

- *Agreed-upon minimum prices that are often higher than those set by the market.* This is in recognition that agricultural commodity market prices, thanks to things like subsidies and monopoly conditions, are rarely fair. Farmers are therefore given a living wage for their work.
- *An additional social premium is paid on top of the fair trade price.* This allows producers and farm laborers to collectively implement larger development projects (like the building of new schools). How the money is spent is usually decided democratically, through co-operatives.
- *Purchasing directly from producers.* This reduces the number of profit-taking "middlemen" in the commodity chain and ensures that more of each dollar spent on the goods returns to producers.
- *Making credit available to producers.* As importers from affluent countries typically have greater access to credit than developing-country producers, importers must prefinance a significant portion of the year's harvest.
- *Farmers and workers are democratically organized.* This helps minimize labor abuses (e.g., child and slave labor) and ensures socially responsible production practices.

A decade ago few had heard of "fair trade." Today, the label is almost as widely recognized globally as "organic." The extra income earned by fair trade producers from US sales alone has increased from almost zero in 1998 to roughly US$80 million in 2006 (Conroy 2007). Not blind to this growing popularity, multinational corporations are getting involved with fair trade. Starbucks, for example, generated an estimated fair trade social premium (money that's invested in community projects) of more than £350,000 from sales in the United Kingdom and Ireland alone in 2009 (Fair Trade Foundation 2009).

deed *could not*—feel free. To explain what I mean by this, I evoke an old English aphorism, "Freedom for the pike is death for the minnow." Without the pursuit of positive freedom for all—pikes and minnows alike—the pikes of the world would be clearly advantaged. And how do we actively pursue positive freedom for all? This is where the concept of *constraint*—which can only come from *outside* the market—comes into the picture. There must be some constraints if minnows are to prosper. Positive freedom, in other words, allows us to talk about constraint in the context of freedom without any sense of paradox.

Let's now apply this thinking to free markets, free enterprise, and the like. In order for me to be and feel free (and trade freely), I need some assurances that the pikes of the world will not freely have their way with me. This is why freedom—and, yes, free markets—*requires* some level of extramarket intervention. This intervention need not come solely in the form of government involvement. It can also exist as informal social norms, trust, and a shared sense of cooperation and responsibility. In a word, this constraint—where we seek to govern ourselves as well our sustainable use of the ecological commons—can also emerge out of *community* (community-based governance is discussed more fully in Chapter 11) (Ostrom 1999).

There is nothing radical about this argument. We as citizens routinely support policies that tie our hands, whether through government-mandated retirement savings programs, restrictions on advertisements to children, or restrictions on commodities themselves (Kysar 2010). No one would support a society that allowed, say, unrestricted violence or the selling of poisoned food. Also remember that an argument *for* restrictions is not an argument *against* a market economy (at least of some form). In the words of free-market advocate Tom Friedman, writing in the wake of the 2008 financial collapse, "We need to re-establish the core balance between our markets, ethics and regulations. I don't want to kill the animal spirits that necessarily drive capitalism—but I don't want to be eaten by them either" (2008).

In the end, markets, even "free" ones, work only *because of* regulation. Business as we know it today could not exist without contracts, which are made possible by a web of government-enforced rules and regulations. Regulation even helps businesses function by laying out clear rules about what they can and cannot do. As Harvard business professor Michael Porter argues, *stricter* environmental regulations are actually in the best interests of many firms and countries, as they provide these actors an important competitive advantage—what is known in the business community as the **Porter Hypothesis** (Frohwein and Hansjürgens 2005). The Porter Hypothesis notes that, among other things, regulation spurs innovation, as it creates incentives for firms to adjust to social and environmental realities (like diminishing natural resources). Those nations and regions slow to commit to stricter environmental regulations are therefore doing themselves a grave disservice, a fact they will pay dearly for in the near future as their firms struggle to compete against those better positioned to deal with the economic, social, and ecological realities of this century.

IMPORTANT CONCEPTS

- Environmental Kuznets Curve (EKC)
- fair versus free trade
- first and second contradictions of capitalism
- Forest Transition Theory (FTT)
- Foucauldian governance
- Isaiah Berlin's dual understanding of freedom
- metabolic rift
- neoliberalism
- Pollution Haven Hypothesis (PHH)

- rebound effect and the Jevons paradox
- relative versus absolute efficiency
- total cost accounting
- treadmill of production
- world-systems theory

DISCUSSION QUESTIONS

1. Have you ever invested in a more energy-efficient technology only to change your behavior and thus offset some (if not all) of those efficiency gains (as I did, as mentioned earlier, when I switched all the incandescent bulbs in my house for CFLs)?
2. In order for capitalism to be sustainable over the long term, what is going to need to happen?
3. Is the treadmill of production an optimistic or pessimistic theoretical framework? Why?
4. What are your thoughts on the position taken about how free markets actually *presuppose* a degree of restraint and government intervention in order to be free?

SUGGESTED ADDITIONAL READINGS

Foster, J. B. 2007. "The Ecology of Destruction." *Monthly Review* 58(9). Retrieved August 30, 2012 (http://monthlyreview.org/2007/02/01/the-ecology-of-destruction).

Owen, D. 2010. "Annals of Environmentalism: The Efficiency Dilemma." *New Yorker,* December 20, 78.

Wold, M. 2012. "Beyond 'Free' or 'Fair' Trade: Mexican Farmers Go Local." *YES!,* January 23. Retrieved August 30, 2012 (http://www.yesmagazine.org/peace-justice/beyond-free-or-fair-trade-mexican-farmers-go-local).

RELEVANT INTERNET LINKS

- http://www.env-econ.net/
  An interesting, independently managed website on subjects related to environmental economics.
- http://www.transfairusa.org/what-is-fair-trade
  Address to Fair Trade USA.

SUGGESTED VIDEOS

- *Capitalism: A Love Story* (2009)
  A critical look at the current economic order in the United States specifically.
- *The Corporation* (2003)
  A documentary that takes an extensive look at the modern-day corporation, in terms of, among other things, its legal status, its behavior toward people, and its impacts on the environment.
- *The Dark Side of Chocolate* (2010)
  A team of journalists investigates how human trafficking and child labor in the Ivory Coast fuel the worldwide chocolate industry.

- *There's No Tomorrow* (2012)
  http://topdocumentaryfilms.com/theres-no-tomorrow/. A half-hour animated documentary about resource depletion, energy, and the impossibility of infinite growth on a
  finite planet.
- *You Can't Be Neutral on a Moving Train* (2004)
  Soon to be a classic, this film chronicles the life and times of the great twentieth-century
  public intellectual Howard Zinn.

Governance: Biases
and Blind Spots

Informational and governance challenges make ecological sustainability a daunting enough goal at the national level. With globalization . . . let's just say the barriers to sustainability—*real* sustainability—increase exponentially. Making supplies of resources and absorption capacities simultaneously available to demand, as we have done, dulls the incentives for states to act in an ecologically responsible matter (Daly 1996). Yet if individual countries will not properly regulate what happens within their borders, no one can do it for them. And there's the rub: whereas today's most pressing environmental problems are global in scope, the regulatory "arms" available to monitor and enforce environmental law and policy weaken considerably when extended beyond their respective geopolitical borders.

This chapter, among other things, is interested in detailing *why* current environmental regulations and policies look like they do. Although there is an air of scientific objectivity to them, they ultimately rest on shifting sand, which is to say their logic is made possible only with the making of some very questionable value judgments. In the Solutions section, alternative and arguably more just and sustainable methods of governance are suggested.

Fast Facts

In 2010 the US Fish and Wildlife Service, which administers one of the world's most potent environmental laws directed at species protection—namely, the Endangered Species Act—extended the law's protections to the polar bear by designating roughly 190,000 square miles of onshore barrier islands in Alaska as "critical habitat." Yet the agency is incapable of doing anything about the leading threat to this creature: climate change (Kazlowski 2008).

Trans-Pacific transportation of pollution from Asia to North America is well documented (Akimoto 2003). Emissions of nitrogen dioxide (NO_2) and sulfur dioxide (SO_2) emanating from East Asia have been increasing at an average rate of roughly 4 percent annually since the 1970s (Fenn et al. 2003). US states are powerless to do anything about this transboundary pollution. Consequently, they must include it in their planning, treating it essentially as if it were their own when seeking to meet federally mandated air-quality standards (Parrish et al. 2011).

What about future generations? If current trends continue, we will leave for our children a world radically different from the one we inhabit today. Global sea levels will rise by 0.8 to 2.0 meters by 2100, which places low-lying countries (like Bangladesh) at severe risk of becoming submerged (US National Academy of Sciences 2011). Following current trends, the future will be less biologically (and hence culturally) diverse, drained of its resources and absorption capacities, and remarkably inequitable (Daly 1996).

Implications

We tried being objective. We tried ripping ourselves out of our political community when assessing and developing environmental policy, to be nowhere and no one while simultaneously everywhere and everyone. We tried to be fair by stripping policy decisions of all ethical consequence and significance. Guided by the so-called comprehensive rationality of cost-benefit analysis, we tried being and doing all these things. Yet for reasons that I will now detail, these goals have neither lived up to their promise nor made the world more sustainable. In fact, they may well have made many things worse.

Welfare Economics and Cost-Benefit Analyses

At its core, cost-benefit analyses are guided by what is known as **welfare economics.** Welfare economics, for those new to the term, is a branch of microeconomics that seeks to evaluate well-being, with the assumption that human well-being is wholly reducible to *economic* well-being. Welfare economics thus ascribe to an extreme form of methodological reductionism, which involves reducing all choices and things to economic terms—usually a dollar amount. Whenever confronted with a choice, it is assumed humans, being the rational creatures we are, will always select the one that brings us the greatest benefit. Even proponents of this approach admit that this process inevitably involves making problematic value assignments. For instance, how does one assign value to biodiversity, a wetland, or a human life? Yet given the risk of regulatory agencies and politicians becoming captured by things like money and persuasive constituents, advocates of the cost-benefit analysis approach insist its objectivity preserves policy analyses' integrity by letting "the facts" decide things and not emotions, values, and subjective interests.

Insurmountable problems, however, remain with this approach. First, the framework is inherently incomplete—after all, it's naive to think all well-being can be reduced to economic well-being (a point I elaborate on in the next chapter). More problematic still, it is incapable of seeing its own flaws, as evidenced by the fact that the approach actually thinks it is objective. Yet facts are incapable of speaking for themselves in matters of public health and environmental sustainability, given the tremendous level of uncertainties involved (see Ethical Question 11.1). *People* have to speak for those facts. And *who* those people are can matter tremendously.

Unpacking "Science"

Funtowicz and Ravetz (1992) provide us with a well-known framework that allows us to move away from a singular view of Science. When speaking of the highly ambiguous nature of today's environmental problems, they acknowledge that decisions can often only take place in a value-laden context. The practice of objective science, they contend, is ill-equipped to deal with any intermingling of facts and values and as such is grossly unprepared as a knowledge system for many of today's environmental problems. They develop their model around the two variables: "systems uncertainty" and "decision stakes" (see Figure 11.1). When dealing with questions that involve low levels of each, they suggest the use of "applied science." When dealing with medium levels of both variables, "professional consultancy" is suggested. And when questions involve high levels of these two variables, "postnormal science" is called for. According to Funtowicz and Ravetz, the way we practice science must change as we move from that of "applied" to that of "postnormal," as scientific questions require the making of additional value judgments. American nuclear physicist Alvin Weinberg noted some forty years ago how there are questions "which can be asked of science and yet which cannot be answered by science" (1972:209). So what should we do? According to Funtowicz and Ravetz, as scientific questions increase in their complexity and systems uncertainty, so too should there be an increase in who is involved in finding answers to them.

FIGURE 11.1 Postnormal Science Diagram

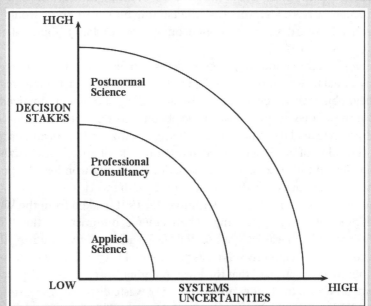

Funtowicz and Ravetz's framework, however, also makes subtle value judgments. For instance, who decides if something falls within the realm of applied science or professional consultancy? Where precisely do we lay down the boundaries between these three types of science? And who decides what constitutes "high" decision stakes? Questions like these are not unique to Funtowicz and Ravetz's model. We confront them every time we make an environmental policy decision.

The **Pareto optimality standard** is a core economic principle driving, and justifying, cost-benefit analyses and welfare economics more generally. The Pareto standard deems a policy acceptable only if at least one individual is better off and no individuals are made worse off. Without passing that minimal bar, a policy will not even be considered. Yet does it matter *who* is made better off? Let say "Policy A" makes Bill Gates and Warren Buffett (and only Gates and Buffet) *minimally* better off and no one worse off, while "Policy B" makes many destitute persons *considerably* better off but costs Gates and Buffet twenty bucks each (which is pocket change for either of them). I know what policy I would root for: Policy B. According to the Pareto optimality standard, however, because it explicitly doesn't care about issues of equity, *who* is being helped is irrelevant. So anyone following the principle would have to choose Policy A, as it harms no one.

While claiming otherwise, this standard also makes normative assumptions: namely, by valuing only living human interests. But there are so many other interests worth valuing, like nonhuman life forms, future generations, and human communities, just to name a few. How are we ever going to make smart policy choices as long as we judge policies with a standard that is vastly prejudicial toward living human interests? In the following quote, Nobel Prize–winning economist Amartya Sen makes plain the aimlessness—or "pointlessness," as Guido Calabresi (1991) famously called it—of this standard: "An economy can be [Pareto] optimal . . . even when some people are rolling in luxury and others are near starvation as long as the starvers cannot be made better off without cutting into the pleasures of the rich. If preventing the burning of Rome would have made Emperor Nero feel worse off, then letting him burn Rome would have been Pareto-optimal. In short, a society or an economy can be Pareto-optimal and still be perfectly disgusting" (1970:22).

The rush for welfare-economic policy analyses to make everything commensurate—that is to say, equal by way of reducing the world to monetary form—may make the approach appear objective, as technically all we are talking about are monetized costs and benefits. But this comes at great cost to society and the environment. One analysis of foreign aid policy calculates that the well-being of citizens in less affluent nations is 1/2,000 of the value of an American citizen (Kopczuk, Slemrod, and Yitzhaki 2005). With such a view of the citizens of poorer nations, is it any wonder why polluting industries and e-waste flow so readily to these parts of the world?

A widely circulated memo, dated December 12, 1991, leaked from the World Bank, articulated precisely such reasoning. Then chief economist for the World Bank Lawrence Summers (who was later appointed US Treasury secretary during the Clinton administration and subsequently served as president of Harvard University) penned the now-infamous memo. It argued that the lower marginal cost of waste disposal in a poor country compared with the higher marginal cost of waste disposal in a waste-producing affluent country justifies the latter polluting the former. The memo further argues that the poorest countries of Africa are vastly underpolluted, as they are underutilizing what affluent countries desperately need, namely, waste sinks.

In appearing to be nonethical, the welfare-economic approach ends up being terribly *un*ethical. In an essay titled "The Rights of Statistical People," Lisa Heinzerling puts the absurdity of this practice in plain sight:

We do not, for example, believe that so long as it is worth $10 million to one person to see another person dead, and so long as current estimates of the value of human life are lower than $10 million, it is acceptable for the first person to shoot and kill the second. . . . Yet when it comes to regulatory programs that prevent deaths—deaths also due to the actions of other people—it has become commonplace to argue that the people doing the harm should be allowed to act so long as it would cost more for them to stop doing the harm than the harm is worth in monetary terms. (2000:189)

When we reduce human life to statistical terms, we deny those people the dignity to be thought of as humans. Similarly, by monetizing ecosystems and nonhuman life, we miss out on the opportunity to value things on their own terms. This can lead to, for example, the view that waste sinks in Africa ought to be filled with pollution from affluent nations just because sinks are substitutable.

It is entirely realistic to expect this approach to assign a lower value to those of lower socioeconomic status as well as to particular racial minorities, as certain ethnic groups are disproportionately overrepresented among lower-income strata. In having lower incomes and thus less buying power, welfare economics sees these people as having less value, literally, than those with higher incomes. Welfare economics therefore *justifies* certain types of environmental racism (Kysar 2010). Yet welfare economists are okay with this, as the outcome "would not be the result of a government decision to take racial characteristics into account; in fact it would not be a product of any group-level discrimination on the government's part" (Sunstein 2004:391). So discrimination that can be justified with statistics is okay? And where's room for justice in all of this? How can we *ever* expect the economically disadvantaged to achieve upward mobility when our policy assessment tools view their lives as having less worth than those that are affluent?

Tyranny of the Present: Discounting

Welfare-economic policy analysis also has a distinct way of looking at the future. To its credit, it is consistent. It utilizes a technique to monetize future well-being, thus making it comparable with well-being today. Enter the practice of discounting.

Following this procedure, an increment of value today is worth more than that same increment in the future. Or, as noted by Cowen and Parfit, at a 5 percent discount rate, "one statistical death next year counts for more than a billion deaths in four hundred years" (1992:147). Seen through this lens, the foot-dragging we've been witnessing in regards to climate change policy starts making sense. Thanks to discounting, it is entirely possible to settle on a policy option that may knowingly result in human extinction hundreds of years from now, but because it also lowers the well-being of some today, it is deemed unacceptable. Douglas Kysar has a wonderful term for this: "tyranny of the present" (2010:148) (see ECOnnection 11.1).

Let's review some of the logic that underlies discounting. Proponents of the practice argue that the procedure is necessary to ensure that current generations maximize their investment of financial *and* natural capital opportunities. This, or so the argument goes, benefits not only the living but also future generations by maximizing the option set

ECOnnection 11.1

Discounting and Forest Management

With harvesting cycles that are often longer than twenty years—and for some tree species they can extend well beyond one hundred years—forestry management is premised upon fairly long time horizons. The discount rate used therefore matters immensely. High discount rates greatly reduce the likelihood of sustainability, as it creates little or no incentive to replant after one rotation, especially as long as there remains a substantial amount of unlogged forest to be exploited (Pearce, Vanclay, and Putz 2002). Lower discount rates, conversely, can make things like replanting incredibly attractive. All this matters enormously, as forestry provides us with so much more than just wood—from potential genetic materials to tourism, biodiversity, and carbon storage. Throughout much of the twentieth century, forestry discount rates were high and discouraged practices that would lead to truly sustainable yields (Hepburn and Koundouri 2007).

bequeathed to them—a type of "trickle forward" reasoning (Kysar 2010:162). But *what* precisely are these benefits we are leaving the future? Answer: monetized well-being. The exact "stuff" left for later generations is irrelevant, according to the welfare-economic policy analysis. As articulated by two prominent welfare economists writing on the topic of sustainable development, "There is no abstract reason to believe that preserving a particular environmental amenity (a forest, a lake) is always better for posterity than other investments that do not involve the environment in particular (expenditures on basic research, reductions in national debt)" (Sunstein and Rowell 2007:203). Remember, at the core of this approach is the assumption of ultimate substitutability among different types of capital. Money is just as good as anything else—in fact *better* because it can be converted into a variety of things (as long as they are not extinct, depleted, or soiled beyond repair).

Eric Neumayer, a prominent welfare economist, has argued that future generations might actually prefer to face higher skin-cancer rates if those risks come in exchange for some greater benefit. As Neumayer explains, "Whether future generations will accept an increase in the rate of skin cancer or not depends on what they get in exchange for it" (1999:40). Even if he's right, how can we possibly know what future generations would accept in exchange for higher rates of skin cancer, and how can we be sure this Faustian bargain is agreeable to all and not just a privileged few? Welfare economists have even managed to justify the discounting of physical deformities, arguing that the cost to care for those deformities is likely to go down. In other words, we ought to value the avoidance of future deformities less than steps toward avoidance today (see, for example, Samida and Weisbach 2007). This argument, however, flatly misrepresents the ethical question at hand. "The nature of the ethical question on the table," remarks Kysar, "is not how to care for or cure a deformity that has already been suffered, but instead whether to inflict the pain in the first place." He continues: "By presuming that there is no ethically relevant distinction between living as a nondeformed individual and living as a deformed individual who has received compensation, the economist's response violated the most fundamental ethical precept, that individuals should not be used without their consent as a mean rather than as ends. Harm is inflicted—future individuals are used and indeed scarified without their consent—in order to promote well-being that they will not enjoy" (2010:170).

The Self-Interested Straw Person

When weighing policy options, the welfare economist also assumes the worst of people. I am talking about the selfish, self-interested depiction of individual behavior assumed by most policy analysts today. Curiously, economists seem to best fit this model, which makes me wonder if this "truth" speaks less about human nature and more about the power of perception, a bit of a case of what we call in the social sciences a self-fulfilling prophesy. It has been shown, for example, that economics majors are more likely than noneconomics students to free ride and are less likely to work cooperatively, just as their discipline would predict (Carter and Irons 1991; Marwell and Ames 1981). One of the dangers of this assumption comes across in international relations. Because national governments are believed to be an aggregate of self-interested people, international policy not surprisingly assumes states to be equally selfish. This stance is of tremendous policy consequence as far as the environment is concerned.

For example, through this lens international relations are viewed as occurring in a space of self-interested competition, leaving no room for anything like cooperation. Yet given that so many of our problems are global in character, trust and collaboration are precisely what we need more of. As long as nation-states assume the worst of other nation-states, it is hard to see how global sustainability will ever be practically attained.

We see this continually in international negotiations over climate change. Countries like the United States are unwilling to commit to any greenhouse gas reductions out of a fear that other developing economies will selfishly free ride and do nothing. President George W. Bush was making precisely this point when he said that without "an accord with China, China will produce greenhouse gas emissions that offset anything we do in a brief period of time" (as quoted in Kysar 2010:142). Indeed, this was the crux of the US government's argument in *Massachusetts v. EPA* (2007).

Massachusetts v. EPA is a US Supreme Court case (decided by a vote of five to four in 2007) between twelve US states (and several US cities) and the Environmental Protection Agency (EPA). The former were seeking to force the latter to regulate CO_2 and other greenhouse gases as pollutants. The US government employed a couple of arguments in its defense. The first, building on this free-rider problem, went along the following lines: because it makes no difference at the global level whether the EPA does or does not regulate these emissions, as other countries (most notably China) will continue to pollute at ever-greater levels, why bother with such regulations? The other argument was based on a welfare-economic approach to international relations: namely, forcing the US government to act unilaterally in regard to greenhouse gas emissions "might hamper the President's ability to persuade key developing nations to reduce emissions" (http://www.law.cornell.edu/supremecourt/text/05-1120). In other words, because states do not (and cannot not) work together cooperatively, responding only to various sticks and carrots, the US government would rather wait to regulate its greenhouse gas emissions. This would give it a bargaining chip to play at some future negotiation to show other countries its willingness to reduce greenhouse gas emissions.

President George W. Bush, during a meeting with European leaders in 2007, explained that "each country needs to recognize that we must reduce our greenhouse gases and deal, obviously, with their own internal politics to come up with an effective strategy that hopefully, when added together, . . . leads to a real reduction" (White House n.d.). Given all that's at stake, I should think we need to rely upon more than just "hope" when developing policies at both domestic and international levels. Yet that's what the welfare-economic approach asks us to do: to go it alone and hope that "when added together," our actions in the aggregate will amount to something that resembles global sustainability. That's a lot to ask for.

Solutions

When I discuss with students the various social drivers that underlie today's environmental problems, and equally create impediments to future solutions, many are initially frustrated after having been informed of the points just highlighted. On the one hand, here is a case where we literally just need to change how we think about things. On the other hand, the welfare-economic policy analysis is so entrenched in political, economic, and policy thought that it will require a lot of work to move away from it. The approach is also remarkably efficient at getting the job done, even though its outputs are highly problematic and ultimately unsustainable. There are alternatives, as I now detail, though it will require a collective rolling up of our sleeves if we want to see the welfare-economic policy approach overturned.

From Tragedy to Drama

The assumption that there is a self-interested individual lying at the core of welfare-economic policy analysis is not without some empirical grounding. This caricature is famously detailed in Garret Hardin's classic essay from 1968, "The Tragedy of the Commons." Though well-known, it is worth repeating some of its more relevant passages here: "Picture a pasture open to all. It is to be expected that each herdsman will try to keep as many cattle as possible on the commons. Such an arrangement may work reasonably satisfactorily for centuries because tribal wars, poaching, and disease keep the numbers of both man and beast well below the carrying capacity of the land. Finally, however, comes the day of reckoning, that is, the day when the long-desired goal of social stability becomes a reality. At this point, the inherent logic of the commons remorselessly generates tragedy" (1244).

Assuming that each herdsperson wishes to maximize their gain, they begin to ponder the consequences of adding one more animal to their herd. It quickly dawns on them that the costs and benefits of such an action are unevenly distributed. The herdsperson receives all the proceeds from the sale of the additional animal. Yet the effects of overgrazing are shared by all. It is therefore perfectly rational for, and therefore expected that, herdspersons in such a situation will continually add animals to their herd—*all* herdspersons. And therein lies the tragedy: everyone acting in their own self-interests, when resources are shared and limited, will have catastrophic ends, leading Hardin to conclude, famously, "Freedom in a commons brings ruin to all" (ibid.).

CASE STUDY 11.1

Central Government, Privatization, or Common-Property Regime?

David Sneath (1998) examined levels of grassland degradation in northern China, Mongolia, and Russia. Mongolia has allowed pastoralists to continue practicing their traditional group-property institutions, which involve large-scale movements between seasonal pastures, whereas Russia and China for much of the latter half of the twentieth century moved toward state-owned agricultural collectives with permanent settlements (though in the 1990s China began privatizing some of its pasturelands). Interestingly, the grassland in Mongolia shows far fewer signs of degradation than comparable land in either China or Russia. About 75 percent of the pastureland in the Russian sector studied has been degraded, while more than one-third the Chinese sector shows a significant level of degradation. Yet in the Mongolian sector examined, only one-tenth has suffered degradation.

Yet as Dietz and colleagues (2002) highlight in their thorough review of the commons literature since Hardin's essay, prototypical scenarios—like Hardin's essay—always end up oversimplifying things. Some case studies tell a story similar to Hardin's. Many others have much happier endings.

One of the most relevant critiques leveled at Hardin is that he conflates common-property and open-access regimes. Common-property regimes are ones "where the members of a clearly demarcated group have a legal right to exclude nonmembers of that group from using a resource. Open access regimes (*res nullius*)—including the classic cases of the open seas and the atmosphere—have long been considered in legal doctrine as involving no limits on who is authorized to use a resource" (Ostrom 2000: 335–336). This is an important distinction, as common property should not be mistaken to mean everyone's property (Ciriacy-Wantrup and Bishop 1975). Under common-property regimes, users *already have* use rights that are maintained through thick webs of social relationships. What from the "outside" may look ungoverned (as there may be no formal laws and rules and state-sanctioned monitoring) could actually be very well governed through local customs, trust, and informal social norms (see, for example, Goldman 1998).

It is concerning that resource privatization—one of Hardin's suggestions to avert the tragedy—may in fact be one of the reasons the tragedy is playing out in some parts of world (see Case Study 11.1). Late-twentieth-century policy reforms are transforming common-property regimes into either state government–owned or private-property regimes. When this happens, however, especially in developing nations, rarely are sufficient moneys and resources devoted to the monitoring of these now non-common-property resources. "Thus, what had been de facto common property with some limitation on access and use patterns become de jure government [or individual] property—but due to the lack of enforcement, it frequently became de facto open access" (Dietz et al. 2002:13).

The late Elinor Ostrom and her various collaborators have extensively documented that common-property resource governance need not end tragically. As it turns out, we are not as self-centered as the welfare-economic approach makes us out to be. There are many examples of long-enduring and sustainable common-property situations from around the world. Sustainable self-governance requires the development of rules and institutions that define such things as the physical boundaries of the property held in common, who has access to the resource, a sustainable rate of extraction and use, the methods for monitoring the resource, a system for resolving conflicts, and suitable sanctions and punishments for transgressions. Robert Netting (1981), in his classic study of a Swiss Alpine village, identifies five environmental variables that contribute to a resource being held as common rather than private property:

- the value of harvestable resource is low per unit of area
- what can be harvested varies considerably over time
- investment in improvements yield relatively small increases in productivity of resource
- overall costs can be reduced if activities (e.g., herding or processing dairy products) can be shared collectively
- infrastructure cost (e.g., fences and buildings) can be reduced if built on a larger scale

Perhaps the largest omission in Hardin's essay, and precisely why we are not as self-centered as the welfare-economic caricature assumes, is the fact that people *talk to one another*. The role of face-to-face interaction in building social capital and establishing those aforementioned thick social relationships that can rein in otherwise selfish behavior is well documented in the social science literature (Flora 2008; Flora et al. 2009; Pretty and Ward 2001; social capital was introduced in Chapter 7). Some interesting laboratory experiments have been conducted to better understand the role that communication plays in averting tragedy-like outcomes. The verdict: the ability to communicate and coordinate drastically alters outcomes.

Group communication fosters the formation of group identity and therefore reduces the likelihood of selfish behaviors. Individuals instead are more willing to think in terms of what's best for the collective versus what's exclusively best for them (Orbell, van de Kragt, and R. Dawes 1988; Ostrom, Gardner, and Walker 1994).

When individuals are placed in a situation where they cannot communicate with others, they are more likely to act selfishly with regard to the use of shared resources (Ostrom et al. 1994).

More recently, research has gone beyond studying resources at a particular scalar level, looking instead at common-property resources that cut across many levels. One obvious difference between global and local resources is the extent of the former and inherent difficulties associated with monitoring and enforcing sustainable use patterns (Dietz et al. 2002). Building and maintaining social capital between social groups from different continents with different backgrounds also complicate matters. Some common-property resources—like fresh water in an international basin or marine ecosystems—are best viewed in an international context. Their effective management therefore depends on the cooperation of appropriate international institutions and national, regional, and local institutions (Ostrom et al. 1999).

CASE STUDY 11.2

Reducing Emissions from Deforestation and Forest Degradation

Reducing Emissions from Deforestation and Forest Degradation (REDD) is a collaborative international initiative under negotiation within the UN climate talks and other international forums that will help to compensate governments, communities, companies, and individuals in low-income countries for actions that protect forests. Forests not only absorb CO_2 from the atmosphere, but when destroyed or degraded also release large amounts of this greenhouse gas, contributing significantly to global warming. It is estimated that forest loss contributes as much as 15 percent of annual greenhouse gas emissions, a figure roughly equivalent to the entire global transportation sector. And when forest and peat-land degradation are included in estimates, the figure increases to 20 percent (van der Werf et al. 2009).

REDD is expected to eventually involve the transfer to developing countries of some US$15–25 billion annually through a variety of performance-based mechanisms. One of the negotiating sticking points at the moment involves deciding what precisely receiving countries can do with that money. A number of governments, for example, want that money used to purchase remote sensing technologies for purposes of monitoring, assessment, reporting, and verification of carbon credits. Others hope to see a large portion of the money used for social development projects, particularly for the indigenous and forest-dependent peoples who will effectively be the stewards of the forests. Down the road, the hope is that REDD can be extended to cover emissions from agricultural practices (Global Witness 2010).

For this to work, effective governance structures must exist. This means not only the existence of coherent policy, laws, and regulations but also the effective implementation and enforcement of those policies, laws, and regulations. In order to give the scheme legitimacy, there must also be transparent and accountable decision making and institutions so as to ensure the program functions equitably and incorporates checks and balances. This transparency and accountability will also foster trust across scales (Saunders and Reeve 2010). Building this capacity, however, will take time. Take, for example, the development of the Philippine national REDD strategy. It has developed an eleven-year timeline to go from local capacity building to regional capacity building to eventually national performance-based implementation and compensation.

Ultimately, the evidence indicates that while complicating matters, the global character of some of today's environmental problems should not be viewed as a guaranteed ticket to a world of despair (Fisher 2004; see Case Study 11.2). Elinor Ostrom (who was awarded the 2009 Nobel Prize in Economic Sciences for her work on this very subject) and collaborators explain the future potential of global governance as follows:

> The lessons from successful examples of CPR [common-property resource] management provide starting points for addressing future challenges. Some of these will be institutional, such as multilevel institutions that build on and complement

local and regional institutions to focus on truly global problems. Others will build from improved technology. For example, more accurate long-range weather forecasts could facilitate improvements in irrigation management, or advances in fish tracking could allow more accurate population estimates and harvest management. . . . In the end, building from the lessons of past successes will require forms of communication, information, and trust that are broad and deep beyond precedent, but not beyond possibility. . . . There is much to learn from successful efforts as well as from failures. (Ostrom et al. 1999:282).

Absolute Sustainability

Welfare-economic policy analyses have a very narrow understanding of "sustainability." According to proponents of this approach, it is necessary to ensure that current generations maximize their investment opportunities in the hope that benefits will trickle "forward" to later generations. Yet *what* are these benefits that we're leaving the future? The precise "stuff," as I have mentioned, is irrelevant (see Sunstein and Rowell 2007:203). Rather, what matters under this calculus is monetary value. This gives the approach the veneer of objectivity by removing from the decision-making process subjective values and emotions—after all, we're "just" talking about dollars and cents.

Clearly, however, *stuff* matters. To repeat a familiar adage: you can't eat GDP. Yet our welfare economist has a response to this: the perfect substitutability assumption. When resources become scare, the higher market price will force innovation and lead, eventually, to suitable substitutes. Although the assumption might hold for some goods, like fuel (biofuels substituting for gasoline) and certain foods (high fructose corn syrup substituting for sugar), no one can seriously hold out similar hope for marine ecosystems, the ozone layer, clean air, and endangered species.

I return to my earlier call for absolute sustainability. Thomas Jefferson famously wrote in a letter to James Madison in 1789 that "the earth belongs in usufruct to the living" (as quoted in Sloan 1993:281). (*Usufruct* means to have a legal right to enjoy and profit from something that belongs to another.) Given that the survival of (future) billions rides on our actions today, it seems like we do indeed have something akin to a duty to leave a sufficient amount of "stuff" intact and minimally adulterated for the future. Monetary wealth will indeed protect some in the future from climate change and provide some with fish if the marine ecosystem were to collapse. Yet I am far less worried about the well-being of the world's future affluent; they will very likely have the resources to protect and take care of themselves. It's the welfare of the other 99 percent of the world's population who will have considerably less that concerns me.

How, then, should we fold future generations into our thinking? Clearly, they cannot speak for themselves. Some economic theorists have begun to argue that the widely used *constant* discount rates are unjustified. When you set a fixed annual discount rate at, say, 5 percent, it is entirely possible to reject a policy option that may knowingly save the human race from extinction hundreds of years from now on the basis that it also lowers the well-being of some today. As opposed to the constant discount rate, some have suggested that the correct social discount rate should decrease with time, beginning, for example, for a short time at 3.5 percent and declining over the long run to 1 percent or less (Hepburn and Koundouri 2007).

There are also some nondiscounting options. Schelling (1995), for example, argues we should make investments explicitly for future peoples just like we do with foreign aid today (future aid?). One benefit of this approach is that it brings the subject of future well-being into the sphere of public consciousness, as opposed to the standard practice, which is generally to never talk about future generations unless it is politically expedient to do so. Of course, this practice does not guarantee anything for future generations, as evidenced by the recent sharp declines in foreign aid by most affluent nations. And it could conceivably make matters worse for the future, as it could provide justification for even more egregiously unsustainable behavior under the guise that "we're aiding the future in other ways."

Others have suggested abandoning discounting altogether for something more democratic in character. Kopp and Portney (1999), for instance, propose mock referenda, where a random sample of the population is presented with a detailed description of the likely effects, current and future, of the various proposed policies. The participants would then vote for or against the policy (see also Page 2003). As opposed to the disinterested rationality of the welfare-economic approach, this style of "rationality depends on the virtues of collective problem solving; it considers the reasonableness of ends in relation to the values they embody and the sacrifices we must make to achieve them" (Sagoff 1988:70). Importantly, this approach is not necessarily antithetical to the welfare-economic framework. Things could still be monetized but only after the policy has been chosen. Thus, rather than *determining* the policy selected, "the value will simply be an ancillary effect of a policy choice that was premised on social values" (Kysar 2010:114). This technique could stop the policy foot-dragging that currently exists around climate change. I try something similar to this with my students. They are presented with reports that calculate projected costs associated with the taking of major steps to mitigate humans' greenhouse gas emissions and to adapt to changes already under way. They are then given other estimates as to the costs to society if nothing is done. This is followed by a conversation about the "value" of future generations and the impacts climate change could have upon them. After these future costs are vaguely established (we never seem to settle on a fixed figure), I ask my students how they compare to the costs associated with implementing aggressive climate change policy today. Taking action today *always* proves the most cost-effective option.

The Precautionary Principle

There was a time in the United States when we talked more about environmental rights than optimal trade-offs, of steward obligations than discounted welfare maximization, and of international cooperation than global competitiveness (Kysar 2010). The Endangered Species Act of 1973, for instance, placed the value of species at "incalculable," thereby, for a time, excluding from consideration *any* economic calculus. Similarly, the UN Environment Programme Participation Act of 1973 declared it "is the policy of the United States to participate in coordinated international efforts to solve environmental problems of global international concern" (United States Code 2002:159). As written in the National Environmental Policy Act of 1969, the US Congress recognized that it is the responsibility of the federal government to, among other things, "fulfill the responsibilities of each generation as trustee of the environment for succeeding generations." Finally, going back in time still further, we have the Delaney Clause. This 1958 amendment to the Food, Drugs, and Cosmetic Act of 1938 states that "the Secretary of the Food and Drug Administration shall not approve for use in food any chemical additive found to induce cancer in man, or, after tests, found to induce cancer in animals" (as recorded in Merrill 1997:313). Note the definitiveness of this language. There is no room for the comparing of an additive's health risks with its perceived economic benefits.

We currently assume the worse of people and the best of the technologies that are created at the hands of these self-centered, selfish people. When it comes to assessing the potential threats of novel technologies and setting up environmental, health, and safety regulations, the tendency, especially in the United States, is to take the position of "innocent until proven guilty." This represents, at its most basic level, the traditional risk assessment. Risk assessment, in effect, places the onus on regulatory agencies and the general public to prove that a given technology or industrial activity is not safe. Or, to put it another way, we have to falsify the statement "It's safe." This places us in a noticeably different regulatory environment from where we were when, say, the Delaney Clause was in full effect (see ECOnnection 11.2).

An alternative to the traditional risk assessment is the precautionary principle. The precautionary principle is generally recognized as having emerged in the 1970s, though its ethos dates back to the Hippocratic Oath, which states "First do no harm" (Christoforou 2003). Since then, the precautionary principle has flourished in a variety of settings. Arguably, its first international application came in 1984, at the First International Conference on Protection of the North Sea. From there, it has been integrated into numerous conventions and agreements, including, for example, the Maastricht Treaty on the European Union, the Barcelona Convention, the Global Climate Change Convention, and Principle 15 of the Rio Declaration. One popular definition of the precautionary principle comes from the 1998 Wingspread Statement on the Precautionary Principle: "When an activity raises threats of harm to human health or the environment, precautionary measures should be taken even if some cause and effect relationships are not established scientifically. In this context the proponent of the activity, rather than the public, should bear the burden of proof" (Raffensperger and Tickner 1999:8).

Admittedly, this statement leaves the concept ill-defined, vague, and difficult to translate into practical action (Turner and Hartzell 2004). For instance, what constitutes a "threat"? What about those cases where human well-being is enhanced while the health of the environment is threatened? What does the term *precautionary measures* mean? And who are the "proponents" that this statement refers to: those producing the technology in question, those who benefit from it, or those who may profit from it?

Proponents would argue that the function of such an "open" definition is to ensure that the principle remains variable and contingent, which is admirable given the indeterminate nature of the systems (ecological, social, and so on) that it seeks to protect. Yet in the face of such ambiguity, it then becomes left to interested parties (regulators, industry representatives, environmental advocacy organizations, and the like) to work out the details. What guarantee is there then that powerful actors will not shape those policy specifics to benefit their interests, while excluding the interests of the less powerful? There are two applications of the precautionary principle: one "strong" and one "weak" (Carolan 2007).

The precautionary principle has frequently been interpreted as calling for the absolute proof of safety before new technologies are adopted (this is a popular reading among its critics). This "strong" formulation, for example, can be seen in a statement

ECOnnection 11.2

Regulation: Who Does It Impact?

Environmental sociologist William Freudenburg (2005) dismantles the following six arguments that purport the "necessity" of pollution:

Pollution is economically vital as measured in dollars.
False: Roughly 60 percent of all US toxic releases come from economic sectors that account for less than 5 percent of GDP.

Pollution is economically vital as measured in jobs.
False: Roughly 60 percent of all US toxic releases come from economic sectors that account for less than 1.5 percent of the nation's jobs.

Heavily polluting activities are vital to the economy because they involve specific high-value materials that are impossible to produce without significant environmental damage.
False: Heavily polluting industries are often not involved in the making of "cutting-edge" technologies and often use outdated, inefficient technologies.

Regulated industries would go out of business.
False: Freudenburg (1991), in an earlier study, found that US states rated by national firms as

having bad "business climates" (e.g., because of stringent environmental and related regulations) actually experienced *more economic growth* than states rated more favorably.

Regulated industries would go to countries with weaker standards.
False: Research indicates (e.g., Repetto 1995) that regulated industries have generally not left the country in response to higher regulations. Even in cases where firms in the environmentally regulated sectors had moved their investments abroad, they tended to move not to developing countries with weaker environmental regulations but to other affluent countries.

Regulation would be too hard on the larger economy.
False: The falsification of the latter five arguments causes this one to ring hollow.
Freudenburg (2005:104) argued that these charges are examples of **"diversionary reframing,"** where attention is diverted away from real problems by trying to reframe the debate as being about something else (Freudenburg and Gramling 1994). Critics of heavily polluting industries are therefore said to be "un-American" or "socialists," all in an attempt to make the issue about the critics rather than about the harmful activities being perpetuated on humans and the environment.

by environmental writer Jeremy Leggett when he argued that "the modus operandi we would like to see is: 'Do not emit a substance unless you have proof it will not do harm to the environment'" (1990:459). Thus, whereas traditional risk assessments presume things to be safe until proven guilty (harmful), under this variant of the precautionary principle, the assumption is that technologies are guilty (harmful) until proven safe. In doing this, the responsibility of "proof" is placed on the shoulders of industry versus the general public and regulatory agencies.

In principle, this position is commendable. It holds a certain degree of moral currency by providing what many would consider a fair and just way of regulating technology: namely, those who stand to make millions from a given technology should likewise bear the burden of proof when demonstrating that such profits are not coming at the expense of humans, the environment, or both. Yet there are grave logical problems with this approach: namely, no product could ever meet the required threshold to be allowed onto the market. How does one prove that a given technology will do no harm to either humans or the environment—that is, how does one prove the statement "It's safe"? Karl Popper (1961) famously argued that theories often take the following form: all Xs are Ys. For example: "All snow is white" or "All bodies attract one another with a force proportional to the product of their masses and inversely proportional to the square of their distance apart." To refute such a theoretical form requires that one find a single X that is not also a Y. To prove such a theory, however, would require that one observe every single X to make sure that it is indeed also a Y. Yet this would mean that one must engage in an exhaustive search of not only the entire universe but of the universe from the beginning to the end of time. Logically, therefore, while refutations of theories appear to be at least possible, confirmations (as a basis for "proof") are not.

One way to salvage the precautionary principle is to weaken our interpretation of "proof." Ultimately, nothing in this world is *totally* safe. Water can be lethal when too much is ingested. The same can be said for tea, coffee, apples, oxygen, sunlight. . . . Perhaps, then, a better way of putting it is seeking proof of being reasonably safe (Tickner 2003). With this move, we can now drink water and tea without the fear of regulatory agencies outlawing their use. Yet in doing this, the precautionary principle slips into something noticeably less novel. To speak of something being "reasonably safe" sounds an awful lot like risk assessment's claim of being about establishing "what's a reasonable risk."

Call it what you want: risk assessment, precautionary principle, or precautionary risk management—what we ultimately need are more open decision-making structures. And not just at the point of regulation. Regulation is something we do at the "back end" of the production process, *after* a product has been made. What about the decisions that are made at the "front end" of the production process, *before* a technology has been developed and mass-produced? As sociologist of science Brian Wynne (2002) points out, attempts to improve public participation in risk assessments, while admirable, have served to reinforce attention on only back-end science questions about consequences or risks instead of looking at why such widespread public dissatisfaction exists toward modern technologies in the first place. In short, a democratic regulatory politics should not kick in only after a technology has been developed. It should inform the entire production process, from conceptual cradle to material grave. Doing this will encourage the production of technologies that are not only more just and less risky but also needed and that will enhance social welfare. This is radically different from the current model, which involves producing goods and leaving it up to marketing departments to convince the public they are things they "need."

IMPORTANT CONCEPTS

- discounting
- open-access versus common-property regimes

- postnormal science
- traditional risk assessment versus the precautionary principle
- tragedy of the commons
- welfare economics and cost-benefit analyses

DISCUSSION QUESTIONS

1. How should future generations be factored into our thinking when assessing policy options?
2. As many of today's problems are global, do we need something akin to a global governing body to deal with these threats? What are some of the potential benefits and costs of this scenario?
3. Should we be more cautious in our approach to novel technologies?
4. How does Elinor Ostrom's research (and that of others in the governing-the-commons tradition) give us hope?

SUGGESTED ADDITIONAL READINGS

Dolsak, N., and E. Ostrom, eds. 2003. *The Commons in the New Millennium: Challenges and Adaptation.* Cambridge: MIT Press.

Science. 2003. "Tragedy of the Commons: A Special Issue." Online extras. Retrieved August 30, 2012 (http://www.sciencemag.org/site/feature/misc/webfeat/sotp/commons.xhtml).

Sen, A. 1977. "Rational Fools: A Critique of the Behavioral Foundations of Economic Theory." *Philosophy and Public Affairs* 6(4):317–344.

RELEVANT INTERNET LINKS

- http://www.iied.org/natural-resources/key-issues/forestry/justice-forests-series-short-films
  Two short films—*Tackling Forest Governance* and *Justice in the Forests*—about indigenous forest governance groups.
- http://www.youtube.com/watch?v=ByXM47Ri1Kc
  Elinor Ostrom explains her pathbreaking research.
- http://www.youtube.com/watch?v=MiybUJE2TRo
  An interview by Democracy Now! that takes a more critical look at REDD, which was discussed in Case Study 11.2.

SUGGESTED VIDEOS

- *Bikpela Bagarap (Big Damage)* (2011)
  http://www.bikpelabagarap.com/. Filmed undercover, this documentary reveals the exploitation of forest communities in Papua New Guinea in their own country by Malaysian logging companies and corrupt politicians.
- *Rachel Carson's "Silent Spring"* (1993)
  Though twenty years old, this production from the Public Broadcasting Service's series the American Experience offers an excellent historical lesson for anyone not familiar with this pathbreaking book and its pioneering author.

12

Inequality and Growth:
Prosperity for All

This chapter turns conventional wisdom upside down and inside out. A variety of social theories were detailed in Chapter 10 that attempt to paint a fairly thick causal arrow from growth to environmental degradation. Since Rachel Carson's *Silent Spring*—a book said to have helped spark the modern environmental movement (Lytle 2007)—a widespread understanding has emerged concerning the costs of growth to the environment. Growth nevertheless remains a sacred cow of sorts. Its costs may be great, but the costs of forgoing it, so the thinking goes, are even greater. Environmental degradation remains for many an unfortunate but necessary condition for future prosperity. We've also had some luck at pushing the "limits" further and further out. Some forty years ago, a handful of widely circulated books were published on the subject of rapidly approaching limits, like *Limits to Growth* (Meadows et al. 1972) and *The Population Bomb* (Ehrlich 1968). These dire prophesies have yet to pan out. Their failure is relative rather than absolute. Their underlying premise is not wrong about there being real limits, but we've just managed to delay hitting up against them. To which proponents of economic growth respond: what makes you so sure we will not delay hitting those limits indefinitely?

Critiquing economic growth on the grounds that it destroys the environment might resonate among the already converted. Yet experience has taught me that among the progrowth diehards, another argumentative frame is required. What if I were to tell you that economic growth, beyond a certain point, contributes *nothing* to making us more prosperous, happy, or healthy? After a certain point, economic growth might even become regressive to society's overall well-being (Dietz, Rosa, and York 2012). Ecological economist Herman Daly (1999) calls this **uneconomic growth**: growth that costs us more than it benefits us. In other words, it is "growth" that makes us *less* well off.

For a time I too had thought economic growth was synonymous with prosperity, which made the subject in my mind ethically thorny. On the one hand, I wanted to do right to the environment; on the other, I wanted to do right to humanity. Turns out, it's not a zero-sum game. The environment's gain is ours too, and vice versa. Allow me to explain. . . .

Fast Facts

The average African was approximately eleven times poorer than the average North American, Australian, or New Zealander in 1950. By 2000 they were *nineteen times* poorer (Gilding 2011).

According to the Millennium Ecosystem Assessment (2005), the total capital stock of the world (most notably natural capital) is degrading faster than wealth created in the formal economy. (Released in 2005, the *Millennium Ecosystem Assessment* involved more than thirteen hundred experts and provides one of the most thorough appraisals of the condition and trends in the world's ecosystems and the services they provide.) To put it another way, more value is being destroyed than created—a classic case of uneconomic growth.

Although economic growth appears necessary in the world's poorest countries, its value diminishes tremendously after a country's average income hits roughly fifteen thousand dollars. Beyond this point, neither objective (such as average life expectancy) nor subjective (happiness indicators) measures of quality of life show any prominent improvement (Jackson 2009; Wilkinson and Pickett 2009). Indeed, beyond a certain point, economic growth may make us *less* happy—a fact that appears to hold as much for the affluent in those countries as for the poor (Kasser 2002; New Economics Foundation 2009; Wilkinson and Pickett 2009).

Real income per capita has tripled in the United States since 1950, but the percentage of people reporting themselves to be "very happy" has actually *declined* since the mid-1970s. The average person in Japan is no more satisfied today than they were several decades ago. In the United Kingdom, the percentage reporting to be "very happy" has been steadily declining over the past half century—from 52 percent in 1957 to 36 percent today—even though real incomes have more than doubled. The average citizen in Denmark, Sweden, Ireland, and New Zealand reports a higher level of life satisfaction than their counterpart in the United States even with their significantly lower income level (Jackson 2009). What's going on here?

Implications

It is only a couple of pages into this chapter, and I have already made a number of bold statements. I do not make them casually. They are based on a remarkable array of research conducted over the past ten years. The last seventy years, since the end of World War II, has been a tremendous social experiment. By practically every empirical indicator, this experiment has not gone as planned. I am not arguing that economic growth is in itself bad, just that after a certain point there ceases to be any empirical justification for it as an end in itself.

Rethinking Growth

First, let's look at the relationship between a country's average income and its life expectancy. Once a country surpasses a level where its average citizen makes approximately

FIGURE 12.1 Relationship between Life Expectancy and Average Per Capita Income, Select High-Income Countries

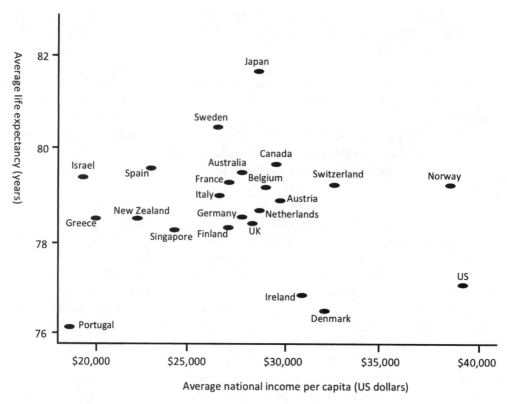

Source: Adapted from Wilkinson and Pickett (2009).

fifteen thousand dollars annually, gains to life expectancy seem to become decoupled from subsequent economic growth. Although gains in life expectancy are still possible, as Figure 12.1 makes clear (which looks only at higher-income countries), they appear to be more about how economic wealth is used (and distributed) than about growth per se. Indeed, some countries manage life expectancies that are higher than the United States with *half* the wealth.

The same holds for more subjective measures. After a certain point, economic growth does nothing to make people feel better off, as documented in Figure 12.2. Yet shouldn't the ultimate goal of "development" be about making us happier and more satisfied about life as a whole? Once we have our basic material needs satisfied, more "stuff" does little to make us happier. Again, any further happiness seems a product of how that additional wealth is used (and distributed) across society as a whole. As with life expectancies, there is remarkable variability across higher-income countries when it comes to how the average citizen feels about being satisfied with life as a whole. We finally have empirical evidence to back up what we've been saying for generations: money doesn't buy happiness.

This stands in stark contrast to conventional macroeconomic theory. Yet even economic theory has a term that recognizes the absurdity of this premise. The **diminishing**

FIGURE 12.2 Relationship between Average Per Capita Income and Percent of Population Reporting Happiness and Satisfaction with Life as a Whole, Select Countries

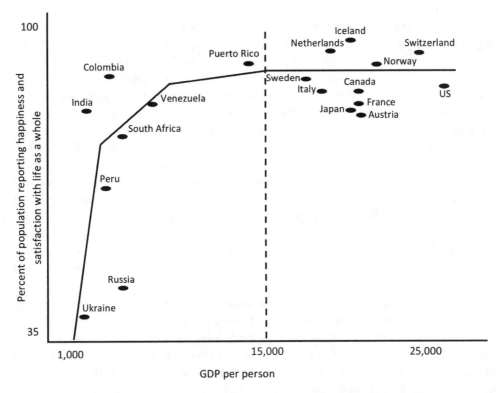

The line indicates the general relationship between *x* and *y* axes when all countries are tabulated. *Source:* Adapted from Jackson (2009) and Wilkinson and Pickett (2010).

marginal utility of stuff, and ultimately of money itself, speaks to the fact that having more of something eventually provides less additional satisfaction. (The so-called law of diminishing marginal utility, plainly stated, is that the more units of something we consume, the less added enjoyment we get from each additional unit.) Although I am getting a bit ahead of myself, this helps us understand why economic growth after a certain point might indeed be *negatively* correlated to happiness. Note in Figure 12.2 how relatively unhappy and unsatisfied the average person is in the wealthiest country of all: the United States. Since 1990, inflation-adjusted per capita expenditures on furniture and household goods in the United States have increased a staggering 300 percent; for apparel, the rate of increase was 80 percent; for vehicles, housing, and food, the figure was 15–20 percent (Schor 2010). During this same period, the United States' ranking on the Human Development Index (HDI), which is discussed in a greater detail later in this chapter, dropped from a respectable second in the world to fifteenth place by 2006. Clearly, all this stuff has done nothing to make the average American better off. This phenomenon of diminishing marginal utility also offers, as others have argued (Jackson 2009), justification for some level of redistribution. When you are starving, any food will bring an immediate bump in your feelings of satisfaction. At the opposite extreme, when a person in the United States is staring at a refrigerator and pantry overflowing with food, a little more will likely bring zero additional satisfaction. It might even be considered a burden, as they now have to find room for it. And for a growing number of people in high-income countries, the actual act of eating has become stressful, as they worry increasingly about obesity and other obesity-related health risks. When talking about this recently in a class, I had a student thoughtfully ask, "Don't we at least need progrowth policies to alleviate poverty? What will happen to them—the poor?" The evidence just does not support the argument that current progrowth policies do much for the poor. For every US$100 of economic growth between 1990 and 2001, a mere *60 cents* went toward poverty reduction for those earning less than US$1 a day (Gilding 2011). The poverty-alleviating logic of growth looks something like this: the rich get richer so the poor can be a little less poor (but still poor in the end).

If you dig a little deeper, the data get even more interesting. The problem with growth as currently practiced is not that it degrades the quality of life for some of the world's inhabitants. It is true that levels of global inequality have never been worse; after all, 3.5 billion people—half the world's population—share just 1 percent of the world's wealth (ibid.; Moellendorf 2009). Yet the rich "suffer" under this system, too—though obviously their suffering is qualitatively different from that of someone in abject poverty. According to the data, economic growth makes life less satisfying for *all* of humanity, rich and poor alike.

Whereas absolute wealth is a poor indicator of a country's level of prosperity, inequality proves to be a strong indicator, as it is negatively correlated to a whole host of prosperity and well-being indicators. This holds even for a nation's affluent. The economically advantaged are better off if the country they live in is more equal. The data on this subject are compelling. More equal societies have fewer health and social problems (see Figure 12.3), treat women and children better, have a greater sense of collective responsibility to those in other countries (see Figure 12.4), have lower rates of mental illnesses, and are more willing to cooperate with international environmental agreements (Wilkinson and Pickett 2009; Wilkinson, Pickett, and De Vogli 2010).

Perhaps it is no coincidence that welfare economics, as detailed in the previous chapter, has found such favor in the United States. More equal countries tend to be more cooperative (Wilkinson and Pickett 2009). The high levels of inequality in the United States offer the perfect environment for a perspective that assumes people are self-interested and selfish. This also helps us make some sense of why most of the industrialized world chose to continue with the Kyoto Protocol despite the noninvolvement of major greenhouse gas–emitting countries like the United States and China. (The Kyoto Protocol is an international agreement linked to the United Nations Framework Convention on Climate Change that sets targets for thirty-seven industrialized countries and the European community for reducing greenhouse gas emissions. Recognizing that developed countries are principally responsible for the majority of greenhouse gas emissions in the atmosphere, the protocol places a heavier burden on developed nations under the principle of "common but differentiated responsibilities." The protocol was adopted in Kyoto, Japan, on December 11, 1997. It entered into force on February 16, 2005.) From a purely self-interested perspective, it makes no sense to do so given that any greenhouse gas reductions under the protocol would easily be offset by nonsignatory countries. Perhaps these countries chose to do so due to a heightened sense of global responsibility

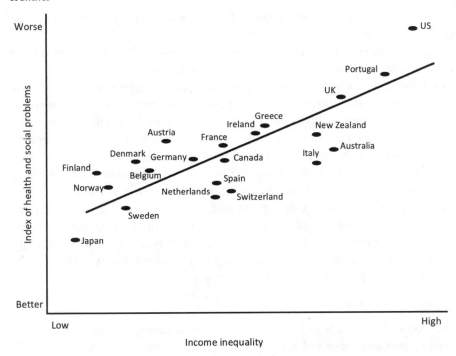

FIGURE 12.3 Relationship Between Health and Social Problems and Income Inequality, Select High-Income Countries

Source: Adapted from Wilkinson and Pickett (2009).

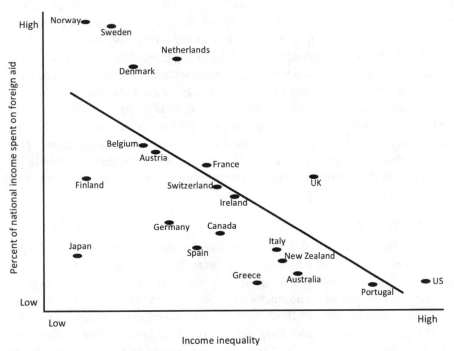

FIGURE 12.4 Relationship Between Foreign Aid Spending and Income Inequality, Select High-Income Countries

Source: Adapted from Wilkinson and Pickett (2009).

(Kysar 2010), a sentiment, perhaps not coincidentally, more likely to be found among more equal societies (Wilkinson and Pickett 2009).

Innovation also appears to be enhanced by equality, as more equal societies have higher levels of patents granted per capita. This may be due in part to their higher levels of social mobility and educational achievement, recognizing that more equal societies are less likely to waste their potential human capital as they provide greater opportunities for all of their members (Wilkinson et al. 2010). Think about this in the context of renewable energy. Those countries first to transition over to renewable-based energy sources will have done so because they are highly adaptable and innovative. Are countries like the United States hindering their ability to make this transition due to their high levels of inequality? In sum, inequality is a tremendous source of inefficiency. The efficiency through which a society utilizes its resources to enhance its well-being increases at low to moderate levels of economic development but *declines* at high levels, particularly when combined with high levels of inequality (Dietz et al. 2012; Knight and Rosa 2011). A high level of inequality in a society is therefore not only morally problematic but bad policy, as it reduces *everyone's* welfare.

The Sociology of Consumption

Why do we consume so much stuff? The following five sociological mechanisms have been linked to escalating levels of consumption: social comparison, creation of self-identity, specialization, sociotechnical systems, and planned obsolescence. I briefly take each in turn, recognizing that this discussion represents the barest of overviews of a richly complex literature (see, for example, Shove, Trentmann, and Wilk 2009).

Social Comparison

More than a century ago Thorstein Veblen ([1899] 1967) introduced us to the now commonplace term "**conspicuous consumption**": the idea that we consume, at least in part, to display to others our social power and status. In centuries past, the displaying of power and status was relatively straightforward, involving things like commanding large armies, possessing huge castles, and ruling over entire societies. Individuals today, however, no longer possess great armies or rule over a peasant class. According to Veblen, we therefore make social statements in other ways, such as by surrounding ourselves with nice things to signal to others our placement in the socioeconomic hierarchy. The mechanism of social comparison also has a ratcheting-up effect on consumption. This occurs as individuals attempt to display a social status above what their household income levels allow as they constantly strive to outdo those around them—a phenomenon commonly known as "keeping up with the Joneses."

Creation of Self-Identity

Consumption is more than just the pursuit of status. It can also have a much deeper function. Our very sense of self is tied to it. The term *lifestyle* is important here, as attachment to groups, according to this argument, is an important source of personal identity. Thus, whether you have chosen, for example, a "green" lifestyle or one of someone who likes to recreate outdoors (both very popular among my students), consumption is tied to both. Association with the green lifestyle might require that you buy, say, organic food, a Toyota Prius, or solar panels for your house—at least these represent recent purchases by a friend of mine who confesses to embrace this lifestyle. If your identity is that of an outdoors person, you might, for example, walk around wearing clothes from Cabela's or Patagonia, depending upon the type of outdoors person you're trying to communicate to others.

Specialization

Henry Ford famously claimed that you could have the Model T automobile in any color as long as that color was black. That mentality reflects the logic of mass production. Today, more producers—perhaps to fit the aforementioned lifestyles and identities they support—are widening their range of what they produce to fit the specialized "needs" of consumers. An example of this is shoes. When my grandmother was growing up in rural Iowa in the 1920s, she had two pairs of shoes: one for work and one for dress. Fast-forward some ninety years to today. Now, two pairs of shoes would never do. We seem instead to "need" a specialized pair of shoes for almost every one of the day's activities: shoes for in the house, shoes for the garden, shoes for the gym (actually, there you'll need numerous different shoes depending on what you're doing), shoes for work, shoes for. . . .

Sociotechnical Systems

This concept reminds us that there are broader sociological reasons that belie the concept of consumer "choice." We should be careful not to look too exclusively at the individual, in other words, to understand why they "choose" to consume as they do. In some instances, that choice is made for them (as earlier discussed when talking about "choosing" to drive). Millions around the world, for example, did not choose to have their nondigital television sets become obsolete as analog television broadcasting is being converted to and replaced by digital television. Similarly, if your grocery store does not carry organic food, you cannot choose to have an organic diet (nor can we say you're choosing a nonorganic diet). We can only "choose" what the sociotechnical system lets us choose.

Planned Obsolescence

After World War II, US automobile manufacturers were facing an uncertain future as more Americans became car owners. Once every household (or at least those that could afford one) owned a car, who would be left to buy new automobiles? The answer was to get people to purchase a new car every couple of years. But how? A well-maintained car would theoretically last decades, perhaps even a person's entire life. How, then, could a car owner be cajoled into choosing to buy a new car even if the one currently owned was—from a functionality standpoint—perfectly fine? Enter planned obsolescence. The idea is quite simple. The goal of planned obsolesce as it applies to automobiles is to make the one you currently have in your garage appear obsolete. This is accomplished with the occasional redesign of the car's interior and exterior so as to literally make your current model appear "old" (even if you just bought it last year). This process is also helped along by incrementally adding "upgrades"—like rearview cameras, eleven-speaker surround sound, and OnStar satellite navigation—and convincing the buyer that they "need" these extra bells and whistles.

Planned obsolescence takes can take other forms, too, like designing devices that cannot be easily taken apart and thus repaired. Apple, for example, realized that they could sell more iPhones if they built the device with an integrated battery (it's soldered into the phone). This therefore requires users to upgrade once the battery wears down, as a phone isn't terribly useful if it can't be away from its charger for longer than an hour. Sure, you could replace the battery, but this will cost you US$79 for a new one, plus US$6.95 for shipping and handling. The iPhone battery replacement process also takes three days. In the meantime, Apple will gladly give you a loaner iPhone while you wait . . . for an additional US$29.

Environmental Justice

Closely related to the above discussion is the subject of environmental justice. As defined by the Environmental Protection Agency, environmental justice is about the "fair treatment and meaningful involvement of all people regardless of race, color, national origin, or income with respect to the development, implementation, and enforcement of environmental laws, regulations, and policies. Fair treatment means that no population, due to policy or economic disempowerment, is forced to bear a disproportionate share of the negative human health or environmental impacts of pollution or environmental consequences resulting from industrial, municipal, and commercial operations or the execution of federal, state, local and tribal programs and policies" (EPA n.d.).

Our understanding of environmental justice has grown as scholarship accumulates, showing the unequal distribution of environmental threats. These threats disparately affect not only those of lower socioeconomic status but also certain ethnic minorities. Pollution-based racial discrimination goes by the name of **environmental racism** (though the concept can be defined much more broadly to include racial discrimination in environmental policy making, enforcement of regulations and laws, in addition to the targeting of communities of color for toxic waste disposal and siting of polluting industries).

The birth of the term *environmental racism* has been traced back to 1982, when civil rights activists organized to stop the US state of North Carolina from dumping 120 million pounds of soil laced with polychlorinated biphenyls in the predominantly African American county of Warren (Bullard 1990; Mohai, Pellow, and Roberts 2009). Out of this was born a new social movement whose aim has been to address concerns ignored by mainstream middle-class white environmentalists. The environmental justice movement heavily (and rightly) criticized the conventional environmental movement for focusing too much on pristine ecological landscapes and not enough on people whose lives are threatened daily by ecological risk.

Some of the earliest research into this subject focused on the location of hazardous waste sites. The first was conducted by the US General Accounting Office in 1983 (GAO 1983). The study documented how African American communities in southern US states hosted a disproportionate share of waste sites. This study was followed famously by the United Church of Christ (UCC) Commission for Racial Justice's national study in 1987 (Chavis and Lee 1987). This pathbreaking study showed that toxic-waste facilities across the United States were far more likely to end up in the backyards of people of color. According to the UCC study, race was the most important factor in predicting where these waste sites were located. In 1990 sociologist Robert Bullard (1990) published the now-classic book *Dumping in Dixie*. This work represents the first comprehensive examination of environmental racism by systematically linking hazardous

ECOnnection 12.1

The Plight of Native Americans

The term *ecocide* has been used to describe the US government's twentieth-century treatment of its Native peoples (Grinde and Johansen 1995; Churchill 2002), a fact that's not entirely denied by the US Department of Defense (DOD 2001): "In order to ensure that it meets its national security mission, DoD operates and trains on vast amounts of land, including American Indian and Alaska Native lands. Evidence of DoD's past use of these lands remains: hazardous materials, unexploded ordnance (UXO), abandoned equipment, unsafe buildings, and debris. This contamination degrades the natural environment and threatens tribal economic, social and cultural welfare."

Fifty years after the conclusion of the so-called Indian Wars, Native Americans were again uprooted from their land when the US government seized more than three hundred thousand acres of the Pine Ridge Reservation in South Dakota (families there were paid three cents an acre). The government wanted this land as a practice bombing range for pilots before being sent off to fight for the Allies in World War II, a practice that laced the environment with contaminants (Bordewich et al. 2007).

The US government continues to unduly burden Native Americans with ecological risks up to this day. A recent analysis looking at closed military bases in the United States found that Native Americans are significantly more likely to be living next to these contaminated spaces than any other ethnic group (Hooks and Smith 2004). One particular risk highlighted by this study is unexploded ordinances, including mines and explosive shells, which have killed, maimed, and injured many. Native Americans continue to be threatened by their environment at levels that would be patently unacceptable to any less marginalized social group.

facility siting with historical patterns of segregation in the southern United States. Bullard documents in exquisite detail how communities of color were deliberately targeted when locations were sought for society's waste (see ECOnnection12.1).

Some twenty-five years after the UCC study, similar findings continue to be made. Some of the recent research utilizes GIS (geographic information system) technology and new methodological techniques to better control for proximity. Employing these new tools, environmental justice scholars in fact "find that the magnitude of racial disparities around hazardous waste facilities is *much greater* than what previous national studies have reported" (Mohai and Saha 2007:343; emphasis added). Those who believe we live in a postracial society will be surprised to learn that the evidence suggests that environmental racism is more pronounced today than it was fifty years ago. One longitudinal study looking at the US state of Michigan from 1950 to 1990 concludes that "whereas significant racial, socioeconomic, and housing disparities at the time of siting were not in evidence for facilities sited prior to 1970, patterns of disparate siting were found for facilities sited after 1970" (Saha and Mohai 2005:618).

Prior to the 1970s, we knew far less about the ecological risks associated with business of usual. The affluent therefore did not have as much reason to oppose living next to industrial facilities. Fortunately, we did not remain ignorant forever about ecological risk. The 1970s marked the beginning of unprecedented growth in public environmental concern and opposition to facilities that bring with them environmental harms. With this came growing opposition to the siting of facilities that threatened environmental and human health. People no longer wanted these operations sited in their backyards. Yet not everyone is in possession of sufficient resources to keep their backyards free of these facilities. Not surprisingly, then, the siting of hazardous waste facilities followed the path of least political resistance. And as inequalities continue to grow in countries like the United States, the "haves" have a lot more to apply to resist polluting industries being sited in their backyards than the "have-nots." Hence, the growing levels of environmental injustice.

Even when controlling for economic and sociopolitical variables, factors uniquely associated with race continue to correlate strongly with the location of the nation's hazardous waste facilities (Mohai et al. 2009). It's hard to believe that in each of those cases, there is overt racial discrimination going on. Perhaps some of this environmental racism is actually an artifact of environmental economism. **Economism**, for those unfamiliar with the term, refers to the act of reducing the world to economic dimensions, a practice, to recall from Chapter 11, lying at the heart of welfare economics (and a specific example of methodological reductionism). When assessing the costs and benefits of policy options, this approach assigns a lower value to those of lower socioeconomic status. As certain ethnic minorities make on average less than other groups, they will be disproportionately penalized by this approach. The welfare-economics approach, in other words, legitimizes environmental racism in some cases.

Whereas early environmental racism studies originated out of the United States, the scope of research in recent years has spanned the world (see Case Study 12.1). Two types of environmental injustice are being increasingly cited: international and global (Roberts and Parks 2007). On the one hand, in reference to the former and as discussed in previous chapters, polluting industries are moving around the world. In doing this, they too often follow the path of least political resistance, which places them squarely in the "backyards" of some of society's most marginalized. Then there are risks that are truly global in character, like climate change (Adger et al. 2006; Roberts and Parks 2007). These threats exacerbate existing inequalities as those best posited (resource-wise) to keep themselves safe are also often those most responsible for the problems in the first place.

Solutions

The solution to the above problems, we know, does not lie in doing away entirely with inequality. People *are* different—in terms of their contributions, skills, and interests—and need to be treated (and rewarded) as such. Differential rewards motivate people to make the world a better place, though clearly people are not motivated by *only* reward, either. Moreover, there are diminishing marginal returns in those rewards. The opportunity to make another ten thousand dollars means a whole lot more to someone currently making ten thousand dollars a year than it does to someone whose annual

CASE STUDY 12.1

Environmental Racism in Cape Town, South Africa

On June 23, 2000, the bulk ore carrier *MV Treasure* sank off the coast of South Africa, spilling more than thirteen hundred tons of bunker oil in a marine ecosystem that supported the largest and third-largest colonies of African penguins worldwide (six years earlier, some ten thousand African penguins were oiled after the sinking of the *Apollo Sea* bulk ore carrier). The world was outraged, prompting environmental organizations from around the world to respond at breakneck speak. Newspapers as far away as North America carried advertisements requesting donations for the army of volunteers who worked tirelessly to clean, rehabilitate, and release the impacted birds and scour their ravaged habitat. Within just a few weeks, almost twenty-five thousand birds had been treated.

At the same time, an equally (or arguably more) calamitous ecological event was occurring on the mainland in Cape Town. If the cameras and volunteers would have ventured just a few miles inland, they would have seen hundreds of thousands of poor, black Capetonians living in some of the most squalid conditions imaginable. Here pollution, sewage, uncollected waste, standing water, disease, and pestilence ravaged those living in these low-income communities. The environment was killing these individuals, just like it had turned against the beloved African penguin. But there was one big difference between the two cases: the world didn't seem to care about those living in the slums. Making this case even more sad is the fact that the postapartheid constitution, finalized in 1996, includes a bill of rights that grants all South Africans the right to an "environment that is not harmful to their health or well-being" and the right to "ecologically sustainable development" (section 24) (McDonald 2005). Apparently, this group is not even viewed by the South African government as worthy of its attention.

salary is a couple of million dollars. At what point, then, is a society's innovative spirit maximized, and after which point does more inequality begin being responsible for more harm than good? This is a question we need to be discussing (see Ethical Question 12.1).

A Postgrowth Society

It's curious why so many continue to be enamored with growth even in the face of mounting evidence that we shouldn't, particularly after a certain point of affluence is attained. John Stuart Mill, one of the founding parents of economics, wrote clearly about the limitations of economic growth: "It is scarcely necessary to remark that a stationary condition of capital and population implies no stationary state of human improvement. There would be as much scope as ever for all kinds of mental culture, and moral and social progress; as much room for improving the Art of Living and much more likelihood of its being improved, when minds cease to be engrossed by the art of getting on" (1848:317).

ETHICAL QUESTION 12.1

Is There a "Right" Level of Inequality?

Although most people believe extreme poverty to be morally wrong, the morality of inequality is far from settled terrain. Most can agree that some inequality is not only fair but best for society, as differential reward (especially when that reward is equally available to all) encourages people to make the world a better place. Empirical evidence (and common sense) also indicates that too much inequality stifles innovation and drive. Where's the incentive when the "haves" have everything and the rest of society has little chance of ever having anything? Getting the level of differential reward "right" is therefore not only an ethical question but also one with profound practical consequences (Gilding 2011).

To help us think through this question, Herman Daly (1996) offers the following instructive observation. He proposes a factor of ten as an inequality ceiling. The military and universities have managed to keep their ratios close to or even below this level while maintaining tremendous drive among individuals within these organizations. In the US military, for instance, the highest-paid generals make

roughly ten times the wages of a private. In a university, the prized rank of distinguished professor brings with it a salary that is roughly six to eight times that of a full time non-tenure track instructor. Compare this to the corporate world. Take Walmart: in 2007 its CEO, H. Lee Scott, made US$29,682,000—that's *1,314 times* more than the company's average full-time workers (IPS 2008). The CEO of Walmart also makes roughly 150 times more than a top-ranking US general and distinguished professor. Is that an efficient and effective distribution of resources? Is the CEO of Walmart 150 times more motivated than US generals and distinguished professors? Do we believe the head of Walmart is delivering 150 times more value to society than a top military commander or, say, a Nobel Prize–winning professor?

One way to frame this discussion is to talk about growing the middle class and expanding opportunities so people can have the freedom and liberty to pursue a life that is meaningful to them. Right now, far too many people lack these basic freedoms.

The great twentieth-century economist John Maynard Keynes (1930), writing some eighty years ago, believed that by the dawn of the twenty-first century, people would be working just a couple of days a week due to the remarkable productivity increases he (correctly) foresaw coming. He predicted (incorrectly) that rather than practicing overconsumption in order to keep everyone working *more* hours (by buying more stuff we would need to work more), we would instead choose to take advantage of those increases in productivity to work less and increase our leisure time. Employment for everyone is possible when the average worker works, for example (depending on the society), twenty hours a week (see Case Study 12.2). In such a scenario, overconsumption is neither possible (as a twenty-hour workweek doesn't allow for it) nor necessarily desired (with everyone in the same boat, the social pressures to overconsume are dramatically weakened). How could Keynes have predicted that we would instead decide

---

CASE STUDY 12.2

Kellogg's Six-Hour Day

Breakfast cereal giant W. K. Kellogg implemented a policy back in 1930 that we could learn from today. In response to the Great Depression, Kellogg made his workforce of fifteen hundred go from a traditional eight-hour to a six-hour workday instead of laying off some three hundred workers. The new arrangement meant everyone had to take a slight pay cut, but Kellogg also initiated production-based bonuses that could offset most of those losses. The policy was an unqualified success. The employees used their newly available time to pursue things of their choosing, which often involved activities that built family, community, and citizenship. In general, employees were happier under this new arrangement (Hunnicutt 1996). They also worked harder. The production of, for example, boxes of shredded whole-wheat biscuits per hour increased from eighty-three to ninety-six once the workday was shortened (Botsman and Rogers 2010).

World War II changed everything. Franklin Roosevelt signed an executive order demanding, among other things, longer workdays so the production needs of a war economy could be met. The labor union initially opposed a policy to return to an eight-hour workday but eventually acquiesced, as they fully expected a return to a six-hour workday after the war's conclusion (Hunnicutt 1996). Workers polled as late as 1946 found that 77 percent of men and 87 percent of women actually preferred a thirty-hour workweek even if it meant lower wages (Fitz 2009). And the longer hours and larger paychecks did little to actually make the employees any better off. As one employee later reported, "Everybody thought they were going to get rich when they got that eight-hour deal and it really didn't make a big difference. . . . Some went out and bought automobiles right quick and they didn't gain much on that because the car took the extra money they had" (as quoted in Botsman and Rogers 2010:46).

---

to continue working longer hours that make us terribly unhappy so we can buy products that do nothing to enhance our well-being while depleting our natural resources and destroying the health of ourselves and our plant. Does that make any sense? Keynes didn't think so either.

More recent still, in 2006, the chair of the UK Financial Services Authority, Lord Adair Turner, argued in an essay titled "Dethroning Growth" that "there is no empirical basis for believing that the aggregate happiness of British people will increase significantly if British GDP per capita grows by 20 per cent over the next ten years" (as quoted in New Economics Foundation 2009:45–46). In the aftermath of the recent global financial crisis, people of all political and economic stripes are revising their definitions of "progress" and "prosperity."

There is an enormous difference between an economy purposefully designed to be indifferent to growth, where prosperity and well-being increase in the absence of economic growth, and a failing growth economy, where growth, prosperity, and well-being all decline while inequality increases. In a failing growth economy, out-of-control un-employment and crushing state, household, and personal debt seriously threaten that society's social and political stability. A failing economy, for instance, helped precipitate the 2011 Egyptian revolution. Conversely, an economy indifferent to growth—even one designed to hold steady and not grow—can avoid all this if intentionally constructed with these ends in mind (Gilding 2011).

How do we do this? We can start by redirecting taxes away from things we generally want (like labor) to things we generally don't want (like pollution and waste). This en-courages employment—a key difference from a failing growth economy—and discour-ages wasteful resource use and dependence, which can help buffer an economy from the shocks that come when access to those resources is disrupted (ibid.). We can also institute policies that encourage a shorter workweek. The government already regulates how much children can work. Why can't it do the same with everyone? By working less, we will also spend less. And as growth is no longer an imperative, we can tighten access to credit, thereby reducing or eliminating entirely personal debt. What would you choose, if given the choice: being caught on what Juliet Schor (1992) has termed the **work-spend cycle** (where we work to spend, which in turn requires us to work more) or having an extra month (or more) of vacation time a year to spend with family and friends? If you are anything like the people whom I have asked this question, you very likely will prefer the latter.

As noted earlier, once we're well fed, clothed, adequately sheltered, educated, and feel generally secure, happiness comes from something other than just more stuff and additional wealth. By working less, we will have time to finally engage in those activities that truly make us happy. We will have time to engage in "mental culture" and "social progress" and improve overall the "Art of Living," to borrow terms used by John Stuart Mill. Decades of social capital research point to the benefits that accrue to individuals and society as a whole when people have the opportunity to engage with one another on a personal level (see Putnam 2001). Moving away from our current obsession with growth will also address the aforementioned problems associated with rabid inequality. As the late Henry Wallich (former governor of the US Federal Reserve) famously put it, "Growth is a substitute for equality of income. So long as there is growth there is hope, and that makes large income differential tolerable" (1972:62).

Do not hold out hope either in so-called service-based, postindustrial, or information-based economies. *Postindustrial* does not mean *postpollution*. These societies are built on an economy whereby manufacturing is reduced through trade, while consumption skyrockets (with the help of an expanding financial sector so we can buy all this stuff). When all ecological impacts are actually accounted for, most service- or information-based economies are at least as resource hungry as industrial economies. We will also have to rethink how we do leisure and recreation in this new economy. As currently practiced, these sectors are terribly energy and resource intensive, responsible for ap-proximately 25 percent of all energy and carbon emissions attributable to UK consumers (Jackson 2009). They are also becoming incredibly expensive. Today many worry about whether they can afford the next big trip (Rojek 2010). I guess that's why I increasingly hear people comment when on vacation that they need a vacation from their vacation. In a postgrowth economy, leisure will once again be leisurely.

It is also worth asking why leisure today must involve going *to* someplace. Or perhaps it is more accurate to characterize it as getting *away*—after all, that's often how we characterize vacations. Maybe, if we enhanced the attractiveness of communities, we could reduce the "need" to travel to distant places. This would not only be a tremendous ecological gain, recognizing the significant environmental footprint associated with air travel and everything else one does when touring a distant land, but also help dampen the need we feel to (over) work, as we would no longer have this large expense looming over the horizon. And over the long term, this would have a virtuous effect. At present, contemporary communities are so lowly regarded that they offer few inducements to encourage people to stick around when they have free time. Making communities places we actually *want* to be will keep people within the community and thus further enhance the social and ecological dynamics of this space still further.

One recent modeling attempt by a Canadian economist illustrates how economic stabilization (growth of less than 0.1 percent annually) can successfully occur, though the entire transition will take a couple of decades (Victor 2008). Under the modeled Canadian scenario, unemployment and poverty were halved, the debt-to-GDP ratio was reduced by some 75 percent, and greenhouse gas emissions for the nation were cut 20 percent. The model revealed a couple of important insights. Changes to investment and the structure of the labor market have to be handled carefully to make a postgrowth society work. While net business investment was reduced in the modeled scenario, there was also a significant shift in investment to public goods through changes in taxation and public spending. The model supports the point made earlier that it is not wealth per se that improves societal well-being and resilience but how that money is spent and distributed. Unemployment was avoided both by reducing the average number of working hours (while assuming that labor productivity continues to increase) and by sharing the work more equally across the available workforce. As certain European labor policies have already shown, reducing the working week is a relatively simple solution to the challenge of maintaining full employment with nonincreasing output (Jackson 2009).

Although it is difficult for some to conceive of how firms can flourish without growth, consider that this is precisely how small businesses—like so-called "mom-and-pop" establishments—have operated for centuries. Firms under this model have costs and revenues. When profits are earned, some are reinvested back into the firm to replace or upgrade worn-out equipment. The goal is not to "grow" but rather to reduce costs in the hope of increasing profits. As Juliet Schor (2010) notes, firms can be quite successful in the market when they offer better quality for a given price, a strategy that can be easily hindered when owners become obsessed by growth. Continual expansion is neither necessary nor sufficient for firm profitability.

The point that prosperity comes not from wealth but from the efficient utilization of resources lies at the heart of alternative measures to GDP. Throughout much of the twentieth century, GDP was the gold-standard measure of progress and prosperity, as it was long assumed that growth could deliver unlimited happiness. Knowing now that it does not, alternative measures of process and prosperity are being developed. One of the most popular alternative measures is the Human Development Index. The HDI factors in a country's life expectancy as well as measures of literacy, education, and standards of living. The HDI was originally devised by the Pakistani economist Mahbub

FIGURE 12.5 Human Development Index Plotted Against Ecological Footprint

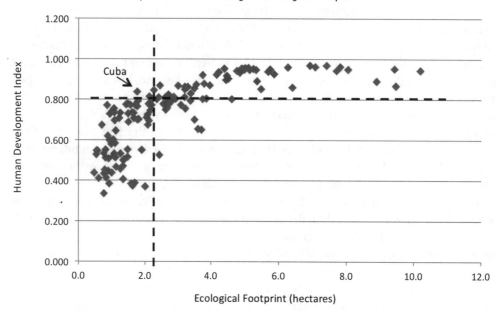

The Human Development Index is calculated on a scale from 0 to 1, where 0 is the lowest and 1 is the highest.

ul-Haq and Indian economist Amartya Sen in 1990. Its goal, in the words of Mahbub ul-Haq, is to give "human capital"—*humanity* (versus money)—"the attention it deserves" when talking about and implementing policies directed at this nebulous thing we call development (1995:3). The HDI is now used widely in the international development community and by organizations like the United Nations. In line with all that has already been discussed, beyond a certain level of affluence, wealth has no correlation to a country's HDI ranking.

In recent years, attempts have also been made to combine HDI with ecological indicators, as presently HDI ignores environmental variables. Figure 12.5 provides an example of this, plotting countries according to their HDI ranking and ecological footprint. Note the wide disparity between countries with high HDI scores and ecological footprints behind those corresponding levels of well-being. One country has managed to produce a high HDI score within the parameters of what ecological-footprint scholars deem to be a truly sustainable economy (a footprint of 2.1 hectares per person or less): Cuba.

Another widely cited measure of progress, which takes into account a country's ecological condition, is the Happy Planet Index (HPI). The fundamental premise of the HPI is the acknowledgment that real prosperity can be said to have been reached only when the well-being of humankind does not come at the earth's expense (New Economics Foundation 2009). HPI scores range from 0 to 100. High scores reflect a society with high life expectancy, high life satisfaction, and a low ecological footprint. This measure turns convention on its head. For example, the United States ranks an unflattering 114th place, while Costa Rica comes out on top. Costa Ricans live slightly longer than Americans, report having much higher levels of life satisfaction, and do all this with an ecological footprint that is less than a quarter the size of the average US citizen. The HPI also supports the argument that it is not environmental throughput (a.k.a. growth) that makes a society great. For example, Vietnam and Cameroon have the same ecological footprints (1.3 hectares). Yet whereas the average resident of Cameroon does not live past 50 years and reports low life satisfaction, the average Vietnamese lives as long as most Europeans (73.7 years) and reports being happier than the average South Korean (ibid.).

Development as Freedom, Justice, and Empowerment

There is also good reason to believe readjustments to developmental policies and practices like those just mentioned would go a long way toward alleviating many of the environmental injustices described earlier. To work through this, I'll turn to Amartya Sen's thoughts on the subject and in particular his theory of justice when he speaks specifically on the pitfalls that come with making economic growth an end in itself. What makes Sen's approach to justice so interesting is his focus on capabilities, which are necessary for people to function fully in the lives they choose. It is Sen's contention that justice should not be about the distribution of goods and services but should be about how individuals are able to utilize those goods and services so they can flourish. In Sen's words, the "focus has to be, in this analysis, on the freedoms generated by commodities, rather than on the commodities seen on their own" (1999:74). Our current focus on economic growth, conversely, cares nothing about what commodities do for people; all that matters is that commodities are produced and sold. In sum, Sen's focus on capabilities forces us to ask what is needed to transform mere economic growth into a truly prosperous life while also considering what might interrupt the process.

This discussion also links up with something discussed back in Chapter 10 when I wrote about Berlin's dual understanding of freedom, as Sen (1993) draws inspiration from Berlin in his writings on the subject. Prosperity requires positive rights, like the right to utilize goods and services in ways that allow people to flourish. But it also, and equally, requires negative rights, such as the right to live in an environment where that process is not interrupted by, say, toxic waste, environmental racism, patriarchy, or runaway inequality. Instead of offering a universal set of capabilities, Sen believes the communities in question are best positioned to decide what it is they value and the life they wish to live: "[The] problem is not with listing important capabilities, but with insisting on one pre-determined canonical list of capabilities, chosen by theorists without any general social discussion or public reasoning. To have such a fixed list, emanating entirely from pure theory, is to deny the possibility of fruitful public participation on what should be included and why" (2005:158; see ECOnnection 12.2).

Environmental justice movements have much in common with Sen's theory of justice and his emphasis on capabilities. This is especially the case of movements originating in low-income countries, where the development priorities of outsiders have threatened the functioning of local communities (Schlosberg and Carruthers 2010). One key component of almost any type of environmental justice activism is building community capacity and facilitating community empowerment (Cole and Foster 2001; see Case Study 12.3).

Community Capitals Framework

There are a variety of ways to translate Sen's thinking about capabilities into a pragmatic developmental program. The HDI represents one attempt to put Sen's thoughts into practice. Yet arguably, any developmental approach that works to empower—rather than just enrich—squares well with Sen's writings.

Take the community capitals framework. According to this approach, sustainable development is the product of a triple bottom line, involving economic, social, and environmental accountability (Flora 2008). These three sustainability pillars come together when a variety of capitals are present in sufficient degree. Those capitals include natural, built, financial, political, social, human, and cultural capitals. Although equally important in the achievement of the aforementioned triple bottom line, investments in social and human capitals in particular, research shows, can produce a "spiraling up" effect that leads to the enhancement of all capitals over time (Emery and Flora 2006). We can see in Table 12.1 the role of the various capitals at play in rural development and how they build upon each other. A community capitals approach expands our understanding of "return on investment," noting that it should be measured in terms of an increase in *all* capitals, rather than just in terms of economic growth (financial capital). Furthermore, community capitals research firmly believes in involving people so they can direct change from within a community, a point that also fits with Sen's point that only the communities—through debate and public reasoning—can determine what's best for them.

TABLE 12.1 Seven Capitals and Their Role in Creating Sustainable and Just Communities

CAPITAL	DEFINITION	ROLE IN CREATING SUSTAINABLE AND JUST COMMUNITIES
Natural	The natural biophysical assets of any given locale—can include natural resources (e.g., water, soil, air, minerals), amenities (e.g., trout streams and sandy beaches), and natural beauty.	These assets, when utilized in a manner cognizant of ecological limits, represent the ecological productive base for the long-term prosperity of other capitals.
Cultural	Institutionalized (widely shared) cultural symbols—attitudes, preferences, beliefs—that shape how we see the world, what we take for granted, and possible alternatives for social change.	By investing in cultural diversity (and including those who are traditionally excluded) biodiversity and different ways of approaching change can be utilized to the enhancement of all capitals.
Human	Includes the skills, knowledge, and abilities of the people within a community to enhance local as well as access outside resources.	Increasing the knowledge base of a community will help that community bolster its other capitals.
Social	The social glue of a community—includes levels of mutual trust, reciprocity, and a sense of shared identity and future.	A social lubricant in that it makes the enhancement of the other capitals considerably easier.
Political	Access to structures of power and power brokers as well as the ability to influence the rules and regulations that shape access to resources.	Political access greatly enhances a community's ability to bolster other capitals.
Financial	The financial resources available to invest in things like community capacity building and social entrepreneurship	Financial resources can help pay for the maintenance and accumulation of other capitals.
Built	Infrastructure (also includes built "natural" areas, like reconstituted wetlands, ski runs, and artificial coral reefs).	Infrastructure supports other capitals.

Source: Adapted from Flora (2008) and Flora et al. (2009).

CASE STUDY 12.3

The Metales Plant in Tijuana, Mexico

Owned by San Diego–based New Frontier Trading Corporation, the Metales and Derivados battery-recycling plant in Tijuana began smelting in 1972 to recover lead and copper from automobile batteries and other sources. One 1990 study of a local water source found lead and cadmium levels three thousand times and one thousand times, respectively, higher than US standards (Carruthers 2008). The plant was eventually closed in 1994, after repeated noncompliance of environmental regulations. The owners of the plant promptly headed north, to San Diego, California, beyond the reach of Mexican authorities, leaving behind more than six thousand metric tons of lead slag and an additional twenty-four thousand tons of mixed hazardous waste (such as antimony, arsenic, cadmium, and copper) (ibid.; Hendricks, 2010). The Federal Ministry for Environmental Protection (PROFEPA) took control of the site, building a containment wall, and covered the slag with plastic tarps to prevent air exposure. Activists and some scientists, however, argued that such measures did little to protect the health of local residents, a point that later became obvious as the containment wall eroded and the plastic tarp degraded.

In 1998 local residents formed an alliance with the San Diego–based Environmental Health Coalition and began holding news conferences, vigils, and protests while also launching letter-writing and direct-action campaigns. After more than five years of hard work and network building—what Sen might call ground-up *capability* building—the activists were able to finally pressure the EPA and its Mexican counterpart, the PROFEPA, to find funding for a cleanup strategy. In June 2004, the activists and the Mexican government signed an agreement for the site's cleanup, a promise that has largely been fulfilled (Carruthers 2008).

Evidence of capability building in the environmental justice movement is ubiquitous, especially at the local level. We must not forget, however, that one community's environmental justice movement victory is another's hazardous-waste facility, as these "successes" typically just displace an unwanted land use onto another community (see, for example, Bullard 2005; Brulle and Pellow 2006; Mohai et al. 2009). The movement has also succeeded in making meaningful changes at the national level. Perhaps the most celebrated US example is President Clinton's Executive Order 12898, which mandates all federal agencies to ensure environmental justice in their operations. Another example is the EPA's National Environmental Justice Advisory Council, which is meant to provide advice and oversight of its environmental justice activities (though the effectiveness of this council has long been questioned by environmental justice scholars and activists). Although a lot of work remains to be done, the movement as a whole *has* empowered communities throughout the United States (and increasingly throughout the world), making "it extremely difficult for firms to locate incinerators, landfills, and related LULUs [locally unwanted land uses] anywhere in the nation without a political struggle" (Brulle and Pellow 2006:111).

IMPORTANT CONCEPTS

- Amartya Sen's theory of justice
- community capitals framework
- conspicuous consumption
- environmental justice
- five sociological mechanisms of consumption
- Happy Planet Index (HPI)
- Human Development Index (HDI)
- limits to growth and post-growth

DISCUSSION QUESTIONS

- What could you change about your own life that would both improve your well-being and reduce your ecological footprint? What's stopping you from making the change?
- As long as we create waste, we are going to have to put that waste somewhere. How do we keep that waste from finding its way into the backyards of *any* marginalized population?
- What do "progress" and "prosperity" mean to you?
- What conditions would have to be met for an economy to grow indefinitely? In such a scenario, would our happiness and well-being increase indefinitely too?

SUGGESTED ADDITIONAL READINGS

Fitz, D. 2009. "What's Wrong with a 30 Hour Work Week." *Z Magazine,* July. Retrieved August 30, 2012 (http://www.zcommunications.org/whats-wrong-with-a-30-hour-work-week-by -don-fitz).

Mohai, P., D. Pellow, and J. T. Roberts. 2009. "Environmental Justice." *Annual Reviews Environmental Resources* 34:405–430.

New Economics Foundation. 2009. "The Un-happy Planet Index 2.0." London: New Economics Foundation. Retrieved August 30, 2012 (http://www.happyplanetindex.org/public -data/files/happy-planet-index-2-0.pdf).

Wilkinson, R., K. Pickett, and R. De Vogli. 2010. "Equality, Sustainability, and Quality of Life." *BMJ* 341(November 27):1138–1140.

RELEVANT INTERNET LINKS

- http://g-mond.parisschoolofeconomics.eu/topincomes/
  The World Top Incomes Database. An excellent resource that illustrates how inequality levels have changed for many countries.
- http://www.happyplanetindex.org/
  Home of the Happy Planet Index.
- http://hdr.undp.org/en/statistics/
  Get the latest Human Development Index data and rankings here.

- http://steadystaterevolution.org/
  Site filled with information (reports, videos, blog posts, and so on) about the steady-state economy.
- http://www.ted.com/talks/nic_marks_the_happy_planet_index.html
  Nic Marks of the New Economics Foundations gives a "TED Talk" titled "The Happy Planet Index."

SUGGESTED VIDEOS

- *The 11th Hour* (2008)
  Leonardo DiCaprio presents practical solutions for ecological problems as we run up against the limits to growth.
- *Growthbusters: Hooked on Growth* (2011)
  A documentary that questions society's most fundamental beliefs about prosperity.
- *The Light Bulb Conspiracy*
  http://dotsub.com/view/aed3b8b2–1889–4df5-ae63-ad85f5572f27. Documents the strategic use of planned obsolesce over the past one hundred years to increase the purchase frequency of consumer goods.
- *Maxed Out* (2006)
  Highlights the downside of consumer debt.
- *Tipping Point: The Age of the Oil Sands* (2011)
  For years, residents in a small community in northern Alberta, Canada, have been plagued by rare forms of cancer. This film chronicles their struggle as they attempt to get answers from the oil industry that is operating upstream from them.

PART IV

SHIFTING THE FOCUS TO RESULTS

13

From Our Beliefs to Our Behaviors: Pragmatic Environmentalism in Action

We come now to the final social driver that I address: us. Sometimes in sociology we get so caught up talking about structures, capital, organizations, and the like that we forget that people "mutually constitute"—to evoke a popular term among agency and structure theorists—those things that otherwise seem to have such power over us. In this chapter, I take a closer look at understandings, perceptions, and attitudes relevant to the problems and solutions discussed throughout this book, noting that these seemingly "mental" artifacts are fundamentally sociological as they affect and are an effect of one's socioecological environment. Any positive change has to ultimately start with us. This point is important, as it takes us back to where this book began: talking about pragmatic environmentalism. The chapter concludes by revisiting this concept.

Fast Facts

Democrats have consistently expressed more concern about climate change than Republicans in the United States, a divide that has grown particularly pronounced in recent years (Dunlap and McCright 2008; McCright and Dunlap 2011b).

A study by Edward Mailbach and colleagues sheds light on the subject of how political ideology moderates views toward climate change in the United States. Their "Six Americas study" breaks the US population into six distinct climate change groups: alarmed (18 percent of the total US population), concerned (33 percent), cautious (19 percent), disengaged (12 percent), doubtful (11 percent), and dismissive (7 percent). One's religious and political beliefs were found to shape considerably which group one fell into. For example, those who were "alarmed" were far more likely to be politically liberal, compared to those identified as "dismissive," who were overwhelmingly conservative (see Figure 13.1). The authors of the study sum up their findings as follows: "The segments that are more concerned about global warming tend to be more politically liberal

FIGURE 13.1   Relationship of Political Ideology to View of Climate Change Source

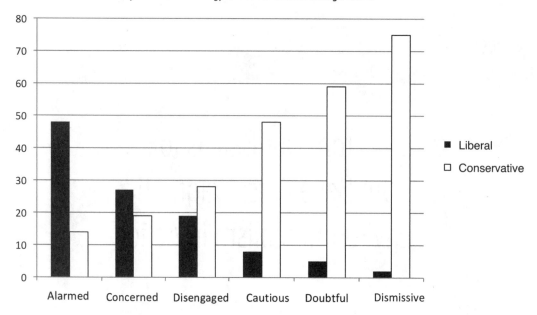

Source: Adapted from Mailbach et al. (2009).

and to hold strong egalitarian and environmental values. The less concerned segments are more politically conservative, hold anti-egalitarian and strongly individualistic values, and are more likely to be evangelical with strongly traditional religious beliefs" (2009:24).

A study with twenty-two authors, from five continents, recently looked at television food advertisements directed at children (B. Kelly et al. 2010). Ads for highly processed, nutritiously shallow foods accounted for between 53 and 87 percent of all food advertisements recorded. The rate of advertisements for these foods was higher during children's peak viewing times.

Marketing textbooks estimate that the average North American is exposed to one thousand advertisements every day (Arens 2005), though other advertising insiders have given numbers as high as three thousand (Alexander, Crompton, and Shrubsole 2011).

The US Department of Health (2008) reviewed research examining links between advertising and tobacco use. The review found a clear causal relationship between tobacco advertising and promotion and increased tobacco use, further evidence that advertising does not just redistribute consumption between brands but increases overall demand.

Implications

As detailed in this section, what and how we think is of tremendous sociological consequence. Unfortunately, there is not enough space to offer an exhaustive account of how and why attitudes and understandings are sociologically relevant to matters relating to the environment and proenvironmental behaviors. Instead, I concentrate on three quite different subjects, looking at how we think about "nature," the roots of climate denial, and the values and attitudes that help drive consumerism.

Knowledge and Worldviews

A lot has been written about how Western philosophy itself, going all the way back to the ancient Greeks (Whitehead 1964), is responsible for bestowing upon nature a type of secondary status (see, for example, Carolan 2008a; Ingold 2000; Zwart 1997). According to this **worldview** (which refers to a fundamental cognitive orientation shared by individuals within which is rooted the entirety of their knowledge), nature is inherently alien to us; while we perceive it, we dwell in a realm separate from it. This creates, in the words of the great twentieth-century philosopher Alfred North Whitehead, "the nature apprehended in awareness and the nature [a.k.a. Nature] which is the cause of awareness" (1964:30–31). Western philosophy thus leaves us with an understanding of the universe as being filled with nothing more than dead, static matter—as exemplified, for instance, in the writings of Newton. The living and dynamic in this philosophical outlook reside only in human consciousness. This separation between thought (mind) and matter (body) has perplexed philosophers for centuries—and more recently even some environmental sociologists. How is it that these two realms interact if indeed they are truly independent of each other (see Ethical Question 13.1)? Such a division inevitably creates the need for a third thing that connects the two. Yet the slope this creates is a slippery one, for what then connects this third thing to the other two?

By making nature something separate from us—and the human condition more generally—we've objectified it. **Ecofeminism** offers a rich literature detailing the historical link between the objectification of women and the objectification of nature. *The Death of Nature* (Merchant 1980) argues that casting nature in the female gender (e.g., Mother Nature) strips it of activity and renders it passive, just as casting women as being closer to nature (as, for example, the "nurturing" sex) has had similar effects. As Merchant argues, "As women's womb had symbolically yielded to the forceps, so nature's womb harbored secretes that through technology could be wrested from her grasp for use in the improvement of the human condition" (ibid.:169).

Metaphysics aside, I'm also convinced that our understandings of nature are in part a consequence of our relationship to this realm (Carolan 2008b, 2011a). Knowledge, after all, is relational. Take, for example, the Batek, one of the indigenous ethnic minorities of peninsular Malaysia. These hunting and gathering "people of the forest" (a self-imposed identity [Tuck-Po 2004:50]) have lived in this space for centuries. For them, concepts like "nature" and "forest" are multivariate categories, depending largely on who is living within this environment. And there is always a *who* in their understandings of nature, as evidenced by the fact that they do not even have a word for *wilderness* (Tuck-Po 2004). Or take research examining how understandings of nature differ between the Menominee (Wisconsin's oldest continuous residents) and their Anglo-European neighbors. Whereas children of European descent expressed problems recognizing that people are animals, the Menominee children grasped this idea fully (Medin and Atran 2004). As for the adults, Anglo-Europeans cited the importance of teaching their children that nature needs to be protected and if possible protected from

ETHICAL QUESTION 13.1

Is Pollution Natural?

Ecologically minded scholars like to talk about breaking free of the dichotomies of Western thought (e.g., mind-body, society-nature, human-animal, and so on). Yet where does that leave something like pollution? If humans are really part of nature (rather than separate from it), doesn't the same then hold for the *effects* of human activity? Pushing the question further: what about human-induced climate change? If humans and all their activities are natural, wouldn't anthropomorphically driven climate change then hold the same status? Is that "natural" too?

The first (and obvious) response to these questions is that we make conceptual distinctions all the time and need to if we want to talk about anything, though we need to be careful how we create those distinctions and be willing to revisit them if they prove problematic or oppressive. (I am doing something a bit unusual here and weighing in on these questions because they can be [and have been] used to undermine the case for taking action toward climate change, and I want to make sure readers have some reasoned responses at their disposal when confronted by such arguments.) A second, slightly more sophisticated, response, would be to point out that the questions

asked above evoke what is known as the "is-ought problem." First articulated by seventieth-century philosopher David Hume, the "problem" goes something like this: just because something *is* doesn't automatically mean it *ought* to be. Or to put it another way: statements of knowledge (e.g., "X is") are not statements of value (e.g., "X is how it ought to be"). For example, the *fact* that women have historically been subservient to men does lead one to logically conclude that they *should* be treated this way. We can therefore say that the fact that life can and has changed the earth's atmosphere for billions of years does not mean humans (as life forms) have a right to do so. To conflate these statements of fact with statements of value is to commit a "**naturalistic fallacy.**" As a statement of value, the question "What impact *should* humans have on climate?" is entirely open for debate. This is why public participation is so crucial when developing environmental policy. Science alone is incapable of translating statements of "what is" (a scientific question) to statements of "what ought to be" (a policy question). Arguably, the best avenue for answering questions of value—questions of what ought to be—is through democratic means.

humans (a viewpoint that places humans outside of nature), whereas Menominee adults stressed to their youth that people are part of nature (Bang, Medin, and Atran 2007). Perhaps not surprisingly, compared to their European neighbors, Menominee children and adults spend more of their time engaged in outdoor practices where the natural world is foregrounded and relatively less time engaged in practices where nature is backgrounded. Researchers point out how "the Menominee ecological orientation in reasoning strategies is paralleled in their framework orientation and practices" (ibid.:13871).

Tuck-Po (2004) explains how the Batek of peninsular Malaysia are able to identify native animals by their calls, a particularly important skill given the dense canopy of the forest, making visual identification nearly impossible. Yet such local knowledge is being lost as embodiments and practices around the world change (recall the earlier discussion of memory banks in Chapter 4). Among the Seri (an indigenous community in the Mexican state of Sonora), the younger generation is losing their ability to identify native animals in photographs due to their reduced interactions with these creatures (Nabhan 1997). Among the Salish people of Washington State, young people are less successful than previous generations at identifying local plants according to their medicinal properties (Turner 1988). At one time, the language of the Rio Grande Pueblos allowed them to distinguish between many types of trees and plants. Today, children increasingly use their native term for *firewood* when speaking of trees and the word *weed* when speaking of herbaceous plants due to having lost the local knowledge of their natural surroundings (Nabhan 1997). Yet it is more than just a problem of languages lost. We are losing the socioecological relationships that language is tethered to, for, as Abram explains, we "learn our native languages not mentally but bodily" (1996:75).

Denial, Ambivalence, and Apathy

In her study of a small community in Norway, Norgaard (2011) finds evidence that a lack of action against climate change is often not the result of poor or incomplete knowledge. Those she interviewed knew climate change was happening. The area had experienced very late snowfall and warmer winter temperatures while she was conducting her research. October, November, and December of that year were 4°C, 5 °C, and 1.5 °C, respectively, warmer than the 30-year average (and the winter as a whole was the second warmest in the past 130 years). Consequently, the local ski area opened late, which had a noticeable negative recreational and economic impact on the community. Moreover, a popular lake used heavily for ice fishing did not freeze.

Literal denial describes when people hold on to beliefs that are demonstrably false (as found among, say, climate change skeptics). Implicatory denial is when we fail to respond according to the moral and rational codes of the day (most citizens of Nazi Germany could be placed in this category). Norgaard's work describes another type of denial: how thinking about climate change raises disturbing emotions of fear about the future, guilt, and a sense of helplessness, which are resisted collectively through participation in such cultural practices as emotion management, norms of conversation, and the use of narratives to justify past and current actions. This type of denial, the ability to *collectively* ignore disturbing information, points to (among other things) the role of emotion in social movements and political action and highlights how global warming raises new threats to the workings of democracy. Norgaard explains how denial allowed citizens of this small community to acknowledge climate change while also pushing it from their conscious mind. One tactic was blame shifting. Many of her respondents were quick to blame, for example, "Amerika" and the Bush administration (the US president at the time). When asked about Norway's role in climate change, as the world's second-largest exporter of oil, they were quick to dismiss this fact as insignificant (though the subject did make some uncomfortable).

Norgaard reminds us that "citizens of wealthy nations who fail to respond to the issue of climate change benefit from their denial in short-run economic terms." She continues, "They also benefit by avoiding the emotional and psychological entanglement and identity conflicts that may arise from knowing that one is doing 'the wrong thing'"

(2006:336). Many who live in affluent nations can also afford to deny climate change. Although the subjects of Norgaard's study will not escape the consequences of climate change, their social positioning was such that climate change will profoundly affect people in less affluent nations long before it drastically alters the lives of those she interviewed in Norway.

The roots of climate denial have also been shown to be fed by political ideology and can span (and in turn be further reinforced by) countermovements. A **countermovement** is a social movement that arises to explicitly oppose an existing social movement. Meyer and Staggenborg (1996:1635) point to three conditions that lead to "openings" for countermovements: the original movement shows signs of success, the interests of some population are threatened by the original movement's goals, and political allies are available to aid oppositional mobilization. Jacques and colleagues (2008) look to these conditions to understand why the conservative movement in the United States launched a major countermovement against the environmental movement in the 1990s.

Environmentalism emerged as a global movement in the early 1990s with the aid of such events as the 1992 Earth Summit in Rio. This, combined with the fall of the Soviet Union, prompted the conservative movement to switch its talk of the "red scare" to a "green scare." The Republican takeover of Congress in 1994 also gave the countermovement access to political allies. Last, and perhaps most significantly, as environmentalists began calling for significant changes, the countermovement sought to brand environmentalism as a threat to not only economic progress but also the "American way of life." Jacques and colleagues also point to the role that conservative think tanks (CTT) have played in creating counterenvironmental knowledge and thereby espouse **environmental skepticism**—a position that attempts to undermine knowledge claims supporting the argument that environmental problems are real and that they are the result of human activity. Their search of English-language environmentally skeptical books published between 1972 (nothing prior to this could be found) and 2005 found 92.2 percent to have a clear link to one or more CTTs, due to author affiliation, because the book was published by a CTT, or, the most often scenario, both.

McCright and Dunlap (2011a, 2011b) recently shed light on why political values matter when it comes to shaping views on climate change. They point to, among other things, research showing that political conservatives are more likely to justify and be apologetic for the status quo (even when it comes to climate change), whereas liberals are more open to critiques toward business-as-usual attitudes. Climate change also represents an existential threat to conservatives' faith in industrial capitalism and unfettered economic growth. This is especially the case when talk of global warming turns to the creation of internationally binding treaties to curb greenhouse gas emissions and the like. Such proposals are viewed as antithetical to many key ideas conservatives hold dear, such as beliefs about American exceptionalism, free markets, and minimal governmental regulation. It's not an understatement to say climate change threatens the entire worldview of conservatives, rocking their political philosophy to its core.

Climate deniers are not only conservative but also white and male, have higher than average incomes, and are overly confident in their views no matter how demonstrably false those views are (McCright and Dunlap 2011a). This privileged position helps explain their blind confidence that climate change will never happen. According to McCright and Dunlap, "Conservative white males have disproportionately occupied positions of power within our economic system. Given the expansive challenge that climate change poses to the industrial capitalist economic system, it should not be surprising that conservative white males' strong system-justifying attitudes would be triggered to deny climate change" (2011a:1166). Having all these resources at their disposal also makes it far less likely that they will be severely threatened anytime soon by the harms caused by climate change, so they can afford to be skeptical (Klein 2011).

Our failure to act on climate change has also been attributed to ambivalence (the concept of ambivalence has also been discussed in the context of sustainable transitions [e.g., Shove and Walker 2007] and the rise of personal air travel [Cohen, M. 2010]). Ambivalence is not the same as indifference, though the two terms are often used interchangeably. When someone is said to be ambivalent, they possess feelings, attitudes, and beliefs that are in tension with each other. **Sociological ambivalence** "focuses on the ways in which ambivalence comes to be built into the structure of social statuses and role" (Merton 1976:5). A slightly more elaborate definition explains sociological ambivalence as referring "to incompatible or contradictory normative expectations or attitudes, beliefs, and behavior assigned to a status or to a set of statuses in a society or even incorporated into a single status" (Stebbins 1967:247).

Tying this back to climate change, I offer a couple of quotes from some of my own research on the subject:

> I care about the environment, biodiversity, conservation, all that. That's one hat I wear, as an environmentalist. But like everyone else I wear other hats: dad, democratic, entrepreneur, husband. . . . They [these different statuses] come with different expectations. For example, while I care about the environment I care about my kids more. So when faced with driving my daughter to school four miles each way in the winter and putting her on a bike, because we can't bus her, I'm going to pick the car. Yes, it has a bigger carbon footprint than a bike but my hat of dad outweighs that of environmentalist. (Carolan 2010b:317)

> I mean, we live in a society that makes it next to impossible to do the right thing as far as the environment is concerned. We have to drive. We're pinched for time so we need modern labor saving conveniences . . . I could live in a thatched hut in the forest but I have responsibilities to my family that keep me from rejecting the modern lifestyle, even though this lifestyle has considerable ecological implications. (ibid.)

For both of these self-identified "environmentalists," ambivalence toward climate change does not mean indifference. Both professed caring for the environment and worrying about greenhouse gas emissions and climate change. Rather, the ambivalence emerged out of a perceived tension between what respondents *wanted* to do and what they believed they *could do* within the existing socio-organizational structures of society. The first person quoted also makes reference to what sociologists call "**role strain**": tensions that emerge when expectations from holding multiple roles clash. The roles "environmentalist" and "dad" are often complementary—after all, environmentalists are deeply concerned about leaving a healthy planet for future generations. Yet sometimes those roles conflict, like when freezing temperatures (and concerns about exposure) momentarily elevate the "dad" role above that of "environmentalist" and result in the bike being left at home in exchange for fossil fuel–based mobility (namely, the car).

Sociological denial and ambivalence might also tell us something about the apathy being reported by recent surveys when it comes to today's environmental problems. One such study found levels of "informedness, confidence in scientists, and personal efficacy" regarding climate change interact such that the "more informed respondents both feel less personally responsible for global warming, and also show less concern for global warming" (Kellstedt, Zahran, and Vedlitz 2008:113). As others have suggested, perhaps apathy isn't about caring too little but a paralysis that arises out of caring too much for too many different things (Lertzman 2010). Some of this apathy can also be attributed to the fact that people are more likely to tune out those problems they feel they have no control over (Stern 2000).

Consumerism, Advertising, and Status Attainment

The following stunning admission is taken from an article by Rory Sutherland, vice chairman of the marketing firm Ogilvy UK and then president of the Institute of Practitioners in Advertising: "The truth is that marketing raises enormous ethical questions every day—at least it does if you're doing it right. If this were not the case, the only possible explanations are either that you believe marketers are too ineffectual to make any difference, or you believe that marketing activities only affect people at the level of conscious argument. Neither of these possibilities appeals to me. *I would rather be thought of as evil than useless*" (2010:59; emphasis added).

Decades of studies note how advertising promotes rabid consumerism (see, for example, Galbraith 1958). After all, economic growth relies upon the unending creation of insatiable needs. As Ezra Mishan, longtime professor of economics at the London School of Economics, famously noted a half century ago: "Therefore to continue to regard the market, in an affluent and growing economy, as primarily a 'want-satisfying' mechanism is to close one's eyes to the more important fact, that it is has become a want-*creating* mechanism" (1967:149; emphasis in the original). We also know that advertising further reinforces the values it reflects by "normalizing" them. On this point, talking specifically about smoking, Rory Sutherland further confessed, "While I can accept that the purpose of tobacco advertising was not to encourage people to smoke, I find it astounding that anyone could barefacedly suggest that cigarette posters seen everywhere did not serve to normalise the habit" (2010:59).

A growing body of research examines links between "intrinsic" and "extrinsic" values and consumption. Intrinsic values refer to aspects of life that we find inherently rewarding, whereas the reward of extrinsic values lies in the validation given to us by others. When you place greater importance on extrinsic values, you are more likely to express prejudice toward others, be less concerned about the environment and human rights, and express lower levels of personal well-being and happiness (Alexander et al. 2011; Kasser 2002; Roccas and Sagiv 2010). Adolescents who strongly endorse extrinsic values report being less likely to turn off lights in unused rooms, recycle, and engage in other proenvironmental behaviors (Kasser 2005). Other studies report a strong positive correlation between the ecological footprints of adults and their possession of extrinsic values (Brown and Kasser 2005). So which values do you suppose advertisers target? The vast majority of advertising is directed at appealing to extrinsic values, the very val-

ECOnnection 13.1

Consumer Involvement, Television, and Children's Well-Being

Utilizing structural equation modeling—which provides an understanding of causality between variables—Juliet Schor set out to understand how television use, consumer involvement, parental attitudes, and well-being are interrelated. The arrows of causality were clear: "Psychologically healthy children will be made worse off if they become more enmeshed in the culture of getting and spending. Children with emotional problems will be helped if they disengage from the worlds that corporations are constructing for them" (2005:167). Schor found that children who spend more time watching television and using other media become more involved in consumer culture. And as children become more involved in consumer culture, their well-being decreases, in terms of depression, anxiety, and self-esteem. Higher involvement in consumer culture also worsens the relationship children have with their parents, and as that relationship deteriorates, their levels of depression and anxiety increase while self-esteem decreases. Consumer culture thus packs a powerful one-two punch for the well-being of children. It negatively impacts them directly through their consumer involvement and indirectly through the deleterious effect that involvement has upon their relations with parents.

ues associated with lower motivation to address social and environmental problems (Alexander et al. 2011). Advertisers have also learned that it is possible to advertise so-called green products through an appeal to extrinsic values, like using a famous celebrity to advertise the latest hybrid car. Such a marketing campaign promotes extrinsic values by encouraging status competition and social comparison.

What are the cumulative effects of being endlessly seduced into becoming envious, status-seeking hyperconsumers who are looking for our next "happiness fix" with a swipe of the credit card or click of the mouse? Obviously, we do not rush to purchase everything we see advertised. But if almost every advertisement we see seeks to fuel our extrinsic values, it's reasonable to think this is going to have a measurable effect on people over the long term. Perhaps, to refer back to a point discussed in the previous chapter, this helps partially explain why so many in the United States report such low levels of well-being and happiness, because of Americans' overexposure to advertisements directed at appeals to extrinsic values. A study examined the impact of the use of *Channel One*—a daily ten-minute news bulletin with two minutes of advertisements—in US schools (Greenberg and Brand 1993). It compared the importance attached to extrinsic values in teenagers from two neighboring schools with very similar student and parent demographics: one had *Channel One;* the other did not. Teenagers enrolled at the school with *Channel One* had much higher levels of extrinsic values than the control group (see ECOnnection 13.1). This corroborates more recent research pointing to links between hours of watching television and a lack of concern about environmental problems and an increased prevalence of extrinsic values (Good 2007; Schor 2005).

A lot of television is watched in the United States. It is also, as discussed in the previous chapter, a society with excessive levels of inequality. This is a powerful double whammy, as we know that inequality is perhaps the greatest driver of overconsumption (Wilkinson and Pickett 2009). For one thing, status competition drives hyperconsumerism. Second, inequality—by heightening the distance between the "haves" from the "have-nots" and thus increasing the status of being a "have"—intensifies status competition. Throw endless hours of television watching into this mix, and you have an environment ripe for materialism that we see in affluent countries today.

Solutions

Changing how we think about things is no small feat. Fortunately, we have the benefit of decades of excellent social science research and illustrative examples from other countries to light our way. The task ahead may be daunting, but it's most definitely possible.

Advertisements, Freedom, and the Public Good

Although the majority of parents feel they are primarily responsible for their children, they do not feel they alone own this responsibility, especially when it comes to competing with the deep pockets of multinational corporations and advertising firms who are trying to get into the minds (and wallets) of today's youth. The vast majority of parents thus favor restrictions on advertising aimed at children. These sentiments have been found among parents in countries as diverse as, for example, the United States (Schor 2005), the Netherlands (van der Voort, Nikken, and van Lil 1992), and China (Chan and McNeal 2003).

Consumption is a thoroughly social activity. Once we accept this undeniable empirical truth, the argument against the regulation of advertisements falls apart. That argument goes something along the lines of the following: in the name of protecting individual freedom, one should being able to buy as much of whatever one likes; after all, the consumer knows best what they need. Establishing that those "needs" are products of social activity diminishes the argument that government intervention takes away from individual freedoms—for example, almost 60 percent of nine- to fourteen-year-olds in one US study explained how they feel pressure to buy stuff in order to fit in (Schor 2005). In fact, it could easily be argued that government intervention *increases* personal freedoms by helping to shield individuals from the dictates of these particular sociological forces.

We could begin by regulating advertisements directed at children, as this population in the classical liberal tradition is often seen as needing more protection than adults. We could also create advertising-free zones. Most places of religious worship are advertisement free. Why can't we do the same with schools and other public places where children are frequently present? Why not limit specific types of advertisement that are clearly meant for children? In Greece, for example, television advertisements for toys are banned from 7 a.m. to 9 p.m. In Norway and Sweden, it is illegal to target through advertisements children under the age of twelve (Kasser 2002). We also need to be aware of the dangers of putting all the responsibility on the shoulders of parents. As market-driven treads increasingly structure social interaction among children and teens, well-meaning parents who place restrictions on their kids' consumption patterns risk setting them up for social exclusion, which does not do their children any good either. Finally, advertisements in countries like the United States are a tax-deductible expense. By spending money on advertisements, which increases brand loyalty and the purchase frequency of the product advertised, firms are also able to reduce their tax liability: a clear win-win scenario for companies. Yet this win comes at the expense of individual and public health. The general public in the United States is subsidizing advertisements. Moreover, the hundreds of millions of dollars saved by firms annually through these deductions could help pay for public services that are currently paid for by taxpayers.

Collaborative Consumption

Aristotle is said to have written that "on the whole, you find wealth much more in use than in ownership" (quoted in Rifkin 2000:76). Kevin Kelly, founder of the influential magazine *Wired*, has argued passionately that "access is better than ownership" (n.d.). We have become so wrapped up in fighting for our "right to own" that we seemed to have forgotten why we wanted to own in the first place: for access and use. We are also guilty of overlooking the fact that markets are not ends in themselves. Markets were developed to solve problems of resource allocation; they were never meant to be the holy grail that they have become. What's important is efficient and fair resource allocation. Markets have long been viewed as the best option to deliver those ends. But what if something better came along?

Michael Spence, a 2001 Nobel laureate for economics and a senior fellow at Stanford's Hoover Institution, wrote a recent article in *Forbes* titled "Markets Aren't Everything" (2009). In this piece, Spence celebrates the work of scholars like Elinor Ostrom, who have highlighted how common-property resources can quite effectively be managed without the aid of formal markets. As Ostrom (1999) and others (e.g., Dietz et al. 2002) have detailed, common-property resources (e.g., forests) have been effectively managed—in some cases for centuries—thanks to things like informal social norms, trust, and social capital. Yet what if, in this age of social media, Twitter, and the Internet more generally, something like a traditional commons is forming for consumers?

A generation ago, the thought of the nonmarket coordination of large groups of people from around the world for purposes of resource allocation seemed absurd. The transaction costs of such an endeavor were too great. If you had something and wanted to get rid of it, your options were limited. You could put an ad in the paper or place fliers on community bulletin boards around your neighborhood. And even if someone would get back to you, the chance of a successful transaction was low (they might have wanted a different color, model, and so on). That has all changed, which explains why the godfather of *Wired* is proclaiming the virtues of access over ownership. For many consumer items, we no longer need the market. Enter what has become known as "collaborative consumption."

One example of collaborative consumption is **peer-to-peer renting**: the process of one private individual renting an underused item of theirs to another individual (a.k.a. P2P renting). There are a number of peer-to-peer sites that create a low–transaction cost environment, allowing a type of commons to appear, like irent2you.com, rentmineonline.com, and iletyou.com. These sites enable individuals to make use of those underused goods we all are guilty of having by renting them to others, which in turn keeps those

---

CASE STUDY 13.1

UsedCardboardBoxes.com

In 2002 Marty Metro started an innovative business venture that buys and sells used cardboard boxes—called, fittingly, UsedCardboard Boxes.com. The business model is simple: to "rescue" boxes from firms all around the United States. By 2006 the company expanded by opening eight more warehouses, in addition to the original one in Los Angeles. Today, the company guarantees the delivery of moving kits (which cost approximately 40 percent less than if one were to buy brand-new materials) to any address in the continental United States in two days or less. Metro has also started a free service, called freecardboardboxes.com, which matches people in communities who have boxes to give with people in need of boxes (Botsman and Rogers 2010).

---

renters from purchasing the goods new (see Case Study 13.1). It has been estimated that if the United States shifted a mere fifth of its household spending from purchasing to renting, the country would cut CO_2 emissions by roughly 2 percent (or 13 million tons) annually (Botsman and Rogers 2010).

Another example of providing access rather than ownership is Zipcar, the world's largest **car sharing** company. Car sharing is a short-term (often by the hour) car rental model where the cars are scattered throughout a community to improve access rather than all being centrally housed at one location (as is the case with traditional car rentals). Zipcar allows members to reserve a car for as little as one hour. Reservations can be made online or even through a mobile phone app. The cars are widely available in communities serviced by Zipcar, so access is often not a problem for members (I can even see two Zipcars from my university office window). The service is currently available in twenty-eight North American states and provinces as well as in the United Kingdom. As of September 2011, the company reported having 650,000 members.

In July 2009, Zipcar started its "Low-Car Diet Challenge," involving 250 persons (some who admitted to being addicted to their cars) from thirteen cities. All participants agreed to put their car keys away for one month and use public transportation, bikes, and their legs to get around. And when driving a car was necessary, they were asked to use a Zipcar, as they were all given a membership. After the challenge they were surveyed. As it turns out, they reduced their vehicle miles traveled by 66 percent, while increasing the miles they walked and biked by 93 and 132 percent, respectively. Almost half of the participants also reported losing weight. And perhaps most important, 61 percent said they planned to continue with their new transportation habits (Botsman and Rogers 2010).

There is an old saying: when you walk around with a hammer, everything starts looking like a nail. Similarly, when you have a car in your garage, every trip starts looking like it can only be accomplished with an automobile. This explains why average car users save an estimated US$600 a month and reduce vehicle miles traveled by 44 percent

CASE STUDY 13.2

*The Carrotmob
(a.k.a. Buycott)*

Rather than punish stores and firms for their environmental atrocities, why not reward those for their proenvironmental actions with mass purchases? "Traditional activism revolves around conflict," explains Schulkin (quoted in Caplan 2009). Schulkin is the founder of a fledgling movement of activist consumers employing a kind of reverse boycott that he calls a **carrotmob**. Simply defined, the carrotmob is a type of consumer activism based on the idea of using carrots (or incentives) to reward businesses for engaging in socially or environmentally responsible practices. Instead of creating enemies, a carrotmob focuses on positive cooperation. Schulkin solicited bids from twenty-three stores in the area to find which business would promise to spend the highest percentage of the carrotmob's profits on more energy-

efficient lighting. In return, Schulkin promised to deliver, with the help of social media and social networks, a horde of consumers who pledged to buy stuff from the highest bidder, things that these consumers would have had to purchase anyway (namely, household and food items). The buycott occurred on March 29, 2008, when hundreds of green-minded patrons waited their turn in an hourlong line to spend their money at K&D Market (a local convenience store). In all, the carrotmob spent more than $9,200, and K&D Market, in turn, promised to spend 22 percent of the day's revenue on energy-efficient lighting (which was enough to make all the improvements recommended by an energy auditor). Since then, carrotmobs have spread to ten other US cities and Finland and France (ibid.; Smith, 2008).

when they switch to car sharing (Keegan 2009). Some of these savings no doubt come from not being responsible for expenses tied to owning a car (e.g., title and insurance). Yet some also come from the fact that car sharing makes you rethink whether a car is necessary for any particular trip. When people share cars, they begin to realize they don't actually need them as much as originally thought. One estimate claims that in some markets, every car-sharing vehicle takes up to eight owned vehicles off the road (Botsman and Rogers 2010).

Let's also not forget about the *social* value added through collaborative consumption. When you consume collaboratively, you build social networks, nurture trust, and generate social capital (see Case Study Box 13.1). As a sociologist, I cannot deny the social nature of shopping. Yet when we shop, we do not really establish any new social networks. We might build trust and a sense of camaraderie among the family and friends we are shopping with, though, equally, shopping has been shown to create animosity and jealousy among even loved ones who shop together (Stillerman 2004). The tentative early evidence suggests that collaborative consumption not only strengthens already existing (a.k.a. "strong") ties but also builds new (a.k.a. "weak") ones between people with different backgrounds (Drogen 2011). Perhaps these ties could even be used to further push for social change by way of consumer activism, such as through traditional boycotts or more recently through "buycotts" (see Case Study 13.2).

ECOnnection 13.2
The New Environmental Paradigm (NEP)

The New Environmental Paradigm (NEP) has been called "the most widely used measure of EA [environmental attitudes] since its publication in 1978" (Hawcroft and Milfont 2010:144). The original scale was first published in 1978 by Dunlap and Van Liere and consisted of twelve items (eight pro-NEP and four anti-NEP) on a four-point Likert scale (anchored by "strongly agree" and "strongly disagree"). The higher the NEP score, the greater an individual's level of environmental beliefs (or ecological worldview) (Dunlap 2008). In 2000 Dunlap and colleagues revised the NEP scale. The revised scale consists of fifteen items (eight pro-NEP and seven anti-NEP). Table 13.1 displays the twelve and fifteen items from the original and revised scales, respectively.

Economists have found the NEP scale to be an accurate predictor of willingness to pay in **contingent valuation** studies (see, for example, Cooper, Poe, and Bateman 2004; Kotchen and Reiling, 2000). (Contingent valuation, for those unfamiliar with the term, is a survey-based economic technique for placing a value on nonmarket resources.) The NEP scale has also been shown to predict both reported and observed behavior (see, for example, Casey and Scott 2006; Olli, Grendstad, and Wollebaek 2001). A growing body of evidence also indicates that environmental educational programs can lead to an increase in NEP scores among children (Manoli, Johnson, and Dunlap 2007) and college students (Rideout 2005; Woodworth, Steen-Adams, and Mittal 2011).

Globalization of Environmental Concern

Here's some good news: there appears to be a global diffusion of views and values concerning environmental protection (Brechin 1999; Dunlap and York 2008; Mohai, Simões, and Brechin 2010). Environmental concern has been defined by Dunlap and Jones as "the degree to which people are aware of problems regarding the environment and support efforts to solve them and/or indicate a willingness to contribute personally to their solution" (2002:485). As environmental attitudes are often taken to be synonymous with environmental concern (Dunlap and Jones 2002; Ester 1981), I will use the two concepts interchangeably (see ECOnnection 13.2).

Until recently, there was quite a debate between scholars about the globalization of environmental concern. Conventional wisdom had long assumed that widespread citizen concern for environmental quality was confined to wealthy nations. This presumption was grounded in the belief that residents of poor countries are too preoccupied with their "material" needs to support the "postmaterialist" value of environmental protection. The most famous champion of this view is Ronald Inglehart. Inglehart grounds his argument in two theories: Maslow's hierarchy of human needs and Mannheim's socialization hypothesis. Maslow argued that "higher-order" needs (e.g., concern for the environment) cannot be fully developed in people worried where their next meal is going to come from (a "lower-order" material need), whereas Mannheim's socialization

TABLE 13.1 New Environmental Paradigm (NEP), Original and Revised

ORIGINAL NEP (1978)	REVISED NEP (2000)
1) We are approaching the limit of the number of people the earth can support.	1) We are approaching the limit of the number of people the earth can support.
2) The balance of nature is very delicate and easily upset.	2) Humans have the right to modify the natural environment to suit their needs.
3) Humans have the right to modify the natural environment to suit their needs.	3) When humans interfere with nature it often produces disastrous consequences.
4) Mankind was created to rule over the rest of nature.	4) Human ingenuity will insure that we do NOT make the earth unlivable.
5) When humans interfere with nature it often produces disastrous consequences.	5) Humans are severely abusing the environment.
6) Plants and animals exist primarily to be used by humans.	6) The earth has plenty of natural resources if we just learn how to develop them.
7) To maintain a healthy economy we will have to develop a "steady-state" economy where industrial growth is controlled.	7) Plants and animals have as much right as humans to exist.
8) Humans must live in harmony with nature in order to survive.	8) The balance of nature is strong enough to cope with the impacts of modern industrial nations.
9) The earth is like a spaceship with only limited room and resources.	9) Despite our special abilities humans are still subject to the laws of nature.
10) Humans need not adapt to the natural environment because they can remake it to suit their needs.	10) The so-called "ecological crisis" facing humankind has been greatly exaggerated.
11) There are limits to growth beyond which our industrialized society cannot expand.	11) The earth is like a spaceship with very limited room and resources.
12) Mankind is severely abusing the environment.	12) Humans were meant to rule over the rest of nature.
	13) The balance of nature is very delicate and easily upset.
	14) Humans will eventually learn enough about how nature works to be able to control it.
	15) If things continue on their present course, we will soon experience a major catastrophe.

In the original NEP, agreement with points 3, 4, 6, and 10 reflects an anti-NEP sentiment, while agreement with points 1, 2, 5, 7, 8, 9, 11, and 12 reflects a pro-NEP sentiment. In the revised NEP, agreement with the even-numbered points reflects anti-NEP opinions, while agreement with odd numbers reflects pro-NEP opinions. *Source:* Adapted from Dunlap and Van Liere (1978) and Dunlap et al. (2000).

hypothesis holds that "one's basic values reflect the conditions that prevailed during one's pre-adult years" (Inglehart 1990:68). With these two theories in tow, Inglehart argues that individuals residing in affluent countries will hold more postmaterialist values and that these values will grow due to generational cohort replacement (Inglehart 1990, 1997). Inglehart's argument was (and still is) attractive in some political corners, as it justifies the status quo and the belief—no matter how disconnected it is from empirical reality—that continued economic development will eventually lead all nations toward socially and politically tolerant, environmentally sustainable, and postmaterial futures (Dunlap and York 2008).

Recent research has not been kind to Inglehart's postmaterialism thesis. Take, for example, the results of the twenty-four-nation "Health of the Planet" survey (ibid.). Of the fourteen different measures of environmental concern employed, seven were found to be *negatively* related with national affluence. In other words, they indicated higher levels of environmental concern among residents of poor countries. As Dunlap and York explain, "Citizens of poorer nations were significantly more likely to (1) express personal concern about environmental problems, (2) rate the quality of their national environments as poor, (3) rate the quality of their community environments as poor, (4) perceive environmental problems as health threats at present (5) and in the future, (6) rate six community-level environmental problems as serious, and (7) express support for six governmental environmental protection programs" (2008:534).

More recent still, a twenty-five-country analysis found that willingness to sacrifice to protect the environment is not unique to wealthy nations (Mostafa in press). Even more devastating to the postmaterialism thesis, the study found that a country's ranking on a postmaterialism index was *negatively* correlated to proenvironmental intentions. Put another way, postmaterialist values were associated with *less* environmentalism.

The big question is what's driving this global diffusion of environmental concern. Some argue, like Inglehart, that whatever environmental concern resides in less affluent countries is the result of local, "objective" environmental degradation. If your local environment is poisoned, so the argument goes, then of course you're going to express some concern about the environment. If this were true, then residents of poor nations should rate local environmental problems as more serious than their counterparts in affluent nations (where local environmental conditions are presumably better), whereas developed nations should rate global problems as more serious. Steve Brechin (1999) set out to test this hypothesis and found only partial support for it. Although citizens of less affluent nations rated local problems as more serious than their more affluent counterparts, ratings of global problems do not differ significantly between rich and poor nations.

Another variable deserving mention is democracy. As democracy grows in a country, so grows not only environmental concern but also environmental associations, which increases opportunities for activism and group formation (Longhofer and Schofer 2010). Information spreads easier in a democracy than in an autocracy (Payne 1995). Democracies also tend to be more responsive to the environmental needs of the public than nondemocracies (Quan and Reuveny 2006). After examining more than one hundred countries, Quan and Reuveny (2006) conclude that, relative to less democratic countries, more democratic countries emit less CO_2 per capita, less NO_2 per capita, and less organic pollution in water; experience lower deforestation rates and less land degradation; and have higher percentages of forested land.

I also wonder what effect inequality has upon levels of environmental concern within a country, to draw upon a variable discussed extensively in the previous chapter. We know, for example, that more equal societies have a greater sense of collective responsibility to those in other countries and that business leaders in more equal countries are more likely to agree that their governments should cooperate with international environmental agreements (Wilkinson and Pickett 2009). I would therefore not be surprised if more equal societies also have higher levels of environmental concern. That would explain why some studies find that citizens of wealthier countries are no more or less concerned about environmental issues than those from poorer nations (Brechin 1999), while others find a negative correlation between national affluence and environmental concern (Dunlap and Mertig 1997; Gelissen 2007). Perhaps "level of societal inequality" ought to be looked at in future studies gauging levels of global environmental concern.

Proenvironmental Behavior

We know from decades of research that there is no magic bullet that triggers environmentally significant behavior (Kollmuss and Agyeman 2002; Stern 2000). Gardner and Stern (1996), for instance, examined four types of intervention: religious and moral appeals, education to change attitudes, efforts to change the incentive structure of behavior by providing various types of rewards and penalties, and community management (e.g., the establishment of norms, shared rules, and expectations). Each type was found to have some success at changing behavior, with moral and educational approaches performing the least well. Without question, the most effective behavioral change strategy involved combinations of intervention types. In another study, incentives and education were found to be more effective when combined than the sum of the two interventions when carried out separately (Stern 1999).

A now-classic study in environmental behavior from the 1980s found that even when electric utility companies subsidized 93 percent of the cost of home insulation, consumer response to the program varied wildly across the regions studied, from 1 to almost 20 percent (Stern et al. 1986). Something other than the subsidy had to be accounting for the different insulation-adoption rates. Researchers found that in addition to reducing financial barriers, utilities also needed to provide information about how insulation can improve household energy efficiency as well as help direct consumers to a reliable contractor.

Social norms (those standards of behavior shared by a social group) also play a significant role in changing behaviors. We typically like to think of ourselves as "normal," especially in relationship to our personally perceived reference group(s). If we think our reference group is doing X, then we are more likely to start doing X too. One study explored the role of social norms in shaping hotel guests' participation in the now ubiquitous towel-reuse program (Goldstein, Cialdini, and V. Griskevicius 2008). Two signs were created asking for participation: one focused on the importance of environmental protection; the other conveyed a descriptive norm informing readers that the majority of other guests participate in the program at least once during their stay. The sign containing the descriptive norm yielded a noticeably higher towel-reuse rate (44.1 percent) than the one focusing only on environmental protection (35.1 percent).

What's remarkable about social norms is that they seem to have the capacity to elicit behavioral changes without any changes in values or attitudes. I would like to discuss briefly one example where behavioral change occurred *absent attitudinal change*. This case study involves high schools from the school district where I live, Fort Collins, Colorado (Shelley et al. 2011, 2012).

Over a period of eight years, Rocky Mountain High School (which first opened in 1973) was able to reduce its electrical energy consumption to levels below that of the recently built (2005) LEED-certified Fossil Ridge High School. (LEED stands for Leadership in Energy and Environmental Design and involves a rating system for the design, construction, and operation of green buildings, homes, and neighborhoods.) Although the LEED school was built for energy efficiency, it consumed electricity at a higher rate (6.24 kWh/ft2) than the much older Rocky Mountain High School (4.79 kWh/ft2) in 2007 due to the latter's highly successful energy-conservation efforts. What did Rocky Mountain High School do to achieve these impressive results, where they were able to cut their electrical energy consumption in half over the span of a few years? As indicated by earlier research, no single thing led to the behavioral changes. The authors of this study cite a number of factors:

- *Physical structures were added in the school that "communicated environmental values."* Examples of this include the recycling center, the "Thanks a Watt" signs above electrical switches, and the clearly marked waste and recycling bins. Making these changes made it easy to be "green," regardless of one's actual beliefs.
- *Everyone was made a vested stakeholder.* Giving staff and students a voice in the process enhanced their desire to see the project become a success and increased their willingness to work toward that end.
- *Providing communication and feedback also proved important.* Providing students and staff with regular reports on their energy consumption, as well on how their consumption compared to other schools in the district, kept them vested in the project.

As mentioned, none of the respondents conveyed an actual change in their attitudes. Nevertheless, "even without a sense of environmental concern and without engaging in environmentally responsible behaviors at home, they participated in energy conservation and other efforts (such as recycling) within the organizational setting" (Shelley et al. 2011:338).

Pragmatic Environmentalism

Pragmatic social theorists—as well as environmentalists—take actors' agency and creativity seriously. As a theoretical tradition, pragmatism offers an alternative to overt social structuralism (an approach giving priority to structures) and methodological individualism (an approach giving priority to individuals). Instead, it emphasizes the dynamic emergent interplay between the process of constructing and reconstructing meaning through action and routine, on the one hand, and structures and the environment, on the other. John Dewey, the great American philosopher and an early developer of pragmatism, worried about the interests, beliefs, and ideologies of elites becoming "fixed" and assuming a taken-for-granted status within the political and the dominant social cultures. To combat this, he prescribed the technique of "experimentalism," which essentially involves the recruiting of the broader public to constantly reflect upon and question conventional habits and beliefs. Dewey believed this constituted an important first step in breaking up imposed rules of order and action that is necessary if meaningful social change is to occur. The most likely time for established rules to be reformed, Dewey argued, is when existing institutions fail. During these moments, "publics" form that are commonly united through a shared threat or actual harm (think of the possible "publics" that could be organized as a response to climate change!). Thus, social and environmental problems are inherently *hopeful,* in the sense that they create openings for creativity, change, and an enlivened democracy.

And what of those who choose not to be initially enrolled in this collective activity? Fortunately, there are many ways to engage people in selecting proenvironmental behaviors without having to make them into so-called environmentalists. For example, let's say we are able to get people to choose to leave their car in the garage (or perhaps not even buy one). As long as they are doing this, does it really matter—at least initially—what their attitudes toward the environment (or even automobiles) are? Anna Peterson (2009) reminds us that attitudes and values have the potential to change in radical ways in response to behavioral changes. She gives the example of the 1954 US Supreme Court decision *Brown v. Board of Education of Topeka,* the landmark court ruling that struck down the infamous "separate but equal" rule made famous in the *Plessy v. Ferguson* US Supreme Courting ruling from 1899. Peterson points out that "while school desegregation certainly did not end racism, it has had a significant effect on the lives and values of both white and black southerners," ultimately concluding that "Brown generated major shifts in values that probably would not have occurred had institutions and practices not changed first." She goes on to suggest that an "environmental *Brown v. Board of Education*" could, over time, help generate "environmental values as well as positive practical results" (2009:132).

Something else we've learned over the past couple of decades is that getting people *talking and working together* is an immensely powerful force. The late Elinor Ostrom, as mentioned in an earlier chapter, won a Nobel Prize in Economics in 2009 for her tireless research on precisely this point, though the idea that "thick" social networks can overwhelm desires to act selfishly has been articulated by social and political theorists for quite some time (see, for example, Eckersley 1992; Dryzek 1990; Habermas 1962). Sometimes the formation of these collectivities is abrupt and immediate: think of the speed at which a shared global "public" formed in the wake of September 11. More often, however, their formation is a slow grind, even for threats that are global and significant in scope (like climate change). In the end, *people* are going to have to do the work—structures are not going to change themselves. What are you going to do?

IMPORTANT CONCEPTS

- climate change denial
- collaborative consumption
- consumerism
- globalization of environmental concern
- Inglehart's postmaterialism thesis
- "intrinsic" and "extrinsic" values
- New Environmental Paradigm (NEP)
- postmaterialism thesis
- pragmatic environmentalism

DISCUSSION QUESTIONS

1. We have long practiced a type of collaborative consumption with public libraries. Why do we not collaboratively consume more stuff (beyond books, movies, and music)?
2. In what ways do some of your own proenvironmental attitudes not match up with certain behaviors? Why do you think this "gap" exists?
3. What are your thoughts on Kevin Kelly's (founder of *Wired* magazine) argument that "access is better than ownership"?
4. To revisit a question first posed at the end of Chapter 2: why do some continue to deny the existence of anthropogenic climate change? What are your thoughts on some of the explanations given above to this question?

SUGGESTED ADDITIONAL READINGS

Dunlap, R. 2008. "The New Environmental Paradigm Scale: From Marginality to Worldwide Use." *Journal of Environmental Education* 40(1):3–18.

Klein, N. 2011. "Capitalism vs. the Climate." *Nation,* November 9. Retrieved August 30, 2012 (http://www.thenation.com/article/164497/capitalism-vs-climate?page=0,5).

Roberts, D. 2011. "Sharing and Caring: The Implications of Collaborative Consumption." *Grist,* May 4. Retrieved August 30, 2012 (http://grist.org/living/2011–05–03-sharing-and-caring-the-implications-of-collaborative-consumption/).

Schor, J. 2005. *Born to Buy.* New York: Scribner.

Stern, P. 2000. "Toward a Coherent Theory of Environmentally Significant Behavior." *Journal of Social Issues* 56:407–424.

RELEVANT INTERNET LINKS

- http://www.scorai.org/
  Address of the Sustainable Consumption Research and Action Initiative (SCORAI). SCORAI is a network of academics and practitioners interested in better understanding the interface of material consumption, human fulfillment, lifestyle satisfaction, and macroeconomic and technological change.
- http://www.ted.com/talks/rachel_botsman_the_case_for_collaborative_consumption.html
  "TED Talk" by Rachel Botsman, one of the authors of *What's Mine Is Yours: The Rise of Collaborative Consumption* (Botsman and Rogers 2010).
- http://www.youtube.com/watch?v=2I5u9rfUSLA
  Link to video of the earlier-mentioned "Six Americas study."
- http://www.youtube.com/watch?v=AsCbcmE07Zg
  Interview on CNN of UsedCardboardBoxes.com founder Marty Metro, who was introduced in Case Study 13.1.

SUGGESTED VIDEOS

- *Czech Dream* (2004)
  A highly original Czechoslovakian documentary about two film students who pull off a remarkable hoax that culminates in the "opening event" of a fake supermarket.

- *Everything's Cool* (2006)
  A film about the most dangerous rift ever to emerge between scientific understanding and political action: global warming.
- *No Impact Man* (2008)
  A story of a family who goes off-grid for one year in New York City in order to minimize their environmental impact.

Glossary

Abject poverty: Most severe state of poverty. Those living in this state cannot meet basic needs for food, water, shelter, sanitation, and health care.

Adaptation (climate change): Actions taken to adjust socioecological systems in response to existing or predicted climatic effects to reduce harmful effects.

Agrobiodiversity: All forms of life directly relevant to agriculture, including crops and livestock but also many other organisms, such as soil, fauna, weeds, pests, and predators.

Anaerobic decomposition: The breaking down of biodegradable material by microorganisms in an environment lacking oxygen.

Apolitical ecology: When conventional explanations do not fully account for the asymmetries in power that first created a problem materially and then later define it as a "problem" to be solved by the same system that gave birth to it.

Arable land: Land that can be cultivated to grow crops.

Biochar: Charcoal derived from a thermochemical decomposition of organic material at heightened temperatures in the absence of oxygen. Biochar is used to improve soil fertility and sequester carbon. Biochar oil and gas by-products can also be used as biofuels.

Biocultural diversity: Cultural diversity does not merely parallel biological diversity but is profoundly interrelated with it.

Biodiversity hot spots: A biogeographic region with a significant reservoir of biodiversity that is under threat from humans.

Biofortification: The breeding (and increasingly genetic engineering) of plants with the aim of higher micronutrient content.

Biohazards: Environmental threats resulting from biological agents or conditions.

Biopiracy: The loss of biocultural diversity through legal—and sometimes illegal—means.

Birthrate: The ratio of live births to total population of a specified community, usually expressed per 1,000 population per year.

"Bonding" social capital: Social ties that link people together who are primarily alike according to established characteristics.

"Bridging" social capital: Social ties that link people together across social cleavages.

Buyer power: An effect that results when a market has numerous sellers but only one buyer (or a few).

Cap and trade: A scheme that involves the trading of a limited number of emission allowances. A regulatory authority establishes this limit, which is typically lower than the historical level of emissions.

Carbon credits: Units of carbon emissions that can be purchased or sold to meet compliance with carbon emission cap.

Carbon intensity: The amount of CO_2 emitted for each unit of economic output produced.

Carbon offsets: Reduction in emissions of carbon dioxide (or greenhouse gases more generally) in order to compensate for (or "offset") an emission released elsewhere.

Carbon tax: Tax on fossil fuels that seeks to reduce the emission of carbon dioxide.

Carrotmob: A type of consumer activism based on the idea of using carrots (or incentives) to reward businesses for engaging in socially or environmentally responsible practices.

Car sharing: A short-term (often by the hour) car rental model where the cars are scattered throughout a community to improve access rather than all being centrally housed at one location (as is the case with traditional car rentals).

Clean coal: Defined by the coal industry as any technologies that improve the environmental performance of coal-based electricity plants, which include equipment that increases the operational efficiency of power plants as well as technologies that reduce emissions. Elsewhere, it refers to the CO_2 capture and (long-term) storage of emissions.

Climate change: A change in climate patterns due to human activity like burning fossil fuels.

Climate change refugees: Populations that have been displaced due to climate change.

Coase theorem: When property rights are involved, parties naturally gravitate toward the most efficient and mutually beneficial outcome.

Collective coverage: Proportion of an area serviced by the municipal waste stream.

Commodity chain: The collective networks that encompass the beginning and end of a product's life cycle.

Community severance: The physical or social separation of an individual from the rest of the community.

Conspicuous consumption: The idea that we consume, at least in part, to display to others our social power and status.

Contingent valuation: A survey-based economic technique for placing a value on nonmarket resources.

Convention on Biological Diversity: An international legally binding treaty that entered into force in 1993. The convention has three main goals: conservation of biological diversity, sustainable use of biological resources, and fair and equitable sharing of benefits arising from genetic resources.

Cornucopian: Someone who believes unending progress, economic growth, and material abundance can be had with advancements in technology.

Countermovements: A social movement that arises to explicitly oppose an existing social movement.

Crop wild relatives: Wild ancestors of crop plants and other species closely related to crops.

Cultural hot spots: A biogeographic region with a significant reservoir of cultural diversity that is under threat of extinction.

Daylighting: The practice of uncovering previously concealed natural amenities.

Dead zones: The name given to bodies of water with low levels of dissolved oxygen.

Decoupling: The ability for an economy to grow without corresponding increases in environmental pressure.

Demographic inertia: A well-documented demographic phenomenon relating to how a time lag is to be expected before the full effects of changes to a fertility rate are seen.

Demographic transition model: A model detailing the historical changes in birth- and death rates for explaining rapid population growth. A country is said to have passed through the demographic transition when it moves from a condition of high birth- and death rates (and a relatively small population) to low birth- and death rates (and a relatively large population).

Desalinization: The removal of salt and other minerals from saline water.

Diminishing marginal utility: The more units of something we consume, the less added enjoyment we get from each additional unit.

Disability-adjusted life-years: The sum of years of potential life lost due to premature mortality and the years of productive life lost due to disability.

Disease vectors: An organism—such as a mosquito or tick—that carries disease-causing microorganisms from one host to another.

Diversionary reframing: Diverted attention away from real problems by trying to reframe the debate as being about something else.

Down-cycling: The process of converting waste into new materials or products of lesser quality and decreased functionality.

Ecofeminism: An area of study that examines the historical (and present) links between the objectification of women and the objectification of Nature.

Economism: The act of reducing the world to economic dimensions.

Ecosystem services: The processes by which the environment produces resources that we often take for granted (but we need for our survival), such as clean air and water, timber, habitat for fisheries, and pollination of native and agricultural plants.

Efficiency shifting: When money and resources saved through energy efficiency merely get shifted and consumed on other goods and services.

Embodied energy: The sum total of the energy utilized throughout an entire product life cycle.

Energy intensity: The amount of energy required to produce each unit of the world's economic output.

Environmental racism: Racial discrimination in environmental policy making, enforcement of regulations and laws, in addition to the targeting of communities of color for toxic waste disposal and siting of polluting industries.

Environmental skepticism: A position that attempts to undermine knowledge claims supporting the argument that environmental problems are real and that they are the result of human activity.

Exponential growth: Constant growth in a system where the amount added is proportional to the amount present. Thus, as the system expands, so too does the proportional amount that is added.

Ex situ: Sampling, transferring, and storage of a species in a place other than the original location in which it was found, like a zoo or seed bank.

Extended producer responsibility: Holding the manufacturer responsible for a product beyond the time of sale, thereby relieving consumers, governments, future generations, and the environment from the costs associated with landfilling and recycling hazardous materials.

Externality: Cost or benefit not transmitted through prices and incurred by a party who did not agree to the action causing the cost or benefit.

Family planning: Services that could include educational, social, or medical services that empower individuals to make choices around reproduction.

Feed-in tariff: A price intervention where the electric utilities are required by law or regulation to buy renewable electricity at fixed prices that are set above the market price.

Food system: The entire array of activities—from input production and distribution to on-farm activities, marketing, processing, wholesale, and retail—that connect seed (and gene) to the mouths of consumers.

Footprint shifting (life cycle): Making efficiency gains at one point in a commodity's life cycle while creating a larger environmental load at another point.

Fracking: a method of extracting natural gas from deep wells (also known as hydraulic fracturing).

Full irrigation: The amount of water needed to achieve maximum yield.

Greenhouse effect: When a portion of the sun's radiation that enters the atmosphere is absorbed by the planet's atmosphere thanks to greenhouse gases like CO_2 rather than being reradiated back into space.

Greenhouse gases: Any gases in the atmosphere that absorb and emit radiation within the thermal infrared range.

Green revolution: A series of strategies developed during the mid- to late twentieth century to combat starvation by expanding the global production of staple food crops through crop breeding.

Habitat fragmentation: The emergence of discontinuities (or fragmentation) in an organism's preferred environment (or habitat).

Heat island effect: Because concrete, tarmac, and other common construction materials absorb heat readily, built-up areas tend to be warmer than nearby rural areas.

Hypoxia: A state when oxygen concentrations in a body of water fall below the level necessary to sustain most animal life.

Indigenous knowledge: Knowledge unique to a given community, culture, or society.

Informal settlements: Unplanned groups of housing that are constructed on land illegally or that are not in compliance with current building regulations (or both).

In situ: The management of a species at the location of discovery.

Intergovernmental Panel on Climate Change: Established by two UN organizations, the United Nations Environment Programme and the World Meteorological Organization, in 1988 to provide scientific assessments on issues relating to climate change. With the IPCC as the internationally accepted authority on the subject, the world's governments look to it as the official advisory body on climate change.

Irrigation efficiency: The ratio of water that evaporates to what saturates in the soil.

Islandization (habitat): The breaking up of habitats without wildlife corridors to connect them.

Kyoto Protocol: An international treaty brokered by the UN, signed in 1997, that binds signatory nations to reduce their emissions of greenhouse gases. At Kyoto (where the agreement was first signed), nations agreed to cut their emissions of six greenhouse gases by an average of 5 percent overall, compared with 1990 levels, in what was termed the first commitment period, which was to end in 2012.

Landfill: A method of solid waste disposal where refuse is buried between layers of dirt.

Low-elevation coastal zones: Areas within ten meters of mean sea level.

Market concentration: The dominance of a particular market by a few large firms as a result of acquisition, mergers, and other processes.

Market environmentalism: Emphasizes markets as a solution to environmental problems.

Mechanical revolution: The gradual substitution of capital for labor in agriculture.

Megacities: Cities with more than 10 million residents.

Micronutrient malnutrition: A condition defined as a diet lacking in sufficient quantities of micronutrients.

Mitigation: Making reductions in the concentration of greenhouse gases by reducing their sources, increasing sink capacity, or both.

Monocultures: An agricultural practice of producing a single plant species over a wide area for a number of consecutive years.

Mountaintop removal mining: Clearing upper-elevation forests (typically at the summit of mountains), stripping the ground of topsoil, and utilizing explosives to break up rocks to expose underlying (yet relatively shallow) coal seams.

Municipal solid waste: All solid waste originating from homes, industries, businesses, demolition, land clearing, and construction.

Natural capital: Assets indispensable for human survival and economic activity provided by the ecosystem.

Naturalistic fallacy: When statements of fact are conflated with statements of value.

Neoliberalism: A set of economic practices grounded in the belief that human well-being is best advanced by limiting (if not eliminating) government and liberating individual entrepreneurial freedoms within legal and institutional frameworks that support strong private property rights, free markets, and free trade.

Neo-Malthusians: Those who advocate for the control of population growth.

Nongovernmental organizations: Any legally constituted organization that operates independently from any government.

Nonpoint-source pollution: Pollution that is more diffuse, making the source harder to pinpoint.

Normal accidents: A failure that is inevitable, given the manner in which particular human and technological systems are organized.

One-child policy (China): First introduced in 1978, this policy restricts married urban couples to one child, though exceptions are allowed (such as for rural couples and certain ethic minorities).

Organic systems (agriculture): A farm-management system that seeks to enhance biodiversity while minimizing the use of off-farm inputs.

Pareto optimality standard: Deems a policy acceptable only if at least one individual is better off and no individuals are made worse off.

Pay-as-you-drive auto insurance: Where one's insurance rate (but not coverage) is contingent upon, among other things, the amount of miles driven.

Peer-to-peer renting: The process of one private individual renting an underused item of theirs to another individual.

Pigovian taxes: A tax levied on companies that pollute or create excess social costs (called negative externalities).

Point-source pollution: Pollution with an identifiable source.

Polycultures: Small, diverse farms that raise grains, fruits, vegetables, and livestock.

Popular epidemiology: A type of citizen science in which laypeople are involved and requires a lower level of statistical confidence when claiming the existence of causal links.

Porter Hypothesis: Regulation spurs innovation, as it creates incentives for firms to adjust to social and environmental realities.

Pronatal social norms: Individual attitudes and societal expectations that promote high fertility rates.

Role strain: Tensions that emerge when expectations from holding multiple roles clash.

Salinization: The buildup of salt in soil and groundwater.

Sequestering CO2: The act of removing CO_2 from the atmosphere and holding it in a sink.

Sink (greenhouse gas): A natural or artificial reservoir—like a forest—that holds and stores greenhouses gases for an indefinite period, thus preventing their accumulation in the atmosphere.

Social constructivism: An approach that focuses entirely on the sociologically dependent knowledge of a phenomenon rather than on any inherent qualities that the thing possesses itself.

Social norms: Standards of behavior shared by a social group.

Sociological ambivalence: Incompatible or contradictory normative expectations or attitudes, beliefs, and behavior that people feel due to their holding multiple statuses (or when a single status has contradictory expectations).

Sociological imagination: A way of thinking that involves making connections between the particular and the general over time and across scales.

Species problem: The inherent ambiguity surrounding the use and definition of the species concept.

Street hierarchy: Eliminates connections between streets by funneling traffic "up" the hierarchy, from cul-de-sac streets to primary or secondary "collector" streets, arterial streets, and ultimately highways.

Strip-mining: The removal of soil and rock overlying the mineral deposit.

Structure of agriculture: How farms, rural populations, and agribusiness firms are arranged to produce and distribute food and fiber.

Terminator technology: Genetically engineered seed that produce sterile plants.

Type I error: Concluding there is a causal link when there is not one.

Type II error: Concluding there is not a causal link when there is one.

Uneconomic growth: Growth that costs us more than it benefits us.

Urban sprawl: The spreading of urban development into areas adjoining cities.

Vertical farming: The practice of farming "up," rather than "out."

Virtual water: Water used during the growing, making, or manufacturing of a given commodity.

Volatile organic compounds: Compounds that evaporate from housekeeping, maintenance, and building products made with organic chemicals.

Vulnerable road users: As defined by the WHO, this population includes pedestrians, cyclists, and users of motorized two-wheel vehicles.

Water footprint: An indicator of freshwater use that looks at both direct and indirect water use of a consumer or producer.

Water privatization: Treating water like any other commodity and leaving questions of access and sanitation to market mechanisms.

Welfare economics: A branch of microeconomics that seeks to evaluate well-being, with the assumption that human well-being is wholly reducible to economic well-being.

Wildlife corridors: Areas of habitat connecting wildlife populations and larger islands of habitat.

Work-spend cycle: Where we work to spend, which in turn requires us to work more.

Worldview: A fundamental cognitive orientation shared by individuals within which is rooted the entirety of their knowledge.

References

Abram, D. 1996. *The Spell of the Sensuous.* New York: Pantheon Books.

Adger, N., J. Paavola, S. Huq, and M. J. Mace. 2006. *Fairness in Adaptation to Climate Change.* Cambridge: MIT Press.

Agapow, P., O. Bininda-Emonds, K. Crandall, J. Gittleman, G. Mace, J. Marshall, and A. Purvis. 2004. "The Impact of Species Concept on Biodiversity Studies." *Quarterly Review of Biology* 79:161–179.

Akimoto, H. 2003. "Global Air Quality and Pollution." *Science* 302(1716):1716–1719.

Alderman, H., J. Behrman, and J. Hoddinott. 2003. "Nutrition, Malnutrition, and Economic Growth." Pan American Health Organization Report. Retrieved April 10, 2012 (http://idbgroup.org/res/publications/pubfiles/pubS-867.pdf).

Alderman, H., J. Hoddinott, and B. Kinsey. 2006. "Long-Term Consequences of Early Childhood Malnutrition." *Oxford Economic Papers* 58(3):450–474.

Alexander, J., T. Crompton, and G. Shrubsole. 2011. "Think of Me as Evil: Opening the Ethical Debates in Advertising." Public Interest Research Centre (PIRC) and WWF-UK. Retrieved April 6, 2012 (http://assets.wwf.org.uk/downloads/think_of_me_as_evil.pdf).

Allsopp, M., W. de Lange, and R. Veldtman. 2008. "Valuing Insect Pollination Services with Cost Replacement." *PLoS One* 3(9):1–8.

Altieri, M. [1987] 1995. *Agroecology: The Science of Sustainable Agriculture.* Boulder, CO: Westview Press.

———. 1999. "Applying Agroecology to Enhance the Productivity of Peasant Farming Systems in Latin America." *Environment, Development, and Sustainability* 1:197–217.

Altieri, M., and C. Nicholls. 2008. "Scaling Up Agroecological Approaches for Food Sovereignty in Latin America." *Development* 51(4):472–480.

American Coalition for Clean Coal Electricity. N.d. "Frequently Asked Questions." Washington, DC: American Coalition for Clean Coal and Electricity. Retrieved June 7, 2012 (http://www.americaspower.org/FAQ).

American Public Health Association. 2010. "The Hidden Health Costs of Transportation." Washington, DC: American Public Health Association. Retrieved April 6, 2012 (http://www.apha.org/NR/rdonlyres/E71B4070-9B9D-4EE1-8F43-349D21414962/0/FINALHidden HealthCostsShortNewBackCover.pdf).

Angel, S., S. Sheppard, and D. Civco. 2005. *The Dynamics of Global Urban Expansion.* Washington, DC: Transport and Urban Development Department, the World Bank. Retrieved March 27, 2012 (http://siteresources.worldbank.org/INTURBANDEVELOPMENT /Resources/dynamics_urban_expansion.pdf).

Anuradha, R. 2001. "IPRs: Implications for Biodiversity and Local and Indigenous Communities." *Review of European Community and International Environmental Law* 10(1):27–36.

Arens, W. 2005. *Contemporary Advertising*. Columbus, OH: McGraw-Hill.

Arnold, E., and J. Larsen. 2006. "Bottled Water: Pouring Resources Down the Drain." Washington, DC: Earth Policy Institute. Retrieved March 11, 2012 (http://www.earth-policy.org /plan_b_updates/2006/update51).

Attari, S., M. DeKayb, C. Davidson, and W. Bruine de Bruin. 2010. "Public Perceptions of Energy Consumption and Savings." *PNAS* 107(37):16054–16059.

Azios, T. 2008. "The Battle over Bottled vs. Tap Water." *Christian Science Monitor,* January 17. Retrieved March 22, 2012 (http://www.csmonitor.com/Environment/2008/0117/p15s03 -sten.html).

Babbitt, C., and A. Lindner. 2005. "A Life Cycle Inventory of Coal Used for Electricity Production in Florida." *Journal of Cleaner Production* 13:903–912.

Bachram, H. 2004. "Climate Fraud and Carbon Colonialism: The New Trade in Greenhouse Gases." *Capitalism Nature Socialism* 15(4):5–20.

Badgley, C., J. Moghtader, E. Quintero, E. Zakem, M. Chappell, K. Aviles-Vazquez, A. Samulon, and I. Perfecto. 2007. "Organic Agriculture and the Global Food Supply." *Renewable Agriculture and Food Systems* 22:86–108.

Balmford, A., R. Green, and J. Scharlemann. 2005. "Sparing Land for Nature: Exploring the Potential Impact of Changes in Agricultural Yield on the Area Needed for Crop Production." *Global Change Biology* 11:1594–1605.

Banerjee, A., and E. Duflo. 2011. "More than 1 Billion People Are Hungry in the World: But What If the Experts Are Wrong." *Foreign Policy* (May–June). Retrieved October 1, 2012 (http://www.foreignpolicy.com/articles/2011/04/25/more_than_1_billion_people_are _khungry_in_the_world?page=full).

Bang, M., D. Medin, and S. Atran. 2007. "Cultural Mosaics and Mental Models of Nature." *Proceedings of the National Academy of Sciences* 104(35):13868–13874.

Banister, D., and A. Bowling. 2004. "Quality of Life for the Elderly: The Transport Dimension." *Transport Policy* 11(2):105–115.

Barlow, M. 2007. *Blue Covenant: The Global Water Crisis and the Coming Battle for the Right to Water*. New York: New Press.

Barnard, N. 2010. "Trends in Food Availability, 1909–2007." *American Journal of Clinical Nutrition* 91:1530S–1536S.

Barnett, T., and D. Pierce. 2008. "When Will Lake Mead Go Dry?" *Water Resources Research* 40:1–10. Retrieved March 10, 2012 (http://www.colorado.edu/geography/geomorph/geog _5241_f10/barnett_08.pdf).

Barros, V. 2006. "Vulnerability to Floods in the Metropolitan Region of Buenos Aires Under Future Climate Change." April. AIACC Working Paper no. 26, Washington, DC. Retrieved September 19, 2011 (http://www.aiaccproject.org/working_papers/Working%20Papers /AIACC_WP26_Barros%20(rev)%201.pdf).

Bartlett, S., D. Dodman, J. Hardoy, D. Satterthwaite, and C. Tacol. 2009. "Social Aspects of Climate Change in Rural Areas in Low and Middle Income Nations." Contribution to the World Bank. Retrieved March 15, 2012 (http://www.dbsa.org/Vulindlela/Papers%20Library /Session1_Satterthwaite.pdf).

Baskoro, Faisal Maliki. 2011. "Air Travel to Grow by 13% by Next Year, Industry Says." *Jakarta Globe*, December 8. Retrieved June 26, 2012 (http://www.thejakartaglobe.com/business/air -travel-to-grow-by-13-next-year-industry-says/483569).

Bateman, C. 2010. "A Colossal Fracking Mess." *Vanity Fair*, June 21. Retrieved March 24, 2012 (http://www.vanityfair.com/business/features/2010/06/fracking-in-pennsylvania-201006).

Battisti, D., and R. Naylor. 2009. "Historical Warning of Future Food Insecurity." *Science* 323:240–244.

Bayani, O. 2010. "U.S. Can Save $41.1billion Annually Through Building Retrofits." *Ecoseed.org*, October 12. Retrieved August 24, 2012 (http://www.ecoseed.org/business/14085-u-s-can -save-41-1-billion-annually-through-building-retrofits).

BBC. 2003. "Argentina Fights Flood Waters." *BBC News*, May 2. Retrieved March 15, 2012 (http://news.bbc.co.uk/2/hi/americas/2994301.stm).

Bell, M., and P. Lowe. 2000. "Regulated Freedoms: The Market and the State, Agriculture, and the Environment." *Journal of Rural Studies* 16:285–294.

Bell, S., and R. York. 2010. "Community Economic Identity: The Coal Industry and Ideology Construction in West Virginia." *Rural Sociology* 75(1):111–143.

Berlin, I. [1958] 1969. *Four Essays on Liberty*. London: Oxford University Press.

Bhattacharyya, S. 2011. *Energy Economics: Concepts, Issues, Markets, and Governance*. New York: Springer.

Biermann, F., and I. Boas. 2010. "Preparing for a Warmer World: Towards a Global Governance System to Protect Climate Refugees." *Global Environmental Politics* 10(1):60–88.

Biggers, J. 2008. "'Clean' Coal? Don't Try to Shovel That." *Washington Post*, March 2. Retrieved March 23, 2012 (http://www.washingtonpost.com/wp-dyn/content/article/2008/02/29 /AR2008022903390.html).

Black, W. 2010. *Sustainable Transportation: Problems and Solutions*. New York: Guilford Press.

Bluhm, G., N. Berglind, E. Nordling, and M. Rosenlund. 2007. "Road Traffic Noise and Hypertension." *Occupational and Environmental Medicine* 64(2):122–126.

Bohra-Mishra, P., and D. Massey. 2011. "Environmental Degradation and Out-migration: New Evidence from Nepal." In *Climate Change and Migration*, edited by E. Piguet, P. de Guchteneire, and A. Pecoud, 74–101. Paris: Cambridge University Press, UNESCO.

Bokowa, A. 2010. "The Review of Odour Legislation." *Proceedings of the Water Environment Federation* 20:492–511.

Bolles, A. 1878. *Industrial History of the United States*. Norwich, CT: Henry Bill.

Bordewich, F., R. Klein, P. Smith, M. Buckingham, and E. Winograde. 2007. *No Reservations: Native American History and Culture in Contemporary Art*. Ridgefield, CT: Aldrich Contemporary Art Museum.

Bordoff, J., and P. Noel. 2008. "Pay-as-You-Drive Auto Insurance: A Simple Way to Reduce Driving-Related Harms and Increase Equity." Discussion paper 2008–2009, July. Washington, DC: Brookings Institution. Retrieved April 12, 2012 (http://www.brookings.edu/~ /media/Files/rc/papers/2008/07_payd_bordoffnoel/07_payd_bordoffnoel_pb.pdf).

Borras, S. 2008. "La Via Campesina and Its Global Campaign for Agrarian Reform. In *Transnational Agrarian Movements Confronting Globalization*, edited by S. Borras, M. Edelman, and C. Kay, 92–122. Malden, MA: Blackwell.

Boserup, E. 1965. *The Conditions of Agricultural Growth: The Economics of Agrarian Change under Population Pressure*. Chicago: Aldine.

Botsman, R., and R. Rogers. 2010. *What's Mine Is Yours: The Rise of Collaborative Consumption*. New York: Harper.

Boulding, K. 1966. "The Economics of the Coming Spaceship Earth." In *Environmental Quality in a Growing Economy*, edited by H. Jarrett, 3–15. New York: Harper and Row.

Brechin, S. 1999. "Objective Problems, Subjective Values, and Global Environmentalism: Evaluating the Postmaterialist Argument and Challenging a New Explanation." *Social Science Quarterly* 80:793–809.

Bremner, B., and N. Lakshman. 2006. "Behind the Coke-Pepsi Pesticide Scare." *Business Week*, August, 24. Retrieved March 20, 2012 (http://www.businessweek.com/globalbiz/content /aug2006/gb20060824_932216.htm).

Brockington, D., and K. Schmidt-Soltau. 2004. "The Social and Environmental Impacts of Wilderness and Development." *Oryx* 3(2):140–142.

Brown, K., and T. Kasser. 2005. "Are Psychological and Ecological Well-Being Compatible? The Role of Values, Mindfulness, and Lifestyle." *Social Indicators Research* 74:349–368.

Brown, L. 2009. *Plan B 4.0: Mobilizing to Save Civilization.* New York: W. W. Norton.

Brown, P., and E. Mikkelsen. 1997. *No Safe Place.* Berkeley and Los Angeles: University of California Press.

Bruinsma, J. 2009. "The Resource Outlook to 2050: By How Much Do Land, Water, and Crop Yields Need to Increase by 2050?" FAO expert meeting, "How to Feed the World in 2050." Rome. Retrieved March 28, 2011 (ftp://ftp.fao.org/docrep/fao/012/ak971e/ak971e00.pdf).

Brulle, R., and D. Pellow. 2006. "Environmental Justice: Human Health and Environmental Inequalities." *Annual Reviews of Public Health* 27:103–124.

Bullard, R. 1990. *Dumping in Dixie: Race, Class, and Environmental Quality.* Boulder, CO: Westview Press.

———, ed. 2005. *The Quest for Environmental Justice: Human Rights and the Politics of Pollution.* San Francisco: Sierra Club Books.

Bullock, C. 2008. "The Economic and Social Aspects of Biodiversity." Government of Ireland, Dublin, Ireland. Retrieved March 19, 2012 (http://www.environ.ie/en/Heritage/PublicationsDocuments/FileDownLoad,17321,en.pdf).

Caballero, B. 2002. "Global Patterns of Child Health: The Role of Nutrition." *Annuals of Nutrition and Metabolism* 46:3–7.

Calabresi, G. 1991. "The Pointlessness of Pareto: Carrying Coase Further." *Yale Law Journal* 100(5):1211–1237.

Canfield, D., A. Glazer, and P. Falkowski. 2010. "The Evolution and Future of Earth's Nitrogen Cycle." *Science* 330:192–196.

Caplan, J. 2009. "Shoppers, Unite! Carrot Mobs Are Cooler than Boycotts." *Time,* May 15. Retrieved April 9, 2012 (http://www.time.com/time/magazine/article/0,9171,1901467,00.html).

Carbon Mitigation Initiative. 2011. *Carbon Mitigation Initiative: Annual Report, 2010.* Princeton, NJ: Princeton University. Retrieved March 2, 2012 (http://cmi.princeton.edu/annual_reports/pdfs/2010.pdf).

Cardinale, B. 2011. "Biodiversity Improves Water Quality Through Niche Partitioning." *Nature* 472:86–89.

Carolan, M. 2005a. "Realism Without Reductionism: Toward an Ecologically Embedded Sociology." *Human Ecology Review* 12(1):1–20.

———. 2005b. "Society, Biology, and Ecology: Bringing Nature Back into Sociology's Disciplinary Narrative." *Organization and Environment* 18:393–421.

———. 2007. "The Precautionary Principle and Traditional Risk Assessment: Rethinking How We Assess and Mitigate Environmental Threats." *Organization and Environment* 20(1):5–24.

———. 2008a. "I Do Therefore There Is: Enlivening Socio-environmental Theory." *Environmental Politics* 18(1):1–17.

———. 2008b. "More-than-Representational Knowledge/s of the Countryside: How We Think as Bodies." *Sociologia Ruralis* 48(4):408–422.

———. 2008c. "When Good Smells Go Bad: A Socio-historical Understanding of Agricultural Odor Pollution." *Environment and Planning A* 40(5):1235–1249.

———. 2009. "The Costs and Benefits of Biofuels: A Review of Recent Peer-Reviewed Research and a Sociological Look Ahead." *Environmental Practice* 11:17–24.

———. 2010a. *Decentering Biotechnology: Assemblages Built and Assemblages Masked.* Burlington, VT: Ashgate.

———. 2010b. "Sociological Ambivalence and Climate Change." *Local Environment* 15(4):309–321.

———. 2011a. *Embodied Food Politics.* Burlington, VT: Ashgate.

———. 2011b. *The Real Cost of Cheap Food.* London and New York: Earthscan.

———. 2012. *The Sociology of Food and Agriculture.* London and New York: Earthscan/Routledge.

Carruthers, D. 2008. "The Globalization of Environmental Justice: Lessons from the US-Mexico Border." *Society and Natural Resources* 21:556–568.

Carter, J., and M. Irons. 1991. "Are Economists Different, and If So, Why?" *Journal of Economic Perspectives* 5(2):171–177.

Casey, P., and K. Scott. 2006. "Environmental Concern and Behavior in an Australian Sample Within an Ecocentric-Anthropocentric Framework." *Australian Journal of Psychology* 58:57–67.

Catton, W., and R. Dunlap. 1978. "Environmental Sociology: A New Paradigm." *American Sociologist* 13:41–49.

Chamon, M., P. Mauro, and Y. Okawa. 2008. "Mass Car Ownership in the Emerging Market Giants." *Economic Policy* 23(54):243–296.

Chan, K., and J. McNeal. 2003. "Parental Concern About Television Viewing and Children's Advertising in China." *International Journal of Public Opinion Research* 15(2):151–166.

Chavis, B., and C. Lee. 1987. *Toxic Wastes and Race in the United States.* New York: United Church Christ.

Chazan, G. 2011. "Biofuels Industry Battles Past Bumps in the Road." *Wall Street Journal*, April 7. Retrieved April 8, 2011 (http://online.wsj.com/article/SB10001424052748703662804576 188851797909800.html?mod=googlenews_wsj).

Chen, C., J. Harries, H. Brindley, and M. Ringer. 2007. "Spectral Signatures of Climate Change in the Earth's Infrared Spectrum Between 1970 and 2006." Fifteenth American Meteorological Society Satellite Meteorology and Oceanography Conference, Amsterdam, September. Retrieved March 21, 2012 (http://www.eumetsat.eu/Home/Main/Publications /Conference_and_Workshop_Proce edings/groups/cps/documents/document/pdf_conf _p50_s9_01_harries_v.pdf).

Chen, H., B. Jia, and S. Lau. 2008. "Sustainable Urban Form for Chinese Compact Cities: Challenges of a Rapid Urbanized Economy." *Habitat International* 32(1):28–40

Chozick, A. 2012. "To Draw Reluctant Young Buyers, G.M. Turns to MTV." *New York Times,* March 22.

Chrischilles, E., R. Ahrens, A. Kuehl, K. Kelly, P. Thorne, L. Burmeister, and J. Merchant. 2004. "Asthma Prevalence and Morbidity Among Rural Iowa Schoolchildren." *Journal of Allergy and Clinical Immunology* 113(1):66–71.

Christoforou, T. 2003. "The Precautionary Principle in European Community Law and Science." In *Precaution: Environmental Science and Preventive Public Policy,* edited by J. Tickner, 241–262. Washington, DC: Island Press.

Churchill, W. 2002. *Struggle for the Land: Native North American Resistance to Genocide, Ecocide, and Colonization.* San Francisco, CA: City Lights.

CIA. 2010. *CIA World Fact Book, 2010.* Washington, DC: Central Intelligence Agency.

Ciriacy-Wantrup, S., and R. Bishop. 1975. "Common Property as a Concept in Natural Resource Policy." *National Resources Journal* 15(4):713–727.

Clapp, J. 2002. "Distancing of Waste: Overconsumption in a Global Economy." In *Confronting Consumption,* edited by T. Princen, M. Maniates, and K. Coca, 155–176. Cambridge: MIT Press.

Clark, B., and R. York. 2005. "Carbon Metabolism: Global Capitalism, Climate Change, and the Biospheric Rift." *Theory and Society* 34:391–428.

Clausen, R. 2005. "The Metabolic Rift and Marine Ecology: An Analysis of the Ocean Crisis Within Capitalist Production." *Organization and Environment* 19(2):422–444.

Clausen, R., and R. York. 2008. "Global Biodiversity Decline of Marine and Freshwater Fish: A Cross-national Analysis of Economic, Demographic, and Ecological Influences." *Social Science Research* 37(4):1310–1320.

Climate Refugees. 2010. *Climate Refugees: The Human Face of Climate Change.* Documentary, distributed by Video Project.

Coase, R. 1960. "The Problem of Social Cost." *Journal of Law and Economics* 3:1–44.

Cochrane, W. 1958. *Farming Prices: Myth and Reality.* Minneapolis: University of Minnesota Press.

Coffey, M. 2005. "Lake Victoria Water and Sanitation Water Initiative: Solid Waste Management Systems for Kisii and Homa Bay." Report by M. Coffey on visit to Kisii and Homa Bay, UN Habitat Contract no. 4798. Retrieved March 30, 2012 (http://www.unhabitat.org /downloads/docs/6165_51256_LVWATSAN%20KENYA%20SWM.pdf).

Cohen, M. 2010. "Destination Unknown: Pursing Sustainable Mobility in the Face of Rival Societal Aspirations." *Research Policy* 39:459–470.

———. 2012. "The Future of Automobile Society: A Socio-technical Transitions Perspective." *Technology Analysis and Strategic Management* 24(4):377–390.

Cohen, S. 2010. "Growing Public Support for Sustainability." *Huffington Post*, April 19. Retrieved May 17, 2012 (http://www.huffingtonpost.com/steven-cohen/growing-public-support-fo_b _542600.html).

Colbert, T. 2000. "Iowa Farmers and Mechanical Corn Pickers, 1900–1952." *Agricultural History* 74(2):530–544.

Cole, L., and S. Foster. 2001. *From the Ground Up: Environmental Racism and the Rise of the Environmental Justice Movement.* New York: New York University Press.

Condon, P. 2010. *Seven Rules for Sustainable Communities.* Washington, DC: Island Press.

Conover, D., and S. Munch. 2002. "Sustaining Fisheries Yields over Evolutionary Time Scales." *Science* 297:94–96.

Conroy, M. 2007. *Branded! How the Certification Revolution Is Transforming Corporations.* Gabriola Island, BC: New Society.

Conservation Measures Partnership. N.d. "Threats Taxonomy." Retrieved May 17, 2012 (http:// www.conservationmeasures.org/initiatives/threats-actions-taxonomies/threats-taxonomy).

Constance, D., and R. Tuinstra. 2005. "Corporate Chickens and Community Conflict in East Texas: Growers' and Neighbors' Views on the Impacts of the Industrial Broiler Production." *Culture and Agriculture* 27(1):45–60.

Cooley, H. 2009a. "Tampa Bay Desalination Plant: An Update." In *The World's Water, 2008–2009*, edited by P. Gleick, 123–126. Washington, DC: Island Press.

———. 2009b. "Water Management in a Changing Climate." In *The World's Water, 2008–2009*, edited by P. Gleick, 39–56. Washington, DC: Island Press.

Cooper, P., G. Poe, and I. Bateman. 2004. "The Structure of Motivation for Contingent Values: A Case Study of Lake Water Quality Improvement." *Ecological Economics* 50:69–82.

Cordell, D., J.-O. Drangert, and S. White. 2009. "The Story of Phosphorus: Global Food Security and Food for Thought." *Global Environmental Change* 19:292–305.

Costanza, R., R. d'Arge, R. de Groot, S. Farber, M. Grasso, B. Hannon, S. Naeem, K. Limburg, J. Paruelo, R. O'Neill, R. Raskin, P. Sutton, and M. van den Belt. 1997. "The Value of the World's Ecosystem Services and Natural Capital." *Nature* 387:253–260.

Cowen, T., and D. Parfit. 1992. "Against the Social Discount Rate." In *Philosophy, Politics, and Society*, edited by P. Laslett and J. Fishkin, 144–161. New Haven, CT: Yale University Press.

Cox, C., A. Hug, and N. Bruzelius. 2011. "Losing Ground." Washington, DC: Environmental Working Group. Retrieved April 15, 2012 (http://static.ewg.org/reports/2010/losingground /pdf/losingground_report.pdf).

Cox, J. 2009. "What Is Vertical Farming?" *On Earth,* November 6. Retrieved April 1, 2012 (http://www.onearth.org/community-blog/what-is-vertical-farming).

Cravens, G. 2008. *Power to Save the World: The Truth About Nuclear Energy.* New York: Vintage.

Crutzen, P. 2006. "Albedo Enhancement by Stratospheric Sulfur Injections: A Contribution to Resolve a Policy Dilemma?" *Climate Change* 77(3–4):211–220.

Cunha, L. 2009. "Water: A Human Right or an Economic Resource?" In *Water Ethics,* edited by M. Ramón Llamas, L. Martínez-Cortina, and A. Mukherji, 97–113. Boca Raton, FL: CRC Press.

Currie, G., and J. Stanley. 2008. "Investigating Links Between Social Capital and Public Transport." *Transport Reviews* 28(4):529–546.

Daily Mail Reporter. 2008. "EU Forces Market Trader to Pulp Thousands of Kiwi Fruit Because They're One Millimeter Too Small." *Daily Mail Reporter,* June 27. Retrieved March 3, 2012 (http://www.dailymail.co.uk/news/article-1029715/EU-forces-market-trader-pulp-thousands -kiwi-fruit-theyre-ONE-MILLIMETRE-small.html).

Daly, H. 1996. *Beyond Growth: The Economics of Sustainable Development.* Boston: Beacon Press.

———. 1999. *Ecological Economics and the Ecology of Economics.* Northhampton, MA: Edward Elgar.

Dankelman, I. 2010. "Introduction: Exploring Gender, Environment, and Climate Change." In *Gender and Climate Change,* edited by I. Dankelman, 1–18. London: Earthscan.

Dasgupta, P. 2006. "Nature in Economics." *Environmental Resource Economics* 39:1–7.

Dasgupta, S., B. Laplante, H. Wang, and D. Wheeler. 2002. "Confronting the Environmental Kuznets Curve." *Journal of Economic Perspectives* 16(1):147–168.

Defra. 2011. "Waste Data Overview." Department for Environment, Food, and Rural Affairs, UK, June. Retrieved March 28, 2012 (http://www.defra.gov.uk/statistics/files/20110617-waste -data-overview.pdf).

Demirbas, A., and M. Demirbas. 2010. *Algae Energy: Algae as a New Source of Biodiesel.* New York: Springer.

Desmarais, A. 2008. "The Power of Peasants: Reflections on the Meanings of *La Vía Campesina.*" *Journal of Rural Studies* 24:138–149.

Desneux, N., A. Decourtye, and J.-M. Delpuech. 2007. "The Sublethal Effects of Pesticides on Beneficial Arthropods." *Annual Review of Entomology* 52:81–106.

Despommier, D. 2010. *The Vertical Farm: Feeding the World in the 21st Century.* New York: Thomas Dunne Books.

Desrochers, P., and H. Shimizu. 2008. *Yes, We Have No Bananas: A Critique of the "Food Miles" Perspective.* Policy Primer no. 8. Washington, DC: Mercatus Center, George Mason University.

Diamond, J. 2006. *Collapse: How Societies Choose to Fail or Succeed.* New York: Penguin.

Diaz, R., and J. Rosenberg. 2008. "Spreading Dead Zones and Consequences for Marine Ecosystems." *Science* 321(5891):926–929.

Dickens, P. 2001. "Linking the Social and Natural Sciences: Is Capital Modifying Human Biology in Its Own Image?" *Sociology* 35:93–110.

———. 2004. *Society and Nature: Changing Our Environment, Changing Ourselves.* Malden, MA: Polity Press.

Dickens, P., and J. Ormrod. 2007. *Cosmic Society: Towards a Sociology of the Universe.* New York and London: Routledge.

Dietz, T., and E. Rosa. 1994. "Rethinking the Environmental Impacts of Population, Affluence, and Technology." *Human Ecology Review* 1:277–300.

Dietz, T., N. Dolsak, E. Ostrom, and P. Stern. 2002. *The Drama of the Commons.* Washington, DC: National Academies Press.

Dietz, T., G. Gardner, J. Gilligan, P. Stern, and M. Vandenbergh. 2009. "Household Actions Can Provide a Behavioral Wedge to Rapidly Reduce US Carbon Emissions." *PNAS* 106(44):18452–18456.

Dietz, T., E. Rosa, and R. York. 2012. "Environmentally Efficient Well-Being: Is There a Kuznets Curve?" *Environmental Geography* 32:21–28.

Dixon, H., and D. Broom. 2007. *The Seven Deadly Sins of Obesity.* Sydney, Australia: UNSW Press.

DOD. 2001. "American Indian and Alaska Native Initiatives." In *Fiscal Year 2001 Defense Environmental Quality Program Annual Report to Congress.* Retrieved March 29, 2012 (http://www.denix.osd.mil/arc/EQFY2001.cfm).

Dodman, D. 2009. "Urban Form, Greenhouse Gas Emissions, and Climate Vulnerability." In *Population Dynamics and Climate Change,* edited by J. Guzmán, G. Martine, G. McGranahan, D. Schensul, and C. Tacoli, 64–79. New York: UNFPA and IIED.

Domingo, J., and M. Nadal. 2009. "Domestic Waste Composting Facilities: A Review of Human Health Risks." *Environment International* 35:382–389.

Donham, K., S. Wing, D. Osterberg, J. Flora, C. Hodne, K. Thu, and P. Thorne. 2007. "Community Health and Socioeconomic Issues Surrounding Concentrated Animal Feeding Operations." *Environmental Health Perspectives* 115(2):317–320.

Douglas, M., S. Watkins, D. Gorman, and M. Higgins. 2011. "Are Cars the New Tobacco?" *Journal of Public Health* 33(2):160–169.

Downs, A. 1962. "The Law of Peak-Hour Express-Way Congestion." *Traffic Quarterly* 16(3):393–409.

Drake, J. 2000. *Downshifting: How to Work Less and Enjoy Life More.* San Francisco: Berrett-Koehler.

Drogen, L. 2011. "Social Capital and Collaborative Consumption." Surview Capital, January 13. Retrieved April 9, 2012 (http://www.leighdrogen.com/social-capital-and-collaborative-consumption/).

Drummond, M., and T. Loveland. 2010. "Land-Use Pressure and a Transition to Forest-Cover Loss in the Eastern United States." *BioScience* 60(4):286–298.

Dryzek, J. 1990. *Discursive Democracy: Politics, Policy, and Political Science.* New York: Cambridge University Press.

Dunlap, R. 2008. "The New Environmental Paradigm Scale: From Marginality to Worldwide Use." *Journal of Environmental Education* 40(1):3–18.

———. 2010. "The Maturation and Diversification of Environmental Sociology: From Constructivism and Realism to Agnosticism and Pragmatism." In *The International Handbook of Environmental Sociology,* edited by M. Redclift and G. Woodgate, 15–32. Northampton, MA: Edward Elgar.

Dunlap, R., and R. Jones. 2002. "Environmental Concern: Conceptual and Measurement Issues." In *Handbook of Environmental Sociology,* edited by R. Dunlap and W. Michelson, 482–524. Westport, CT: Greenwood Press.

Dunlap, R., and A. McCright. 2008. "A Widening Gap: Republican and Democratic Views on Climate Change." *Environment* 50(5):26–35.

Dunlap, R., and A. Mertig. 1997. "Global Environmental Concern: An Anomaly for Postmaterialism." *Social Science Quarterly* 78:24–29.

Dunlap, R., and K. Van Liere. 1978. "The New Environmental Paradigm." *Journal of Environmental Education* 9:10–19.

Dunlap, R., K. Van Liere, A. Mertig, and R. Jones. 2000. "Measuring Endorsement of the New Ecological Paradigm: A Revised NEP Scale." *Journal of Social Issues* 56:425–442.

Dunlap, R., and R. York. 2008. "The Globalization of Environmental Concern and the Limits of the Postmaterialist Values Explanation." *Sociological Quarterly* 49:529–563.

Duranton, G., and M. Turner. 2009. "The Fundamental Law of Road Congestion: Evidence from US Cities." Cambridge, MA: National Bureau of Economic Research, NBER Working Paper no. 15376, September. Retrieved April 11, 2012 (http://www.nber.org/papers/w15376.pdf).

Eccleston, C., and F. March. 2011. *Global Environment Policy: Concepts, Principles, and Practice.* Boca Raton, FL: CRC Press.

Eckersley, R. 1992. *Environmentalism and Political Theory: Towards an Ecocentric Approach.* London: University College London Press.

Economist. 2008. "Running Dry." August 21. Retrieved March 11, 2012 (http://www.economist.com/node/11966993).

———. 2011a. "China Still Looking to Win the Future." February 2. Retrieved March 30, 2012 (http://www.economist.com/blogs/freeexchange/2011/02/infrastructure).

———. 2011b. "The 9-Billion People Question: A Special Report on Feeding the World." February 26. Retrieved March 28, 2012 (http://www.economist.com/surveys/download SurveyPDF.cfm?id=18205243&surveyCode=%254e%2541&submit=View+PDF).

Edmonds Institute. 2006. "Out of Brazil: A Peanut Worth Billions (to the US)." Edmonds, WA: Edmonds Institute, March. Retrieved August 26, 2012 (http://www.edmonds- institute.org/outofbrazil.pdf).

Edney, M. 1997. *Mapping an Empire: The Geographical Construction of British India, 1765–1843.* Chicago: University of Chicago Press.

Ehrhardt-Martinez, K., E. Crenshaw, and J. Jenkins. 2002. "Deforestation and the Environmental Kuznets Curve: A Cross-national Investigation of Intervening Mechanisms." *Social Science Quarterly* 83(1):226–243.

Ehrlich, P. 1968. *The Population Bomb.* San Francisco: Sierra Club.

Ehrlich, P., and J. Holden. 1971. "Impact of Population Growth." *Science* 171:1212–1217.

EIA. 2011. "International Energy Outlook, 2011." Washington, DC: US Energy Information Administration. Retrieved March 19, 2012 (http://205.254.135.24/forecasts/ieo/pdf/0484(2011).pdf).

Ekelund, R., and R. Hébert. 1997. *A History of Economic Theory and Method.* 4th ed. New York: McGraw-Hill.

Emery, M., and C. Flora. 2006. "Spiraling-Up: Mapping Community Transformation with Community Capitals Framework." *Community Development* 37(1):19–35.

English, M., K. Solomon, and G. Hoffman. 2002. "A Paradigm Shift in Irrigation Management." *Journal of Irrigation and Drainage Engineering* (September–October):267–277.

ENS. 2011. "First Recycler Indicated for Exporting Toxic E-waste." Environmental News Service, September 16. Retrieved May 18, 2012 (http://www.ens-newswire.com/ens/sep2011/2011-09-16-094.html).

EPA. 2004. "Risk Management Evaluation for Concentrated Animal Feeding Operation." Washington, DC: US Environmental Protection Agency, Office of Research and Development. Retrieved April 20, 2012 (http://www.epa.gov/nrmrl/pubs/600r04042/600r04042.pdf).

———. 2009. "Municipal Solid Waste in the United States." EPA 530-R-10-012. Washington, DC: US Environmental Protection Agency, December. Retrieved March 23, 2012 (http://www.epa.gov/wastes/nonhaz/municipal/pubs/msw2009rpt.pdf).

———. 2011. "Inventory of US Greenhouse Gas Emission and Sinks, 1990–2009." EPA 430-R-11-005. Washington, DC: US Environmental Protection Agency, Office of Atmospheric Programs, April. Retrieved March 29, 2012 (http://epa.gov/climatechange/emissions/downloads11/US-GHG-Inventory-2011-Executive-Summary.pdf).

———. N.d. "Environmental Justice Key Terms." Washington, DC: Environmental Protection Agency. Retrieved July 3, 2012 (http://www.epa.gov/region07/ej/definitions.htm).

Eskelanda, G., and A. Harrison. 2003. "Moving to Greener Pastures? Multinationals and the Pollution Haven Hypothesis." *Journal of Development Economics* 70:1–23.

Ester, P. 1981. "Environmental Concern in the Netherlands." In *Progress in Resource Management and Environment Planning*, edited by T. O'Riordan and R. Turner, 81–108. Chicester: John Wiley and Sons.

EWG. 2008. "Bottled Water Quality Investigation: 10 Major Brands and 38 Pollutants." Washington, DC: Environmental Work Group. Retrieved March 11, 2012 (http://www.ewg.org/reports/BottledWater/Bottled-Water-Quality-Investigation).

Ewing, R., R. Brownson, and D. Berringan. 2006. "Relationship Between Urban Sprawl and Weight of United States Youth." *American Journal of Preventative Medicine* 31(6):464–474.

Ewing, R., T. Schmid, R. Killingsworth, A. Zlot, and S. Raudenbush. 2003. "Relationship Between Urban Sprawl and Physical Activity, Obesity, and Morbidity." *American Journal of Health Promotion* 18(1):47–57.

Fair Trade Foundation. 2009. "Starbucks Serves Up Its First Fairtrade Lattes and Cappuccinos Across the UK and Ireland." Press Release, September 2. Retrieved October 3, 2011 (http://www.fairtrade.org.uk/press_office/press_releases_and_statements/september_2009/starbucks_serves_up_its_first_fairtrade_lattes_and_cappuccinos.aspx).

FAO. 2002. "Reducing Poverty and Hunger: The Critical Role of Financing for Food, Agriculture, and Rural Development." Food and Agriculture Organization, International Fund for Agricultural Development, World Food Program. Retrieved June 7, 2012 (http://www.fao.org/docrep/003/Y6265e/y6265e00.htm).

———. 2004. "Building on Gender, Agrobiodiversity, and Local Knowledge." Rome: Food and Agriculture Organization of United Nations. Retrieved March 7, 2012 (ftp://ftp.fao.org/docrep/fao/007/y5609e/y5609e00.pdf).

———. 2008. "Climate Change and Food Security." Rome: Food and Agriculture Organization of the United Nations. Retrieved March 25, 2012 (http://www.fao.org/forestry/15538–079b31d45081fe9c3dbc6ff34de4807e4.pdf).

Fenn, M., R. Haeuber, G. Tonnesen, J. Baron, S. Grossman-Clarke, D. Hope, D. Jaffe, S. Copeland, L. Geiser, H. Rueth, and J. Sickman. 2003. "Nitrogen Emissions, Deposition, and Monitoring in the Western United States." *BioScience* 53(4):391–403.

Finetto, C., C. Lobascio, and A. Rapisarda. 2010. "Concept of LUNAR Farm: Food and Revitalization Module." *Acta Astronautica* 66(9–10):1329–1340.

Fisher, D. 2004. *National Governance and the Global Climate Change Regime.* New York: Rowman and Littlefield.

Fisher, W. 1943. "The Bengal Famine: 50,000 Indians Weekly Succumb to Disease and Starvation in Spreading Catastrophe." *Life* 15(21):16–20.

Fitz, D. 2009. "What's Wrong with a 30-Hour Work Week?" *Z Magazine*, July. Retrieved April 3, 2012 (http://www.zcommunications.org/whats-wrong-with-a-30-hour-work-week-by-don-fitz).

Fleming, D. 2007. "The Lean Guide to Nuclear Energy: A Lifecycle in Trouble. London: Lean Economy Connection. Retrieved March 24, 2012 (http://www.theleaneconomyconnection.net/nuclear/Nuclear.pdf).

Flora, C. 2008. "Social Capital and Community Problem Solving Combining Local and Scientific Knowledge to Fight Invasive Species." *Learning Communities* 2:30–39.

Flora, C., M. Livingston, I. Honyestewa, and H. Koiyaquaptewa. 2009. "Understanding Access to and Use of Traditional Foods by Hopi Women." *Journal of Hunger and Environmental Nutrition* 4:158–171.

Food and Water Watch. 2009. "All Bottled Up: Nestle's Pursuit of Community Water, Food, and Water." Washington, DC: Food and Water Watch. Retrieved March 11, 2012 (http://www.foodandwaterwatch.org/reports/all-bottled-up/).

Forgie, V., P. Horsley, and J. Johnston. 2001. "Facilitating Community-Based Conservation Initiatives." Science for Conservation Report no. 169, Wellington, New Zealand: Department of Conservation, March. Retrieved March 6, 2012 (http://www.doc.govt.nz/upload/documents/science-and-technical/Sfc169.pdf).

Forman, R., D. Sperling, J. Bissonette, A. Clevenger, C. Cutshall, V. Dale, L. Fahrig, R. France, C. Goldman, K. Heanue, J. Jones, F. Swanson, T. Turrentine, and T. Winter. 2002. *Road Ecology: Science and Solutions.* Washington, DC: Island Press.

Foster, J. B. 1999. "Marx's Theory of Metabolic Rift: Classical Foundations for Environmental Sociology." *American Journal of Sociology* 105(2):366–405.

———. 2005. "The Treadmill of Accumulation: Schnaiberg's Environment and Marxian Political Economy." *Organization and Environment* 18(1):7–18.

Frank, L., M. Andresen, and T. Schmid. 2004. "Obesity Relationships with Community Design, Physical Activity, and Time Spent in Cars." *American Journal of Preventative Medicine* 27:87–96.

Fraser, C. 2009. *Rewilding the World.* New York: Henry Holt.

Freeman, L. 2001. "The Effects of Sprawl on Neighborhood Social Ties: An Explanatory Analysis." *Journal of the American Planning Association* 67(1): 69–77.

Freudenburg, W. 1991. "A Good Business Climate as Bad Economic News?" *Society and Natural Resources* 3:313–331.

———. 2005. "Privileged Access, Privileged Accounts: Toward a Socially Structured Theory of Resources and Discourses." *Social Forces* 94(1):89–114.

Freudenburg, W., and R. Gramling. 1994. *Oil in Troubled Waters: Perceptions, Politics, and the Battle over Offshore Oil.* New York: SUNY Press.

Frey, S. 1998. "The Hazardous Waste Stream in the World System." In *Space and Transportation in the World-System,* edited by P. Ciccantell and S. Bunker, 84–103. Westport, CT: Greenwood Press.

Friedman, T. 2008. "The Great Unraveling." *New York Times,* December 16. Retrieved November 18, 2011 (http://www.nytimes.com/2008/12/17/opinion/17friedman.html).

Frohwein T., and B. Hansjürgens. 2005. "Chemicals Regulation and the Porter Hypothesis: A Critical Review of the New European Chemicals Regulation." *Journal of Business Chemistry* 2(1):19–36.

Fukuda-Parr, S. 2003. "The Human Development Paradigm." *Feminist Economics* 9(2–3):301–317.

Fullerton, D., and L. Gan. 2005. "Cost-Effective Policies to Reduce Vehicle Emissions." *American Economic Review* 95(2):300–304.

Funtowicz, S., and J. Ravetz. 1992. "Three Types of Risk Assessment and the Emergence of Post Normal Science." In *Social Theories of Risk,* edited by S. Krimsky and D. Golding, 230–251. New York: Praeger.

Gagnon, L., C. Belanger, and Y. Uchiyama. 2002. "Lifecycle Assessment of Electricity Generation Options: The Status of Research in Year 2001." *Energy Policy* 30:1267–1278.

Galbraith, K. 1958. *The Affluent Society.* New York: Penguin.

GAO. 1983. "Siting of Hazardous Waste Landfills and Their Correlation with Racial and Economic Status of Surrounding Communities." Washington, DC: US Government Printing Office.

Gardner, G., and P. Stern. 1996. *Environmental Problems and Human Behavior.* Boston: Allyn and Bacon.

———. 2008. "The Short List." *Environment Magazine* 50(5):12–25.

Gelissen, J. 2007. "Explaining Popular Support for Environmental Protection: A Multi-level Analysis of 50 Nations." *Environment and Behavior* 39:392–415.

Geurs, K., W. Boon, and B. Van Wee. 2009. "Social Impacts of Transport: Literature Review and the State of the Practice of Transport Appraisal in the Netherlands and the UK." *Transport Reviews* 29(1):69–90.

Gilbert, R., and C. O'Brien. 2005. "Child- and Youth-Friendly Land-Use and Transport Planning Guidelines." Plymouth, UK: University of Plymouth, Centre for Sustainable Transportation. Retrieved September 10, 2012 (http://cst.uwinnipeg.ca/documents/Guidelines _ON.pdf).

Gilding, P. 2011. *The Great Disruption.* New York: Bloomsbury Press.

Gleick, P. 1996. "Basic Water Requirements for Human Activities: Meeting Basic Needs." *Water International* 21:83–92.

Gliessman, S. 1998. "Agroecology: Ecological Process in Sustainable Agriculture." Ann Arbor, MI: Ann Arbor Press.

Global Witness. 2010. "Understanding REDD+: The Role of Governance, Enforcement, and Safeguards in Reducing Emissions from Deforestation and Forest Degradation." London: Global Witness, November. Retrieved April 14, 2012 (http://www.globalwitness.org/sites /default/files/library/Understanding%20REDD+.pdf).

Godfray, H., J. Beddington, I. Crute, L. Hadded, D. Lawrence, J. Muir, J. Pretty, S. Robinson, S. Thomas, and C. Toulmin. 2010. "Food Security: The Challenge of Feeding 9 Billion People." *Science* 327:812–818.

Goldman, M., ed. 1998. *Privatizing Nature: Political Struggles for the Global Commons.* New Brunswick, NJ: Rutgers University Press.

———. 2007. "How 'Water for All' Policy Becomes Hegemonic: The Power of the World Bank and Its Transnational Policy Networks." *Geoforum* 38:786–800.

Goldschmidt, W. 1978. *As You Sow: Three Studies in the Social Consequences of Agribusiness.* Montclair, NJ: Allanheld, Osmun.

Goldstein, N., R. Cialdini, and V. Griskevicius. 2008. "A Room with a Viewpoint: Using Social Norms to Motivate Environmental Conservation in Hotels." *Journal of Consumer Research* 35(3):472–482.

Gooch, M., A. Felfel, and N. Marenick. 2010. "Food Waste in Canada." Guelph, Canada: George Morris Center, University of Guelph. Retrieved March 16, 2012 (http://www.vcmtools.ca /pdf/Food%20Waste%20in%20Canada%20120910.pdf).

Good, J. 2007. "Shop 'til We Drop? Television, Materialism, and Attitudes About the Natural Environment." *Mass Communication and Society* 10:365–383.

Goodland, R., and J. Anhang. 2009. "Livestock and Climate Change." *World Watch Magazine* (November–December):10–19.

Goodwin, P. 2012. "Three Views on Peak Car." *World Transportation Policy and Practice* 17(4):8–17.

Gouveia, N., S. Hajat, and B. Armstrong. 2003. "Socioeconomic Differentials in the Temperature–Mortality Relationship in São Paulo, Brazil." *International Journal of Epidemiology* 32:390–397.

GPI. N.d. "Mining Impacts." Amsterdam: Greenpeace International. Retrieved June 7, 2012 (http:// www.greenpeace.org/international/en/campaigns/climate-change/coal/Mining-impacts/).

Green Advocacy Ghana. 2011. "Ghana E-waste Country Assessment." SBC E-waste Africa Project. Retrieved March 18, 2011 (http://ewasteguide.info/files/Amoyaw-Osei_2011 _GreenAd-Empa.pdf).

Greenberg, B. S. and Brand, J. E. (1993). Television news and advertising in schools: The "Channel One" controversy. *Journal of Communication,* 43(1), 143–151.

Griggs, J., and J. Harries. 2004. "Comparison of Spectrally Resolved Outgoing Longwave Data Between 1970 and Present." *Proceedings of the SPIE* 5543:164–174.

Grinde, D., and B. Johansen. 1995. *Ecocide of Native America: Environmental Destruction of Indian Lands and Peoples.* Santa Fe, NM: Clear Lights.

Grossman, G., and A. Krueger. 1994. *Economic Growth and the Environment.* NBER Working Paper no. W4364. Cambridge, MA: National Bureau of Economic Research.

Grundwald, M. 2008. "The Clean Energy Scam." *Time*, March 27. Retrieved March 5, 2012 (http://www.time.com/time/magazine/article/0,9171,1725975,00.html).

Gupta, R., and A. Seth. 2007. "A Review of Resource Conserving Technologies for Sustainable Management of the Wheat-Cropping Systems of the Indo-Gangetic Plains (IGP)." *Crop Production* 26(3):436–447.

Habermas, J. 1962. *The Structural Transformation of the Public Sphere.* Darmstadt, German: Hermann Luchterhand Verlag.

Hall, R., and D. Papell. 2005. *Macroeconomics: Economic Growth, Fluctuations, and Policy.* New York: W. W. Norton.

Hamilton, C. 2010. *Requiem for a Species.* London: Earthscan.

Hanson, V. 2011. "California's Water Wars." *Los Angeles Times*, August 7. Retrieved March 21, 2012 (http://articles.latimes.com/2011/aug/07/opinion/la-oe-hanson-california-water-wars-ce20110807).

Haq, M. ul-. 1995. *Reflections on Human Development.* New York: Oxford University Press.

Hardin, G. 1968. "The Tragedy of the Commons." *Science* 162:1243–1248.

Harley, B. 1989. "Deconstructing the Map." *Cartographica* 26:1–20.

Harries, J., H. Brindley, P. Sagoo, and R. Bantges. 2001. "Increases in Greenhouse Forcing Inferred from the Outgoing Longwave Radiation Spectra of the Earth in 1970 and 1997." *Nature* 410:355–357.

Harris, L., and H. Hazen. 2006. "Power of Maps: (Counter) Mapping for Conservation." *ACME: An International E-Journal for Critical Geographies* 4:99–130.

Hartmann, B. 2010. "Rethinking Climate Refugees and Climate Conflict: Rhetoric, Reality, and the Politics of Policy Discourse." *Journal of International Development* 22(2):233–246.

Harvey, D. 2005. *Brief History of Neoliberalism.* New York: Oxford University Press.

Harvey, P., and R. Reed. 2006. "Community-Managed Water Supplies in Africa: Sustainable or Dispensable?" *Community Development Journal* 42(3):365–378.

Hatfield, J., L. McMullen, and C. Jones. 2009. "Nitrate-Nitrogen Patterns in the Raccoon River Basin Related to Agricultural Practices." *Journal of Soil and Water Conservation* 64(3):190–199.

Hatherly, J. 2008. "Transit Riders Turn Boring Commute into a Social Community on Wheels: 'Bus Buddies' Use Hour-Long Ride for Fun and Games." *Victoria Times Colonist*, December 28. Retrieved April 10, 2012 (http://www.canada.com/victoriatimescolonist/news/capital_van_isl/story.html?id=85608a98–6f70–43f8–9c2c-bc6f0af69b1d).

Hawcroft, L., and T. Milfont. 2010. "The Use (and Abuse) of the New Environmental Paradigm Scale over the Last 30 Years: A Meta-Analysis." *Journal of Environmental Psychology* 30:143–158.

Hazen, H., and P. Anthamatten. 2004. "Representation of Ecoregions by Protected Areas at the Global Scale." *Physical Geography* 25:499–512.

Hegarty, S. 2010. "Why Family Planning Saves Lives." *Guardian*, November 19. Retrieved September 30, 2011 (http://www.guardian.co.uk/journalismcompetition/ethiopia-contraception).

Heinzerling, L. 2000. "The Rights of Statistical People." *Harvard Environmental Law Review* 24:189–207.

Heiskanen, E., M. Johnson, S. Robinson, E. Vadovics, and M. Saastamoinen. 2010. "Low-Carbon Communities as a Context for Individual Behavioral Change." *Energy Policy* 38:7586–7595.

Hendricks, T. 2010. *The Wind Doesn't Need a Passport: Stories from the US-Mexico Borderlands.* Berkeley and Los Angeles: University of California Press.

Hendryx, M., and M. Ahern. 2008. "Relations Between Health Indicators and Residential Proximity to Coal Mining in West Virginia." *American Journal of Public Health* 98(4):669–671.

Hepburn, C., and P. Koundouri. 2007. "Recent Advances in Discounting: Implications for Forest Economics." *Journal of Forest Economics* 13(2–3):169–189.

Hertsgaard, M. 2010. "The Grapes of Wrath: Climate Change and the Wine Industry." *PBS.org*, April 30. Retrieved March 16, 2012 (http://www.pbs.org/wnet/need-to-know/economy /the-grapes-of-wrath-climate-change-and-the-wine-industry/263/).

Heschong, L., R. Wright, and S. Okura. 2002. "Daylighting Impacts on Human Performance in School." *Journal of the Illuminating Engineering Society* 3:101–114.

Hey, J. 2001. *Genes, Categories, and Species: The Evolutionary and Cognitive Causes of the Species Problem.* New York: Oxford University Press.

Hoddinott, J., and B. Kinsey. 2001. "Child Growth in the Time of Drought." *Oxford Bulletin of Economics and Statistics* 63(4):409–436.

Hoekstra, A., and A. Chapagain. 2007. "Water Footprints of Nations: Water Use by People as a Function of Their Consumption Pattern." *Water Resources Management* 21(1):35–48.

Hoffmann, M. 2011. *Climate Governance at the Crossroads: Experimenting with a Global Response After Kyoto.* New York: Oxford University Press.

Holdrege, C., and S. Talbott. 2008. *Beyond Biotechnology: The Barren Promise of Genetic Engineering.* Lexington: University Press of Kentucky.

Hooks, G., and C. Smith. 2004. "The Treadmill of Destruction: National Sacrifice Areas and Native Americans." *American Sociological Review* 69(4):558–575.

Hopkins, J., and N. Maxted. 2011. "Crop Wild Relatives: Plant Conservation for Food Security." Natural England Research Report NERR037. Sheffield: Natural England. Retrieved March 7, 2012 (http://www.cropwildrelatives.org/fileadmin/www.cropwildrelatives.org/documents /NaturalEnglandResearchReportNERR037.pdf).

House of Commons. 2010a. *The Regulation of Geoengineering: Fifth Report of Session 2009–10.* London: Parliament, House of Commons, Science and Technology Committee.

———. 2010b. *Taxes and Charges on Road Users: Sixth Report of Session 2008–09.* London: Parliament, House of Commons, Transport Committee.

Howard, P. 2009. "Visualizing Consolidation in the Global Seed Industry, 1996–2008." *Sustainability* 1:1266–1287.

Huff, E. 2011. "Global Cost of Chronic Disease Treatment to Top $47 Trillion by 2030, More than Triple Current US National Debt." *Nature News.com*, September 22. Retrieved April 5, 2012 (http://www.naturalnews.com/033651_chronic_disease_expenditures.html).

Hughes, T. 1969. "Technological Momentum in History: Hydrogenation in Germany, 1898–1933." *Past and Present* 44(1):106–132.

Hunnicutt, B. 1996. *Kellogg's Six-Hour Day.* Philadelphia: Temple University Press.

Hunter, L., and E. David. 2011. "Climate Change and Migration: Considering Gender Dimensions." In *Climate Change and Migration,* edited by E. Piguet, P. de Guchteneire, and A. Pecoud, 306–330. Paris: Cambridge University Press, UNESCO.

Hunter, M., and J. Gibbs. 2007. *Fundamentals of Conservation Biology.* 3rd ed. Malden, MA: Blackwell.

Hurst, D. 2010. "Growers Go Bananas over Waste." *Brisbane Times,* January 7. Retrieved March 30, 2012 (http://www.brisbanetimes.com.au/business/growers-go-bananas-over-waste -20100106-lu7q.html).

Hutchinson, A. 2008. "Is Recycling Worth It? PM Investigates Its Economic and Environmental Impact." *Popular Mechanics,* November 13. Retrieved March 28, 2012 (http://www .popularmechanics.com/science/environment/recycling/4291566).

Hvistendahl, M. 2008. "China's Three Gorges Dam: An Environmental Catastrophe." *Scientific American,* March 25. Retrieved April 25, 2012 (http://www.scientificamerican.com /article.cfm?id=chinas-three-gorges-dam-disaster).

IAEA. N.d. "Nuclear Re-Think." Vienna: International Atomic Energy Agency. Retrieved June 7, 2012 (http://www.iaea.org/Publications/Magazines/Bulletin/Bull481/htmls/nuclear_rethink .html).

ICTSD. 2010. "Food Giant Nestlé Accused of Biopiracy." *Bridges Trade BioRes: International Center for Trade and Sustainable Development (ICTSD)* 10(10):3. Retrieved March 3, 2012 (http://ictsd.org/downloads/biores/biores10-10.pdf).

India Planning Committee. 2008. *Kerala Development Report.* New Delhi: Academic Foundation.

Inglehart, R. 1990. *Culture Shift in Advanced Industrial Society.* Princeton, NJ: Princeton University Press.

———. 1997. *Modernization and Postmodernization: Cultural, Economic, and Political Change in 43 Societies.* Princeton, NJ: Princeton University Press.

Ingold, T. 2000. *The Perception of the Environment: Essays on Livelihood, Dwelling, and Skill.* New York: Routledge.

Institute for Lifecycle Energy Analysis. 2002. "Reusable Versus Disposable Cups." Seattle: Institute for Lifecycle Energy Analysis. Retrieved March 31, 2012 (http:// sustainability.tufts.edu/downloads/Comparativelifecyclecosts.pdf).

InterAcademy Council. 2003. "Realising the Promise and Potential of African Agriculture: Science and Technology Strategies for Improving Agricultural Productivity and Food Security in Africa." Amsterdam: InterAcademy Council. Retrieved April 15, 2012 (http://www.cgiar .org/pdf/agm04/agm04_iacpanel_execsumm.pdf).

IPC. N.d. "What Is IPC?" International Planning Committee for Food Sovereignty. Retrieved June 7, 2012 (http://www.foodsovereignty.org/Aboutus/WhatisIPC.aspx).

IPCC. 2007. *Climate Change 2007: Mitigation of Climate Change.* Cambridge: Cambridge University Press.

IPS. 2008. "Executive Excess, 2008: How Average Taxpayers Subsidize Runaway Pay." Washington, DC: Institution for Policy Studies. Retrieved April 28, 2012 (http:///www .faireconomy.org/files/executive_excess_2008.pdf).

IRIN. 2008. "Afghanistan: Medical Waste Poses Health Risk in Urban Area." Retrieved May 18, 2012 (http://www.irinnews.org/report.aspx?reportid=80902).

Ismail, Z., and T. Fakir. 2004. "Trademarks or Trade Barriers? Indigenous Knowledge and the Flaws in the Global IPR System." *International Journal of Social Economics* 31(1–2):173–194.

IUCN. 2006. "IUCN Red List of Threatened Species." Gland, Switzerland: International Union for Conservation of Nature. Retrieved March 7, 2012 (http://www.iucnredlist.org).

———. 2010. *Addressing Climate Change: Issues and Solutions from Around the World.* Gland, Switzerland: International Union for Conservation of Nature.

Jacobson, M., and M. Delucchi. 2009. "A Plan to Power 100 Percent of the Planet with Renewables." *Scientific American,* October 26. Retrieved March 26, 2012 (http://www .scientificamerican.com/article.cfm?id=a-path-to-sustainable-energy-by-2030).

Jackson, T. 2009. *Prosperity Without Growth.* London: Earthscan.

———. 2011. "'Peak Stuff' Message Is Cold Comfort." *Guardian,* November 1. Retrieved April 1, 2012 (http://www.guardian.co.uk/environment/2011/nov/01/peak-stuff-message-green -ktechnology?intcmp=239).

Jacques, P., R. Dunlap, and M. Freeman. 2008. "The Organisation of Denial: Conservative Think Tanks and Environmental Skepticism." *Environmental Politics* 17(3):349–385.

Jaramillo, P., W. Griffin, and H. Matthews. 2007. "Comparative Life-Cycle Air Emissions of Coal, Domestic Natural Gas, LNG, and SNG for Electricity Generation." *Environmental Science and Technology* 41(17):6290–6296.

Jebaraj, P. 2011. "Development of Bt Brinjal: A Case of Bio-Piracy." *Hindu,* August 10. Retrieved March 19, 2012 (http://www.thehindu.com/todays-paper/article2341585.ece).

Jenerette, G., and Larrisa Larsen. 2006. "A Global Perspective on Changing Sustainable Urban Water Supplies." *Global and Planetary Change* 50:202–211.

Jevons, W. 1865. *The Coal Question.* London: Macmillan.

Jindal, R., B. Swallow, and J. Kerr. 2008. "Forestry-Based Carbon Sequestration Projects in Africa: Potential Benefits and Challenges." *Natural Resources Forum* 32:116–130.

Jones, T. 2005. "How Much Goes Where? The Corner on Food Loss." *BioCycle* (July):2–3.

Jorgenson, A. 2006. "Unequal Ecological Exchange and Environmental Degradation: A Theoretical Proposition and Cross-national Study of Deforestation, 1990–2000." *Rural Sociology* 71(4):681–712.

Jorgenson, A., and B. Clark. 2012. "Are the Economy and the Environment Decoupling? A Comparative International Study, 1960–2005." *American Journal of Sociology* 118:1–44.

Kahn, J., and J. Yardley. 2007. "As China Roars, Pollution Reaches Deadly Extremes." *New York Times,* August 26. Retrieved April 7, 2012 (http://www.nytimes.com/2007/08/26/world/asia /26china.html?pagewanted=print).

Kasser, T. 2002. *The High Price of Materialism.* Cambridge: MIT Press.

———. 2005. "Frugality, Generosity, and Materialism in Children and Adolescents." In *What Do Children Need to Flourish? Conceptualizing and Measuring Indicators of Positive Development,* edited by K. Moore and L. Lippman, 357–373. New York: Springer Science.

Katz, J. 2008. "Poor Haitians Resort to Eating Mud." *National Geographic,* January 30. Retrieved April 7, 2012 (http://news.nationalgeographic.com/news/2008/01/080130-AP-haiti -eatin.html).

Kazlowski, S. 2008. *The Last Polar Bear: Facing the Truth of a Warming World.* Seattle: Mountaineers Books.

Kearsley, A., and M. Riddel. 2010. "A Further Inquiry into the Pollution Haven Hypothesis and the Environmental Kuznets Curve." *Ecological Economics* 69:905–919.

Keegan, P. 2009. "Zipcar: The Best New Idea in Business." *CNNMoney,* August 27. Retrieved April 9, 2012 (http://money.cnn.com/2009/08/26/news/companies/zipcar_car_rentals .fortune/).

Kellstedt, P., S. Zahran, and A. Vedlitz. 2008. "Personal Efficacy, the Information Environment, and Attitudes Toward Global Warming and Climate Change in the United States." *Risk Analysis* 28(1):113–126.

Kelly, B., J. Halford, E. Boyland, K. Chapman, I. Bautista-Castaño, C. Berg, M. Caroli, B. Cook, J. Coutinho, T. Effertz, E. Grammatikaki, K. Keller, R. Leung, Y. Manios, R. Monteiro, C. Pedley, H. Prell, K. Raine, E. Recine, L. Serra-Majem, S. Singh, and C. Summerbell. 2010. "Television Food Advertising to Children: A Global Perspective." *American Journal of Public Health* 100(9):1730–1736.

Kelly, K. N.d. "Access Is Better than Ownership." *Exponential Times.* Retrieved July 3, 2012 (http://www.exponentialtimes.net/videos/access-better-ownership-0).

Kemfert, C. 2005. "Global Climate Protection: Immediate Action Will Avert Higher Costs." *German Institute for Economic Research Weekly Report* 1(12):135–141.

Kempton, W., C. Harris, J. Keith, and J. Weihl. 1985. "Do Consumers Know What Works in Energy Conservation?" In *Families and the Energy Transition,* edited by J. Byrne, D. Schulz, and M. Sussman, 115–132. New York: Haworth Press.

Kernan, M., R. Battarbee, and B. Moss, eds. 2010. *Climate Change Impacts on Fresh Water Systems.* Hoboben, NJ: Blackwell.

Keynes, J. M. 1930. "Economic Possibilities of Our Grandchildren." In *John Maynard Keynes, Essays in Persuasion,* 358–373. 1963. Reprint, New York: W. W. Norton.

Khan, S., M. Hanjra, and J. Mu. 2009. "Water Management and Crop Production for Food Security in China: A Review." *Agricultural Water Management* 96(3):349–360.

Kirkham, M. 2011. *Elevated Carbon Dioxide: Impacts on Soil and Plant Water Relations.* Boca Raton, FL: CRC Press.

Klein, N. 2011. "Capitalism vs. the Climate." *Nation,* November 9. Retrieved April 18, 2012 (http://www.thenation.com/article/164497/capitalism-vs-climate?page=0,5).

Knight, K., and E. Rosa. 2011. "The Environmental Efficiency of Well-Being: A Cross-national Analysis." *Social Science Research* 40:931–949.

Koeppel, D. 2007. *Banana: The Fate of the Fruit That Changed the World.* New York: Hudson Street Press.

Kollmuss, A., and J. Agyeman. 2002. "Mind the Gap: Why Do People Act Environmentally and What Are the Barriers to Pro-environmental Behavior?" *Environmental Education Research* 8(2):239–260.

Kopczuk, W., J. Slemrod, and S. Yitzhaki. 2005. "The Limitations of Decentralized World Redistribution: An Optimal Taxation Approach." *European Economic Review* 49(4):1051–1079.

Kopp, R., and P. Portney. 1999. "Mock Referenda for Intergenerational Decisionmaking." In *Discounting and Intergenerational Equity*, edited by P. Portney and J. Weyant, 87–98. Washington, DC: Resources for the Future.

Kotchen, M., and S. Reiling. 2000. "Environmental Attitudes, Motivations, and Contingent Valuation of Nonuse Values." *Ecological Economics* 32:93–107.

Kozloff, N. 2010. *No Rain in the Amazon: How South America's Climate Change Affects the Entire Planet.* New York: Palgrave.

Kumar, D., and O. P. Singh. 2005. "Virtual Water in Global Food and Water Policy Making: Is There a Need for Rethinking?" *Water Resources Management* 19:759–789.

Kuznets, S. 1955. "Economic Growth and Income Inequality." *American Economic Review* 45(1):1–28.

Kysar, D. 2010. *Regulating from Nowhere: Environmental Law and the Search for Objectivity.* New Haven, CT: Yale University Press.

LAB. N.d. "Ride for the Environment." Washington, DC: League of American Bicyclists. Retrieved June 6, 2012 (http://www.bikeleague.org/resources/why/environment.php).

Lamba, N., and H. Krahn. 2003. "Social Capital and Refugee Resettlement: The Social Networks of Refugees in Canada." *Journal of International Migration and Integration* 4(3):335–360.

Larrick, R., and J. Soll. 2008. "The MPG Illusion." *Science* 320:1593–1594.

La Via Campesina. 2008. "Declaration of Maputo." Fifth International Conference of La Via Campesina, October 19–22. Retrieved April 17, 2012 (http://viacampesinanorteamerica .org/en/viacampesina/conferencias/V%20conferencia%20Declaration%20of%20Maputo .pdf).

La Viña, A., and L. Ang. 2011. "Implementing the REDD-Plus Safeguards: The Role of Social Accountability." Affiliated Network on Social Accountability, East Asia and the Pacific, Working Paper, Philippines, September. Retrieved April 14, 2012 (http://www.theredddesk .org/sites/default/files/resources/pdf/2011/implementing_the_redd_safeguards_the_role _of_social_accountability.pdf).

Leach, A., and J. Mumford. 2008. "Pesticide Environmental Accounting: A Method for Assessing the External Costs of Individual Pesticide Applications." *Environmental Pollution* 151:139–147.

Leggett, J. 1990. "Global Warming: A Greenpeace View." In *Global Warming: A Greenpeace Report,* edited by J. Leggett, 457–480. Oxford: Oxford University Press.

Lehmann, J. 2007. "A Handful of Carbon." *Nature* 447(May 10):143–144.

Leiserowitz, A., N. Smith, and J. Marlon. 2010. "Americans' Knowledge of Climate Change." New Haven, CT: Yale University, Yale Project on Climate Change Communication. Retrieved September 10, 2012 (http://environment.yale.edu/climate/files/ClimateChange Knowledge2010.pdf).

Lenne, J., and D. Wood. 2011. *Agrobiodiversity Management for Food Security: A Critical Review.* Cambridge, MA: CABI International.

Leonard, A. 2010. *The Story of Stuff.* New York: Free Press.

Lertzman, R. 2010. "The Myth of Apathy: Psychosocial Dimensions of Environmental Degradation." PhD thesis, Cardiff University.

Levins, H. 2006. "A Whole-System View of Agriculture, People, and the Rest of Nature." In *Agroecology and the Struggle for Food Sovereignty in the Americas,* edited by A. Cohn, J. Cook, M. Fernández, R. Reider, and C. Steward, 34–49. London: International Institute for Environment and Development (IIED). Retrieved April 22, 2012 (http://pubs.iied.org/pdfs /14506IIED.pdf).

Lindhqvist, T., and K. Lidgren. 1990. "Modeller för Förlängt Producentansvar (Model for Extended Producer Responsibility)." In *Från vaggan till Graven: Sex Studier av Varors Miljöpåverkan (From the Cradle to the Grave: Six Studies of the Environmental Impacts of Products)*, 7–44. DS1991:9. Stockholm: Ministry of the Environment.

Litman, T. 2010. "Community Cohesion as a Transport Planning Objective." Victoria Transport Policy Institute, Victoria, BC, April 15. Retrieved April 10, 2012 (http://www.vtpi.org /cohesion.pdf).

Liu J., G. Daily, P. Ehrlich, and G. Luck. 2003. "Effects of Household Dynamics on Resource Consumption and Biodiversity." *Nature* 421:530–533.

Liu, J., and H. Savenije. 2008. "Food Consumption Patterns and Their Effects on Water Requirements in China." *Hydrology and Earth System Science* 12:887–898.

Lobao, L., and C. Stofferahn. 2008. "The Community Effect of Industrial Farming: Social Science Research and Challenges to Corporate Farming Laws." *Agriculture and Human Values* 25:219–240.

Lomax, T., D. Schrank, S. Turner, L. Geng, Y. Li, and N. Koncz. 2011. "Real-Timing the 2010 Urban Mobility Report." College Station: University Transportation Center for Mobility, Texas Transportation Institute, Texas A&M University System. Retrieved October 5, 2011 (http://utcm.tamu.edu/publications/final_reports/Lomax_10-65-55.pdf).

Longhofer, W., and E. Schofer. 2010. "National and Global Origins of Environmental Association." *American Sociological Review* 75(4):505–533.

Lonsdorf, K. 2011. "From Freeways to Waterways: What Los Angeles Can Learn from Soule." KCET, August 9. Retrieved April 11, 2012 (http://www.kcet.org/socal/departures /landofsunshine/la-river/from-freeways-to-waterways-what-los-angeles-can-learn-from -seoul.html).

Lovejoy, T. 1980. "A Projection of Species Extinctions." In *The Global 2000 Report to the President,* edited by G. Barney, 2:328–373. Washington, DC: US Government Printing Office.

Lovins, L. H., and B. Cohen. 2011. *Natural Capitalism: Capitalism in the Age of Climate Change.* New York: Hill and Wang.

Luber, G., and M. McGeehin. 2008. "The Health Impacts of Climate Change: Climate Change and Extreme Heat Events." *American Journal of Preventative Medicine* 35(5):429–435.

Lytle, M. 2007. *The Gentle Subversive: Rachel Carlson and the Rise of the Environmental Movement.* New York: Oxford University Press.

MacKay, D. 2009. *Sustainable Energy: Without Hot Air.* Cambridge: UIT Press.

MacKenzie, D., and G. Spinardi. 1995. "Tacit Knowledge, Weapons Design, and the Uninvention of Nuclear Weapons." *American Journal of Sociology* 101(1):44–99.

Maffi, L., and E. Woodley. 2010. *Biocultural Diversity Conservation: A Global Sourcebook.* London: Earthscan.

Mailbach, E., C. Roser-Renouf, and A. Leiserowitz. 2009. "Global Warming's Six Americas, 2009: An Audience Segmentation Analysis." Yale Project on Climate Change and the George Mason University Center for Climate Change Communication. Retrieved September 10, 2012 (http://www.americanprogress.org/issues/2009/05/pdf/6americas.pdf).

Maibach, E., L. Steg, and J. Anable. 2009. "Promoting Physical Activity and Reducing Climate Change: Opportunities to Replace Short Car Trips with Active Transportation." *Preventative Medicine* 49:326–327.

Manoli, C., B. Johnson, and R. Dunlap. 2007. "Assessing Children's Environmental Worldviews: Modifying and Validating the New Ecological Paradigm Scale for Use with Children." *Journal of Environmental Education* 38(4):3–13.

Marín, L., R. Sandoval, F. Tagle, E. Sanchez, and W. Martinez. 2009. "Water as a Human Right and as an Economic Resource: An Example from Mexico." In *Water Ethics,* edited by M. Llamas, L. Martínez-Cortina, and A. Mukherji, 115–125. Boca Raton, FL: CRC Press.

Marinelli, J. 2011. "Landscape for Life." Report funded by the United States Botanic Garden and the Lady Bird Johnson Wildflower Center at the University of Texas at Austin. Retrieved March 8, 2012 (http://www.landscapeforlife.org/publications/LFL_Workbooks_Print _downloadable.pdf).

Markovich, J., and K. Lucas. 2011. "The Social and Distributional Impacts of Transport: A Literature Review." Working Paper no. 1055. Oxford: Transport Studies Unit, School of Geography and the Environment, Oxford University, August. Retrieved April 9, 2012 (http:// www.tsu.ox.ac.uk/pubs/1055-markovich-lucas.pdf).

Martine, G. 2009. "Population Dynamics and Policies in the Context of Global Climate Change." In *Population Dynamics and Climate Change,* edited by J. Guzmán, G. Martine, G. McGranahan, D. Schensul, and C. Tacoli, 9–30. New York: UNFPA and IIED.

Martínez-Torres, M., and P. Rosset. 2010. "La Vía Campesina: The Birth and Evolution of a Transnational Social Movement." *Journal of Peasant Studies* 37:149–175.

Marwell, G., and R. Ames. 1981. "Economists Free Ride, Does Anyone Else?" *Journal of Public Economics* 15:295–310.

Marx, K. [1863–1865] 1981. *Capital.* Vol. 3. New York: Vintage.

———. [1863] 1976. *Capital.* Vol. 1, Vintage, New York.

Marx, K., and F. Engels. [1848] 1978. "Manifesto of the Communist Party." In *The Marx-Engels Reader,* 469–500. New York: W. W. Norton.

Maser, C. 2009. *Earth in Our Care: Ecology, Economy, and Sustainability.* New Brunswick, NJ: Rutgers University Press.

Mason, R. 2011. "Plans for UK's First 'Clean Coal' Plant Collapse over £1.5bn Cost." *London Telegraph,* October 20. Retrieved March 23, 2012 (http://www.telegraph.co.uk/finance /newsbysector/energy/8837141/Plans-for-UKs-first-clean-coal-plant-collapse-over-1.5bn -cost.html).

Mather, A. 1990. *Global Forest Resources.* London: Bellhaven Press.

———. 1992. "The Forest Transition." *Area* 24:367–379.

May, E. 1973. "Extensive Oxygen Depletion in Mobile Bay, Alabama." *Limnology and Oceanography* 18:353–366.

Mayden, R. 1997. "A Hierarchy of Species Concepts: The Denouement in the Saga of the Species Problem." In *Species: The Units of Biodiversity,* edited by M. Claridge, H. Dawah, and M. Wilson, 381–424. New York: Chapman and Hall.

McCright, A., and R. Dunlap. 2011a. "Cool Dudes: The Denial of Climate Change Among Conservative White Males in the United States." *Global Environmental Change* 21(4):1163–1172.

———. 2011b. "The Politicization of Climate Change and Polarization in the American Public's View of Global Warming, 2001–2010." *Sociological Quarterly* 52:155–194.

McDonald, D. 2005. "Environmental Racism and Neoliberal Disorder in South Africa." In *The Quest for Environmental Justice: Human Rights and the Politics of Pollution,* edited by Robert Bullard, 255–278. San Francisco: Sierra Club Books.

McGranahan, G., D. Balk, and B. Anderson. 2007. "The Rising Tide: Assessing the Risks of Climate Change and Human Settlements in Low Elevation Coastal Zones." *Environment and Urbanization* 19(1):17–37.

McKenzie-Mohr, D. 2011. *Fostering Sustainable Behavior: An Introduction to Community Based Social Marketing.* Gabriola Island, BC: New Society.

McMichael, P. 2006. "Peasant Prospects in the Neoliberal Age." *New Political Economy* 11(3):407–418.

———. 2009. "Banking on Agriculture: A Review of the World Development Report, 2008." *Journal of Agrarian Change* 9(2):235–246.

McNeill, D. 2011. "Why the Fukushima Disaster Is Worse than Chernobyl." *Independent,* August 29. Retrieved June 7, 2012 (http://www.independent.co.uk/news/world/asia/why-the-fukushima-disaster-is-worse-than-chernobyl-2345542.html).

Meadows, D., D. Meadows, J. Randers, and W. Behrens. 1972. *The Limits to Growth.* New York: Universe Books.

Medin, D., and S. Atran. 2004. "The Native Mind: Biological Categorization and Reasoning in Development and Across Cultures." *Psychological Review* 111(4):960–983.

Meijaard, E., and V. Nijman. 2003. "Primate Hotspots on Borneo: Predictive Value for General Biodiversity and the Effects of Taxonomy." *Conservation Biology* 17:725–732.

Menon, G. 1991. "Ecological Transition and the Changing Context of Women's Work in Tribal India." *Purusartha* 14:291–314.

Merchant, C. 1980. *The Death of Nature: Women, Ecology, and the Scientific Revolution.* San Francisco: HarperCollins.

Merrill, R. 1997. "Food Safety Regulation: Reforming the Delaney Clause." *Annual Review of Public Health* 18:313–340.

Merton, R. 1976. *Sociological Ambivalence, and Other Essays.* New York: Free Press.

Meyer, D. S., and S. Staggenborg. 1996. "Movements, Countermovements, and the Structure of Political Opportunity." *American Journal of Sociology* 101:1628–1660.

Mill, J. S. 1848. *Principles of Political Economy.* Boston: Charles C. Little and James Brown.

Millennium Ecosystem Assessment. 2005. *Ecosystems and Human Well-Being: Synthesis.* Washington, DC: Island Press

Miller, T., and S. Spoolman. 2010. *Environmental Science.* Belmont, CA: Brooks/Cole.

Mirabelli M., S. Wing, S. Marshall, and T. Wilcosky. 2006. "Asthma Symptoms Among Adolescents Who Attend Public Schools That Are Located Near Confined Swine Feeding Operations." *Pediatrics* 118:e66–e75.

Mishan, E. 1967. *The Costs of Economic Growth.* Middlesex, MA: Penguin Books.

MIT. 2007. "The Future of Coal." Cambridge: Massachusetts Institute of Technology. Retrieved March 23, 2012 (http://web.mit.edu/coal/The_Future_of_Coal.pdf).

Moellendorf, D. 2009. *Global Inequality Matters.* New York: Palgrave Macmillan.

Mohai, P., D. Pellow, and J. T. Roberts. 2009. "Environmental Justice." *Annual Reviews Environmental Resources* 34:405–430.

Mohai, P., and R. Saha. 2007. "Racial Inequality in the Distribution of Hazardous Waste: A National-Level Reassessment." *Social Problems* 54(3):343–370.

Mohai, P., S. Simões, and S. Brechin. 2010. "Environmental Concerns, Values, and Meanings in the Beijing and Detroit Metropolitan Areas." *International Sociology* 25(6):778–817.

Moore, M., and P. Foster. 2011. "China to Create Largest Mega City in the World with 42 Million People." *Telegraph,* January 24. Retrieved March 30, 2012 (http://www.telegraph.co.uk/news/worldnews/asia/china/8278315/China-to-create-largest-mega-city-in-the-world-with-42-million-people.html).

Morris, J. 2005. "Comparative LCAs for Curbside Recycling Versus Either Landfilling or Incineration with Energy Recovery." *International Journal of Life Cycle Assessment* 10(4):273–284.

Mostafa, M. In press. "Wealth, Post-materialism and Consumers' Pro-environmental Intentions: A Multilevel Analysis Across 25 Nations." *Sustainable Development.*

Mougeot, L. 2005. "Introduction: Urban Agriculture and Millennium Development Goals." In *Agropolis: The Social, Political, and Environmental Dimensions of Urban Agriculture,* edited by L. Mougeot, 1–29. London: Earthscan.

MST. N.d. "What Is the MST?" Friends of the MST. Retrieved June 7, 2012 (http://www.mstbrazil.org/).

Murray, J. 2011. "Japan's Feed-In Tariff Bill Clears Parliamentary Hurdle." *Business Green,* August 23. Retrieved March 26, 2012 (http://www.businessgreen.com/bg/news/2103716/japans-feed-tariff-clears-parliamentary-hurdle).

Myrskyla, M., H.-P. Kphler, and F. Billari. 2009. "Advances in Development Reverse Fertility Declines." *Nature* 460:471–743.

Myers, N., and J. Kent. 2005. *The New Atlas of Planet Management.* Berkeley and Los Angeles: University of California Press.

Nabhan, G. 1985. "Native American Crop Diversity, Genetic Resource Conservation, and the Policy of Neglect." *Agriculture and Human Values* 11(3):14–17.

———. 1997. *Cultures of Habitat.* Washington, DC: Counterpoint.

———. 2009. *Coming Home to Eat: The Pleasures and Politics of Local Foods.* New York: W. W. Norton.

Nash, J. 2007. "Consuming Interests: Water, Rum, and Coca-Cola from Ritual Propitiation to Corporate Expropriation in Highland Chiapas." *Cultural Anthropology* 22(4):621–639.

National Geographic. N.d. "Water Foot Print Calculator." Retrieved March 28, 2012 (http://environment.nationalgeographic.com/environment/freshwater/water-footprint-calculator/).

National Research Council. 2011. *Renewable Fuel Standard: Potential Economic and Environmental Effects of U.S. Biofuel Policy.* Washington, DC: National Academies Press.

Nazarea, V. 2005. *Heirloom Seeds and Their Keepers: Marginality and Memory in the Conservation of Biological Diversity.* Tucson: University of Arizona Press.

NEI. N.d. "World Statistics." Washington, DC: Nuclear Energy Institute. Retrieved June 7, 2012 (http://www.nei.org/resourcesandstats/nuclear_statistics/worldstatistics/).

Netting, R. 1981. *Balancing on an Alp: Ecological Change and Continuity in a Swiss Mountain Community.* New York: Cambridge University Press.

Neumayer, E. 1999. "Global Warming: Discounting Is Not the Issue, but Substitutability Is." *Energy Policy* 27:33–34.

Neumayer, E., and T. Plumper. 2007. *The Gendered Nature of Natural Disasters.* London: London School of Economics, University of Essex, and Max-Planck Institute of Economics.

New Economics Foundation. 2009. "The Un–Happy Planet Index 2.0." London: New Economics Foundation. Retrieved April 22, 2012 (http://www.happyplanetindex.org/public-data/files/happy-planet-index-2-0.pdf).

Newman, A. 2011. "N.J. to Leave Regional Cap-and-Trade Scheme." *New American,* May 31. Retrieved March 25, 2012 (http://www.thenewamerican.com/tech-mainmenu-30/environment/7689-nj-to-leave-regional-cap-and-trade-scheme).

NHDES. N.d. "Time It Takes for Garbage to Decompose in the Environment." New Hampshire Department of Environmental Services. Retrieved March 28, 2012 (http://des.nh.gov/organization/divisions/water/wmb/coastal/trash/documents/marine_debris.pdf).

Nicholls, A., and C. Opal. 2005. *Fair Trade: Market Drive Ethical Consumption.* Thousand Oaks, CA: Sage.

Nielsen. 2009. "More than Half the Homes in US Have Three or More TVs." *Nielsen Wire,* July. Retrieved May 18, 2012 (http://blog.nielsen.com/nielsenwire/media_entertainment/more-than-half-the-homes-in-us-have-three-or-more-tvs/).

NMA. N.d. "Most Requested Statistics." Washington, DC: National Mining Association. Retrieved June 7, 2012 (http://www.nma.org/pdf/c_most_requested.pdf).

NOAA. 2008. "NOAA and Louisiana Scientists Predict Largest Gulf of Mexico 'Dead Zone' on Record This Summer." Washington, DC: National Oceanic and Atmospheric Administration, US Commerce Department. Retrieved April 14, 2012 (http://www.noaanews.noaa.gov/stories2008/20080715_deadzone.html).

Norgaard, K. 2006. "'We Don't Really Want to Know': Environmental Justice and Socially Organized Denial of Global Warming in Norway." *Organization and Environment* 19(3):347–370.

———. 2011. *Living in Denial: Climate Change, Emotions, and Everyday Life.* Cambridge: MIT Press.

NPR. 2011. "Among the Costs of War: Billions a Year in A.C.?" *National Public Radio,* June 25. Retrieved June March 24, 2012 (http://www.npr.org/2011/06/25/137414737/among-the-costs-of-war-20b-in-air-conditioning).

NRDC. 1999. "Bottled Water: Pure Drink or Pure Hype?" National Resources Defense Council, petition to the US Food and Drug Administration. Retrieved March 11, 2012 (http://www.nrdc.org/water/drinking/bw/bwinx.asp).

Nuclear Energy Agency. 2010. "Nuclear Energy and Addressing Climate Change." Nuclear Energy Agency, November. Retrieved March 24, 2012 (http://www.oecd-nea.org/press/in-perspective/2010-addressing-climate-change.pdf).

O'Brian, E. 2006. "Habitat Fragmentation Due to Transport Infrastructure." In *The Ecology of Transport,* edited by J. Davenport and J. Davenport, 191–203. Dordrecht, the Netherlands: Springer.

O'Connor, J. 1998. *Natural Causes: Essays in Ecological Marxism.* New York: Guildford Press.

OECD. 2010a. *OECD Factbook 2010: Economic, Environmental, and Social Statistics.* Paris: Organization for Economic Cooperation and Development.

———. 2010b. "Tackling Inequalities in Brazil, China, India, and South America." Paris: Organization for Economic Cooperation and Development.

Ogino, A., H. Orito, K. Shimada, and H. Hirooka. 2007. "Evaluating Environmental Impacts of the Japanese Beef Cow-Calf System by the Life Cycle Assessment Method." *Animal Science Journal* 78:424–432.

Ó Gráda, C. 2007. "Making Famine History." *Journal of Economic Literature* 45(1):5–38.

Oliver-Smith, A. 2009. "Climate Change and Populations Displacement: Disasters and Diasporas in the Twenty-First Century." In *Anthropology and Climate Change: From Encounters to Actions,* edited by S. Crate and M. Nuttall, 116–136. Walnut Creek, CA: Left Coast Press.

Olli, E., G. Grendstad, and D. Wollebaek. 2001. "Correlates of Environmental Behaviors: Bringing Back Social Context." *Environment and Behavior* 33:181–208.

Orbell, J., A. van de Kragt, and R. Dawes. 1988. "Explaining Discussion-Induced Cooperation in Social Dilemmas." *Journal of Personality and Social Psychology* 54:811–819.

Oregon State University. 2009. "Family Planning: A Major Environmental Emphasis." University Relations and Marketing, July 31. Retrieved March 27, 2012 (http://oregonstate.edu/ua/ncs/archives/2009/jul/family-planning-major-environmental-emphasis).

Oreskes, N. 2004. "Beyond the Ivory Tower: The Scientific Consensus on Climate Change." *Science* 306:1686.

Osborn, S., A. Vengosh, N. Warner, and R. Jackson. 2011. "Methane Contamination of Drinking Water Accompanying Gas-Well Drilling and Hydraulic Fracturing." *Proceedings of the National Academy of Sciences USA* (advance online publication).

Ostrom, E. 1999. *Governing the Commons: The Evolution of Institutions for Collective Action.* New York: Cambridge University Press.

———. 2000. "Private and Common Property Rights." In *Encyclopedia of Law and Economics,* edited by B. Bouckaert and G. De Geest, 3:332–379. London: Edward Elgar.

Ostrom, E., J. Burger, C. Field, R. Norgaard, and D. Policansky. 1999. "Revisiting the Commons: Local Lessons, Global Challenges." *Science* 284(5412):278–282.

Ostrom, E., R. Gardner, and J. Walker. 1994. *Rules, Games, and Common-Pool Resources.* Ann Arbor: University of Michigan Press.

Owen, D. 2011. *The Conundrum.* New York: Riverhead Books.

Pacala, S., and R. Socolow. 2004. "Stabilization Wedges: Solving the Climate Problem for the Next 50 Years with Current Technologies." *Science* 305:968–72.

Page, T. 2003. "Balancing Efficiency and Equity in Long-run Decision-making." *International Journal of Sustainable Development*(6), 70–86.

Palaniappan, M. 2009. "Millennium Development Goals: Charting Progress and the Way Forward." In *The World's Water, 2008–2009,* edited by P. Gleick, 57–78. Washington, DC: Island Press.

Palmer, M., E. Bernhardt, W. Schlesinger, K. Eshleman, E. Foufoula-Georgiou, M. Hendryx, A. Lemly, G. Likens, O. Loucks, M. Power, P. White, P. Wilcock. 2010. "Mountaintop Mining Consequences." *Science* 327 (January 8):148–149.

Parrish, D., H. Singh, L. Molina, and S. Madronich. 2011. "Air Quality Progress in North American Megacities: A Review." *Atmospheric Environment* 45:7015–7025.

Parry, I. 2005. "Is Pay-as-You-Drive Insurance a Better Way to Reduce Gasoline than Gasoline Taxes?" *American Economic Review* 95(2):288–293.

Paschenko, C. 2011. "Bay Thrives with Help from Desalination." *Daily News,* September 6. Retrieved March 22, 2012 (http://galvestondailynews.com/story/255950).

Payne, R. 1995. "Freedom and the Environment." *Journal of Democracy* 6:41–55.

Pearce, D., J. Vanclay, and F. Putz. 2002. "A Sustainable Forest Future?" In *Economic Valuation in Developing Countries,* edited by D. Pearce, C. Pearce, and C. Palmer, 112–145. Cheltenham: Edward Elgar.

Pehnt, M. 2006. "Dynamic Lifecycle Assessment of Renewable Energy Technologies." *Renewable Energy* 31:55–71.

Pellow, D., A. Schnailberg, and A. Weinburg. 2000. "Putting the Ecological Modernization Thesis to the Test: The Promises and Performance of Urban Recycling." In *Ecological Modernizaton Around the World: Perspectives and Critical Debates,* edited by A. Mol and D. Sonnenfeld, 109–137. Portland, OR: Frank Cass.

Perfecto, I., J. Vandermeer, and A. Wright. 2009. *Nature's Matrix: Linking Agriculture, Conservation, and Food Sovereignty.* London, Earthscan.

Perkins, S. 2011. "Methane Threat to Drinking Water." *Nature,* May 9. Retrieved March 24, 2012 (http://www.nature.com/news/2011/110509/full/news.2011.278.html).

Perrow, C. 1984. *Normal Accidents: Living with High Risk Technologies.* Princeton, NJ: Princeton University Press.

———. 2010. "Organizations and Global Warming." In *Routledge Handbook of Climate Change and Society,* edited by C. Lever-Tracy, 59–77. New York: Routledge.

Perry, T. 2005. "Recycling Behind Bars." *IEEE Spectrum,* June. Retrieved March 1, 2012 (http://spectrum.ieee.org/green-tech/conservation/recycling-behind-bars/2).

Peterson, A. 2009. *Everyday Ethics and Social Change: The Education of Desire.* New York: Columbia University Press.

Peterson, A., and A. Navarro-Siguenza. 1999. "Alternative Species Concepts as Bases for Determining Priority Conservation Areas." *Conservation Biology* 13:427–431.

Peterson, E. 2009. *A Billion Dollars a Day: The Economics and Politics of Agricultural Subsides.* Malden, MA: Wiley-Blackwell.

Pfaff, A., and R. Walker. 2010. "Regional Interdependence and Forest 'Transitions': Substitute Deforestation Limits the Relevance of Local Reversals." *Land Use Policy* 27:119–127.

Pfeffer, M. 1983. Social Origins of Three Systems of Farm Production in the United States." *Rural Sociology* 48(4):540–562.

Pickering, A. 1999. *Constructing Quarks: A Sociological History of Particle Physics.* Chicago: University of Chicago Press.

Pidgeon, N. 2011. "In Retrospect: Normal Accidents." *Nature* 477(7365):404–405.

Pigou, A. 1912. *Wealth and Welfare.* London: Macmillan.

Pimentel, D. 2005. "Environmental and Economic Costs of the Application of Pesticides Primarily in the United States." *Environment, Development, and Sustainability* 7:229–252.

Pimentel, D., J. Krummel, D. Gallahan, J. Hough, A. Merrill, I. Schreiner, P. Vittum, F. Koziol, E. Back, D. Yen, and S. Fiance. 1978. "Benefits and Costs of Pesticide Use in United States Food Production." *BioScience* 28(772):778–784.

Pimentel, D., S. Williamson, C. Alexander, O. Gonzolel-Pegan, C. Kontak, and S. Mulkey. 2008. "Reducing Energy Inputs in the US Food System." *Human Ecology* 36:459–471.

Popper, K. [1934] 1961. *The Logic of Scientific Discovery.* New York: Science Editions.

Potera, C. 2008. "Corn Ethanol Goal Revives Dead Zone Concerns." *Environmental Health Perspectives* 116(6):A242–A243.

Pradhan, E., K. West, J. Katz, S. LeClerq, S. Khatry, and S. Shrestha. 2007. "Risk of Flood-Related Mortality in Nepal." *Disasters* 31(1):57–70.

Pretty, J., ed. 2004. *Pesticide Detox: Towards a More Sustainable Agriculture.* London: Earth scan.

Pretty, J., C. Brett, D. Gee, R. E. Hine, C. F. Mason, J. I. L. Morison, M. Rayment, G. van der Bijl, and T. Dobbs. 2001. "Policy Challenges and Priorities for Internalizing the Externalities of Agriculture." *Journal of Environmental Planning and Management* 44(2):263–283.

Pretty, J., and H. Waibel. 2005. "Paying the Price: The Full Cost of Pesticides." In *The Pesticide Detox,* edited by J. Pretty, 39–54. London: Earthscan.

Pretty, J., and H. Ward. 2001. "Social Capital and the Environment." *World Development* 29(2):209–227.

Putnam, R. 2001. *Bowling Alone.* New York: Simon and Schuster.

PWC. 2011. "PWC's Autofacts Forecasts 2012 Global Automotive Assembly to Increase to 83.5 Million Units." New York: PricewaterhouseCoopers, August 3. Retrieved April 7, 2012 (http://www.pwc.com/us/en/press-releases/2011/pwcs-autofacts-forecasts-2012.jhtml).

Qadir, M., B. Sharma, A. Bruggeman, R. Choukr-allah, and F. Karajeh. 2007. "Nonconventional Water Resources and Opportunities for Water Augmentation to Achieve Food Security in Water Scarce Countries." *Agricultural Water Management* 87:2–22.

Quan, L., and R. Reuveny. 2006. "Democracy and Environmental Deregulation." *International Studies Quarterly* 50:935–956.

Rabobank Group. 2010. "Sustainability and Security of the Global Food Supply Chain." Retrieved April 7, 2012 (http://www.rabobank.nl/images/rabobanksustainability_29286998 .pdf?ra_resize=yes&ra_width=800&ra_height=600&ra_toolbar=yes&ra_locationbar=yes).

Radon, K., A. Schulze, V. Ehrenstein, R. van Strien, G. Praml, and D. Nowak. 2007. "Environmental Exposure to Confined Animal Feeding Operations and Respiratory Health of Neighboring Residents." *Epidemiology* 18:300–308.

Raffensperger, C., and J. Tickner, eds. 1999. *Protecting Public Health and the Environment: Implementing the Precautionary Principle.* Washington, DC: Island Press.

Ravallion, M., S. Chen, and P. Sangraula. 2007. "New Evidence on the Urbanization of Global Poverty." Policy Research Working Paper 4199. Washington, DC: World Bank. Retrieved April 8, 2012 (http://siteresources.worldbank.org/INTWDR2008/Resources/2795087-1191427986785/RavallionMEtAl_UrbanizationOfGlobalPoverty.pdf).

Raynolds, L., D. Murray, and J. Wilkinson. 2007. *Fair Trade: The Challenges of Transforming Globalization.* New York: Routledge.

Redwood, M. 2010. "Commentary: Food Price and Volatility and the Urban Poor." In *Urban Agriculture: Diverse Activities and Benefits for City Society,* edited by C. Pearson, 5–6. London: Earthscan.

Rees, W. 2009. "True Cost Economics." In *Berkshire Encyclopedia of Sustainability,* edited by C. Laszlo, 468–471. Great Barrington, MA: Berkshire Publishing Group.

REN21. 2010. *Renewables 2010: Status Report, Renewable Action Policy Network for the 21st Century (REN21).* Paris: REN21 Secretariat.

Repetto, R. 1995. *Jobs, Competitiveness, and Environmental Regulation: What Are the Real Issues?* Washington, DC: World Resources Institute.

Reuveny, R. 2007. "Climate Change–Induced Migration and Violent Conflict." *Political Geography* 26:656–673.

Revi, A. 2008. "Climate Change Risk: An Adaptation and Mitigation Agenda for India Cities." *Environment and Urbanization* 20(1):207–229.

Revkin, A. 2009. "Peeling Back Pavement to Expose Watery Havens." *New York Times,* July 17. Retrieved April 11, 2012 (http://www.nytimes.com/2009/07/17/world/asia/17daylight .html?pagewanted=all).

Rhoades, R., and V. Nazarea. 2006. "Reconciling Local and Global Agendas in Sustainable Development." *Journal of Mountain Science* 3(4):334–346.

Rideout, B. 2005. "The Effect of a Brief Environmental Problems Module on Endorsement of the New Ecological Paradigm in College Students." *Journal of Environmental Education* 37(1):3–11.

Riffle, C. 2011. "Can Cities Lead the Way in Cutting Greenhouse Gas Emissions?" *Guardian,* June 7. Retrieved May 18, 2012 (http://www.guardian.co.uk/sustainable-business/blog /cities-lead-cutting-greenhouse-gas-emissions).

Rifkin, J. 2000. *The Age of Access.* New York: Tarcher.

———. 2003. *The Hydrogen Economy: The Creation of the Worldwide Energy Web and the Redistribution of Power on Earth.* New York: Penguin.

Robbins, P. 2012. *Political Ecology.* 2nd ed. Malden, MA: John Wiley and Son.

Roberto, K. 2003. *How to Do Hydroponics.* 4th ed. Lindenhurst, NY: Futuregarden.

Roberts, J. T., and P. Grimes. 1997. "Carbon Intensity and Economic Development, 1962–1971: A Brief Exploration of the Environmental Kuznets Curve." *World Development* 25:191–198.

Roberts J. T., and B. Parks. 2007. *A Climate of Injustice: Global Inequality, North-South Politics, and Climate Change.* Cambridge: MIT Press.

Roccas, S., and L. Sagiv. 2010. "Personal Values and Behaviour: Taking the Cultural Context into Account." *Social and Personality Psychology Compass* 4:30–41.

Rodwan, J. 2009." Confronting Challenges: US and International Bottled Water Developments and Statistics for 2008." *Bottled Water Reporter* (April–May):12–18. Retrieved March 11, 2012 (http://www.bottledwater.org/public/2008%20Market%20Report%20Findings%20 reported%20in%20April%202009.pdf).

Rogers, P. 2003. "Effective Water Governance." TAC Background Papers no. 7. Stockholm, Sweden. Retrieved March 12, 2012 (http://citeseerx.ist.psu.edu/viewdoc/download?doi =10.1.1.130.2714&rep=rep1&type=pdf).

Rogers, P. and Hall, A. 2003. "Effective Water Governance," Global Water Paternership Technical Committee, TEC background paper No 7, Stockholm, Sweden, http://www.tnmckc .org/upload/document/bdp/2/2.7/GWP/TEC-7.pdf, last accessed November 17, 2012.

Rogers, P., R. Bhatia, and A. Huber. 1998. "Water as a Social and Economic Good: How to Put the Principle into Practice." TAC Background Papers no. 2. Stockholm, Sweden. Retrieved March 23, 2012 (http://info.worldbank.org/etools/docs/library/80637/IWRM4_TEC02 -WaterAsSocialEconGood-Rogers.pdf).

Rojek, C. 2010. *The Labour of Leisure: The Culture of Free Time.* Thousand Oaks, CA: Sage.

Rosa, E., and T. Dietz. 1998. "Climate Change and Society: Speculation, Construction, and Scientific Investigations." *International Sociology* 13:421–455.

Rossem, C., N. Tojo, and T. Lindhqvist. 2006. "Extended Producer Responsibility." Report commissioned by Greenpeace International, Friends of the Earth Europe, and the European Environmental Bureau. Retrieved March 4, 2012 (http://www.greenpeace.org/international /PageFiles/24472/epr.pdf).

Rothschild, D. 2007. *The Life Earth Global Warming Survival Handbook.* New York: Rodale Books.

Sagoff, M. 1988. *The Economy of the Earth.* New York: Cambridge University Press.

Saha, R., and P. Mohai. 2005. "Historical Context and Hazardous Waste Facility Siting: Understanding Temporal Patterns in Michigan." *Social Problems* 52(4):618–648.

Samida, D., and D. Weisbach. 2007. "Paretian Intergenerational Discounting." *University of Chicago Law Review* 74(1):145–170.

Sander, T. 2002. "Social Capital and New Urbanism: Leading a Civic Horse to Water?" *National Civic Review* 91(3):213–234.

Satterthwaite, D. 2009. "Urban Form, Greenhouse Gas Emissions, and Climate Vulnerability." In *Population Dynamics and Climate Change,* edited by J. Guzmán, G. Martine, G. Mc-Granahan, D. Schensul, and C. Tacoli, 64–79. New York: UNFPA and IIED.

Saunders, J., and R. Reeve. 2010. "Monitoring Governance for Implementation of REDD+." Monitoring Governance Safeguards in REDD+ Expert Workshop, London, May 24–25. Retrieved April 14, 2012 (http://www.fao.org/climatechange/21147-0514db68f6b31fda61d9b95fdf2b70093.pdf).

Schade, C., and D. Pimentel. 2010. "Population Crash: Prospects for Famine in the Twenty-First Century." *Environment, Development and Sustainability* 12(2):245–262.

Schelling, T. 1995. "Intergenerational Discounting." *Energy Policy* 23:395–401.

Schiller, P., E. Bruun, and J. Kenworthy. 2010. *An Introduction to Sustainable Transportation: Policy, Planning, and Implementation.* London: Earthscan.

Schipper, L. 2011. "Automobile Use, Fuel Economy, and CO_2 Emissions in Industrialized Countries." *Transportation Policy* 18:358–372.

Schlosberg, D., and D. Carruthers. 2010. "Indigenous Struggles, Environmental Justice, and Community Capabilities." *Global Environmental Politics* 10(4):12–35.

Schnaiberg, A. 1980. *The Environment: From Surplus to Scarcity.* New York: Oxford University Press.

Schnaiberg, A., and K. Gould. 1994. *Environment and Society: The Enduring Conflict.* New York: St. Martin's.

Schor, J. 1992. *The Overworked American.* New York: Basic Books.

———. 2005. *Born to Buy.* New York: Scribner.

———. 2010. *Plenitude: The New Economics of True Wealth.* New York: Penguin.

Schreckenberg, K., and C. Luttrell. 2009. "Participatory Forest Management: A Route to Poverty Reduction?" *International Forestry Review* 11(2):221–238.

Science. 2011. "The Legacy of Three Gorges Dam." *Science* 333(6044)817.

Seckler, D. 1996. "The New Era of Water Resources Management: From 'Dry' to 'Wet' Water Savings," research report, International Irrigation Management Institute, Colombo, Sri Lanka, www.iwmi.cgiar.org/Publications/IWMI_Research_Reports/PDF/pub001/REPORT01.pdf, last accessed 17 November 2012.

Seipel, M., M. Hamed, J. Sanford Rikoon, and Anna M. Kleiner. 1998. *The Impact of Large-Scale Hog Confinement Facility Sightings on Rural Property Values.* Conference proceedings, Agricultural Systems and the Environment, Des Moines, Iowa, July. Ames: Iowa State University.

Sen, A. 1970. *Collective Choice and Social Welfare.* San Francisco: Holden-Day.

———. 1981. *Poverty and Famines: An Essay on Entitlement and Deprivation.* New York: Oxford University Press.

———. 1984. "The Living Standard." *Oxford Economic Papers* 36:74–90.

———. 1993. "Markets and Freedom." *Oxford Economic Papers* 45:519–541.

———. 1994. "Population and Reasoning." Working Paper Series no. 94.06. Cambridge, MA: Harvard Center for Population and Development Studies, Harvard School of Public Health, Harvard University.

———. 1999. *Development as Freedom.* New York: Anchor.

———. 2005. "Human Rights and Capabilities." *Journal of Human Development* 6(2):151–166.

Seshadri, S. 2001. "Prevalence of Micronutrient Deficiency Particularly of Iron, Zinc, and Folic Acid in Pregnant Women in South East Asia." *British Journal of Nutrition* 85:S87–S92.

Shelley, C., J. Cross, W. Franzen, P. Hall, and S. Reeve. 2011. "Reducing Energy Consumption and Creating a Conservation Culture in Organizations: A Case Study of One Public School District." *Environment and Behavior* 4(3):316–343.

———. 2012. "How to Go Green: Creating a Conservation Culture in a Public High School Through Education, Modeling, and Communication." *Journal of Environmental Education* 43(3):143–161.

Shove, E., F. Trentmann, and R. Wilk. 2009. *Time, Consumption, and Everyday Life: Practice, Materiality, and Culture.* New York: Berg.

Shove, E., and G. Walker. 2007. "CAUTION! Transitions Ahead: Politics, Practice, and Sustainable Transition Management." *Environment and Planning A* 39:763–770.

Simon, J. 1981. *The Ultimate Resource.* Princeton, NJ: Princeton University Press.

Skousen, M. 2011. *Econopower: How a New Generation of Economists Is Transforming the World.* New York: Wiley.

Sloan, H. 1993. "The Earth Belongs in Usufruct to the Living." In *Jeffersonian Legacies,* edited by P. Onuf, 281–315. Charlottesville: University Press of Virginia.

Smil, V. 2004. *China's Past, China's Future: Energy, Food, Environment.* New York: Routledge.

Smith, C. 2008. "Ready, Set, Shop!" *San Francisco Magazine,* May 12. Retrieved April 9, 2012 (http://www.modernluxury.com/san-francisco/story/ready-set-shop-0).

Smith, E. 2001. "On the Coevolution of Cultural, Linguistic, and Biological Diversity." In *Biocultural Diversity: Linking Language, Knowledge, and the Environment,* edited by L. Maffi, 95–117. Washington, DC: Smithsonian Institution Press.

Smith, E., and L. Marín. 2005. "Water and the Rural Poor in Latin America: The Case of Tlamacazapa, Guerrero, Mexico." *Hydrogeology Journal* 13:346–349.

Sneath, D. 1998. "State Policy and Pasture Degradation in Inner Asia." *Science* 281(5380):1147–1148.

Socolow, R. 2011. "Wedges Reaffirmed." *Bulletin of the Atomic Scientists,* September 27. Retrieved March 22, 2012 (http://www.thebulletin.org/web-edition/features/wedges-reaffirmed).

Soleri, D., and D. Cleveland. 1993. "Hopi Crop Diversity and Change." *Journal of Enthobiology* 13(2):203–231.

Sovacool, B. 2008. "Valuing the Greenhouse Gas Emissions from Nuclear Power: A Critical Survey." *Energy Policy* 36:2950–2963.

Spence, M. 2009. "Markets Aren't Everything." *Forbes,* October 12. Retrieved April 9, 2012 (http://www.forbes.com/2009/10/12/economics-nobel-elinor-ostrom-oliver-williamson-opinions-contributors-michael-spence.html).

Sperling, D., and D. Gordon. 2009. *Two Billion Cars: Driving Towards Sustainability.* New York: Oxford University Press.

Spilsbury, R. 2010. *Deforestation Crisis.* New York: Rosen.

Stack, L. 2009. "For Egypt's Christians, Pig Cull Has Lasting Effects." *Christian Science Monitor,* September 3. Retrieved March 22, 2012 (http://www.csmonitor.com/World/Middle-East/2009/0903/p17s01-wome.html).

Stansfeld, S., C. Clark, R. Cameron, T. Alfred, J. Head, M. Haines, I. van Kamp, E. van Kempen, and I. Lopez-Barrio. 2009. "Aircraft and Road Traffic Noise Exposure and Children's Mental Health." *Journal of Environmental Psychology* 29(2):203–207.

Stansfeld, S., and M. Matheson. 2003. "Noise Pollution: Non-auditory Effects on Health." *British Medical Bulletin* 68:243–257.

Stebbins, R. 1967. "A Note on the Concept of Role Distance." *American Journal of Sociology* 73(2):247–250.

Stehfest, E., L. Bouwman, D. Vurren, M. Elzen, B. Eickhout, and P. Kabat. 2009. "Climate Benefits of a Changing Diet." *Climate Change* 95:83–102.

Stepp J., S. Cervone, H. Castaneda, A. Lasseter, G. Stocks, and Y. Gichon. 2004. "Development of a GIS for Global Biocultural Diversity." *Policy Matters* 13:267–270.

Sterling, E., and E. Vintinner. 2008. "How Much Is Left? An Overview of the Crisis." In *Water Consciousness,* edited by Tara Lohan, 14–25. San Francisco: Alternet Books.

Stern, P. 1999. "Information, Incentives, and Pro-environmental Consumer Behavior." *Journal of Consumer Policy* 22:461–478.

———. 2000. "Toward a Coherent Theory of Environmentally Significant Behavior." *Journal of Social Issues* 56:407–424.

Stern, P., E. Aronson, J. Darley, D. Hill, E. Hirst, W. Kempton, and T. Wilbanks. 1986. "The Effectiveness of Incentives for Residential Energy Conservation." *Evaluation Review* 10(2):147–176.

Sterne, J. 2007. "Out with the Trash: On the Future of New Media." In *Residual Media,* edited by Charles Acland, 16–31. Minneapolis: University of Minnesota Press.

Stillerman, J. 2004. "Gender, Class, and Generational Contexts for Consumption in Contemporary Chile." *Journal of Consumer Culture* 4(1):51–78.

Stofferahn, C. 2006. "Industrialized Farming and Its Relationship to Community Well-Being: An Update of a 2000 Report by Linda Lobao." Bismarck: prepared for the State of North Dakota, Office of the Attorney General, September.

Stone, B. 2008. "Urban Sprawl and Air Quality in Large US Cities." *Journal of Environmental Management* 86:688–698.

Stuart, T. 2009. *Waste: Uncovering the Global Food Scandal.* New York: W. W. Norton.

Sunstein, C. 2004. "Valuing Life: A Plea for Disaggregation." *Duke Law Journal* 54:384–445.

Sunstein, C., and A. Rowell. 2007. "On Discounting Regulatory Benefits: Risk, Money, and Intergenerational Equity." *University of Chicago Law Review* 74(1):171–208.

Sutherland, R. 2010. "We Can't Run Away from the Ethical Debates in Marketing." *Market Leader,* January. Retrieved April 8, 2012 (http://www.marketing-society.org.uk/SiteCollectionDocuments/knowledge-zone/market-leader/january-2010.pdf).

Sutton, M., C. Howard, J. Erisman, G. Billen, A. Bleeker, P. Grennfelt, H. van Grinsven, and B. Grizzetti. 2011. *The European Nitrogen Assessment: Sources, Effects, and Policy Perspectives.* Cambridge: Cambridge University Press.

Swartz, S., and S. Oster. 2010. "China Tops US in Energy Use." *Wall Street Journal,* July 18. Retrieved March 22, 2012 (http://online.wsj.com/article/SB10001424052748703720504575376712353150310.html).

Swift, P., D. Painter, and M. Goldstein. 2006. "Residential Street Typology and Injury Accident Frequency." VMT Congress of New Urbanism. Retrieved April 11, 2012 (http://massengale.typepad.com/venustas/files/SwiftSafetyStudy.pdf).

Szasz, A. 2007. *Shopping Our Way to Safety: How We Changed from Protecting the Environment to Protecting Ourselves.* Minneapolis: University of Minnesota Press.

Taylor, D., C. Taylor, and J. Taylor. 2012. *Empowerment on an Unsustainable Planet.* New York: Oxford University Press.

Taylor, J., and P. Van Doren. 2011. "Nuclear Power in the Dock." *Forbes,* April 5. Retrieved March 24, 2012 (http://www.forbes.com/2011/04/04/nuclear-energy-economy-opinions-jerry-taylor-peter-van-doren.html).

Terry, G. 2009. "No Climate Justice Without Gender Justice: An Overview of the Issues." *Gender and Development* 17(1):5–18.

Thompson, M. 1979. *Rubbish Theory.* New York: Oxford University Press.

Thornes, J., W. Bloss, S. Bouzarovski, X. Cai, L. Chapman, J. Clark, S. Dessai, S. Du, D. van der Horst, M. Kendall, C. Kidda, and S. Randalls. 2010. "Communicating the Value of Atmospheric Services." *Meteorological Applications* 17:243–250.

Tickner, J. 2003. "The Role of Environmental Science in Precautionary Decision Making." In *Precaution: Environmental Science and Preventive Public Policy*, edited by J. Tickner, 3–20. Washington, DC: Island Press.

Toulmin, C. 2009. *Climate Change in Africa*. New York: Zed Books.

Trinh, L., J. Watson, N. Huec, N. Ded, N. Minhe, P. Chuf, B. Sthapit, and P. Eyzaguirre. 2003. "Agrobiodiversity Conservation and Development in Vietnamese Home Gardens." *Agriculture, Ecosystem, and Environment* 97:317–344.

Tripp, R. 2001. "Can Biotechnology Reach the Poor? The Adequacy of Information and Seed Delivery." *Food Policy* 26:249–264.

Trotman, R. 2008. "The Benefits of Community Conservation: A Literature Review." Report prepared for the Auckland, New Zealand, Regional Council, December. Retrieved March 6, 2012 (http://www.arc.govt.nz/albany/fms/main/Documents/Auckland/Volunteers/Benefits%20of%20community%20conservation.pdf).

Trzupek, R. 2011. "Natural Gas Will Repower America." *Real Clear Energy*, October 18. Retrieved March 23, 2012 (http://www.realclearenergy.org/articles/2011/10/18/natural_gas_will_repower_america_106319.html).

TSA. 2010. "Information." Washington, DC: Transportation Security Administration. Retrieved June 26, 2012 (http://blog.tsa.gov/2010/11/tsa-myth-or-fact-leaked-images.html).

Tuck-Po, L. 2004. *Changing Pathways*. Lanham, MD: Lexington Books.

Tudge, C. 2010. "How to Raise Livestock—and How Not To." In *The Meat Crisis*, edited by J. D'Silva and J. Webster, 9–21. London: Earthscan.

Turner, D., and L. Hartzell. 2004. "The Lack of Clarity in the Precautionary Principle." *Environmental Values* 13:449–460.

Turner, N. 1988. "The Importance of a Rose." *American Anthropologist* 90(2):272–290.

UNEP. 2007. *Declaration of the Rights of Indigenous People*. New York: United Nations General Assembly, Sixty-First Session.

———. 2008. *State and Trends of the Environment, 1987–2007*. New York: United Nations Environmental Program. Retrieved March 5, 2011 (http://www.unep.org/geo/geo4/report/02_Atmosphere.pdf).

———. 2009. "Recycling: From E-waste to Resources." United Nations Environment Program, July. Retrieved March 18, 2012 (http://www.unep.org/PDF/PressReleases/E-Waste_publication_screen_FINALVERSION-sml.pdf).

UNESCO. 2003. "Water for People, Water for Life." First United Nations World Water Development Report. Paris: United Nations Educational, Scientific, and Cultural Organization. Retrieved March 22, 2012 (http://www.unesco.org/water/wwap/wwdr/wwdr1).

———. 2009. "World Water Development Report." Paris: United Nations Educational, Scientific, and Cultural Organization. Retrieved March 23, 2012 (http://www.unesco.org/water/wwap/wwdr/wwdr3/pdf/WWDR3_Water_in_a_Changing_World.pdf).

UNHCR. 2010. "Global Trends, 2010." Geneva: United Nations High Commissioner for Refugees. Retrieved March 17, 2012 (http://www.unhcr.org/4dfa11499.html).

UNICEF. 2011. "Reduce Child Mortality." Retrieved May 20, 2012 (http://www.unicef.org/mdg/childmortality.html).

UNICEF, WTO, and WFP. 2007. "Preventing and Controlling Micronutrient Deficiencies in Populations Affected by an Emergency: Joint Statement." Retrieved April 9, 2012 (http://www.helid.desastres.net/en/d/Js13449e/1.html).

United Nations. 2002. "General Comment no. 15." New York: Economic and Social Council, United Nations. Retrieved March 22, 2012 (http://www.citizen.org/documents/ACF2B4B.pdf).

United Nations 2004 World Population to 2020, *Economic and Social Affairs*, United Nations, New York, http://www.un.org/esa/population/publications/longrange2/WorldPop2300final.pdf, last accessed November 17, 2012.

———. 2005. "Fact Sheet 7: Mega Cities." Working Paper no. ESA/P/WP/200. New York: UN Department of Economic and Social Affairs, Population Division. Retrieved September 10, 2012 (http://www.un.org/esa/population/publications/WUP2005/2005WUP_FS7.pdf).

———. 2006. "Human Development Report, 2006." New York: United Nations Development Programme. Retrieved March 16, 2012 (http://hdr.undp.org/en/media/HDR06-complete.pdf).

———. 2009. "Water in a Changing World." Third UN World Water Development Report. Retrieved March 19, 2012 (http://www.unesco.org/water/wwap/wwdr/wwdr3/pdf/WWDR3 _Water_in_a_Changing_World.pdf).

———. 2010. *Solid Waste Management in the World's Cities.* London: Earthscan.

———. N.d. "Statistics: Graphs and Maps, UN Water." New York: United Nations. Retrieved March 28, 2012 (http://www.unwater.org/statistics_san.html).

United Nations Development Programme. 1990. *Human Development Report, 1990.* New York: Oxford University Press.

United States Code. 2002. *United States Code, 2000: Title 22, Foreign Relations and Intercourse.* Washington, DC: US Government Printing Office.

USDA. N.d. "Organic Production/Organic Food: Information Access Tools." Washington, DC: US Department of Agriculture. Retrieved June 7, 2012 (http://www.nal.usda.gov/afsic/pubs /ofp/ofp.shtml).

US Department of Health. 2008. "The Role of the Media in Promoting and Reducing Tobacco Use." NCI Tobacco Control Monograph Series no. 19. Washington, DC: US Department of Health, National Cancer Institute. Retrieved April 6, 2012 (http://cancercontrol.cancer.gov /tcrb/monographs/19/docs/M19MajorConclusionsFactSheet.pdf).

US Department of Labor. 2010. "More than 75 Percent of American Households Own Computers." May 2010. Retrieved May 18, 2012 (http://www.bls.gov/opub/focus/volume1 _number4/cex_1_4.htm).

US National Academy of Sciences. 2008. "What You Need to Know About Energy." Washington, DC: National Academy of Sciences. Retrieved March 22, 2012 (https://download .nap.edu/login.php?record_id=12204&page=%2Fcatalog.php%3Frecord_id%3D12204).

———. 2011. *Climate Change, the Indoor Environment, and Health.* Washington, DC: National Academies Press.

van den Bosch, R. 1978. *The Pesticide Conspiracy.* Garden City, NY: Doubleday.

Vandergeest, P. 1996. "Mapping Nature: Territorialization of Forest Rights in Thailand." *Society and Natural Resources* 9:159–175.

van der Voort, T., P. Nikken, and J. van Lil. 1992. "Determinants of Parental Guidance of Children's Television Viewing: A Dutch Replication Study." *Journal of Broadcasting and Electronic Media* 36(1):61–74.

van der Werf, G. D. Morton, R. DeFries, J. Olivier, P. Kasibhatla, R. Jackson, G. Collatz, and J. Randerson. 2009. "CO_2 Emissions from Forest Loss." *Nature Geoscience* 2:737–738.

Veblen, T. [1899] 1967. *The Theory of the Leisure Class: An Economic Study of Institutions.* New York: Funk and Wagnalls.

Vedwan, N. 2007. "Pesticides in Coca-Cola and Pepsi: Consumerism, Brand Image, and Public Interest in a Globalizing India." *Cultural Anthropology* 22(4):659–684.

Vernooy, R., and Y. Song. 2004. "New Approaches to Supporting the Agricultural Biodiversity Important for Sustainable Rural Livelihoods." *International Journal of Agricultural Sustainability* 2(1):55–66.

Vickrey, W. 1968. "Automobile Accidents, Tort Law, Externalities, and Insurance: An Economist's Critique." *Law and Contemporary Problems* 33:464–487.

Victor, P. 2008. *Managing Without Growth: Slower by Design, Not Disaster.* Northampton, MA: Edward Elgar.

Vijayan, V. 1987. *Keoladeo National Park Ecology Study.* Bombay: Bombay Natural History Society.

———. 1991. *Keoladeo National Park Ecology Study, 1980–1990.* Bombay: Bombay Natural History Society.

Vrijheid, M. 2000. "Health Effects of Residence Near Hazardous Waste Landfill Sites: A Review of Epidemiologic Literature." *Environmental Health Perspectives* 108(Supp. 1):101–112.

Wagenet, L., and M. Pfeffer. 2007. "Organizing Citizen Engagement for Democratic Environmental Planning." *Society and Natural Resources* 20(9):801–813.

Wainwright, M. 2009. "Supermarket Offers and Food Waste Targeted in Government's Food Strategy." *Guardian*, August 10. Retrieved March 3, 2012 (http://www.guardian.co.uk /environment/2009/aug/10/food-security-climate-change).

Wallich, H. 1972. "Zero Growth." *Newsweek*, January 24, 62.

Watkiss, P., T. Downing, C. Handley, and R. Butterfield. 2005. "The Impacts and Costs of Climate Change." Final Report to DG Environment, September. Retrieved March 24, 2012 (http://europa.eu.int/comm/environment/climat/studies.htm).

Watts, J. 2011. "Fukushima Disaster: It's Not Over Yet." *Guardian*, September 9. Retrieved March 24, 2012 (http://www.guardian.co.uk/world/2011/sep/09/fukushima-japan-nuclear -disaster-aftermath).

WEDO. 2008. "Gender, Climate Change, and Human Security: Lessons from Bangladesh, Ghana, and Senegal." Women's Environment and Development Organization, May. Retrieved March 15, 2012 (http://www.wedo.org/wp-content/uploads/hsn-study-final-may-20–2008.pdf).

Weeratunge, N., and K. Snyder. 2009. "Gleaner, Fisher, Trader, Processor: Understanding Gendered Employment in the Fisheries and Aquaculture Sector." Paper presented at the FAO-IFAD-ILO Workshop on Gaps, Trends, and Current Research in Gender Dimensions of Agricultural and Rural Employment, Rome, March 31–April 2. Retrieved March 5, 2012 (http://www.fao-ilo.org/fileadmin/user_upload/fao_ilo/pdf/Papers/Weeratunge -final.pdf).

Weinberg, A. 1972. "Science and Trans-Science." *Minerva* 10:209–222.

Weis, T. 2007. *The Global Food Economy: The Battle for the Future of Farming.* New York: Zed Books.

Welsh, R., and R. Graham. 1999. "A New Paradigm for World Agriculture." *Field Crops Research* 60:1–10.

———. 2004. "Breeding for Micronutrients in Staple Food Crops from a Human Perspective." *Journal of Experimental Botany* 55(396):353–364.

Westhead, R. 2010. "A New Issues Percolates Throughout India: How Much to Charge for Water?" *Toronto Star*, August 16. Retrieved March 15, 2012 (http://www.thestar.com/news /world/india/article/848255—a-new-issue-percolatesthroughout-india-how-much-to -charge-for-water).

White, M., N. Diffenbaugh, G. Jones, J. Pal, and F. Giorg. 2006. "Extreme Heat Reduces and Shifts United States Premium Wine Production in the 21st Century." *PNAS* 103(30):11217–11222.

White, S., and D. Cordell. 2008. "Peak Phosphorus: The Sequel to Peak Oil." Information Sheet Two, Global Phosphorus Research Initiative. Retrieved April 12, 2012 (http:// phosphorusfutures.net/peak-phosphorus).

Whitehead, A. N. [1920] 1964. *Concept of Nature.* Cambridge: Cambridge University Press.

Whitehead, L., A. Upward, P. Friedel, G. Cox, and M. Mossman. 2010. "Using Core Sunlight to Improve Illumination Quality and Increase Energy Efficiency of Commercial Buildings." Proceedings of the ASME Fourth International Conference on Energy Sustainability, Phoenix, AZ, May 17–22, 2010. Retrieved March 24, 2012 (http://www.phas.ubc.ca/ssp /howdoesitwork/ASME_2010_paper.pdf).

White House. N.d. Transcript. Retrieved November 12, 2011 (http://www.google.com/url?sa =t&rct=j&q=bush%20%22each%20country%20needs%20to%20recognize%20that%20 we%20must%20reduce%20our%20greenhouse%22%20%22when%20added%22&source=web& cd=6&ved=0CDkQFjAF&url=http%3A%2F%2Fwww.eurunion.org%2Fpartner%2Fsummit%2

FSummit20070430%2FBush-Merkel-BarrosoPrConf070430.doc&ei=esm-TvuhHYatiAKq3t T5Ag&usg=AFQjCNF4IFLODvpWbbj5esdokSfayDGprg).

WHO. 2009. "Global Status Report on Road Safety: Time for Action." Geneva: World Health Organization. Retrieved April 7, 2012 (http://whqlibdoc.who.int/publications/2009 /9789241563840_eng.pdf).

———. 2011. "Burden of Disease from Environmental Noise: Quantification of Healthy Life Years Lost in Europe." Geneva: World Health Organization. Retrieved April 7, 2012 (http:// www.euro.who.int/__data/assets/pdf_file/0008/136466/e94888.pdf).

———. 2012. "Media Center: Malaria." Geneva: World Health Organization. Retrieved May 20, 2012 (http://www.who.int/mediacentre/factsheets/fs094/en/).

———. N.d.a. "DALYs / YLDs Definition." Geneva: World Health Organization. Retrieved June 6, 2012 (http://www.who.int/mental_health/management/depression/daly/en/).

———. N.d.b. "WHO Definition of Health." Geneva: World Health Organization. Retrieved May 19, 2012 (http://www.who.int/about/definition/en/print.html).

Wilkinson, R., and K. Pickett. 2009. *The Spirit Level: Why More Equal Societies Are Almost Always Better.* New York: Penguin Books.

Wilkinson, R., K. Pickett, and R. De Vogli. 2010. "Equality, Sustainability, and Quality of Life." *BMJ* 341(November 27):1138–1140.

Williamson, T. 2002. "Sprawl, Politics, and Participation: A Preliminary Analysis." *National Civic Review* 91(3):235–244.

Wilson, E. [1992] 1999. *The Diversity of Life.* New York: W. W. Norton.

Wily, L. 1999. "Moving Forward in African Community Forestry: Trading Power, Not Use Rights." *Society and Natural Resources* 12(1):49–61.

Wise, T. 2012. "The Cost to Mexico of U.S. Corn Ethanol Expansion." Global Development and Environment Institute, Working Paper no. 12–01. Medford, MA: Tufts University.

WNA. N.d. "World Nuclear Power Reactors and Uranium Requirements." London: World Nuclear Association. Retrieved June 7, 2012 (http://www.world-nuclear.org/info/reactors.html).

Wood, D. 1993. "The Power of Maps." *Scientific American* (May):88–94.

Woodworth, B., M. Steen-Adams, and P. Mittal. 2011. "Role of an Environmental Studies Course on the Formation of Environmental Worldviews: A Case Study of a Core Curriculum Requirement Using the NEP Scale." *Journal of Environmental Studies and Sciences* 1(2):126–137.

World Bank. 2007. "The Cost of Pollution in China." Washington, DC: World Bank. Retrieved April 7, 2012 (http://siteresources.worldbank.org/INTEAPREGTOPENVIRONMENT /Resources/China_Cost_of_Pollution.pdf).

———. 2008. *World Development Indicators, 2008.* Washington, DC: World Bank.

World Coal Association. N.d. "Coal." London: World Coal Association. Retrieved June 7, 2012 (http://www.worldcoal.org/coal/).

Worldwatch Institute. 2010. *State of the World, 2010: Transforming Cultures.* New York: W. W. Norton.

Wynne, B. 2002. "Risk and Environment as Legitimatory Discourses of Technology: Reflectivity Inside and Out?" *Current Sociology* 50:459–477.

Xing, Y., Z. Li, Y. Fan, and H. Hou. 2010. "Biohydrogen Production from Dairy Manures with Acidification Pretreatment by Anaerobic Fermentation." *Environmental Science and Pollution Research* 17(2):392–399.

Yang, J. 2011. "China's Energy Consumption Rises." *Wall Street Journal,* February 28. Retrieved March 22, 2012 (http://online.wsj.com/article/SB10001424052748704615504576171922 168262078.html).

York, R. 2006. Review of *Cultures of Environmentalism,* by Steve Yearly. *Organization and Environment* 19:142–144.

———. 2010. "The Paradox at the Heart of Modernity: The Carbon Efficiency of the Global Economy." *International Journal of Sociology* 40(2):6–22.

York, R., E. Rosa, and T. Dietz. 2003. "Footprints on the Earth: The Environmental Consequences of Modernity." *American Sociological Review* 68(2):279–300.

———. 2004. "The Ecological Footprint Intensity of National Economies." *Journal of Industrial Ecology* 8(4):139–154.

Zezza, A., and L. Tasciotti. 2010. "Urban Agriculture, Poverty, and Food Security: Empirical Evidence from a Sample of Developing Countries." *Food Policy* 35:265–273.

Zhang, W., T. Ricketts, C. Kremen, K. Carney, and S. Swinton. 2007. "Ecosystem Services and Dis-services to Agriculture." *Ecological Economics* 64(2):253–260.

Zhaoa, Z., and R. Kaestnerb. 2010. "Effects of Urban Sprawl on Obesity." *Journal of Health Economics* 29:779–787.

Zwart, H. 1997. What Is an Animal? A Philosophical Reflection on the Possibility of a Moral Relationship with Animals." *Environmental Values* 6:377–392.

Index

Please note: Page numbers denoting special boxes and formatting appear with the following abbreviations: (cs) for Case Study; (eco) for ECOnnection; (eq) for Ethical Question; (tbl) for table; (fig) for figure; and (img) for image.